On Heidegger's
Nazism and
Philosophy

On Heidegger's Nazism and Philosophy

Tom Rockmore

University of California Press

Berkeley / Los Angeles / Oxford

University of California Press
Berkeley and Los Angeles, California

University of California Press
Oxford, England

Copyright © 1992 by the Regents of the
University of California

Library of Congress Cataloging-in-Publication
Data

Rockmore, Tom, 1942–
    On Heidegger's Nazism and philosophy / by
Tom Rockmore.
        p.   cm.
    Includes bibliographical references and index.
    ISBN 0-520-07711-3 (hard : alk. paper)
    1. Heidegger, Martin, 1889–
1976.   2. National socialism.
  I. Title.
  B3279.H49R62   1992
  193—dc20   91-22072
                                            CIP

Printed in the United States of America

1 2 3 4 5 6 7 8 9

The point of revisiting Heidegger's involvement with Nazism is not primarily to pass judgment on the past. Nor is it born of a desire, as Heidegger once suggested, to attack the man because one cannot attack his works. Quite the contrary. The point is precisely to sift the works for what might still be of value, and what is not. To do that, one must reread his works—particularly but not exclusively those from 1933 on—with strict attention to the political movement with which Heidegger himself chose to link his ideas. To do less than that is, I believe, finally not to understand him at all.

Thomas Sheehan, "Heidegger and the Nazis," *The New York Review of Books*, 16 June 1988

Wer denkt gross, muss gross irren.

Martin Heidegger, *Aus der Erfahrung des Denkens*

It is always well to divorce an artist from his work and to take him less seriously than it. He is, after all, only a condition of the work, the soil from which it grows, perhaps only the manure of that soil. Thus he is, in most cases, something that must be forgotten if one wants to enter into the full enjoyment of the work.

Nietzsche, *The Genealogy of Morals*

Zum Schluss möchte ich Sie bitten, zu bedenken, dass auch heute eine falsche Propaganda besteht, z.B. dass Gerüchte herumgetragen werden, die der Wahrheit widersprechen. Es sind mir geradezu unsinnige Verleumdungen über mich und meine Arbeit bekannt geworden.

Letter from Heidegger to Marcuse, 20 January 1948

Contents

Acknowledgments

I owe an important debt to the increasing number of scholars, some of them with a considerable investment in Heidegger scholarship, who continue to seek the truth, even when it contradicts Heideggerian strategies for dealing with Heidegger's Nazism. To this general debt I would add more specific ones incurred to two anonymous readers of the manuscript, to Michael Zimmerman for helpful comments on the initial draft, to Debra Bergoffen, who read a draft of the chapter on Nietzsche, and to Theodore Kisiel, who commented on the entire final draft. None of them is responsible for the views expressed here. But I gratefully acknowledge that their attention to detail has saved me from numerous slips and in general helped me to strengthen the argument.

I gratefully acknowledge as well that discussion with Joseph Margolis has provided insight useful in writing this book. His willingness to collaborate in bringing Farias's study of *Heidegger and Nazism* into English started me on the road that led to this book. Nicolas Tertulian initially called this problem to my attention. Edward Dimendberg, Philosophy Editor at the University of California Press, whose faith in this project made it possible, has been a constant pleasure to work with. His own insightful suggestions have improved the manuscript. I am grateful as well for the excellent copyediting by Nicholas Goodhue, which generally improved the manuscript and detected several errors. As always, I am deeply indebted to my family in ways that I cannot simply or even adequately express.

Acknowledgments

Introduction: On Heidegger's Nazism and Philosophy

This book considers the nature and philosophical significance of the controversial relation between Heidegger's philosophy and his Nazism. The significance of this relation is clear in virtue of the importance of Heidegger's philosophical thought and its widespread influence not only in the philosophical discussion but throughout the cultural life of this century. Heidegger's supporters and even his most ardent critics agree that Heidegger's thought is important and cannot merely be dismissed. Heidegger is often held to be one of the most important contemporary philosophers, even the most important philosopher of this century, maybe even one of the small handful of truly great philosophers in the history of the philosophical tradition.

Heidegger is certainly the most influential philosopher of our time. Heidegger's influence is widely felt in contemporary philosophy: in negative fashion in Husserl's final phase; in the positions[1] of Gadamer and Derrida, his two closest students; in the thought of Herbert Marcuse, the first Heideggerian Marxist; in the phenomenological theories of Jean-Paul Sartre, Maurice Merleau-Ponty, Emmanuel Levinas, and Paul Ricoeur; and more distantly in the writings of Foucault, Apel, Habermas, and Rorty, as well as in those of a host of other figures such as Hans Jonas, Hannah Arendt, and Leszek Kolakowski. The Heidegger literature has by now taken on such proportions that no one, not even the most industrious student, can possibly read it all. Heidegger is now widely present in the discussions in Germany, even more so in the United States, but above all in France, where for several decades he has functioned as the main "French" philosopher, the unacknowledged but omnipresent master thinker whose thought continues to form the horizon of French philosophical thinking.

Heidegger's influence, which is by no means limited to philosophy, is widely apparent throughout the recent discussion: in theology in the work of Paul Tillich, Rudolf Bultmann, and Karl Rahner; in psychoanalysis in the work of Jacques Lacan, Ludwig Binswanger, and Medard Boss; in literary theory through Paul de Man; in feminism through Gayatri Spivak; in ecology through Albert Borgmann and Wolfgang Schirmacher; in political theory through Fred Dallmayr; and so on. The list of those influenced by Heidegger, which is impressive, rivals in scope that of such other conceptual giants of this century as Freud and Weber.

Obviously, the impressive nature of Heidegger's thought and its extraordinary influence do not diminish but rather only raise the stakes of the present discussion. In view of the growing knowledge of the historical record and the ongoing publication of Heidegger's writings, one can overlook, or choose to ignore, but can no longer deny, the relation between his Nazism and his philosophy. To "bracket" this issue, simply to turn away from the problem, to refuse to confront it, is silently to accept what a number have seen as the totalitarian dimension in one of the most important theories of this century, itself largely marked by totalitarianisms of the right and the left, a theory apparently lacking in the resources necessary to come to grips with totalitarianism. In confronting Heidegger's Nazism, one inevitably questions as well the philosophical and wider intellectual discussion of our time and its ability to think the connection between philosophy and politics.

The link between Heidegger's thought and politics has been known for many years. Its discussion began in the 1940s in the pages of the French intellectual journal, *Les Temps Modernes,* in a controversy initiated by Karl Löwith, Heidegger's former student and later colleague.[2] The initial phase of the debate ended quickly, but the theme has continued to resurface at intervals. It has recently received a fresh impetus in publications by Ott[3] and Farias.[4] The merit of Farias's book, in part based on Ott's research, is that for the first time it has brought the Heidegger affair to the attention of the wider intellectual readership.

Since a relation between Heidegger's thought and his Nazism has been known for more than half a century, one must ask why it has not been studied earlier in greater depth. The reasons include the relative success at what can charitably be described as damage control on the part of his most fervent admirers—those for whom he can apparently do no wrong, or at least none of lasting consequence for his thought—as well as a lack of insight into its philosophical significance. But the recent discussion has provided sustained attention to the series of issues surrounding Heidegger's thought and politics. It is now too late to put the genie back in the bottle, to deflect attention away from this relation, since the publications by Farias and Ott raise this issue in a way that in good faith cannot simply be ignored.

Everything about this relation is subject to dispute. It has been asserted that it is philosophically insignificant, since the struggle concerning Heidegger is merely symptomatic of a weakness of contemporary thought. It has been claimed that Heidegger was not a Nazi, or at least not in any ordinary sense. It has been suggested that we must differentiate between Heidegger the thinker and Heidegger the man, for the former cannot be judged in relation to the latter. It has been argued that information recently made available is not new and was already known to any serious student. It has been held that everything that Heidegger ever did or wrote was Nazi to the core. It has been maintained that Heidegger's only problem was that he never said he was sorry, that he never excused himself or asked for forgiveness. Finally, it has been maintained with all the seriousness of the professional scholar, in a way recalling many a theological dispute, that Heidegger's thought is so difficult that only one wholly immersed in it, at the extreme only a true believer committed to his vision, could possibly understand it. Yet if it can only be comprehended by a "true" believer, then Heidegger's Nazism is beyond criticism or evaluation of any kind, since no "true" believer will criticize it.

The view of the present study is that all of the above claims about the relation of Heidegger's thought and his Nazism are false. Attention focused on Heidegger's Nazi inclinations by Farias, Ott, and others (e.g., Pöggeler, Marten, Sheehan, Vietta, Lacoue-Labarthe, Derrida, Bourdieu, Schwan, Janicaud, Zimmerman, Wolin, Thomä, etc.) has created a momentum of its own. It has been realized that Heidegger's Nazism raises important moral and political issues that cannot simply be evaded and that must be faced as part of the continuing process of determining what is live and what is dead in Heidegger's thought. It is not inaccurate to say that as a result of recent discussion, at least two things have become clear: First, the problem cannot simply be denied since one can no longer even pretend to understand Heidegger's philosophy, certainly beginning in 1933, if one fails to take into account his Nazism. In a word, serious study of Heidegger's thought can no longer evade the theme of Heidegger's Nazism. Second, the issues posed by Heidegger's unprecedented turn to Nazism on philosophical grounds, and the way the theme has been received in the discussion of his thought, point beyond his position to raise queries about the nature of philosophy and even the responsibility of intellectuals.

The complex topic of Heidegger's thought and politics concerns what we know about his actions and philosophy as they bear on his Nazism, including Heidegger's own explanation of his turn toward National Socialism, as well as the roots of that turn in his position and the later development of his thought. It includes as well the way in which this theme has been received in the Heidegger discussion over many years, in an often bitter dispute between his partisans and detractors, between those who invoke special rules for a German genius (e.g., Gadamer), and those who maintain the same rules for all. It further includes the significance of this affair for the philosophical discipline itself. We must inquire whether Heidegger's turn to Nazism is sui generis, an aberration uncharacteristic of the discipline, which hence casts no light at all on it, or whether, on the contrary, it in some sense illuminates philosophy.

This question is actually a series of questions, one of which can be stated as follows: Did Heidegger's effort to lead the German nation fail in 1933–1934 because he misjudged the appropriateness of National Socialism, or rather because philosophy is inapt to play a political role, or rather finally because, as Heidegger later came to believe, it is simply not useful? It is also relevant to inquire how and why he turned to Nazism. The obvious fact that—as Rorty, Habermas, and others have pointed out—Heidegger was an important thinker but a Nazi requires scrutiny. We cannot merely dismiss it, since it is as close to true as any claim about a philosopher can be; but we cannot act as if it were unimportant, since our view of Heidegger's position cannot ignore his own statement that he turned to National Socialism on the basis of his philosophical thought. This admission leads to a provocative question: can a theory be great which leads to the political abomination of National Socialism? Since Heidegger is not just any thinker but by all standards an exceptional one, his Nazism is exceptionally troublesome. In Heidegger we have an example of a supposedly great philosopher, according to Levinas, the author of the most important treatise since Hegel's *Phenomenology of Spirit*.[5] Then there is the light that Heidegger's turn to Nazism and its reception in the literature throw on the philosophical discipline: what is the social relevance of philosophy if it can and in fact does lead to such ends? In other words, how can great thought lead to great evil? Or is it that in the claim of conceptual greatness, we are greatly mistaken?

The interpretation of the link between Heidegger's philosophy and Nazism points toward the relation between thought and time. It has been usual in the philosophical tradition to maintain that philosophy is in but not of time, since it is independent of its context. On the contrary, Marxism argues that philosophy can be reduced to its context. The present work denies these two antithetical claims in favor of a third, more difficult approach according to which philosophy is in part dependent on, and in part independent of, the context in which it arises. This view accords with Heidegger's understanding of Dasein as existence and as transcendent. It will be applied here in order to comprehend Heidegger's Nazism in terms of his philosophical thought, and his thought as dependent on and reflective of its social, historical, political, and philosophical background. A main theme of this book is that Heidegger's philosophical thought and his Nazism are interdependent and cannot be separated, more precisely, that he turned to National Socialism on the basis of his philosophy and that his later evolution is largely determined by his continuing concern with Nazism.

Not unnaturally, some of Heidegger's closest students, following Heidegger's lead, have long sought to conceal the Nazism lodged in his thought. The present effort to reveal and to consider the nature and philosophical significance of Heidegger's Nazism will need to break sharply with all the various ways in which Heidegger and his students have sought to conceal this aspect of his thought. It will rely on three general principles. To begin with, it will part company with the view that in order to discuss Heidegger at all one must be an expert in his thought, a master of his position able to quote chapter and verse at the drop of a manuscript, even capable on demand of adducing unpublished material in support of an argument.

Unquestionably, it is necessary to be informed about Heidegger's thought in order to comprehend the nature and philosophical significance of his Nazism. But the work to follow will not seek to imitate the massively detailed commentaries on the main thinkers in the tradition, or the equivalent analyses of Heidegger's thought. If the requirement of detailed expert commentary does not always function as a strategy to preclude significant criticism, in the main it only helps to foreclose the possibility of raising the significant philosophical issues. I am convinced that the relevant issues of Heidegger's Nazism, and probably any basic aspect of his thought, can be addressed in the intersubjective conceptual space common to the majority of philosophers and many intellectuals of all kinds. In this specific sense, whatever the peculiarities of Heidegger's position, which should not be denied, it is "available" to discussion in roughly the same way as others.

Second, we must refuse the distinction, cherished equally by Heideggerians and philosophers of all kinds, between Heidegger the thinker and Heidegger the man, Heidegger the great philosopher and Heidegger the intellectual's peasant solidly rooted in the soil of his beloved

Schwarzwald. The supposed distinction between Heidegger and his thought obviously reflects a separation of theory from practice, well rooted in traditional philosophical theory and practice. In virtue of their concern to separate what they think from what they do, philosophers resemble those in other lines of work, who are frequently unwilling to act on their views. The result is a peculiar form of inaction, or insistence on theory, which philosophers from Aristotle over Hegel to Heidegger have often identified with action, even with its highest form. Philosophers, who speak eloquently of the truth, are only rarely willing to break a lance for truth. The example of Socrates, who died for an idea which he regarded as more important than life itself, is overshadowed by the more typical case of Spinoza, who prudently refused to descend into the arena lest he compromise his freedom of thought.

In the discussion of Heidegger's Nazism, the distinction between Heidegger the man and Heidegger the philosopher is frequently invoked by his students in order to save, if not the man, at least his thought. This distinction underlies the frequent admission that Heidegger was a rather dreadful person, a concession that functions strategically to protect his thought against the defects of his character. Yet if Heidegger's philosophical thought and his turn to Nazism are continuous in any ordinary sense, if one admits that his identification with National Socialism was motivated by his philosophical theory, as Heidegger himself suggests, then a critique of his actions immediately reflects on his view.

It is relatively easy to criticize Heidegger's identification with Nazism since on the practical plane there is nothing to distinguish it from that of anyone else, with the exception of its possible relation—still contested by many, on occasion still even denied—to the position of an important thinker. If one thinks that there is something reprehensible about a close association with Nazism, or denouncing one's colleagues as politically unreliable, or trying to devise a Nazi theory of higher education, or maintaining a theoretical commitment to Nazism as an ideal after National Socialism had failed in practice, then it is important to return from the actions themselves to the view behind them. On the contrary, if we are willing to admit that theory is divorced from practice, as Heidegger's students insist, then the defense of his thought is simplified. For one can simply admit that Heidegger was not a very nice man, that he did a number of reprehensible things in connection with Nazism, while denying that any of his actions reflect on his position. And we can further express our dismay that Heidegger never simply excused his Nazi connection or expressed shame for his own past, since his stoic refusal to admit any involvement at all would, then, be the only problem.

I will resist the effort to drive a conceptual wedge between Heidegger the man and Heidegger the thinker for two reasons. On the one hand, theory and practice are never wholly separate and hence cannot be disjoined. At least implicitly, practice of any kind always reflects a theoretical perspective. In all cases, action follows from, and is on occasion justified by, an attitude, a reason, an intention, an aim, or even a passion. Even such extreme views as the conviction of the Italian Fascists that one should act first and create a justification for the actions after the fact, or the German *Führerprinzip* according to which the will of the *Führer* is a sufficient justification for any action at all, make action depend on a prior theory.

On the other hand, the defense of Heidegger's position in terms of an alleged split between the man and his thought is inconsistent with Heidegger's own view of the matter. Obviously, it contradicts his clear claim that his theory must be judged by his actions. It further runs counter to the understanding, basic to his fundamental ontology, of Dasein as existence. In *Being and Time,* he repeatedly affirms the priority of existence, or the practical dimension in the wider sense of the term, over theory of any kind on the grounds that the precognitive dimension is prior to, and provides the basis for, the cognitive level. Heidegger's insistence that theory is meaningful only within the practical framework precisely denies the kind of separation of theory from practice which some of his followers introduce in order to defend his position in spite of his Nazism. In short, this defense must be resisted since if it succeeds it fails, because the condition of its success is precisely to deny a fundamental aspect of the position it is invoked to defend.

Further, we will consider Heidegger the thinker as in part a man of his times, whose times offer insight into his theory. Now Heidegger can be construed as deflecting attention from the relation of his thought to time, in particular to his own time, in his repeated insistence that his own thought is limited to the problem of Being, the *Seinsfrage.* Certainly, many writers on Heidegger have understood his position in this way, including the vast majority of commentators who discuss Heidegger's thought merely in terms of his texts without reference to the wider context that forms their background. In this sense, those who discuss Heidegger are repeating the view, itself a staple of the philosophical tradition at least since Plato, that thought is in time but not of time, as if a philosopher were somehow able to escape from time itself.

I believe this deflection should be resisted. To begin with, there is the general point, mentioned above, that all thought, including Heidegger's, is related to time. Thought cannot easily, in fact perhaps never wholly, be isolated from time. Perhaps even such familiar assertions as $7 + 5 = 12$ are not devoid of reference to time and place. Certainly, Heidegger's own view is specifically related to the period in which it arose, and cannot adequately be understood merely through attention to factors supposedly independent of the historical context, such as the problem of the meaning of Being. I am convinced that Heidegger's theory reflects a variety of contemporary influences, some of which he may not have been fully aware of, such as the role of a conservative, nationalistic form of Roman Catholicism in southwestern Germany in his youth, stressed by Ott, Farias, and most recently Thomä;[6] the widespread concern, which he seems to have shared, for Germany, the defeated party in the First World War, to recover as a nation and to assume what many thought was the manifest German destiny; the reintroduction of destiny as an explanatory factor of historical change by Spengler; the interest in the concept of the *Volk* as it was developed in nineteenth-century Germany; and Heidegger's own desire to assume an ever-greater role in the German university system as the central thinker of his day, even to reform the university system according to his own view of higher education. These and other factors are ingredient in Heidegger's theory, and knowledge of them offers insight into Heidegger's position. Conversely, to follow the traditional philosophical view that thought is independent of time, in this case to fail to take these and other factors into account, is to close off important roads of access to Heidegger's position.

Heidegger's own insistence on the contextuality of thought within existence, in which it arises, and by which it is limited, suggests that his own philosophical theory can fairly be understood in this way and cannot be understood otherwise. There is an obvious analogy between Heidegger's understanding of the contextuality of thought and Hegel's view of philosophy as its own time captured in thought. Hegel sees philosophy as both immanent and transcendent, as an analysis of what occurs on a higher conceptual plane. This duality of immanence and transcendence is reproduced in Heidegger's position in his understanding of Dasein, or human being, as existence and in his insistence on the dimension of transcendence. As early as his dissertation and in later writings, Heidegger continued to insist that human being was not only present in but also able to transcend its situation. But Heidegger goes further than Hegel in an important respect, since he follows Husserl's concept of the horizon, for instance in his insistence in *Being and Time* on the world as in effect the horizon for all interpretation. The point is not to perform a reduction on Heidegger's position by reducing it to its situation, since no philosophical theory is merely a reflection of the circumstances in which it arises. But since theories are also not independent of such circumstances, one can—in fact, in my view, one must—utilize an awareness of the role of that situation in the constitution of the theory as a clue to its interpretation. As concerns Heidegger, an awareness of such factors is helpful to understand his position in ways that might not be as evident if we restrict ourselves merely to the *Seinsfrage*.

Although it is my intention here to study Heidegger's Nazism, I do not intend to provide a study of Nazism as such. For present purposes it is unnecessary to consider the nature of Nazism in detail, which, as an amorphous collection of doctrines that never assumed canonical shape, is in any case notoriously difficult to define.[7] It will be sufficient to center this discussion on a doctrine which Heidegger shared with National Socialism as well as preceding forms of *Volk* ideology: the historical realization of the German *Volk*. I am less interested in Heidegger's acceptance of the *Führer* principle, an important element in the legal framework of the Nazi state, such as it was, than in the constant presence of a metaphysical commitment to the German *Volk* as a central historical goal in his thought, a commitment which, like the theme of a fugue, is consistently renewed at regular intervals beginning in 1933. It is, I believe, this concern—in conjunction with Heidegger's underlying interest in Being—which drew him to National Socialism. This concern remains constant throughout his career and determines the later development of his position, the evolution of which cannot otherwise be grasped.

The present inquiry into Heidegger's Nazism conflicts in two ways with the reigning temper of philosophy. On the one hand, it associates philosophy with history, whereas a major current in the modern tradition is to drive a wedge not only between philosophy and the history of philosophy but also between thought and history. Although there are exceptions, such as Hegel, most philosophers adopt a nonhistorical perspective on the grounds that truth is not historical. Yet if philosophy is to tell us about the world as given in experience, if it is to make good on its claim to grasp the nature of experience as a historical process, it must in some sense emerge within it and actually be historical. Philosophy cannot, then, sever the link to history and pretend to know it. Hence, in a deep sense a discussion of Heidegger's Nazism cannot be successful in isolation from a study of the link between his thought and his times.

On the other hand, the skepticism about truth as historical has given rise to skepticism about historical truth. The rise of deconstructionism, clearly influenced by Heidegger's position, is a form of skepticism with obvious historical implications. The very idea of historical truth has recently been placed in doubt by one of Heidegger's admirers, Paul de Man, who was notoriously concerned to conceal his own political past:

[I]t is always possible to face up to any experience (to excuse any guilt), because the experience always exists simultaneously as fictional discourse and as empirical event and it is never possible to decide which one of the two possibilities is the right one. The indecision makes it possible to excuse the bleakest of crimes because, as a fiction, it escapes from the constraints of guilt and innocence.[8]

The implication of de Man's view—which is by no means unprecedented, since it is common also, say, to Stalinism—is that we can treat the past as a fiction that can be rewritten at will in order to correct or even to erase what has taken place, to expunge inconvenient events from the historical record. But Heidegger's very idea that revealing is accompanied by concealing implies the obverse doctrine, that concealing is linked to revealing, or at least to its possibility. Despite Leopold von Ranke, it may not be possible to recover the past as it really happened, whatever that means. Yet in my view, there is indeed a kind of historical truth, a possibility of determining the historical record which justifies a refusal of historical skepticism and undercuts the efforts of many to conceal the past. A premise that underlies the present discussion is that despite Heidegger's lengthy effort to hide, to distort, and to misrepresent the nature of his commitment to Nazism, his very deception reveals itself as a deception as well as the truth about it if we will only examine his thought with sufficient care.

The discussion of the nature and philosophical consequences of Heidegger's Nazism unfolds in eight chapters. The first chapter, which is procedural, considers the proper approach to reveal the Nazism concealed in his thought. It is argued that his Nazism is concealed in his philosophy; it is further argued that through an "official view" of the matter Heidegger and a number of his followers have contrived to conceal his Nazism in a manner similar to that in which, in his belief, the original Greek insight into Being was later covered up. Chapter 2 studies in detail the famous rectoral address, in which Heidegger turns publicly to Nazism and seeks to ground politics in philosophy, in order, as Jaspers and, following him, Pöggeler have said, to lead the leaders. The speech, which is more often mentioned than analyzed, is studied in continuity with such background factors as the romantic reaction against the *Aufklärung,* the *völkisch* intellectual movement, the decline of the Weimar Republic, and Heidegger's view of inauthentic boredom as the predominant mood at the end of the Weimar period. The intrinsic link between Heidegger's philosophical thought and his turn to politics is analyzed in terms of concepts of authenticity, resoluteness, Being-with, destiny, fate, and so on. There is detailed attention to the quasi-Platonic aspect of Heidegger's understanding of the relation between politics and philosophy, his reliance on von Papen, his crucial misrendering of a Platonic text, and other relevant factors.

The third chapter discusses the effort, ultimately rooted in Heidegger's own fabrication of an "official" view of his relation to Nazism, to contain the damage to his reputation. The "official" view provides the basis for Heidegger's largely successful effort to minimize his Nazi turn as transitory whereas it was permanent, as unrelated to his thought from which it in fact followed closely, as unimportant for the later turning in his thought which it basically influenced, and so on. This phase of the discussion is mainly devoted to careful scrutiny of Heidegger's detailed account of his relation to Nazism as rector of the University of Freiburg in a posthumously published article, "The Rectorate 1933/34: Facts and Thoughts." Heidegger's discussion of his political turn is more often invoked than discussed. Analysis of this text, crucial for an understanding of Heidegger's political turn, shows that it reveals what it is meant to conceal: an enduring commitment to Nazism on the basis of his thought. Attention is given to the nature of Heidegger's philosophical attachment to Nazism, and its grounding in his concept of the destiny of the German people. Heidegger's sophistical effort to reinterpret the idea of *Kampf,* which he related to Clausewitz in the *Rektoratsrede,* and by implication to *Mein Kampf,* as a disguised allusion to Heraclitus is studied carefully.

Chapters 4 and 5 provide detailed discussion of Heidegger's first Hölderlin lecture series; of his recently published, unfinished work, for some his masterpiece, *Contributions to Philosophy* (*Beiträge zur Philosophie*), composed in 1936–1938 during his Nietzsche lecture courses; and of the Nietzsche lectures themselves. Following Heidegger's own suggestions, some of his followers (e.g., Aubenque, Vietta) maintain that in these places Heidegger decisively criticizes National Socialism. Yet close analysis of these texts reveals that Heidegger criticizes Nazism not as a political practice but for its alleged insufficiency as an ontological theory, that is, as a grasp of Being as such. It further reveals his continued insistence on the realization of the historical destiny of the German *Volk,* a point that originally led him to Nazism and which he never abandoned. Here, we find the emergence of a new conception of silence as no longer an authentic aspect of speech but the ground of authentic speech, a change tending to justify his own silence about Nazism and the Holocaust. Detailed discussion of the famous turning in his thought shows that it is composed of a series of elements, including, as part of his later "post-metaphysical" antihumanism, a turning away from personal responsibility—earlier stressed in the notion of resoluteness—in the later emphasis on Being as the ultimate historical agent.

The sixth chapter takes up the genesis and nature of Heidegger's theory of technology, which some writers (e.g., Caputo) see as his permanent legacy. Attention is focused on Heidegger's conception of technology as an effort to carry further a supposedly incomplete attempt by National Socialism to confront technology and modernity. The discussion, which criticizes Heidegger's nonanthropological understanding of modern technology as inadequate, shows that Heidegger does not break with, but carries further, his view of Nazism in his writing on technology. It further demonstrates the inadequacy of Heidegger's grasp, even after the Second World War, of National Socialism as a response to technology.

It is perhaps understandable on human grounds that Heidegger concealed his relation to Nazism. But since relevant material has long been available, no credit can be accorded to his followers for their continued obstruction of efforts to understand this relation. The seventh chapter reviews the reception of Heidegger's Nazism, with special attention to the obscurantist tendencies of the French discussion. In the discussion of Heidegger's politics, the French debate stands out as an ongoing effort, over many years, to examine, but mainly to defend, Heidegger's position. It is argued that Heidegger's thought has come to form the horizon of French philosophical thought, which has in turn obstructed the concern to understand the philosophical component of his Nazism.

The conclusion affirms an "organic" relation between Heidegger's philosophical thought and his commitment to real and ideal forms of Nazism. It compares the "organic" interpretation to other interpretations of the link between Heidegger's thought and politics. It considers the problem which the reception of Heidegger's political engagement poses for the reception of his thought, for philosophy in general, and for the responsibility of intellectuals. It is stressed that Heidegger's philosophy ought not to be rejected merely in terms of his political engagement but that his thought also cannot be understood apart from that engagement, which must figure prominently in the reception of his theory of Being. It is further stressed that Heidegger shares with Nazism an interest in authenticity, interpreted as the destiny of the German people, which he did not and literally could not renounce without renouncing an aspect of his thought unchanged in its later evolution, or turning. Heidegger's insensitivity to human being, which he apparently found meaningful only as a means to the authentic thought of Being, appears as a philosophical component of his insensitivity to Nazism. The book ends with a reflection on the paradox of Heidegger, an important thinker, perhaps a great philosopher, but unable to discern the character of National Socialism, a leading example of absolute evil. It is suggested that Heidegger's example calls in question the widely held view of the socially indispensable character of philosophic reason. If the ethical component is not present in the beginning, it will not be present at the end; and it was not present in—in fact, it was specifically excluded from—Heidegger's "antihumanist" meditation on Being. The concern to respect nature but the insensitivity to human being, the turn to Nazism, the continued adherence to the destiny of the German *Volk,* Heidegger's antihumanism and inability to understand Nazism even after the Second

World War, all follow from his nearly obsessive care about the authentic thought of Being.

It is appropriate to anticipate two related objections. On the one hand, there is the obvious criticism, long a staple of the Heideggerian defense of Heidegger's thought, that whoever criticizes the master is insufficiently versed in the position. Let me immediately concede the strategic strength of this defense, to which, in my opinion, there is no fully satisfactory response. It is appropriate to acknowledge the permanent possibility of skepticism about the analysis of a philosophical position. Any effort to allay doubts about the grasp of a theory can always be met by raising further doubts. But at a certain point, criticism cannot merely be evaded by suggestions that the critic is insufficiently versed in the topic and must be met directly. Readers will need to decide whether on balance this essay demonstrates a grasp of Heidegger's position sufficient to permit the analysis developed below.

On the other hand, there is the objection based not on lack of knowledge but possible prejudice, such as prejudice with regard to Heidegger's thought, even the imputation of prejudice for raising the question of the philosophical significance of Heidegger's Nazism.[9] The possibility of prejudice is certainly enhanced in a discussion of Nazism. I have no illusions that my rereading of these texts will convince all observers, some of whom will certainly find—indeed, how could it be otherwise?— that my discussion reflects my own prejudices. The issue of how to react to possible prejudice is an important hermeneutical theme. In reaction to the Enlightenment concern with pure reason, Gadamer, Heidegger's closest student, has tried to rehabilitate the concept of prejudice (*Vorurteil*) through the Hegelian move that we should be prejudiced against prejudice. In this case, I hold that nothing is to be gained by being open to prejudice, mine or that of anyone else. There can be no guarantee that all prejudice has been overcome. But if one must be prejudiced, which I do not concede, let us at least, with Aristotle, be prejudiced in favor of the truth.

The link between Heidegger's Nazism and his philosophical thought is the topic of an expanding literature in a variety of languages. It is necessary to present a reasonably broad account of the debate about Heidegger's politics, especially the discussion in languages other than English, for the reader to have a sense of the complex, controversial issues at stake and the relevant texts. It is useful to pull together the wider debate that has now become so broad as to be difficult to survey quickly if at all. The importance of an awareness of the prior discussion of the topic is brought home by a strategy to defend Heidegger now emerging in the American discussion, as well as elsewhere, which consists in bracketing the entire literature on the relation between Heidegger's philosophy and his Nazism in order to discuss his position in total isolation from his politics,[10] and his political turning in independence of what is now known about it.[11] In the same way as Heidegger later urged the idea of a *Verwindung* of metaphysics, the idea clearly is to confront the problem posed by the discussion of Heidegger's Nazism, not by responding to the available discussion and textual analyses, but by simply turning one's back on it.[12] Now only a philosopher could possibly hold that knowledge is irrelevant to judgment[13] or even prevents one from arriving at a proper understanding. Yet others, deeply committed to Heidegger's thought, have properly seen that Heidegger's receptivity to Nazism requires careful study since at this late date we cannot continue business as usual if we desire to understand Heidegger's thought.[14]

In the present case, the relevant material includes not only Heidegger's exoteric writings, in which he set out his official view of the matter, but his esoteric texts, including pertinent portions of his published writings and of his lectures and correspondence, certain background materials, and the full range of writings by Heidegger's defenders and critics. Hence, one criterion on which to judge this essay is its relative success in presenting a representative sample of the relevant materials, including materials that contradict my own reading of the issues as well as the main features of the previous debate. Another criterion is an appropriate treatment, not of Heidegger's thought in general, surely an enormous task, but of those portions of Heidegger's corpus which bear on the problem at issue here. Finally, one must consider the degree of insight offered by the overall conceptual framework proposed here into the wider theme of Heidegger's Nazism and philosophy. It is one thing to collect themes in the secondary discussion and in Heidegger's writings relevant to a grasp of the link between his Nazism and philosophy, and something else to weave the various strands together in an appropriate fabric, a comprehensive theory. A measure of the usefulness of this essay is its capacity to embrace and explain, but not to explain away, all that is now known, and to provide a place for what as yet remains unknown about Heidegger's turning toward National Socialism and the permanent place thereafter of Nazism in the further evolution of his philosophical thought. If it is not too much to ask, it is my hope that in this way it will be possible to focus the debate, not on a careless word or a phrase, as a means of evading the issues, but on a careful discussion, as serious as the serious nature of the theme permits, of the many issues raised by the deeply rooted, permanent commitment to National Socialism in the philosophical position of one of the most important thinkers of our time.

1

Revealing Concealed Nazism

The concern of this book is not with Heidegger's position as a whole, but with the link between his Nazism and that position. Now the theme of his Nazism is only in part visible, because it is mainly hidden, or concealed, in Heidegger's philosophy. An important part of our task will be to reveal Heidegger's Nazism in a way that also preserves the capacity for critical judgment. Much of the Heidegger literature is limited to exegesis in which his disciples, who routinely forgo criticism, expound the "revealed truth."[1] On the contrary, the aim of this essay is to describe, to interpret, and, when necessary, to criticize this aspect of his thought.

We can begin with the description of some of the main obstacles impeding access to Heidegger's philosophical thought—in particular, access to his Nazism. Heidegger was concerned to conceal what he was not obliged to reveal about his Nazism, to provide what can charitably be described as an indulgent, even a distorted view of the historical record and of his thought. Some of Heidegger's closest students, above all Karl Löwith, Otto Pöggeler, and more recently Thomas Sheehan, Theodore Kisiel, and Dominique Janicaud, have scrupulously attempted to disclose the nature and significance of his Nazism. Others, convinced of the importance of Heidegger's thought, have on occasion confused, even clearly identified, allegiance to Heidegger's thought and person with the discovery of the truth. In consequence, a certain number of obstacles, conceptual and otherwise, have arisen which impede an objective discussion of Heidegger's Nazism. In order to discuss this topic, it will be useful to identify the main obstacles. Accordingly, this chapter, whose intent is prolegomenal, will be devoted to clearing away some of the conceptual underbrush that has in the meantime grown up around the link between Heidegger's Nazism and his philosophy in order to expose this theme for more detailed study.

Concealing and Revealing

In the modern tradition, two of the best-known views of concealment are found in Marx and Freud. On the one hand, there is the Marxian concept of ideology, not to be identified with its Leninist cousin, or any of the myriad variant forms, according to which what Marxists call "bourgeois thought" tends to conceal the true state of society in order to prevent social change.[2] On the other, there is Freud's view of repression based on the complex libidinal economy of psychoanalysis. Now these two forms of concealment may or may not be relevant to Heidegger's thought. The dual insistence by both Ott and Farias on the significance of Heidegger's background depends on a form of the Freudian claim, not obviously inconsistent with Heidegger's own concept of Dasein, that thought is the conscious tip of an unconscious iceberg. Heidegger never tires of repeating that, as existence, Dasein is prior to a rational approach, which emerges only within existence.

To these two forms of concealment Heidegger opposes his own phenomenological view of the problem in the context of his focus on the problem of the meaning of Being, or *Seinsfrage.* In *Being and Time,* Heidegger maintains that there is nothing "behind" phenomena, although in the main, phenomena are not given and hence must be elicited by phenomenology.[3] He regards what he calls covered-up-ness, literally concealment, as the counterpart of the phenomenon.[4] Phenomenology in his view is then nothing more than the rendering visible of that which is not visible because covered up or hidden, which in turn leads to his characterization of phenomenological description as interpretation, that is, the hermeneutic that elucidates the authentic structures of Being.

For Heidegger, phenomenological hiddenness, perhaps even hiddenness as such, is either accidental or necessary. A necessary form of hiddenness is grounded in the very being of what is to be elucidated. According to Heidegger, a phenomenon is what shows itself and phenomena can in his words be "brought to light," or shown.[5] In *Being and Time,* Heidegger develops a view of truth as disclosure (*Erschlossenheit*) based on the idea that the phenomenon shows itself.[6] He maintains that an assertion of truth presupposes the uncovering of the entity as it is in itself.[7] According to Heidegger, what he calls Being-uncovering (*Entdeckend-sein*) must be literally wrested from the objects.[8] He sums up his view in two points: First, truth belongs to Dasein. Second, Dasein is fundamentally in truth and in untruth.

The theme of concealment remains important in Heidegger's later writing.[9] He further develops his doctrine of concealment in an important essay "On the Essence of Truth" first published in 1943. Here, in the context of the exposition of his view of truth as disclosure, he maintains that concealment is undisclosedness, hence the untruth intrinsic to the essence of truth.[10] Unlike Hegel, Heidegger does not regard untruth as essentially privative. Heidegger maintains that untruth or concealment is inherent in the nature of truth itself, so that disclosure, which reveals, also conceals. He insists that Dasein is marked by a preservation of untruth as mystery, as well as the flight from mystery toward what is readily available, which he designates as errancy. It is only in his late essay, "The End of Philosophy and the Task of Thinking," which appeared in 1964, that the doctrine of truth is denied, or at least basically revised. Here, as part of the effort to leave metaphysics and philosophy behind, he argues that uncovering is not truth but makes truth possible:

> Insofar as truth is understood in the traditional "natural" sense as the correspondence of knowledge with beings demonstrated in beings, but also insofar as truth is interpreted as the certainty of the knowledge of Being, *aletheia*, unconcealment in the sense of the opening may not be equated with truth. Rather, *aletheia*, unconcealment as opening, first grants the possibility of truth.[11]

Concealing in Heidegger's Thought

The present effort to elucidate the hidden dimension and philosophical significance of Heidegger's Nazism need not be, but in fact is, consistent with Heidegger's own view of concealment. Now Heidegger's thought is not distinguished by the very need as such to reveal it, since the study of other positions, particularly original theories, often encounters obstacles, linguistic, conceptual, or other, that impede their comprehension. What distinguishes Heidegger's thought is its link to Nazism, which is unprecedented among thinkers of the first rank and even among important philosophers in this century.

In virtue of its novelty, Heidegger's thought in general, not just the link between his thought and his Nazism, is concealed in a variety of ways. In an obvious sense, a thinker who has something importantly new to say, a novel doctrine to propose, a theory that differs in some significant way from other views, cannot be understood quickly. The reason is simply that ideas are always comprehended against a conceptual horizon, a background that acts as its frame of reference. As soon as a position breaks with the familiar conceptual frameworks, either through the introduction of a new form of thought, the denial of an essential element of what we thought we knew, or the reordering of accepted conceptions, then the usual background that serves to promote comprehension is lacking. If a novel view is quickly "understood," then invariably it is misunderstood. Certainly, one should not confuse the claim that a new idea has been grasped with the grasp itself.[12] It is likely that anyone who can be understood immediately is not a novel thinker, although the converse claim does not hold. It is even more likely that a thinker who makes an original contribution is misunderstood in the short run and only understood, if at all, at a later date, at a temporal remove, when the work necessary to revise the established categories, to open the discussion to new ways of thinking, has had the time to occur. Since Heidegger is a genuinely novel thinker who breaks with established patterns of thought, he is difficult to understand. It is possible that Heidegger's particular philosophical contribution has not yet been understood, or rather has so far been largely misunderstood.[13] Indeed, one of the aims of this discussion is to suggest that despite the immense literature concerning Heidegger's position, the intrinsic political dimension of his theory of Being has not so far been clearly seen.

The novelty of Heidegger's position is only one of the obstacles to its comprehension. The difficulty of Heidegger's language is legendary. Other philosophers, such as Whitehead, have devised novel terms to describe their basic insights, but Heidegger carries this practice to unusual, perhaps unprecedented, lengths. He frequently coins new words to express his ideas, or imparts technical meanings to available vocabulary—which he often uses in odd ways in accordance with the allegedly original meanings supposedly covered up by the later evolution of the language—or even employs a dash or other devices to highlight a part of the word. The result is a vocabulary that often has no usual equivalent in German and even more frequently has no easy rendition into English. An example among many is the term "*Ent-fernung*" for the ordinary German "*Entfernung*," which Macquarrie and Robinson translate by the neologism "deseverance."[14] The fact that many of Heidegger's formulations are at best unclear only heightens the difficulty of understanding.

Heidegger's thought is also difficult to comprehend in part because of the unfinished nature of *Being and Time,* his main treatise. It is well known that the published fragment is part of a much larger work, which never appeared. The extant fragment is difficult to interpret since Heidegger published his study before he had had a chance to give it a final form. A close reading of the text reveals ways in which he changed his mind on fundamental points during the writing of the book. For instance, he insists on a concept of truth as *veritas transcendentalis*,[15] similar to the Husserlian version of the traditional philosophical view of truth, before introducing an obviously incompatible hermeneutical notion of truth.[16] The incompatibility lies in the inability to make out a claim for the traditional philosophical notion of truth as absolute on the basis of the relativistic terrain of hermeneutics.[17] After the book was published, and in particular after Heidegger resigned his post as rector of the University of Freiburg in 1934, he increasingly devoted himself—perhaps under the influence of the intervening political events—to reinterpreting his main text in a long series of later writings. The result is that an already difficult book, bristling with strange neologisms and novel ideas, is rendered even more difficult by Heidegger's repeated efforts to construe his thought from an increasingly greater remove.

Heideggerian Concealment and the History of Philosophy

Heidegger's analysis of Being further conceals its relation to the history of philosophy. Now in part the relation of philosophy to its history has long been concealed through the normative view of philosophy current in the modern tradition. A main impulse at least since Descartes has been the preference for systematic over historical forms of thought. The result is the effort to begin again, finally to make a beginning, finally to make an acceptable beginning in virtue of the preference for a priori over a posteriori types of knowledge, succinctly formulated in Kant's insistence, following Leibniz, on *cognitio ex principiis* over *cognitio ex datis*.[18]

As the title of a well-known book about Heidegger suggests,[19] his entire philosophical career is focused to an unusual degree on a single project, initially identified as the question of the meaning of Being. The term "Being" refers to "Being in general," or the "Being of beings," as distinguished from beings, or entities, such as shoes or ships or sealing wax. Heidegger's conviction that since the early Greeks this question has been forgotten, or covered over, so that he needs to destroy later metaphysics in order to return to the original, and solely valid, form of the question, points both toward and away from the importance of the history of philosophy for Heidegger's position. His assertion that the *Seinsfrage,* or at least the *Seinsfrage* in its authentic form, has been forgotten since early in the philosophical tradition strongly suggests that his own thought cannot depend on other views in the history of philosophy which he seeks to "destroy" as the condition of freeing up the proper approach to Being.[20] Heidegger is unquestionably equipped with a deep, in fact unusual, command of the historical tradition; yet his own argument implies that his theory is independent of the history of philosophy, more precisely of anything that happened in the tradition after the pre-Socratics, or at the latest Aristotle.

The implication that Heidegger's own thought is independent of the history of philosophy since the Greeks—which derives from a strategic move on his part to open the path leading to Being—tends to insulate his position from critical scrutiny. In effect, as a result of this move Heidegger contends that his thought is not only original but sui generis. If it differs not only in degree but in kind from any others, that is, all the other views in earlier and contemporary philosophical discussion, then obviously it cannot be understood or evaluated through comparison with them.

Heidegger's references to later thinkers, particularly in *Being and Time,* are mainly negative. Partly for this reason, Heidegger has been accused of distorting, in fact deliberately concealing, his dependence on previous writers, for instance Kierkegaard.[21] Others have suggested a wider philosophical debt including Nietzsche,[22] Jünger,[23] and others. My own view is that there is a strongly Kantian component in his thought. I think that his study of Being as present under the mode of absence can be regarded as a variant of the Kantian dualistic analysis of noumenon and phenomenon, mediated by such neo-Kantian thinkers as Rickert and Lask. This claim implies that Heidegger's view of Being is circumscribed by the dualistic Kantian framework that structures most later discussion in the German tradition.

Heidegger's strategy to free his position from dependence on the preceding philosophical discussion, a strategy that is neither convincing nor original, impedes the comprehension of his position. An example, among many, of the effort to break with the prior philosophical tradition is Kant's claim, in the famous passage on the Copernican Revolution, that his own position represents a clean break with prior thought.[24] The grounds for Kant's introduction of the Copernican Revolution is that all previous efforts at knowledge have failed and that we need to invoke a new approach, represented by him as systematic. If "critical" means, as it does in Kant's thought, "not dogmatic" but "demonstrable," then we can inquire about the nature of the proof. Now a proof of the critical philosophy is not forthcoming on the a priori, systematic plane it favors, since its claim rests in part on the alleged failure of prior views, that is, on a reading of the history of philosophy. Even Kant's effort to establish the transcendental conditions of the possibility of any knowledge whatsoever is historically tinged, dependent on its relation to other theories in the philosophical tradition.

Heidegger's position is highly dependent on a wide variety of modern philosophers and even some nonphilosophers, such as Hölderlin, Jünger, and others. The dependence of Heidegger's thought on the preceding philosophical tradition is apparent in at least three ways. First, and most generally, we have already noted that all positions depend on prior thought for their evaluation, for their claim to advance the discussion. Second, Heidegger's argument depends on the history of philosophy since he needs to carry out his "destruction" of metaphysics in order to demonstrate the assertion that forms of ontology later than those of the Greeks have taken an incorrect turning in the road to Being. If he cannot show that later views of ontology are incorrect, then his claim to recover the only correct approach to Being, which has meanwhile lain hidden, is undercut. Third, his desire to return to origins, in this case the proposed return to the hidden beginnings of the philosophical discussion of Being, is merely another form of the widespread modern philosophical interest in bringing about an end to the discipline. In that precise sense, Heidegger's view is largely traditional.

Heidegger's Nazism and the Expert Commentator

An account of obstacles to an appreciation of Heidegger's Nazism needs to address the role of the Heidegger discussion in an enormous and still rapidly growing literature. Obviously, the justification for the debate concerning any thinker, including Heidegger, can only be to illuminate and ultimately to evaluate the position in question, which it must seek to reveal rather than to conceal. Unfortunately, the fact that this principle is often honored in the breach because of the evolution of the philosophical discipline itself has contributed in a powerful way to impeding access to Heidegger's thought, particularly to his Nazism.

Philosophy feeds on itself as the condition of its further progress. Despite the recent insistence on the independence of system from history, it is rather obvious that philosophy relies, indeed has always relied, on its preceding tradition for insight and impetus. Now the great philosophers are rarely if ever specialists in the interpretation of one or another body of thought, although their positions often depend on their understanding of a preceding position, as Aristotle depends on Plato, Spinoza depends on Descartes, Kant depends on Leibniz and Hume, and Fichte depends on Kant. But the recent development of philosophy has seen the emergence of the expert commentator, the person whose career is closely linked to the knowledge and interpretation of a single position, whose works he or she tends to know intimately and whose details loom large in the interpretation. This phenomenon is now almost pandemic in the academy, where whole careers are built upon superior knowledge of Dickens, or Proust, or Mozart's music.

The phenomenon of the expert commentator figures largely in the role of Heideggerians in the interpretation of the master's thought. Heideggerians have always claimed, rightly in my view, that Heidegger's thought presents unusual difficulties. Heideggerians have tended to seize on the difficulties of Heidegger's thought in order to make of its interpretation an almost mystical, hieratic process. The result, in imitation of Heidegger's own strategy, is to shield Heidegger's thought from any attempt at criticism.

If the only person who is acknowledged as sufficiently versed in a position, say Heidegger's, is someone whose entire professional career centers on the position in question, then philosophy is no longer the affair of philosophers in general. In modern times, certainly until relatively recently, through the time of the British empiricists, at least until Kant, virtually anyone, such as gifted amateurs like Descartes or Locke, could participate in the discussion on an equal footing. But this changes if the discussion is restricted to experts only, that is, to specialized students of a particular thinker, a particular question, a particular period. The result is to exclude not only the gifted amateur but even the professional philosopher whose lack of the most intimate knowledge of the position is taken to mean that it is in principle beyond his or her grasp.

It is obvious that the rise of the expert commentator tends to reduce or even to eliminate criticism. Here we need to distinguish between the way into philosophy through the study of a position and the professional expert commentator. It is often the case that one will write a dissertation, or even a first book on a given thinker, say on Wittgenstein, about whom one is enthusiastic, and then later change one's mind and reject that view as part of the maturation process of developing one's own point of view. This is very different from the approach of the expert commentator, who is much less likely to reject that about which he or she is expert. Someone whose career is built on detailed knowledge of a given position, for instance a Platonist who really "knows" Plato and the Plato literature in a thorough way, is exceedingly unlikely to offer fundamental criticism that places the entire theory, or even a part of it, in jeopardy. The obvious fact that Heidegger experts inevitably have a heavy professional investment in the importance, even the correctness, of his position explains their widespread reluctance to call it in question in any but the most timid manner.

The reduction of criticism due to the rise of the expert commentator is now widespread in the philosophical discipline at the present time. There is now increasing stress on the creation of specialized societies, with specialized publications, accompanied by specialized professional meetings, as philosophy, in imitation of nearly all forms of academic research, continues to fragment itself. The result is to inhibit philosophical change, even to impede philosophical progress. Obviously, philosophy advances through the scrutiny of previous views, which later thinkers find wanting in one respect or another and which they eventually seek to improve or replace. If the scrutiny of previous views is reduced to minute textual observations, then philosophical progress, such as it is, tends to diminish, even to come to an end. It is not privileged information that at present it is easier to advance in the profession by hanging around well-known colleagues and massaging their egos than by an effort at articulating a fundamental disagreement. Marxists talk about Marxists, Quine scholars dialogue with Quine scholars, Husserlians meet among themselves. But although the contact of experts, a frequent form of the manifestation of the rise of the expert commentator, often produces useful discussion, it inevitably tends as well to reduce the type of basic criticism that enables the discussion to progress beyond the particular view, even the particular form of the particular, under consideration.

There is a pronounced tendency among Heideggerian scholars to limit the Heidegger discussion to themselves. As a consequence the discussion becomes less adventurous, but perhaps more surefooted. This possible advantage is, however, dissipated by the transformation of what at best is a strategy for access to Heidegger's position through expert analysis into a strategy intended to prevent those outside of the Heideggerian fold from criticizing his thought. This tactic, which is much in evidence in the debate on Heidegger's Nazism, takes a number of different forms, including stress on the difficulty of rendering Heidegger's terminology, admittedly difficult by the standards of ordinary academic German, into other languages. I well remember a lecture of one and a half hours I attended devoted merely to the translation of the term "*Gestell*" into French. More recently, the undoubted linguistic unease in the translation of key terms has been transformed into a watershed question, in which defenders of the faith protect the master thinker through the claim that others are incapable of comprehending the central terms of his position. A particularly uncompromising form of this tactic consists in the denial that an outsider either does or possibly could understand the Heideggerian position. Examples include De Waehlens's assertion that Löwith, Heidegger's former student and later colleague, was not sufficiently versed in the thought of the master to criticize it, and Derrida's claim that Farias, who spent a dozen years writing a book about Heidegger's Nazism, could not possibly have spent more than an hour studying Heidegger's thought. A more general form of this tactic is to characterize whatever one says about the master thinker as metaphysics on the theory that Heidegger has somehow gone beyond it. This is tantamount to claiming that, as Ryle used to say, there is a category mistake since a metaphysical statement cannot possibly apply to Heidegger's view.[25]

The tendency to limit the Heideggerian discussion to Heidegger scholars works to preserve the Heideggerian view from prying eyes by rendering it invisible to any but the orthodox believer. To accept this requirement is to place a nearly insuperable obstacle in the path of any effort to come to grips with Heidegger's Nazism. With rare exceptions, the orthodox Heidegger scholar is highly unlikely to offer such criticism, since to do so is to admit that a professional career is focused on a thinker whose relentless pursuit of Being was centrally related to Nazism; and anyone who seriously objects can simply be dismissed as not knowledgeable enough to pass judgment. In effect, Heidegger's thought, like Plato's reality, then becomes a secret visible to men of gold only, something which only they can know and about which others can at best have no more than opinions. In this way, Heidegger's position can be worshiped but not evaluated as philosophy transforms itself into theology.

Heidegger's Nazism

In practice, the discussion of Heidegger in the literature has often constituted a major hindrance to an appreciation of the extent and significance of his Nazism. The obstacles that specifically impede a comprehension of Heidegger's Nazism are of three kinds: those due to Heidegger's largely successful effort to manipulate the discussion of his writings through the presentation of an "official" view of his Nazism and its relation to his thought; those due to the affirmation and development of what I am calling the official view as a specialized aspect of the enormous Heidegger secondary literature; and finally those which are not strictly philosophical at all. Heidegger's own understanding of his Nazism is displayed in an article written in 1945, in the famous *Spiegel* interview, and in hints scattered throughout his later texts. Heidegger's closest followers have developed Heidegger's own view of the matter in the course of the lengthy, often intense debate that continues to oppose Heidegger's critics and defenders on the theme of Heidegger's political views. The concern by some to defend Heidegger's person and thought at all costs has in practice led to further impediments to a grasp of his Nazism that are not always of a strictly philosophical nature, including simple problems of securing appropriate access to the texts.

What we can call "the facts" about Heidegger's Nazism have been known at least in part since the end of the Second World War. They are still not fully known since despite strenuous efforts by a small group of writers, most prominently Schneeberger, Ott, and Farias, efforts are under way to protect Heidegger, or his reputation, by hindering the release of factual material known to exist, above all in Marbach, where the Heidegger Archives are still closed to scholars.[26]

We can begin with that part of the factual material which is not in dispute and which is accepted by all observers. From a factual perspective, we know at least the following: Heidegger initially took up a position at Marburg, and when Husserl retired, Heidegger assumed his chair at the University of Freiburg. In 1933, Heidegger was elected to the post of rector of the University of Freiburg by his colleagues and became a member of the Nazi party. In the spring of that year, on the occasion of taking his position as rector, he gave the rectoral address (*Rektoratsrede*). In 1934 he resigned his position as rector and returned to teaching. After the Second World War, he was interrogated by the Allies and, mainly on the recommendation of Karl Jaspers, prevented from resuming his position in the university, although he was not formally charged with any war crimes. He was later permitted to resume teaching. He continued to write and occasionally to teach until the end of his life. Although he was often asked about the rectoral period, he avoided explicit comment except for two occasions: a posthumously published article, written in 1945; and an interview in 1966 with a popular weekly magazine, *Der Spiegel,* which, on his explicit request, was published only ten years later when he died.

If this were all there were to say, Heidegger's Nazism would not be interesting, certainly not more than faintly so, above all not philosophically interesting. There were many, including a distressing number of philosophers, those strange masters of blindness and insight, who had a brief relation to Nazism for a variety of reasons. Heidegger's relation was, however, different from other such encounters, in fact in some ways unprecedented. Let us now provide a partial enumeration of some of these differences. An obvious factor is the fact that Heidegger stands absolutely alone among the major thinkers of this century as a voluntary adherent of Nazism.[27] If there were no other reason, then the fact that Heidegger was the only important philosopher to become a Nazi is worthy of consideration.

But this is not the only factor, since although Heidegger refused to comment publicly on his Nazism, his writings contain a series of cryptic hints concerning this episode. In his usual ambiguous style, Heidegger indicates that he confronted National Socialism in his writings and left it behind him, something Heideggerians like to stress.[28] Heidegger implies that he has come to grips with Nazism in several texts, including the account of the turning (*Kehre*) in his thought in the "Letter on Humanism"[29] and the remark in the *Spiegel* interview that his initial course on Hölderlin and his courses on Nietzsche were a confrontation (*Ausei-*

nandersetzung) with National Socialism.[30] I believe that Heidegger's version of his Nazism is overly indulgent, tendentious, and misleading. In my view, Heidegger's presentation of his Nazism as essentially meaningless occludes, or conceals, its deep significance for the understanding and evaluation of his view of Being. I hold that the study of the texts themselves presents a rather different view of the matter less favorable to Heidegger and in fact damaging to his thought.

One impediment to a comprehension of Heidegger's Nazism is the misleading series of hints about it in Heidegger's texts, hints that taken together constitute his own "official" view of the situation. In Heidegger's wake, a certain number of his followers have presented a version of events which at most denies, at least minimizes, and in any case further distorts Heidegger's Nazism as well as its relation to his thought. The result has been an effort, extending now over several decades, to construe Heidegger's turn to National Socialism in a way that is not harmful, or at least no more than minimally harmful, to the philosopher. Writers engaged in this task include some of his most important French students, but a number of others, all of whom follow Heidegger's own lead in an effort at what—in language more familiar from the political realm, but appropriate here, since the aim is clearly political—can charitably be called damage control.[31]

A strong statement tending to call in question the life and thought of a major thinker requires strong evidence. One factor is Heidegger's scandalous refusal to comment on his Nazism during his lifetime over a period of more than forty years. Then there is Heidegger's infamous stress on the supposedly misunderstood essence of National Socialism in a work republished in 1953.[32] Further, there is the exchange of letters with Herbert Marcuse, in which Heidegger seemed to justify Nazism, as well as the comparison, in an unpublished lecture on technology, between the Nazi extermination of the Jews and agricultural technology.[33]

Attention to these and other passages in his writings suggests that Heidegger did not engage in a confrontation with National Socialism; on the contrary, he sought to conceal the nature of his original and continued interest in Nazism. His writings, then, call in question his own publicly stated view of the matter and suggest that the "official" view, due to Heidegger and propagated by his disciples, is incomplete, inaccurate, or both. This suggestion is further supported by the role of the Heidegger family in controlling access to his *Nachlass*. Germany, until recently West Germany, has long maintained exceedingly strict restrictions on unauthorized publication. It is, then, relevant to note that the Heidegger family has consistently refused publication of a number of important documents concerning Heidegger's Nazism and restricted access to Heidegger's unpublished work.[34] This restriction even extends to the publication of Heidegger's collected works, now under way. The collected works of a major thinker usually, perhaps even always, contain the extant correspondence. In Heidegger's case, his correspondence would almost certainly provide important evidence for an evaluation of his Nazism, especially through the publication of his correspondence as rector of the University of Freiburg. It is, hence, significant that the edition of his collected works now in preparation, in a clear departure from the practice for the writings of a major thinker, will omit his letters.

The aim of this chapter has been to identify some of the obstacles impeding responsible study of Heidegger's Nazism. It is not meant as, and cannot take the place of, a detailed discussion of the texts themselves. This chapter has shown that the scrutiny of Heidegger's Nazism presents formidable obstacles due to the peculiar nature of his thought, as well as the efforts consistently deployed by himself, certain students, and even his family, to prevent an accurate understanding of his Nazism from emerging and to propagate an interpretation that is more charitable to Heidegger than to the truth. We can add to this complex situation the fact that more than forty-five years after the end of the Second World War many, including a number of Heidegger's disciples, are less than eager to engage in a dispassionate analysis of a difficult period, in which they were personally involved, and to which their relationship remains ambiguous. There is, hence, reason to believe that after some four decades of discussion beginning in the 1940s we still do not fully comprehend the nature of Heidegger's Nazism nor understand its relation to his philosophical thought. The remainder of this essay will be devoted to an elucidation and interpretation of Heidegger's Nazism and an evaluation of its significance for his philosophy, even for philosophy in a wider sense.

2

The Nazi Turning and the
Rectoral Address

The preceding chapter, which was prolegomenal, identified obstacles tending to impede a comprehension of Heidegger's Nazism, above all the smoke screens propagated by Heidegger and his closest followers. This chapter will provide the difficult transition to study of the relevant textual material. It is relatively easy to identify impediments to an understanding of Heidegger's Nazism. It is much more difficult to analyze Heidegger's Nazism and its relation to his philosophical thought. It is an indisputable fact that in the period after the publication of *Being and Time,* the magisterial statement of his fundamental ontology, Heidegger turned to Nazism. The problem that arises can be stated in question form: How are we to understand Heidegger's turn to Nazism? In asking this question, my aim is not to determine the role that Heidegger could conceivably have played in the difficult situation in the later 1920s in Germany in Hitler's rise to power.[1] On the contrary, I am interested in the opposite question: how is Heidegger's Nazi turning related to his philosophical position? It is not sufficient merely to aim at a total explanation of human behavior, at a total grasp of human being.[2] If we are to understand the nature and significance of Heidegger's political turning for his philosophy, then we must study the importance of his philosophy of Being for his Nazism, for his political practice. The difficulty, which is real, is that we do not understand in general how thought relates to practice. In order, then, to understand the link between Heidegger's philosophy and politics, between his fundamental ontology and his Nazism, it will be necessary to devise an explanatory framework.

What I am calling Heidegger's Nazi turning is a complex process that is not reducible to any single event nor even to the endorsement of a single doctrine. Heidegger's private embrace of National Socialism apparently occurred as early as 1931, well before the electoral victory of the NSDAP. His public turn toward Nazism obviously occurred when he joined the Nazi party on 1 May 1933. On a philosophical plane, his Nazi turning took place in the rectoral speech delivered on the occasion of Heidegger's formal assumption of the rectorate of the University of Freiburg. It is important to distinguish between the turn to Nazism and the basis for its occurrence. I believe that Heidegger's Nazi turning can be understood as the result of factors external and internal to his thought, that is, factors that impinged upon him and others in the period toward the end of the Weimar Republic, as well as his philosophical position that arose in this political, social, and historical setting. This chapter will study factors within and outside of Heidegger's fundamental ontology leading to Heidegger's turn toward National Socialism; it will further examine a crucial exoteric document: the rectoral address.

Extraphilosophic Factors in Heidegger's Nazi Turning

Heidegger's turning to Nazism is not explicable through any single factor or type of factor. It has been held that his Nazi turn is due merely to his philosophy or merely to nonphilosophical reasons.[3] In fact, it is the result of both philosophical and extraphilosophical—or, for want of a better term, "existential"—factors. Among the many factors that are cited as influencing the rise of Nazism, beyond Adolf Hitler, are "German philosophy, romantic mysticism, anti-Semitism, the 'stab in the back' argument aimed at the Weimar Republic, German big business, the German economy in the wake of the Versailles treaty, the Prussian tradition, insidious occultism associated with 'ariosophy,' and the threat of Stalinist communism."[4] Factors that led to National Socialism were part of the social, political, and historical background when Heidegger turned to Nazism. Among the many factors ingredient in the wider background in which Heidegger's philosophical position emerged and in which he turned to Nazism, three are particularly important for his own political evolution: the decline of the Weimar Republic, the prevailing conservative political thought, and the *Volk* ideology it expressed.

Historical Background: The Weimar Republic

Since a political engagement does not occur in a social, political, and conceptual vacuum, it is useful to indicate, at least in outline, some of the main features of the social context when Heidegger became rector.[5] The Nazi accession to power occurred against the background of German history. Under Bismarck, the minister of war for Wilhelm I, Germany was unified, Schleswig-Holstein was wrested from Denmark, and Prussia took the place previously occupied by Austria. Germany successfully waged war against France, increased its imperial power, and acquired foreign colonies. The expansion and consolidation of German power came to an abrupt halt with the end of the First World War, culminating in the Treaty of Versailles in June 1919, which was widely perceived as a humiliation by the defeated German population.

The Weimar Republic arose and can be understood against the background of more than a half century of imperialist expansion through war.[6] It was proclaimed on 9 November 1918 in Weimar—the site of the intellectual circle centered around Goethe, one of the greatest humanists in the history of European culture—by the Social Democrat Philipp Scheidemann. The Weimar Republic prospered during the golden twenties, which culminated in the world economic crisis in 1929.[7] The history of the Weimar Republic describes a short period of hope symbolized by the introduction of a republican form of government, in an obvious reaction against the consequences of German imperialism, which then quickly degenerated into one of the worst tyrannies the world has ever known. Whether the hope was ever justified, whether the period of the Weimar Republic was more than a failed effort at the introduction of a liberal democratic form of goverment in the interregnum between two world wars, is a topic of scholarly debate.

Even before the outbreak of economic depression, the Weimar Republic suffered from a series of deep ideological, social, political, and economic problems. The world economic crisis that arose in 1929 led to enormous inflation and staggering unemployment, among other social problems. It was accompanied by an almost palpable sense of decay in the university and many other areas of German life.[8] In Heidegger's philosophy, the influence of this particular problem is visible in Heidegger's analysis, in a lecture course, of the prevailing mood as one of boredom and in the rectoral talk in his concern to defend what he refers to as the essence of the German university. There was further a clear sense of instability, a belief that things could not just continue on the same course, a conviction that something needed to be done, a longing for a solution, even a radical measure to transform the situation in steady deterioration. The final part of the Weimar period has been aptly described, immediately before Hitler took office, as follows: "This, then, was the Weimar Republic in 1932: clear vision and political impotence, fear, suspicion, and moments of irrational hope, among the politicians of the middle, politics as usual, but with everyone else, a sense of emergency."[9]

The reasons for the demise of the Weimar Republic are still not clear. One possibility is the failure to comprehend the growing threat of the imperialism of German monopoly capital.[10] Another is the concern with political freedom as the means to an end rather than an end in itself.[11] Yet another is the perpetration of a conservative revolution from the right.[12] Still others include the polarization between various right- and left-wing extremes, the idea of a democracy not itself democratic—both of which suggest that "the people" in a collective sense was in some sense responsible for the Republic's end—the fascist seizure of power, the interplay of certain forces, and so on.[13] What is known is that the outbreak of a world economic crisis destabilized a weak government, exacerbating social and political tensions, which in turn contributed to an unexpected Nazi electoral victory in July 1932. The end of the Republic less than a decade and a half after it began was hastened when von Papen persuaded Hindenburg to appoint Hitler as chancellor. It finally ended with the resignation of Kurt von Schleicher on 28 January 1933 and the assumption of power by Adolf Hitler on 30 January of that year, which led straight into Nazi tyranny.[14]

The complex series of events that led to the Nazi assumption of power is different from its significance.[15] The German revolution that began in 1933 and led to a second defeat of Germany was only the continuation of the historical process begun under Bismarck, which came to a temporary halt, during the Weimar period, at the end of the First World War. If this is true, then the rise of National Socialism can be regarded as an effort to win a war that had already been lost, to renew with a political approach the momentum temporarily suspended during the Weimar Republic, which unsuccessfully sought to lead Germany in another direction, to restore German self-esteem and confidence—in short, to bring about the historical realization of the German people.[16]

Conservative Political Thought

Heidegger's concern with the contemporary situation can be understood in the context of the interest of German intellectuals in general with modern life. He was one of a large group of German intellectuals who found change unsettling and who in various ways longed for a return to an earlier, more stable social structure.[17] He shared the widespread conservative worldview that emerged after the loss of the First World War, including conservative revolutionary tendencies, visible in his Nazi turning, and the rejection of the liberal democratic conception embodied by the Weimar Republic. He further shared the anticapitalist romanticism that emerged toward the end of the nineteenth century and that can be symbolized by the opposition between *Kultur* and *Zivilisation,* according to which culture in the deep sense required a rejection of modernity.[18] This view is evident in Heidegger's writings in his cult of Greek thought as the true form of philosophy. Yet it is important not to confuse the widespread conservativism of this period with support for National Socialism, which at the peak of its electoral success in the elections of April and July 1932 garnered no more than 37 percent of the popular vote.[19]

Heidegger shared the growing sense of unease widely felt by German intellectuals in the waning days of the Weimar Republic.[20] This intellectual sense of dismay found expression among German intellectuals in a concern to "locate" human being with respect to the present. Two extremes can be represented by Max Scheler, the phenomenologist and Jewish convert to Catholicism, whose thought influenced Heidegger's, and Karl Mannheim, a prominent sociologist who studied with the Marxist Lukács and with Heidegger. In 1928 in the "Author's Preface" to his last uncompleted book, significantly entitled *Man's Place in Nature,* Scheler writes in reference to contemporary work in philosophical anthropology: "In spite of this, however, man is more of a problem to himself at the present time than ever before in all recorded history."[21] Only one year later, from a radically different angle of vision, Mannheim observes that it is "imperative in the present transitional epoch to make use of the intellectual twilight which dominates our epoch and in which all values and points of view appear in their genuine relativity. We must realize once and for all that the meanings which make up our world are simply an historically determined and continuously developing structure in which man develops, and are in no sense absolute."[22]

Heidegger further shared the rejection, following from the concern to seek a third way between liberal democracy and Bolshevism, of modernity as such. Heidegger is already opposed to Cartesianism, a central form of modern philosophy, as early as 1919. Yet modernity is not a problem in Heidegger's fundamental ontology, either in *Being and Time* or in his other early writings. So far as I know, the word "modernity" does not even occur in the book. The question, however, of what Blumenberg has felicitously called the "legitimacy of the modern age" is in retrospect an obvious issue for Heidegger's philosophy.[23] As became clear in the later evolution of his thought—in his rejection of both metaphysics or modern theory and technology or modern practice—his conception of ontology brought him into conflict with anything modern as such. A typical instance is his later comment in a lecture course that the danger we face lies not in the decline of the West but in the acceptance and development of the idea of modernity.[24]

Heidegger's embrace of National Socialism is exceptional only for the importance of his thought and the depth of his commitment. But his failure to oppose Nazism is typical of the behavior of German philosophers in general. It is not well known, in part because German philosophy during the Nazi period has not often been studied, that German philosophy played an equivocal role at this time.[25] It has been said that German philosophy failed in three different ways: in removing or even weakening the barriers against National Socialism, in creating an intellectual atmosphere propitious to it, and in apologizing for it.[26] Certainly, German philosophers both collectively and individually did little to prevent the rise of Nazism.

When one reads the texts from this period, the widespread insensitivity among philosophers to the specific currents, such as anti-Semitism, that shortly led to National Socialism is striking. An example among many is Heidegger's remark in a letter of 1926 to Jaspers, who was married to a Jewish woman, about the concern in the University of Marburg to appoint a non-Jew and if at all possible a German nationalist, a remark that typically evoked no protest from Jaspers.[27] It has been pointed out that many Germans unsympathetic to Hitler's anti-Semitism were willing to cooperate with him to revise the Versailles treaty and in general to strengthen Germany's position in Europe.[28] Indeed, it is a mistake to consider anti-Semitism as the single crucial problem, or maybe even as crucial at all, since it was not one of the central themes in Hitler's rise to power.[29]

Once Nazism had taken power, German philosophers typically either rushed to ingratiate themselves with the National Socialist movement, or at least failed to reject it. When they did reject it, they mainly did so in an ineffectual manner, for instance in Husserl's noble but pathetic call to defend the ancient Greek distinction between knowledge and opinion in order to resist the rise of Nazi barbarism.[30] In retrospect, however, Husserl's rejection of National Socialism, weak as it unfortunately was, shines like a beacon in comparison with the more typical philosophical effort to embrace, or at least to cooperate with, Hitler's movement, above all by Martin Heidegger. It is a matter of record that there is no important protest against Nazism by the German philosophical community.[31] Although this has been explained through the unpolitical nature of German philosophers, in fact many German philosophers who represented themselves as unpolitical were intensely political beings, including Heidegger. In 1933, when Heidegger issued his claim as the rector of the University of Freiburg to be the philosophical *Führer* of National

Socialism, he was only one of numerous philosophers each of whom claimed to provide the only correct idea of the new Nazi state through his own philosophy, including Krieck, Bauemler, Rothacker, Gehlen, and others.[32]

Although Hitler only came to power in 1933, as early as the presidential elections in early 1932 a manifesto of personal support for Hitler was issued by six professors, including a philosopher, Carl August Enge, professor of law (*Rechtsphilosophie*) in Jena and scientific director of the Nietzsche Archives in Jena.[33] Between this initial manifesto and the election of the Reichstag in November 1933, there were no fewer than four other manifestos in which a progressively greater number of philosophers participated.[34] On the occasion of the vote for the Reichstag in November 1933, no fewer than a thousand professors, after an address by Heidegger, publicly acknowledged their support for Hitler and the National Socialist state, including Heidegger, N. Ach, O. F. Bollnow, O. Dittrich, K. Graf Dürckheim, H. Freyer, H.-G. Gadamer, A. Gehlen, J. E. Heyde, E. Jaensch, G. Krüger, F. Krueger, K. Leese, P. Lersch, H. Lipps, F. Lipsius, T. Litt, D. Mahnke, H. Noack, K. J. Obenauer, J. Ritter, H. Sauer, W. Schingnitz, H. Schneider, H. Schwarz, and W. Wirth.[35]

In fact, philosophical support for Hitler began even earlier. For instance, Ernst Krieck, professor of pedagogy, with whom Heidegger later collaborated on the National Socialist reform of German higher education, was disciplined for a pro-Nazi speech in 1931; and when he joined the NSDAP on 1 January 1932, he was suspended. Until the end of 1932, slightly more than 1 percent of the German academic establishment had publicly taken a position for Hitler, including eight philosophers: Enge, Schwarz, Krueger, Krieck, Baeumler, Rothacker, Bornhausen, and Jaensch.[36] Apparently the numbers would have been even larger had other philosophical colleagues, like German academics in general, not held back for tactical considerations.[37] The awareness of political consequences was not misplaced, since a number of academics, including more than thirty philosophers, quickly lost their positions in 1933.[38] Among the philosophers, in April, Max Horkheimer, Karl Mannheim, Paul Tillich, and Siegfried Marck; then in July Ernst von Aster was fired and August Messer and Hans Driesch were forcibly retired; and Bernhard Groethuysen was chased out of the university.[39] Other philosophers who were let go in 1933 include Richard Hönigswald, Ernst Cassirer, Jonas Cohn, Arthur Liebert, Dietrich von Hildebrandt, Helmuth Plessner, Martin Buber, and Theodor Adorno.[40]

From a political perspective, Heidegger largely shared the conservative tendencies prevalent after the First World War, including the basic acceptance, or at least tolerance, of National Socialism with the exception of its biological anti-Semitism, which was declined by most academics, and his participation, surprising for Heidegger, who seems to have had few or no personal heroes, in the Hitler cult. Heidegger followed other conservative intellectuals in rejecting both Bolshevism and liberalism of all kinds. But he carried his cooperation with Nazism further than most other academics, certainly further than any philosopher with the exception of Ernst Krieck. The main difference between Heidegger and all other philosophers, including Krieck, was his impressive ability to express his conservative worldview, itself typical of the conservative mood of the times among intellectuals, in a series of philosophical doctrines. These doctrines, all of which are deeply rooted in his philosophy of Being, include: the rejection of a democratic form of government as antithetical to modern life, particularly evident in the *Spiegel* interview; the philosophical reworking of Schmitt's conception of decisionism, the basis of the *Führer* principle, in his own conception of resoluteness;[41] the rejection of modernity itself in his espousal of Nietzsche's diagnosis of nihilism and European nihilism; and his own later rejection of technology.

The *Volk* and German Romanticism

The concern of conservative German intellectuals, including a large proportion of German academics, to seek a third way between the failed liberalism incarnated by the Weimar Republic and the Bolshevism which they unanimously feared was motivated by both historical and conceptual factors. On the one hand, it was motivated by such historical circumstances as the concern to redeem the German defeat in the First World War, to restore German honor and pride. But it was also spurred on by the reactionary tradition of German *Volk*-thought, with its stress on the historical realization and exaltation of the Germans as German, which impelled both the imperialist movement stemming from Bismarck and the National Socialist conception of the German nation. In *Mein Kampf,* Hitler clearly stressed the fact of belonging to the German *Volk,* namely the conception of nationality (*Volkstum,* from *Volk*), as more important than the state, which was merely a means to the achievement and preservation of the higher form of human being.[42]

The *Volk* perspective, which is older than Nazism, was already an important current in nineteenth-century German thought. It emerged as a romantic response to the general problem of human being in modern society, the so-called *condition humaine,* with important ties to German romanticism and conservative thinking. The *völkisch* perspective, like romanticism with which it is allied, represents an approach to the problems of modern life which eschews rational solutions of any kind, including economic analysis, social reform, and so on, in favor of an emphasis on human being in an often mystical sense. It differs from romanticism, which places primary emphasis on the individual, in the appeal to supraindividual, mystical forces and the stress on the people writ large. The importance of the individual is limited to the belonging to the group, typically the nation or the race, or both. Unlike romanticism, which is often apolitical, *völkisch* thought is typically related to extreme forms of political conservatism and the most virulent types of nationalism.

Völkisch ideas were typically advanced in order to counter widespread alienation held to be characteristic of modern society. The conception of alienation, understood as separation, say the separation of human being from its essence, or essential nature, is older than modernity. It has a long theological lineage, for instance in the idea that Adam and Eve, and human beings in general, were separated from God. In this view, which dominates Christianity, the purpose of human life is to overcome one's separation from the divine by finding the way back to God. This view receives a secularized development in the effort of modern thinkers to "think" the problem of the modern human being. It can be illustrated in a passage about labor that Hegel cites from Adam Smith:

> But the value of labor decreases in the same proportion as the productivity of labor increases. Work becomes thus absolutely more and more dead, it becomes machine-labor, the individual's own skill becomes infinitely limited, and the consciousness of the factory worker is degraded to the utmost level of dullness. The connection between the particular sort of labor and the infinite mass of needs becomes wholly imperceptible, turns into a blind dependence. It thus happens that a far-away operation often affects a whole class of people who have hitherto satisfied their needs through it; all of a sudden it limits [their work], makes it redundant and useless.[43]

The concern with alienation as the condition of human being in modern society is a frequent theme in modern thought in an almost bewildering variety of ways, in literature, art, and philosophy, but also in psychology, psychiatry, sociology, and other disciplines. All of these disciplines are concerned with the recognition and analysis of the phenomenon of alienation and the diagnosis of ways to achieve reconciliation, to heal the perceived dichotomy. This concern is widely present in modern political philosophy, for instance in Hobbes's view of the social contract as a necesssary evil, and in Rousseau's espousal of a political reformulation of society to reach a simple human community that is neither the state of nature nor civilization as we know it. In the period after the French Revolution, the diagnosis and supersession of alienation becomes a main theme in the thought of Hegel.[44] The dual concepts of alienation and reconciliation are important to the views of his main successors: Marx, Kierkegaard, and Nietzsche.[45] Alienation is further a main theme in Heidegger's early position and, under the guise of a concern for the historical realization of the German people, a persistent aspect of all his later thought.

The philosophical concern with the diagnosis and supersession of alienation runs parallel to a similar concern in the romantic movement, including literature, art,[46] and politics. Political romanticism found expression in such diverse tendencies as romantic traditionalism, romantic humanitarianism, and romantic nationalism. In reaction to the French Revolution, a specific form of political romanticism was created in Europe by the fear of revolutionary ideology in the writings of Edmund Burke, Joseph de Maistre, and L. G. A. de Bonald. Philosophically, romanticism has been described as a loosely related set of views consisting in the rejection of rationalism, of the Locke-Hume philosophical axis.[47] Romanticism is said to be typified by a cluster of beliefs including idealization of social relations in contrast with the Enlightenment view, the idea of the state as a social organism, opposition to the thought of the French Revolution, sympathy for Roman Catholicism, and nationalism.[48] It has further been observed that in all its varieties, romanticism celebrates the self.[49]

The idea of the *Volk* features a characteristic romantic response to the problem of the separation, or alienation, supposedly typical of life in modern society. The general idea of *Volksgeist,* or spirit of a people, which cannot be equated with *Volk* ideology, its degenerate, reactionary form, appears in historical investigations, in the writings of such diverse thinkers as Burke, Montesquieu, Hume, and Voltaire. The intellectual genesis of this concept has been traced to three writers:[50] Herder, who refers to the *Geist des Volkes, Geist der Nation,* and *Nationalgeist*; Hegel's coinage of the term *"Volksgeist,"* in the course of early meditations on popular religion and Christianity;[51] and the controversy involving F. K. Savigny and G. F. Puchta, in the historical school of law, about the relation between the national spirit and the legal system. Rotenstreich points out that the idea of a *Volksgeist* provided "a descriptive concept as well as a normative demand of faithfulness"[52] influential in politics, literature, law, and philosophy, as well as the distinction between peoples and their traditions.

The idea of a *Volksgeist* need not, but can, be used for specifically conservative purposes, as witness the later Nazi confusion of the distinctions between *Volksgeist* and race. The concept of the *Volk* is difficult to define, but important to grasp as a central factor in Heidegger's turn toward Nazism. According to Bourdieu, who mainly bases himself on Mosse, the *völkisch* perspective is an attitude toward the world, which resists any objectification, englobing literary, historical, and philosophical sources, as well as biological and philological forms of racism, including a series of confused views regarding phantasms, technology, workers, the elite, the people, and concerning history and country.[53] Mosse stresses the filiation leading from romanticism to the idea of the *Volk*, which he regards as similarly irrational and emotional. He adduces a series of traits as characteristic of right-wing, *völkisch* thought, including the *Volk* as a desired unity beyond contemporary reality, "a more tangible vessel for the life force that flowed from the cosmos," a romantic pantheistic concept of nature, a view of the spirit as limited to a national entity, and a concept of man as not vanquishing or overcoming nature but as living in harmony with it.[54] Heidegger's later exaltation of allegedly misunderstood nature as *physis* through his conception of *Gelassenheit* is, with the exception of the philosophical formulation, typical of the *Volk* perspective. From a quasi-philosophical perspective, the *Volk* point of view reached its dubious high point in the insistence of Alfred Rosenberg, the chief Nazi ideologist, in his analysis of the alleged myth of the twentieth century, on soul as the interior form of race and the racial soul as the effective motor of history.[55]

Romantic thought is essentially antirationalist, directed against the Enlightenment and its legitimate achievements in the defense of reason. Whereas the Enlightenment thinker seeks a rational solution to the problems of society, founded on faith in reason, the disillusioned romantic[56] typically eschews reason in an effort to return into oneself to seek the proper attitude to life and reality. There is a clear connection between the intrinsically romantic effort to resolve the great social and political problems of the day through essentially magical solutions and the essential antirationalism common to all forms of totalitarian thought. Berlin's account of the antirationalistic, romantic approach to human life and action, including the problem of alienation, in the writings of Joseph de Maistre, an early forerunner of fascism, is an accurate description of the *Volk*-ideological approach to modern life which influenced Heidegger's own Nazi turning:

> Human action in his [i.e., Maistre's] sense is justified only when it derives from that tendency in human beings which is directed neither to happiness nor to comfort, nor to neat, logically coherent patterns of life, nor to self-assertion and self-aggrandizement, but to the fulfillment of an unfathomable divine purpose which men cannot, and should not try to, fathom—and which they deny at their peril.[57]

In his own way, Heidegger echoes this concern in his steadfast insistence throughout his entire career on the importance of Being. It is literally through uncognizable Being, which in his view towers over beings, or mere entities, and human being alike, that he sought to comprehend all questions concerning human being now and in the future.

Intraphilosophic Factors in Heidegger's Nazi Turning

Fundamental Ontology, Nazism, and Political Philosophy

The account of external factors in the background has identified factors that impinge on, form the background of, and are reflected in Heidegger's fundamental ontology. There can be no doubt that Heidegger's personal and philosophical position reflect the decline of the Weimar Republic and the intensely conservative tendencies of the period. Both of these factors impelled many other German intellectuals of this period, including numerous German philosophers, toward National Socialism. Yet Heidegger was neither an ordinary German nor even an ordinary German philosopher. Since he differed from all other Germans, including all other German philosophers, in the possession of a philosophical position of unusual importance, we must inquire whether there are still other factors, factors internal to Heidegger's thought, that led him in the direction of Nazism.

As a first step, it is helpful to recall the traditional philosophical view of the relation between philosophy and politics. We owe to Plato the idea that philosophy is a necessary condition for the good life. Philosophy, on this view, differs from other disciplines such as shoemaking or chemistry, in that while the other disciplines contribute to a good life and are useful to that end, philosophy is not only useful but moreover indispensable, for philosophers and only philosophers possess unique insight into reality. To put the point more strongly, the good life may well be possible without shoemakers or chemists; but, according to the traditional view, it is not possible without philosophers. It is, then, different if a businessman or a philosopher turns to Nazism. One cannot demand that a businessman possess knowledge that leads beyond the business world. But a philosopher can be held responsible for his political actions since philosophy is intended to afford insight into the political realm.

It is difficult to square the claim for the specific insight of philosophy into reality, including politics, with the actions of philosophers. The actions of philosophers in times of crisis provide no comfort to those who hold that knowing and doing are intimately related. If Nazism is evil, then it is troubling that German philosophers lined up to become members of the NSDAP. Either philosophy was insufficient to discern the truth in such political circumstances, for instance through a misidentification of Nazism as the good, or knowledge of the truth was insufficient to influence actions as German philosophers flocked to enlist in this cause. Despite philosophical claims for the political utility of their discipline, philosophers have at best an indifferent political record. There is no reason to believe that philosophy as such is either politically indispensable or the source of political insight. Philosophers have certainly not been the model citizens that their superior insight would suggest, although the link between their thought and their actions is often rather tenuous. For instance, Frege's well-known, vicious anti-Semitism seems unrelated to his fundamental contributions to modern logic.[58] On the contrary, the relation between Heidegger's philosophy and his politics is by no means merely contingent, or limited to the impact of external factors, since it follows as well from factors internal to his thought.

The link between Heidegger's thought and his politics is a form of the wider problem of the relation between theory and practice. It is no accident that Heidegger turned to politics, since his philosophy is intrinsically political. Now the claim that fundamental ontology is not only a theory of Being but also political is obviously controversial. The way to understand the relation of *Being and Time* to Heidegger's politics has sharply divided students of his thought. Aubenque has argued that Heidegger's turn to National Socialism is not a political act since it cannot be deduced from his philosophy.[59] Janicaud, following Aubenque, does not deny that fundamental ontology is implicated in Heidegger's politics but insists on the necessarily apolitical status of his thought.[60] On the contrary, Wolin has described Heidegger's political philosophy in detail.[61]

If fundamental ontology is basically political, then there is an intrinsic connection between ontology, as Heidegger understands it, and politics. Since Heidegger never tired of praising the virtues of ancient Greek thought, not surprisingly it provides obvious antecedents of the political dimension of Heidegger's position. Plato's *Republic* describes an ideal state based on the self-realization of the individual through what he or she does best.[62] Aristotle's *Nicomachean Ethics* treats of the good for its own sake, that for the sake of which all actions are taken, which belongs to the science of politics. According to Aristotle, the end of politics is the good for man.[63]

Being and Time is an intensely political book in an Aristotelian sense of the term "politics." It is a book concerned with the good in itself, understood as the concern with fundamental ontology. Heidegger rejects the Aristotelian view of human being, although he accepts the general Aristotelian understanding of practical philosophy.[64] According to Heidegger, concern with the problem of Being is indispensable for the good for human being. For both Aristotle the author of the *Ni-*

comachean Ethics and Heidegger the author of *Being and Time,* the aim is not merely a theoretical treatise but a work with practical intent. Just as ethics belongs to politics, so Aristotle's account of human affairs points beyond itself to the state that completes it.[65] Similarly, fundamental ontology demands a response to the question of the meaning of Being which cannot leave human being indifferent. *Being and Time,* which does not offer a series of political injunctions, is not political in the sense of, say, Machiavelli's *The Prince* or Hobbes's *Leviathan,* or even Kant's "To Perpetual Peace: A Philosophical Sketch." But it is political in another, more basic sense, concerning the realization of human being in the human context. It is, then, no accident that the entire discussion of "Being" in this work culminates in an analysis of historicality (*Geschichtlichkeit*), Heidegger's term for the authentic conception of history, since fundamental ontology and political life are intimately related.[66] Even some thirty years later, after his period as rector, the turning in his thought, and the loss of the Second World War, Heidegger held the same view of the political consequences of the concern with Being. He ends his lectures on the law of sufficient reason with the statement:

> Does the specified criterion, that man is a rational animal, exhaust the essence of man? Is it the last word concerning Being, that Being means ground? Does not the essence of man, does not his belonging to Being, does not the essence of Being itself remain still and ever more urgently worthy of thought? . . . That is the question. That is the world question [Weltfrage] of thought. Its answer will decide what becomes of the earth and of the existence of man on this earth.[67]

The turn to politics in general, including real and ideal forms of Nazism, is obviously rooted in Heidegger's philosophical thought. It is not necessary, nor is it my intention, to demonstrate that fundamental ontology necessarily led to National Socialism as its only possibility. This kind of argument, which is sometimes made in political theory, say to explain the relation between Marx, or Marxism, and Stalinism, is difficult at best.[68] My point is rather that fundamental ontology necessarily leads beyond itself to political practice, and that National Socialism represents one of the types of politics acceptable to Heidegger's philosophical perspective. To put the same point differently, I hold that the link between Heidegger's philosophy and his politics is not necessary, but I also hold that it is not contingent.

It is a matter of record that Heidegger, the philosopher of Being, did turn to Nazi politics. This political turning is not contingent since it was inscribed in the essence of his theory, which called for, even demanded, political practice. The fact that his political turn took the form of Nazism is neither contingent nor necessary, but hardly surprising. It was not necessary in any strict sense and could not therefore be "deduced" since he could possibly have accepted another form of politics. But what in practice took the form of a turning to Nazism was also not contingent, a mere accident as it were, an unfortunate incident, even essentially meaningless as Heidegger later claimed, since the political practice called for by his philosophy in fact suggested either National Socialism or something like it. It is not surprising that Heidegger's philosophy in practice led him toward a Nazi form of political practice. For his position reflected in philosophical dress the same political and social influences of his time which themselves led to Nazism. In short, Heidegger's Nazi turning represents a rather obvious historical confluence, something that comes about at a particular historical moment, a coming together as it were between the external influences on his thought, which also led to Nazism, and his own turning in that direction because of his thought.

Fundamental Ontology and Politics

This general account of factors influencing Heidegger's turn to politics is insufficient without specific textual analysis. As an aid in grasping the specific connection between Heidegger's philosophy and Nazism, we can differentiate three aspects of his thought: his initial philosophical position as described in *Being and Time,* its evolution in the period between *Being and Time* and the Nazi turning, and the political application of his philosophical thought in the rectoral address.

Now it is difficult to describe a philosophical position adequately. In virtue of its original character, no simple description is adequate to the complex nature of Heidegger's thought. It is also not possible to attempt anything like a full description of Heidegger's position.[69] Fortunately, that is not necessary for our purposes here. Since the present discussion is concerned with the relation of Heidegger's thought to Nazism, we can restrict our account of fundamental ontology merely to those concepts which form the background of his turn to practical politics, including the question of Being, or *Seinsfrage;* Dasein, the distinction between authenticity and inauthenticity; and historicity.

Fundamental ontology is intended as a new theory of ontology which takes up the unanswered question of the meaning of Being through a demonstration of "the Interpretation of *time* as the possible horizon for any understanding whatsoever of Being."[70] Heidegger's investigation is based on the ontological difference between Being in general and beings, or entities. The question of the meaning of Being concerns the Being of beings, or entities. "Dasein" is Heidegger's name for human being.[71] According to Heidegger, as a being human being, or Dasein, differs from other entities, either animate or inanimate, since its under-standing of Being is characteristic of it.[72]

In rapid succession, Heidegger sketches the outlines of a view of Dasein. Dasein's way of "Being-ontological" is not tantamount to pos-sessing an ontology, since it is "pre-ontological," that is, a "way that one has an understanding of Being."[73] Dasein always comports itself in terms of its existence, defined as "a possibility of itself; to be itself or not itself."[74] There is, accordingly, a close, in fact a reciprocal, link between Dasein and the *Seinsfrage*. Since existence is the defining trait of Dasein, the analysis of Dasein requires that existence be considered initially. But since Dasein's existence concerns its Being, an analysis of Dasein re-quires a prior analysis of the question of the meaning of Being.[75] Hence, an understanding of human being rests on a conceptually prior grasp of Being. On the contrary, the *Seinsfrage* requires as its condition the analysis of human being. Since Dasein belongs essentially to a world, it possesses an equally primordial understanding of "world" as well as of the entities within it.[76] It follows that the way to respond to the question of the meaning of Being is through an analysis of Dasein: "Therefore, *fundamental ontology,* from which alone all other ontologies can take their rise, must be sought in the *existential analytic of Dasein.*"[77]

So far we have uncovered the reciprocal relationship, the hermeneuti-cal circle so to speak, in the connection between Dasein and Being. Hei-degger's thought here and in succeeding works is resolutely centered on Being, not on human being. He does not intend to provide a philosophi-cal anthropology, much less a complete ontology, of Dasein.[78] In fact, Heidegger's interest in human being is confined solely and wholly to its role in providing access to Being. That this is so is shown in two ways in Heidegger's thought. On the one hand, it is visible in the fact that, following the so-called turning in his thought, he later gives up the idea that we can accede to Being through Dasein in his turn away from human being. In the later phase of his thought, he resolutely attempts to think Being without human being. On the other hand, philosophically speaking, his political turn is not motivated, as might be thought, by a basic concern with human being, since this is never Heidegger's funda-mental philosophical interest. From a philosophical perspective, it is rather motivated by the underlying concern with Being, which itself leads to politics.

In *Being and Time* Heidegger has not yet arrived at the idea that Being can be thought without human being. Here, he insists strongly that Dasein is the clue to Being. Since at this stage of his thought the way to Being necessarily runs through human being, fundamental ontology cannot wholly free itself from "philosophical anthropology," which it needs to address. For that reason, Heidegger inquires into the essential structures of Dasein, which he describes in a preliminary way.[79] Among these essential structures, none is more fundamental than Dasein's understanding of itself in terms of its existence.

According to Heidegger, existence, or the way in which Dasein always understands itself, concerns the possibility to be or not be to itself. He develops this idea in his analysis of the difference between authenticity and inauthenticity. This facet of his view provides a rigorous philosophical statement of the concern with alienation expressed in the traditional German concern with traditional *Volksideologie*. It further offers an alternative to the Marxist conception of alienation.[80] Heidegger's main predecessor in his understanding of authenticity is Kierkegaard.[81]

"Authenticity" can mean "what is really intended."[82] As applied to human being, authenticity concerns a conception of self-realization through a choice of oneself. Heidegger identifies two basic characteristics of Dasein: "the priority of *existentia* over *essentia* and the fact that Dasein is in each case mine."[83] Unlike entities, or mere things, Dasein is intrinsically directed toward the future. It is essentially characterized by the fact that its " 'essence' lies in its 'to be' [Zu-sein]."[84] The Being of Dasein which is in question is in every case its own. On this basis, Heidegger infers that for Dasein the Being that is at issue is its ownmost possibility, namely its possibility either to be or not to be what it essentially is. In an important passage, he asserts that whether Dasein will be or not be its possibility is a matter of choice.

> And because Dasein is in each case essentially its own possibility, it *can*, in its very Being, 'choose' itself and win itself; it can also lose itself and never win itself; or only 'seem' to do so. But only in so far as it is essentially something which can be *authentic*—that is, something of its own—can it have lost itself and not yet won itself.[85]

Authenticity and inauthenticity are correlative concepts. Both are grounded in the notion of mineness. Heidegger is at pains to stress that the difference between authenticity and inauthenticity does not concern the degree of Being. It follows, although he does not say so explicitly, that the difference concerns the type of Being, in other words the way that Dasein is itself. Since in principle Dasein always in a sense understands its own possibility, the way in which one is oneself is a matter of choice.[86] Although surrounded with numerous precautions to distinguish the analytic of Dasein from other endeavors, Heidegger's analysis of Dasein is similar to other theories of human self-realization.[87] For Heidegger, human being cannot be understood as a rational animal on the ancient Greek model or in terms of Christian theology; it must be grasped through its own existence, or innermost possibility, which it necessarily understands and either chooses or fails to choose.

Now for Heidegger, a precondition of the thought of Being in an authentic manner is a break with the established tradition of metaphysical thought. For to follow the tradition on the well-known path of ontology is to accept precisely the view that must be "destroyed" in order to recover the original, correct alternative later covered up. Authentic thought of Being, like authenticity in all its forms, requires a withdrawal from the ordinary, in fact from the public in all its forms, where one mainly follows others, into the private sphere where one follows only oneself. On the conceptual level, this requires that one in effect think for oneself as opposed to remaining on paths already marked out.[88] Hence, if for no other reason, Heidegger's conception of the problem of Being in this work demands that he bring about human authenticity as a condition of the working out of the problem itself.[89]

Authenticity is obviously a key conception in *Being and Time*. There is a clear difference between an idea of authenticity, such as Heidegger's conception, and its practical realization. Special interest attaches to the transition from an understanding of the nature of an authentic person, namely the abstract, or philosophical, theory of authenticity, to actually being authentic in a concrete manner. Heidegger articulates his claim for the transition from a theoretical understanding of human being or Dasein as possibly authentic to authenticity in practice through a number of concepts, above all the notion of resoluteness (*Entschlossenheit*).

Heidegger's argument depends on his basic understanding of human being. He summarizes his view of human being through the enumeration of four basic traits.[90] Disclosedness (*Erschlossenheit*), which belongs to the Being of human being, primarily concerns care (*Sorge*), that is, being in a context at all, and being with whatever is in the context, in Heidegger's language Being-in-the-world and Being alongside entities within-the-world. "Thrownness" is Heidegger's way of indicating that we are dealing with people in concrete situations, not ideal or idealized concepts that function as the subjective pole in a theory of knowledge. "Projection," which also belongs to the Being of human being, is defined as "disclosive Being towards its potentiality for Being."[91] This is Heidegger's designation for the capacity, ingredient in his basic conception of a person, to be aware of one's own capacities, capacities which every individual possesses. "Falling" is the term chosen to indicate that for the most part individuals are not authentic but inauthentic since, although aware of their own possibilities, they fail to choose them.

An awareness of one's capacities, which Heidegger insists we all possess, is merely a precondition to their manifestation. One has to be aware of possibilities in order to bring them about, but the awareness itself is not the same as their manifestation. If a capacity, such as writing music, can only be realized because the person who possesses it is also aware of the fact, then this awareness is a necessary but not a sufficient condition for its realization. If Bach is unaware that he has the ability to write cantatas, he is exceedingly unlikely to do so. Heidegger addresses the problem of the transition to authenticity, given the imputation of a conception of self-awareness, in a notion of resoluteness.

Resoluteness is the key transitional notion, the way in which Heidegger means to mediate between authenticity as a theoretical concept, an ideal for human being as it were, and its practical realization. According to Heidegger, to be resolute is already to be authentic.[92] There is a faint echo here of Kant's idea of pure practical reason. For Kant, to determine oneself to act according to a principle applicable to every possible rational being is already in a sense to be moral; so for Heidegger, merely to be resolute is already to be authentic. The difference, on which Heidegger insists, is that unlike Kant's view of the subject as necessarily separate from the world, for Heidegger a person is already and necessarily in the concrete context. Resoluteness occurs in the life of a particular person, in a particular situation, at a particular time.

As elsewhere in Heidegger's theory, there are authentic and inauthentic forms of resoluteness. To be resolute is to anticipate a possibility, something a person can choose to be, rather like picking out a lifestyle. Now some possibilities are, in Heidegger's view, inessential because not specifically rooted in the essence of the person as such. Although they affect the person's Being, they do not do so in a way that belongs to that person as distinguished from others. Like Plato, Heidegger seems to hold that there are identifiable characteristics which individuals possess and that they ought to realize these characteristics in their actions, to concentrate on what is specific to them. Resoluteness is authentic, then, when it picks out what is uniquely characteristic of that person–in Heidegger's sibylline language, one's "ownmost authentic possibility."[93] Heidegger's conception seems to contain something like a sense of resistance against other temptations or possibilities, almost like Ulysses resisting the blandishments of the sirens.

The conception of resoluteness invoked in order to account for the practical realization of authenticity is at least as abstract as the abstract concept it is intended to mediate. To point out that a person grasps his or her specific potentials is not the same as showing how this is in practice carried out. We don't have any criteria that allow us to identify what is intrinsic to the individual. Unless one holds that an individual who is resolute about being authentic cannot go wrong, or unless resoluteness is itself the authenticity one seeks, then more needs to be said to rule out possible incorrect choices of oneself. Heidegger moves closer to the practical level in his account of historicality, or the authentic conception of history.[94]

Heidegger's convoluted discussion of historicality carries special importance within the book for at least two reasons. First, it is plausible to hold that the work as a whole culminates in this passage, in the account of the transition from a manifold account of forms of human authenticity and inauthenticity to the concretely authentic person or group.[95] Second, Heidegger understands time as the indispensable horizon of Being and Dasein as existence. At this point in the analysis existence and time, human being, and Being come together in a supposedly authentic conception of history.

Heidegger provides additional information about his view of resoluteness in the context of his discussion of historicality (*Geschichtlichkeit*). The idea of authenticity is initially futural in that the possibility to be realized obviously lies in the future as something that can still come about. Heidegger now renders this conception more concrete by insisting that the possibility to be realized in the future is part of the heritage and, hence, lies in the past. Clearly, a heritage is what is transmitted from the past to later generations. For Heidegger, who here anticipates Gadamer's notion of the tradition as itself valuable, what is "good" is a heritage, since goodness makes authenticity possible, and goodness is transmitted in resoluteness.[96] It follows, since authenticity is understood as the realization of the possibility that most intimately belongs to the individual person, that such possibilities are by their nature traditional in character. There is, then, a fiercely conservative strain in Heidegger's view of self-realization as the free choice of oneself, since to realize oneself, to resolutely seize the most intimate possibility available to one in choosing oneself, is finally to extend past tradition; for tradition itself is the vehicle of the "good." In a fundamental sense, the authenticity made possible by resoluteness is not innovative but repetitive in character; it is not the realization of what is new and unprecedented, but rather the repetition of a prior tradition which as such embodies "goodness." In a deep sense, for Heidegger to be authentic is to embrace or to repeat the past in one's own life through a reinstantiation of the tradition. Since Nazism claimed to embody the values of the authentic German, of the German *Volk* as German, there is, then, a profound parallel, providing for an easy transition without any compromise of basic philosophical principles, between Heidegger's conception of authenticity through resoluteness and National Socialism.

Heidegger expands on his conception of the transmission of the tradition as intrinsically good by introducing a series of distinctions concerning heritage and resoluteness. The two basic forms of tradition are fate

(*Schicksal*), which concerns the individual, and destiny (*Geschick*), which affects a group, such as a community or people.[97] Heidegger here notes, as he has done before, that authenticity can be either individual or on the level of the group. What, for lack of a better term, we can call "plural authenticity" can come about if the group authentically shares its heritage and realizes it.[98] When the group shares in an authentic manner that which represents its authentic heritage, then it obviously can be authentic in a plural sense. It is in this sense that he introduces the German idea of the people (*Volk*), namely a community (*Gemeinschaft*), as distinguished presumably from a society, which shares a common heritage, or destiny.[99]

Heidegger further mentions conceptions of the hero, the moment of vision, and loyalty. The conception of the hero (*Held*) is evoked in relation to the authentic repetition of a possibility.[100] We can speculate that the hero is one willing to sacrifice or even die for this cause, that is, the destiny of the *Volk*. Here, Heidegger stresses the notion of struggle in which the hero acts as a model for others, who can follow in his footsteps as it were. It is this notion which he later applied, during his period as rector, in praise of Albert Leo Schlageter, a young man who was earlier hanged for terrorist acts against French and Belgian troops in the Rhineland and whom Heidegger eulogized as a hero.[101] Heidegger further links resoluteness with the moment of vision (*Augenblick*).[102] Like the theological conception of *kairos*, there is a right time, a propitious instant when things come together, so to speak—a moment when an important action is possible, such as the transition to authenticity in practice through the grasp and reenactment of one's heritage on both the levels of the individual and the group. An important aspect of Heidegger's Nazi turning was his conviction that National Socialism offered the historical moment for the realization of the authenticity of the German *Volk*.

This account of the basic structure of *Being and Time* shows that Heidegger's conception of ontology commits him, as a condition of thinking through the problem of the meaning of "Being," to a political understanding of human being, that is, to an idea of the person as mainly inauthentic but as possibly authentic in a concrete fashion. The very concern with fundamental ontology requires a political turn since an authentic thought of Being can only arise on the basis of concrete authenticity. Heidegger's concern with the problem of the meaning of Being is not apolitical; nor is it indifferent to theory and practice in virtue of its concern with the *Seinsfrage*. Rather, the concern with "Being" is itself intrinsically political.

My argument to this point can be summarized as follows. Heidegger's turn to National Socialism, which cannot be denied, was motivated by factors intrinsic and extrinsic to his philosophical position. Extrinsic factors include the general sense of despair in the waning days of the Weimar Republic, the concern with *Volk* ideology, the desire to recover self-respect in the wake of the disastrous defeat in the First World War, and so on. These influences, which were in the air, so to speak, at the time he was working out his fundamental ontology, constitute the wider contemporary context in which his philosophical theory emerged. These extrinsic factors are not merely part of the background but are in fact incorporated into Heidegger's thought in various ways—for instance, in his extensive reflection on the theme of authenticity. The intrinsic factors are those aspects of his philosophical theory which led him toward politics and which further made it possible for him to accept National Socialism. Heidegger's understanding of ontology commits him to a turn to politics, centered on the conception of human authenticity, which demands realization in a political context, as a condition of the authentic thought of Being. Heidegger's turn to Nazism was an obvious attempt to seize a supposedly propitious historical moment. The mere fact that Heidegger's attempt to seize the day was a decision for the darkest night of the human soul should not be invoked to explain his adherence to National Socialism as a mere error of judgment, as a simple mistake, as the kind of mistake anyone, so to speak, could make. The reason is obvious: unlike everyone, or his academic colleagues, or even other philosophers, Heidegger possessed an important philosophical theory, and it is this theory itself which led him from the ivory tower inhabited by German intellectuals toward the political arena.

Ontology and Existence: On the Way to Practice

The turn from the theory of Being in *Being and Time* to political practice did not occur immediately, although it was also not long in coming. Since important thinkers do not always realize the implications of their ideas, and Heidegger was an important thinker, it is possible that he was not immediately aware of the political implications of his study of ontology. Nevertheless, he quickly turned to practice and to politics on the basis of his thought. The initial step out of the ivory tower and into the real world occurred in his discussion of the crisis faced within Germany in the latter part of the Weimar Republic. Since Heidegger was officially concerned only with the problem of Being, he has often been portrayed as an unpolitical person, as uninterested in or unaware of the surrounding world, as the fictional absentminded professor.[103] On the contrary, Heidegger was deeply aware of and interested in contemporary events, as witness numerous references in his lecture courses to happenings of the day. He was specifically disturbed by the general cultural mood prevalent in the later period of the Weimar Republic. His analysis of this existential situation is doubly interesting: as a phase in the transition from fundamental ontology to National Socialism through an initial political turning, and as an effort to confront the contemporary political malaise through his theory of Being.

The significance of Heidegger's remarks on cultural criticism, besides their intrinsic interest, lies in his concern to apply his theory of Being to the analysis of the current existential malaise at a point late in the Weimar Republic, as the incipient economic depression is spreading throughout the world, when all concerned are aware that the experiment in democratic liberalism in the Weimar Republic is in deep trouble, when powerful forces are emerging to challenge both liberalism and communism through a conservative revolution from the right.

Heidegger turns to contemporary society in his lecture course of 1929/ 30, at a point located between the publication of *Being and Time* and prior to the rectoral speech, shortly before his private turning to National Socialism in 1931.[104] The analysis of Being in *Being and Time* offers a theoretical reason for the link of fundamental ontology to politics, which is only mandated theoretically but is not yet carried out. It is in abeyance, waiting to happen so to speak. A transition from theory to practice, but not yet to politics, in effect a practical intermezzo, occurs in Heidegger's analysis of the contemporary political situation in his lecture course. Here, we see Heidegger's effort to come to grips with the really existing social world, in this case the current social situation, from the perspective of his philosophical theory.

Heidegger's attempt to confront the existential situation through an analysis of mood is an application of his fundamental ontology. For Heidegger, everyone always has a mood of some kind, and he understands mood as the actually existing manifestation of the potential for state-of-mind.[105] Heidegger insists that one's state-of-mind, or potential for a given mood, is significant not only to disclose a person as what he or she is but also as an indication of how an individual comes into contact with its world.[106] For this reason, he regards the state-of-mind in general as providing an important clue for existential analysis. In *Being and Time,* Heidegger employs his conception of state-of-mind as a basic clue to elucidate fear and anxiety. In his lecture course, Heidegger switches his attention from fear and anxiety to boredom. In his analysis of the present situation, Heidegger insists that the basic mood of the present is boredom induced by the failure to be an authentic person, which he interprets as a clue to a deeper problem: the problem of Being. In his reading of the contemporary situation, in his diagnosis of the contemporary dependence on slogans, Heidegger maintains that no one is really the master of "the inner greatness" (*der inneren Grösse*) of Dasein.[107]

Heidegger maintains that the deep boredom characteristic of current social life is ontologically significant. The discussion comes to a head in the final paragraph of the first part (§ 38), which bears the significant, but rather clumsy title: "Essential need in general, the missing (self-denial) of the essential distress of our contemporary Dasein as the left-emptiness of the particularly deep boredom." Heidegger leaves no doubt about his bleak view of the contemporary situation, including the decline of the Weimar Republic and worldwide economic depression:

> Everywhere there are deep shakings [Erschütterungen], crises, catastrophes, needs [Nöte]: contemporary social misery, political confusion, the powerlessness of science, the emptiness [Aushöhlung] of art, the ungroundedness of philosophy, the incapacity of religion. Certainly, there are needs everywhere.[108]

In this connection, Heidegger makes five points, each of which contributes to an analysis of the contemporary social crisis and an identification of the role for philosophy in the practical social sphere.

1. The hidden basic mood of the current situation is deep boredom (*tiefe Langeweile*).[109] This is his basic diagnosis of the contemporary social crisis through the application of the conceptions of mood and state-of-mind developed in his fundamental ontology.

2. Everyone is aware of the situation. But others have so far failed to grasp the real nature of the problem since they invariably tend to focus on types of need to the neglect of need as such.[110] Examples of this failure are provided by psychology, including depth psychology and psychoanalysis. Heidegger here offers a methodological critique of other approaches to the understanding of contemporary society through an application of his canonical ontological difference, roughly the difference between the ontological and ontical dimensions.

3. Merely to ask the proper question—more precisely, to raise the question of the basic mood (*Grundstimmung*)—is to perform a crucial service. This questioning does not justify or deal with contemporary human being as human, but rather frees human being's specifically human capacity as Dasein.

> To question concerning *this basic mood* does not mean to justify and to carry on with the present humanness of human beings [Menschheit des Menschen], but to free the humanness in human being, the humanness of human being, that is, to free the *essence* of human being, to permit Dasein in him essentially to become.[111]

4. Heidegger specifies what Dasein can become by drawing attention to the link between his concern with the present time of need and the

question of the meaning of Being raised in his fundamental ontology. To free human being by enabling it to become Dasein is not to place it in an arbitrary situation. It is rather to divest it of its specific burden and, accordingly, to free it. "The freeing of Dasein in human being does not mean to put him into an arbitrary situation [Willkür], but to remove from him his ownmost [eigenste] burden. Only one who can truly give oneself a burden is free."[112]

5. Heidegger understands the proposed questioning as practically important. The proper questioning, which is parenthetically only possible from the perspective of fundamental ontology, is intended to lead us in two directions: to action and to being (*zum Handeln und zum Sein*).[113]

Heidegger's conception of how to minister to the malady of the present day provides insight into his view of human being, including its role in his philosopical theory. His concern is manifest here on two levels, in respect to (1) the dreadful disintegration of contemporary Germany, and (2) his reading of the deeper significance of the present mood. It is, then, significant that, despite his linguistic tip of the hat to the gravity of the momentary situation, his concern is finally not with human being but with Being. Others are obviously shocked by the grave social situation present in the declining phase of the Weimar Republic because of an abiding interest in human being. But here and elsewhere, this more usual humane concern is wholly absent in Heidegger's personal and philosophical perspectives. From a strictly philosophical point of view, it is fair to say that he fastens on the practical situation in order to further fundamental ontology.

Since Dasein is that being concerned with Being, in a word the *Seinsfrage,* to bring about the fulfillment of Dasein is to create the real possibility to grasp Being. For human being to realize itself has nothing to do with its present distress, but everything to do with being an authentic human being, namely that being essentially concerned with Being. It follows that the problem of Being, the center of theoretical concern in his fundamental ontology, is also doubly implicated in his analysis of the present-day situation of Germany: as the conceptual framework of the analysis, and as the problem toward which the contemporary situation points. In short, in rather transparent fashion Heidegger here substitutes his own philosophical concerns for the existential concerns created by the world economic collapse and the decline of the Weimar Republic.

The result of this discussion is to point to a clear dualism in Heidegger's analysis of Being. His fundamental ontology is clearly circular, since the analysis of Being leads to a conception of human being, which is either inauthentic or authentic. An authentic grasp of Being depends on an authentic human being. The interest in human being is, then, twofold: perhaps or at least possibly for the sake of human beings, but finally and most basically for the sake of the understanding of Being. To put the same point in other words, Heidegger's main concern is with Being, not human being; he turns to human being as the way into the problem of Being. Even in his most concrete moments, such as in his application of his theoretical framework to the analysis of contemporary society, his main interest lies in the understanding of Being. This same overriding concern is the main thread of his turn in the rectoral address to Nazism.

From Practice to Politics

Heidegger insists on the importance of mood. We can summarize Heidegger's own mood in the waning period of the Weimar Republic, as revealed in this text, as follows: Obviously, human being is in trouble and the ordinary solutions seem not to have taken hold. Yet the problematic nature of contemporary life is finally due to the turn of human being away from its ownmost possibilities of being, which can only be understood in terms of the problem of Being. For this reason, Dasein must be forced to listen to that which it has refused to hear, to be forced to take up a burden in order to be free. For only in this way can Dasein reach its so-called inner greatness.

The problem of Dasein's inner greatness as an authentic possibility in its moment of need is a precipitating factor in Heidegger's Nazi turning. Everything points to a convergence at this point in Heidegger's development of his concern with the problem of Being as supposedly manifest in the contemporary German social context, the various influences arising through the decline of the Weimar Republic and the strengthened appeal of *Volk* ideology, the reflection of these themes in Heidegger's own philosophical theory, which necessarily provokes a turn to practice, and the practical instantiation of similar themes in National Socialist politics. There is an obvious, profound link between Heidegger's interest in authenticity, the romantic *Volk* idea of the realization of the individual in the state as the true reconciliation of the spirit of the people, and the Nazi idea of the identity or essential unity of the German state and the so-called Aryan race. The idea of the *Volk,* which is not precisely translated as "people," is difficult to define but is important to an understanding of German ideology and Heidegger's attraction to Nazism. One of its main characteristics, which connects it to the romantic reaction to the Enlightenment as an alternative solution to the problems of alienation and reconciliation, is the union, or making whole, of the individual or group with its transcendent spirit, or essence.[114]

This view of the overcoming of alienation through effective historical realization of the spirit of the *Volk* provides a clue to Heidegger's turn to

Nazism. It is not necessary to claim that Heidegger subscribed to a biological theory of race to perceive that for reasons internal to his philosophy, his analysis of the contemporary situation was conducive to acceptance of the conservative *Volk* perspective and the much more extreme National Socialist program. It is, then, no accident that in the rectoral speech Heidegger strongly stresses the concept of spirit. For the concept of the spirit of the people, or *Volksgeist,* of the essence of the German people, provides the link between Heidegger's view of Dasein in the light of his comprehension of Being, the conservative *völkisch* response to the situation of human being in modern society, and the Nazi program.

Fundamental Ontology and National Socialism: The Rectoral Address

The discussion in this chapter to this point has been prolegomenal. I have argued that Heidegger's philosophy of Being is intrinsically political. I have further shown that he turned to practice which he analyzed through the lens of his philosophy. And I have issued a promissory note in the form of the as yet unsupported claim that his turn to Nazism was based in his philosophy. I now want to redeem that promissory note, which is so far no more than that, through a reading of the rectoral address,[115] the main exoteric document of Heidegger's public identification with National Socialism. Now the idea that philosophy is the ground of politics is as old as Plato's *Republic.* I am convinced that Heidegger's approach to politics in his speech is quasi-Platonic, in fact a form of right-wing Platonism. My aim in reading this text is to show not only that Heidegger's turning to National Socialism is based on his philosophical position, but further that his speech can be read in a rather straightforward manner as an effort to found National Socialism in fundamental ontology.

The rectoral address is the text in which Heidegger for the first time publicly associated his own philosophy with National Socialism. The so-called *Rektoratsrede* was a public speech given by Heidegger, the newly elected rector of the University of Freiburg, on 27 May 1933 on the occasion of the ceremonial transfer of the rector's office. Heidegger's inauguration as rector of the University of Freiburg in April 1933 took place immediately after the end of the Weimar Republic when Hitler had already taken power, at the beginning of the new postrepublican period, symbolizing a return to the imperialistic form of German politics. Almost immediately thereafter, there was a suspension of the formal rule of law, of freedom of expression, and of habeas corpus. Civil rights were abrogated and a legal basis was established for a Nazi dicta-torship. Dictatorial powers were voted to Hitler for a period of four years. Most Jews were deprived of civil service jobs, including those in the university. In March, the first concentration camps were established and publicly announced. On 1 April a boycott of all Jewish establish-ments was instituted. In May, there was a burning of "decadent" works by Jews and non-Jews. In the same month, labor unions and then, in July, political parties were banned. In the early summer, the Vatican entered into a treaty, or *Konkordat,* with Hitler, negotiated for the National Socialist government by von Papen, which provided the first official recognition of Hitler's regime.[116]

Heidegger's speech has already attracted extensive attention.[117] Analy-sis of this speech from various perspectives has shown an indebtedness, surprising in this thinker of Being, to some less than lofty sources, such as H. S. Sommerfeldt's study, *Hermann Göring: Ein Lebensbild.*[118] Hei-degger evidently took Göring, the Reichsminister, Innenminister for Prussia, and a leading Hitler associate, as a model for the new German man.[119] Here, it will be useful to consider the specifically philosophical context of Heidegger's speech in order to bring out the relation between his fundamental ontology and his turn to politics.

Heidegger's talk represents his further effort, after his analysis of the social situation in the latter days of the Weimar Republic, to apply his philosophical theory in and to political practice. The rectoral address is a short text, about ten pages in length, elicited by a specific occasion. It is not, however, a merely occasional text, a few well-chosen words with no intrinsic significance, unworthy of further consideration. Rather, it is a philosophical discussion of surprising depth, which largely surpasses the occasion for which it was written, and would be worth studying with care even were it not a main document in Heidegger's turn to National Social-ism. Since the text does not interpret itself, we will need to provide an interpretation.

The significance of Heidegger's speech is suggested by the various ways in which it has been interpreted. It has been read from different, even incompatible, perspectives: as a strategic effort to lead the German university, even to lead the leaders of the Nazi state; as a defense of the German university; as a defense of the Greek concept of science; and in other ways. One should not deny that Heidegger's talk is in part in-tended to perform these tasks, and can hence be described as perform-ing them; but it is more than that. While recognizing that there are grounds for legitimate disagreement with the reading to be advanced here, I will interpret the rectoral speech as a coherent philosophical text in the service of Nazism. I am convinced that Heidegger's talk represents a well-thought-out philosophical effort to put philosophy as he understood it in the service of National Socialism in the first place for what he portrayed as the good of the German people, but ultimately for his own view of Being. In my view, this speech is primarily, and should be regarded as, an effort to apply a philosophical theory, conceived in independence of Nazism and before that movement came to power, within a political context for which Heidegger believed his thought was relevant, indeed essential, in order to bring about a goal Heidegger shared with National Socialism and *Volk* ideology—the historical gathering of the Germans—as well as a goal of his own: the comprehension of Being.

It is, then, reasonable to assume that Heidegger's words on this occasion are not merely strategic, nor merely limited to the immediate situation, but express his own deepest view of the matter, drawing on the entire range of intellectual resources at his command. Although concerned with the alienation of the German *Volk,* with the opportunity supposedly presented for the coming to being of what is specifically German, this is only an intermediate end, that is a means to a further, more important goal, for Heidegger is finally more concerned with Being. It is his ultimate concern with his ontological preoccupation which made it possible for Heidegger, after the decline of real Nazism, to remain faithful to a kind of ideal Nazism. He may, as Löwith suggests, have been fascinated by Hitler.[120] But his abiding fascination was undoubtedly with Being itself, which called forth his commitment to National Socialism as a way station on the road to ontology.

The later thrust of Heidegger's philosophy is decidedly anti-Platonic. Yet in the rectoral address, Heidegger's understanding of philosophy as essential to National Socialism is basically Platonic. There are divergent ways to interpret the Platonic view of philosophy as the final arbiter of knowlege and as the foundation of politics. The Platonic view has from time to time animated philosophers in the history of the tradition, who regarded themselves as responsible for others, even all others, in virtue of their special claim to knowledge. It animated, for example, Fichte, who claimed a responsibility for all Germans:

> And act thou shalt as though
> The destiny of all things German
> Depended on you and your lonely acting,
> And the responsibility were yours.[121]

This Platonic idea of the peculiar responsibilty of philosophers as philosophers can lead in two directions. It is worth recalling that Fichte's words were cited by Kurt Huber, the only philosopher executed by the Nazis, whose participation in the White Rose conspiracy against Hitler cost him his life.[122] Heidegger used the same idea of the cognitive privilege of philosophy to argue for philosophy as the foundation of Nazism. For Heidegger, the philosopher is the necessary component, the conceptual linchpin as it were, for the realization of the National Socialist program. As for Plato, so in this text for Heidegger as well, the necessary condition of the ideal or just state is that it be led by a philosopher.[123] It is, then, consistent to regard his later effort to reject philosophy in favor of a so-called new thinking beyond "philosophy" as doubly determined by the internal evolution of his position as well as by his evident inability to lead the leaders, by his unsuccessful effort to apply philosophy to politics.

Heidegger is not the only philosopher who turned to politics. Perhaps the closest analogy in our time is with the Hungarian Marxist philosopher Lukács.[124] Both the Bolshevist Lukács and the National Socialist Heidegger take a quasi-Platonic stance on the need for philosophy to found politics, and both place their considerable intellectual resources in the service of totalitarian political practice. Heidegger's relation to Nazism resembles Lukács's relation to Marxism-Leninism. It has been said that Lukács provided the philosophical grounding for Leninist politics.[125] It is plausible to regard Heidegger's speech as an effort, based in the extension and interpretation of his own thought, to provide the philosophical grounding for Nazism. In the same way as Lukács turned to politics, from which he later withdrew after the failure of his attempt to translate his thought into practice, so Heidegger also was later marked by his unfortunate effort to descend from the philosophical perch into the political arena. Also like Lukács, Heidegger later abjured the desire to actualize his thought through political action, although he remained faithful to his original political view.

The title of the speech, "The Self-Assertion [Selbstbehauptung] of the German University," records a quadruple commitment: a self-justification; a self-defense, in this case the defense of oneself against the presumed efforts by others to usurp one's place; the self-assertion of the university for a special role to be played by the university in general and the philosophers in particular; and, finally, the self-assertion of the German people through the university.[126] The text begins with the following, crucial statement:

> The assumption of the rectorate is the commitment to the *spiritual* leadership of this institution of higher learning. The following of teachers and students awakens and grows strong only from a true and joint rootedness in the essence of the German university. This essence, however, gains clarity, rank, and power only when first of all and at all times the leaders are themselves led—led by that unyielding spiritual mission that forces the fate of the German people to bear the stamp of its history.[127]

As early as the first sentence, Heidegger lays claim to the traditional role of philosophy in the statement that in assuming the rectorate he commits himself to the spiritual, or intellectual, leadership of the institution of higher learning. A view of spiritual leadership presupposes a conception of spirit. In German philosophy, where the idea of spirit is a leading theme, it refers roughly to a conception of reason as mediated through the social and historical context as the highest point of culture. Spirit is a leading theme in modern German philosophy, for instance in the views of Fichte, Hegel, and Dilthey. For Fichte, the end of life is the development of the spiritual order. In Hegelian idealism, human being differs from nonhuman being through the spiritual dimension, which is manifested in culture. He analyzes the spiritual dimension of existence in magisterial fashion in the *Phenomenology of Spirit.* In part following Droysen, Dilthey insisted on the difference in kind between natural and social sciences, or *Geisteswissenschaften,* literally the sciences of the spirit.

Heidegger develops his claim about the university in the next two sentences by applying his conceptions of the ontological difference, fate, history, the *Volk*[128] or people, truth as disclosure, and so on, all drawn from his fundamental ontology. For Heidegger, the university is an institution composed of teachers and students who are rooted in the so-called essence of the German university. Heidegger names the background for his speech in his reference to the historical fate of the German people. The image he describes is that of an unbroken chain whose links are constituted by the supposed spiritual mission of the Germans within history, the leaders who are led by that mission, their followers composed of other teachers and students, and presumably all other members of the nation.

In invoking the idea of the essence of the university, Heidegger applies his idea of truth as disclosure in a Platonic manner. We recall that Plato insisted on a distinction in kind between reality and appearance and that he further insisted that only philosophers who possessed the inherent mental capabilities honed by appropriate training were able to perceive reality. In quasi-Platonic fashion, Heidegger suggests that the university possesses an essence, as distinguished from its appearance, which he, as a philosopher, is uniquely able to perceive. Others, nonphilosophers, are unable to see the university's essence and hence unable to lead either it or Nazism. Since from his quasi-Platonic angle of vision, the philosopher, incarnating the spirit of the university and the German people, is alone capable of discerning what should be done, Heidegger's demand to lead the university as its spiritual leader, or spiritual *Führer,*[129] is also a claim that only the spiritual, but not the political, leader can lead the state to realize the destiny of the German people.

The Marxist view of the leading role of the party, led by the leader, rests on Marx's conception of the philosopher as the head of the revolution, so to speak—as one whose intellectual qualities provide him with a unique task.[130] Similarly, Heidegger now asserts that the philosopher and only the philosopher is qualified to lead the German revolution initiated by Nazism.

The idea of the historical fate of the German people rests on the concept of fate introduced by Heidegger in *Being and Time*. His appeal to fate and destiny represents a qualified return to the Greek concept of *moira,* to an analysis of history in mythical rather than causal terms,[131] as in the well-known myth of the three fates reported by Plato.[132] There is a clear continuity between the analysis of historicality in *Being and Time* and the initial paragraph of the *Rektoratsrede.* Heidegger here adopts a nonbiological but metaphysical theory of racism—an exaltation of the Germans specifically in virtue of their belonging to the German people, deeply informed by conservative political thought, including *Volk* ideology—as concerns the realization of the German people, at the expense of other peoples if necessary. To this end, he links together two views: his own view of fate and its realization through the decisive action of a people spurred on to achieve its destiny in the choice of itself, in effect to be its ownmost possibilities for being as specified through its heritage, on the one hand; and the Nazi view of the intrinsic destiny of the German people as distinguished from other peoples on the other. In his choice of the title "The Self-Assertion of the German University" for this public talk, Heidegger affirms his intention to bend the philosophical resources of his position to a specific political task in a fourth form of self-assertion: the self-assertion of the German people in the conscious decision, as voiced by the newly elected rector of the University of Freiburg, to seize their own destiny. This destiny will be realized through the leadership of the university, particularly through the central role of philosophy, above all through Heidegger's philosophy within the university. True Nazism, Nazism in the authentic sense, cannot be left to the National Socialists, the exponents of "political science"; it requires a philosopher.

The interpretation of the passage "forces the fate of the German people to bear the stamp of its history" ("Schicksal des deutschen Volkes in das Gepräge seiner Geschichte zwingt") is delicate. In *Being and Time,* Heidegger distinguishes between fate, which refers to the individual, and destiny, which refers to the group, more precisely to the manner in which one relates to others. Heidegger's application of the term "fate" here to the German people, a plural noun, indicates that he regards the Germans as a unity, as a group whose members are intrinsically linked together in a particular manner. What they share is not something like belonging to the same club or living in the same neighborhood. For Heidegger, this linkage is historical; it lies in the common heritage shared by the Germans as German. According to Heidegger, in virtue of their German origins, the Germans partake of a deep relationship that is already determined for them by history. He stresses this point in *Being and Time* with the strong expression "fateful destiny of Dasein" (*das schicksalhafte Geschick des Daseins*), which violates his distinction between fate and destiny, to designate the way in which a person is related to his or her generation.[133] What Heidegger in the rectoral address, in reference to the destiny of the Germans, calls "the stamp of its history" (*Gepräge seiner Geschichte*) is a metaphysical claim about what the Germans are as Germans. For Heidegger, then, the role of the philosopher, what he further designates here as "the unyielding spiritual mission" entrusted to him as the *Führer* of the University of Freiburg, is nothing other than calling the German people back from its lack of awareness into what it, as German, inherently is, that is, Germans with a potential to exhibit their Germanity, to realize their past in their future actions. What I am calling the realization of the Germans as German is Heidegger's metaphysical understanding of the conception of the destiny of the German people to realize themselves in history.

As I read this text, its initial paragraph records Heidegger's clear and forceful public declaration of his intent to provide vital philosophical help and sustenance to the Nazi political program, support which in his eyes is a necessary condition for its realization. It is possible to read this passage in the rectoral address differently. There is a linguistic defense available amounting to a denial of Heidegger's turn toward Nazism in the observation that the word "*Führer*" appears here in the plural. In response, we can note that in the context of his rise to the position of rector shortly after Hitler came to power, Heidegger is proposing to lead the leaders of National Socialism and, finally but unmistakably, Hitler himself. As Pöggeler, following Jaspers, has seen, Heidegger understood the concept of the self-assertion of the German university to mean that he would lead the Nazi revolution.[134] Paradoxically, in his public statement of his desire to bend philosophy to the task of Nazi politics, in his own peculiar expression of philosophical loyalty to the National Socialist revolution, he at the same time sows the seeds of discord between himself and official Nazism in his attempted philosophical usurpation of political hegemony.[135] For Heidegger characteristically depicts himself not in the role of the vassal who pledges fealty but in the role of the feudal lord.

The initial paragraph of the talk provides a clear, forceful, unsettling, in fact frightening statement of Heidegger's intention to ground politics in philosophy by basing Nazism on fundamental ontology. The initial paragraph does not stand alone; it is merely the preamble for the text to follow, which amplifies and completes the main lines set out in the beginning of the document. In the remainder of his speech, Heidegger develops the implications of the supposed need to marry philosophy and politics at this particular moment in German history. He immediately considers the implications of the traditional claim of the university to self-governance, which, he asserts, requires interpretation in terms of who one is, namely the essence of the university, which can be revealed through self-examination only. The university's self-assertion, he states, in a reference to the title of the essay, consists in a common will to the shared will to realize its essence.

In defense of his claim, Heidegger now forges a link between the acknowledged task of the university to defend science, the fate of the German people, and the present historical moment. In the *Republic,* Plato insists on the task of the philosopher to educate and to discipline the other philosophers, the guardians and the tradesmen. Like Plato, Heidegger points successively to the role of the university to ground science as well as to educate and to discipline the leaders and guardians of the German people, in the present historical moment the German Nazi party. "We understand the Germany university as the 'high' school that, grounded in science, by means of science educates and disciplines the leaders and guardians of the fate of the German people."[136]

Heidegger's analysis presupposes a concept of the right time for decisive action, or *kairos,* described under the heading of the moment of vision (*Augenblick*) in *Being and Time*. He insists that both science—whose contemporary source lies in the German university—and the fate of Germany must come together in order to respond to the problem of the present moment. Presumably he has in mind the series of difficulties due to the loss of the First World War, later accentuated by the decline and fall of the Weimar Republic, the same general situation discussed under the heading of boredom in the lecture course of 1929/30.

The idea of a historical turning point has ample philosophical precedent. At the time he composed the *Phenomenology,* Hegel believed that society was at a turning of world history, a period in which fundamental social change was possible, a moment in which the old order was coming to an end and in which it was opportune to seize the day, as it were.[137] Like Hegel, Heidegger thought that history had arrived at a propitious moment in which philosophy can play an important social role. Also like Hegel, Heidegger believes that a people ultimately knows itself in the form of the self-conscious state—according to Heidegger, in the Nazi state. Like Husserl, Heidegger holds that the university can respond to the extreme need of the German people at this supposedly historic moment. But Husserl and Heidegger take diametrically opposed attitudes to National Socialism. Husserl opposed Nazism and desired to utilize the resources of philosophy as science to defeat it; but Heidegger saw philosophical science as a necessary condition to realize the fate of the Germans through National Socialism:

> The will to the essence of the German university is the will to science as will to the historical mission of the German people as a people that knows itself in its state. *Together,* science and German fate must come to power in this will to essence. And they will do so if, and *only* if, we—this body of teachers and students—*on the one hand* expose science to its innermost necessity and, *on the other hand,* are equal to the German fate in its most extreme distress.[138]

Heidegger next turns to a meditation on the nature of science (*Wissenschaft*). Contemporary science is a mere semblance (*Schein*). Science must be understood through its beginnings in Greek philosophy since all science is philosophy. We need to recapture two fundamental traits of the essence of the Greek view of science. Since, as Aeschylus represents Prometheus as saying, "knowledge, however, is far weaker than necessity,"[139] knowledge must be defiant. Heidegger reinforces this view through a series of remarks on the Greek view of theory (*theoria*) as the highest form of activity (*energeia*). His insistence here that theory in the authentic sense is in fact the highest form of activity, as described in the Aristotelian conception, highlights his later claim that the translation of the Greek "*energeia*" as the Latin "*actualitas*" results in the loss of the original insight.[140] Heidegger's point is consistent with his insistence that after the early Greeks metaphysics is on the wrong track, since science in the Greek sense of the term no longer exists in later thought. Speaking in his own voice, he declares that "this active perseverance [that is, science] knows, as it perseveres, about its impotence before fate [Schicksal]."[141]

The passage cited from Aeschylus and its restatement in Heidegger's own words call for three remarks: To begin with, Heidegger's translation is suspect. According to standard sources "*techne*" does not mean "knowledge."[142] At best, it refers to a kind of knowledge, roughly that kind required for "knowing how" as opposed to "knowing that." Second, there is an interesting relation between the view that theory is in itself the highest form of practice and Heidegger's effort to place his philosophy in the service of Nazism. Heidegger is not now arguing, as he later will, that his thought is impractical, of no use.[143] He is arguing that pure theory is practically relevant, in fact indispensable for the good life, in the sense that this view is formulated by Plato and restated by numerous later writers.[144] Further, in retrospect there is a strategic value to Heidegger's insistence that necessity is stronger than knowledge. On this basis, Heidegger later insisted that the failure of his turn to National Socialism did not lie in National Socialism itself, and perhaps not even in his perception of it, but in Being. The idea that Being, not human being, controls human destiny forms the basis of his later nonanthropological view of technology. We perceive, then, in the quotation, and in its restatement by Heidegger, the nascent possibilty of a strategic retreat which Heidegger later undertook.

The meditation on the essence of Greek science is intrinsic to Heidegger's allegiance to Nazism, as he proceeds to demonstrate. We need to recover the original Greek view on the premise that if science is important, its beginning is most important. The original idea of science is significant since its recovery enables us to bend science to the innermost necessity of our being. Heidegger now emphasizes the political force of his view of the preeminence of Greek thought in two ways, through a single sentence that stands apart as a paragraph of its own, and through the appropriate combination of his concept of Dasein with the traditional philosophical concept of spirit and the Nazi concept of the people (*Volk*): "But if we submit to the distant command of the beginning, science must become the fundamental happening of our spiritual being as part of a people [dann muss die Wissenschaft zum Grundgeschehnis unseres geistig-völklichen Daseins werden]."[145] In less sibylline language, Heidegger's statement means that we need to return to the original Greek sense of science within the university, particularly within philosophy, in order to realize the fate of the German nation. If we do so, then, unavoidably, science will become the fundamental happening, which will bring this destiny about. The means for science to bring about German destiny is obviously through the realization of Nazism to which Heidegger has pledged the resources of his thought.

It is striking that Heidegger seems to believe that science in the true sense somehow realizes or could realize itself in Nazism. Heidegger seems literally to believe that science in the ancient Greek sense will realize the Nazi goal, which he also shares, of the gathering of what is authentically German. From this conception it follows loosely that the Greeks would be the authentic forerunners of the German National Socialists. Heidegger was aware of this inference, which he is at pains to refute, perhaps because he later changed his mind about the link between the Greeks and the Nazis. In a lecture course given in the middle of the Second World War, he twice denies that the Greeks are the original Nazis on the grounds that this kind of identification fails to grasp the specificity of National Socialism.[146] Since Heidegger may then have been under political surveillance, it is also possible that he did not change his mind but that in drawing this distinction he merely meant to be prudent in his own way.

What is it precisely that true, or Greek, science is meant to bring about? Heidegger answers this question in a meditation on spirit, which dramatically deepens the link between his own philosophical position and Nazism. According to Heidegger, what he calls the will to the essence of science in the original sense creates for the people the danger of the spiritual world. Heidegger relies on his fundamental ontology when he states that spirit is the resoluteness (*Entschlossenheit*) to the essence of Being. Yet he utilizes the *Blut und Boden* rhetoric of National Socialism[147] when he writes that the "spiritual world of a people" is "the power that most deeply preserves the people's strengths, which are tied to earth and blood powers [seiner erd- und bluthaften Kräfte] as the power of the innermost and widest shaking of its Dasein."[148] Now playing on the relation between the German terms "*Marchschritt*" and "*Schrittgesetz*," roughly "march step" and "law of the step," he emphasizes that the defense of the spiritual world, to be undertaken by the university, will preside over the march already begun by the people into its future history. In sum, the authentic way of Being with respect to German destiny depends on the defense of the ancient Greek concept of science, which alone can and will make possible the desired future of the German people.

Heidegger's view of theory as itself the highest form of practice is merely a restatement of the traditional Greek view of philosophy as the highest form of life. Unlike some thinkers, Heidegger does not maintain that theory is self-realizing, that ideas in some sense literally put themselves into practice.[149] Heidegger finds the means for the realization of his theory in an analysis of the German student movement. His view here anticipates by several decades Herbert Marcuse's theory of the student movement as a radically destabilizing social element.[150] Further extending his military metaphor, Heidegger says that the German students are already on the march in the search for the leaders (*Führer*) through whom to realize their own vocation (*Bestimmung*).

This statement is both self-serving and explosive. Obviously, Heidegger is pointing toward philosophers as the custodians of the ancient conception of science and himself as their titular head. But he is also pointing away from the National Socialist government, above all Hitler, whose leadership he by inference rejects. For Heidegger, in the final analysis only the German university can defend the original Greek concept of science in order to realize the fate of the German people. The crucial role of the students is to bring this goal about. "Out of the resoluteness of the German student body to be equal to the German fate in its most extreme distress, comes a will to the essence of the university."[151] Again like the early Marx, who thought of the philosophers as the head and the proletariat as the heart of the coming communist revolution,[152] Heidegger obviously thinks of the philosophers as the leaders and the students as the followers of the true, philosophically grounded form of the National Socialist revolution.

Heidegger elaborates his view through two further remarks. First, he qualifies the will attributed to the students as the true will, which he now links to the newly promulgated student law (*das neue Studentenrecht*). We are far from Kant's view of the good will as the only intrinsically good thing.[153] For Kant, the good will must determine the principle of its action on a wholly a priori and universalizable basis. For Heidegger, the true will is neither independent, nor free, nor autonomous in Kant's sense, as unconcerned with empirical considerations. On the contrary, for Heidegger the true will is subservient to the *Studentenrecht* intended after 1 May 1933 to apply the so-called *Führerprinzip* in the university. Heidegger's understanding of this idea, which decisively linked all legitimacy to the desires of a single demented individual, is clear in his remarkable proclamation as rector to the German students, published in November 1933: "The *Führer* himself and alone is today and in the future German reality and its law."[154]

Heidegger's acceptance of this principle is significant as an indication of the extent of his enthusiasm for National Socialism at this point, especially as propagated in fact by Hitler and his party colleagues. It further indicates Heidegger's deplorable inability, on the basis of his conception of resoluteness, to distinguish one of its forms from another. In his conception, the important thing is resoluteness as such. Although in theory resoluteness is the call of conscience, in practice there are absolutely no criteria that enable one to recognize where conscience lies, to make a rational choice. The words and deeds of the Nazi dictator are as good as any other form of resoluteness. For a theory that insists on resoluteness at all costs, resoluteness about pushpin is as good as that about poetry, and Nazism is as good as altruism. Heidegger's notion of resoluteness is, then, the ultimate parody of the Kantian idea of moral responsibility based on intellectual maturity and a wholly rational choice of moral principles.

Heidegger's acceptance of the *Führer* principle stands as a clear, unassailable demand to abandon any velleity of critical thought in favor of political orthodoxy. His later attempt to portray his public adherence to this principle as one of a series of compromises he knew he would need to make as rector is unconvincing because it contradicts the idea of free thought, which is a necessary condition of philosophy.[155] His later claim that during his period as rector he believed in the possibility of National Socialism and, for this reason, abandoned the thinker's essential vocation in favor of his work in an official capacity[156] is at best a half truth. For when he pledged his thought to the service of Nazism, he not only abandoned his philosophical research and teaching; he also renounced free thought, which is its proudest possession. If philosophy consists in critical thought, in the demand for the demonstration of proposed claims, in accepting the *Führer* principle Heidegger abjures purely and simply his philosophic calling. There is finally no significant distinction between Heidegger's call for submission to the whim of the *Führer* and Lukács's similar betrayal of reason in the service of Stalinism.[157] As concerns their voluntary subordination of philosophical criticism to political totalitarianism, both thinkers are outstanding examples of the betrayal of reason in our time.

Heidegger's renunciation of the critical role of thought is apparent in his peremptory dismissal of academic freedom. He refers to academic freedom in quotation marks, as inauthentic, in favor of the highest freedom consisting in the giving of the law to oneself. The obvious echo of Kant's categorical imperative is misleading here, since for Heidegger "authentic academic freedom" means that "the German students must give to themselves the new law promulgated by the National Socialist movement." It is difficult to view this statement otherwise than as an injunction to forgo freedom of thought in the ordinary sense by voluntarily submitting to the necessity imposed by a new political reality. In this respect, despite the stress on the call of conscience, there is a less obvious echo of Spinoza's view of freedom as insight into necessity, where "necessity" means "the law of National Socialism."

If Heidegger's new concept of the freedom of the German students is the true view, then the familiar view of academic freedom as the possibility to think and write without constraints is untrue. Heidegger maintains that his new concept creates a specific obligation for German students. "The concept of the freedom of the German student is now brought back to its truth. Henceforth the bond [Bindung] and service [Dienst] of the German student will unfold from this truth."[158] In a clear echo of the triadic structure of the Platonic state, Heidegger now dogmatically asserts the existence of three bonds, which he interprets as services owed by the German students.[159]

First, there is the bond to the community of the people (*Volksgemeinschaft*), presumably to those who share the common German heritage, a bond that is rooted in labor service (*Arbeitsdienst*). The use of the term "*Volksgemeinschaft*" combines a commitment to the *Volk* and to the *Gemeinschaft,* to those who share something in common, by opposition to the *Gesellschaft,* or society. It is overly charitable to think that Heidegger is concerned with all Germans, for instance those who fail to share his view of the importance of the German people. A community in this sense is a mere subset of society composed of those bound together through a common purpose, end, or goal. It follows that the commitment Heidegger exacts from the students is not to society as a whole, not, for instance, to all Germans, but only to those who share the common project. Even if we suppose that Heidegger is interested in people and not only in Being, clearly his interest in the German people is limited only to those ready and willing to accept a particular view of the situation, namely the one he happens to share with National Socialism. His idea of the realization of the German people through philosophy as the ground of National Socialism, hence, includes the familiar National Socialist exclusion of those who happen to reject this program or, by implication, are rejected by it. Although he doesn't spell out his exclusion from the destiny of the Germans of those who might be unhappy with this goal, it obviously is reflected in his peculiar choice of terminology.

Second, there is the bond to the honor and destiny (*Geschick*) of the nation. This is a plural form of resoluteness that concerns a common future as distinguished from the individual. Heidegger grounds this possibility in a brief, undeveloped reference to the possibility of authentic being with one another, evoked in *Being and Time*.[160] This bond is now rendered explicit in the third, decisive bond to the spiritual mission of the German people. For Heidegger, this people influences its own destiny through its world-shaping powers. In this respect, there is an interesting tension, which perhaps reflects Heidegger's genuine ambivalence. On the one hand, he now insists on what a people can do to shape its own destiny, through its adherence to science, the presupposition of Heidegger's call for the members of the academic community to assume their prescribed role in the transformation of German reality. On the other hand, earlier in the same text he has insisted on the relative powerlessness of knowledge before destiny. It is inconsistent to analyze history in terms of destiny and to maintain that a people can be master of its future. At best, as Heidegger later realized after the turning in his thought, one can hold oneself open for a possibility which one cannot oneself realize if historical agency is lodged on some level beyond human being.

According to Heidegger, a people must risk everything in order to be a spiritual people. This idea recalls his insistence in *Being and Time,* in his analysis of death, on the recognition of human finitude as a condition of authenticity.[161] To drive this point home, he now provides a series of metaphors expressing concepts of danger, hardest clarity, highest, widest, and richest knowledge, future destiny, and so on. The effect is to create a sense of struggle in which one's very existence is at stake, a struggle not necessarily for truth but for life itself in the genuine sense. Heidegger's commitment to an "existential" struggle for his view of the proper way to live is further evident during this period by his cooperation in the institution of what can be described as camps for scientific reeducation (*Wissenschaftslager*) more precisely for the reeducation of students and professors to his view of the true commitment to National Socialism.[162] This incident, which recalls the worst excesses of political efforts at mind control, has many historical precedents. Here, it is specifically interesting as an indication of the extent to which Heidegger's philosophical conviction led in political practice. It is difficult to perceive the difference between Heidegger's active cooperation in setting up and running scientific concentration camps on the basis of his fundamental ontology and the use of such means in our time by dictators such as Stalin or Mao.

So far in his talk, Heidegger has stressed the preeminent role of the university for furthering science and, as a consequence, German destiny. He now reinforces this view in three ways:

First, he lists a number of professions. He then states that knowledge does not serve them but that they serve knowledge, although in doing so they carry out the will of the people concerning its very being. "Knowledge does not serve the professions, quite the reverse: the professions effect and administer that highest and essential knowledge of the people concerning its entire being (Dasein)."[163] In the present context, this remark means that the various professions are necessarily subordinated to the home of philosophy in the university, precisely as in Plato's *Republic*.

Second, here and elsewhere in the speech Heidegger stresses the equal primordiality of the three bonds and the three services he has just assigned to the German students. "The three bonds—by the people, to the destiny of the state, in a spiritual mission—are *equally primordial* to the German essence. The three services that stem from it—Labor Service, Armed Service, and Knowledge Service—are equally necessary and of equal rank."[164] The effect of this statement is to heighten the responsibility of the German students to carry out the duties assigned to them by the philosophers.

Third, Heidegger now draws an obvious inference following from his subordination of the students, members of the professions, and presumably everyone else, including the National Socialist regime, to philosophy. Once again he clearly insists on the central role of science in the full sense of the term—here through a self-interpretation of his own term "high school"—because the university alone is able to pursue the destiny of the German people. "*This* science is meant when the essence of the German university is delimited as the 'high' school that, grounded in science, by means of science educates and disciplines the leaders and guardians of the fate of the German people."[165] Obviously, this is an activist view of philosophy. Clearly, Heidegger rejects the traditional idea of philosophy as disinterested science, as exemplified, say, in Aristotle's view of pure theory, in favor of something like the Leninist concept of *partiinost'*. According to Lenin, following Marx, philosophy is an important means to bring about the proletarian goal of abolishing the state. Heidegger, who also regards philosophy as a means to an end, understands its task as to realize German destiny by strengthening the Nazi state.

The stress on science as determined by philosophy presupposes that the university is organized to reflect that view. Heidegger underlines that need but realistically acknowledges that since it took the Greeks three centuries to arrive at an appropriate concept of science, it will not be possible to do so in the current academic year. The distinction of three bonds implicitly raises the question of their relation. Heidegger responds by stating that the type of university he has in mind depends upon the coalescence of the three bonds in a single formative force. He interprets this vision to mean that students and professors alike must necessarily strive toward the essence of science. Through another military metaphor, he insists that both wills confront each other in battle since battle is unavoidable. "The two wills [i.e., that of the student body and of the professors] must confront one another, ready for *battle* [Kampf].[166] All capacities [Vermögen] of will and thought, must be unfolded *through* battle, heightened *in* battle, and preserved *as* battle."[167] Heidegger further heightens his emphasis on battle with a quotation from Carl von Clausewitz, the author of the well-known military treatise *On War:* "I take leave of the frivolous hope of salvation by the hand of accident."[168]

Heidegger's reference to battle is doubly determined here, by his own philosophical position and the political reality of National Socialism. In *Being and Time,* he maintains that the realization of the German people, on which he insists here, requires a battle. "Only in communication and in struggle [Kampf] does the power of destiny become free. Dasein's fateful destiny in and with its 'generation' goes to make up the full authentic happening [Geschehen] of Dasein."[169] His allusions to battle are, hence, consistent with his view that authenticity can come about in no other way.

The idea of battle obviously also refers to Hitler as well. Heidegger does not mention Hitler either here or elsewhere in his speech. But it would be an error to regard the failure to name the Nazi dictator as either decisive or even significant. A direct reference to Hitler would almost be superfluous since indirect references are scattered throughout. In the context of Heidegger's assumption of the rectorate as the spiritual *Führer* of the University of Freiburg almost immediately after the Nazi rise to power, his multiple allusions to battle are also intended as a clear allusion to Hitler's notorious view of the struggle for the realization of the destiny of the German people formulated in *Mein Kampf*.

Heidegger has no doubt about what is correct, about what members of the German academic community should do at this period of German history, at a moment when the NSDAP has risen to power. He portrays this moment as a turning point in world history, as an occasion to seize the future, as it were. In a dramatic passage, fully equal to Spengler[170] at his best, Heidegger shows why he believes that the moment has come to act. "But no one will even ask us whether we do or do not will, when the spiritual strength of the West fails and the joints of the world no longer hold, when this moribund semblance of a culture caves in and suffocates all that remains strong into confusion and lets it suffocate in madness."[171]

Heidegger's conception of Nazism as the way to realize the destiny of the Germans presupposes an ideal of community that can be realized in practice only if each individual contributes to it. Heidegger underscores the need for each person to decide for or against the historical destiny of the German people. "Whether this will happen or no depends alone on whether or not we, as a historical-spiritual people, still and once again will ourselves. Every individual *participates* in this decision, even he, and indeed especially he, who evades it."[172] Since the philosopher speaks for the people, its political leaders and the state, in short for everyone, it is the philosopher who takes the fateful decision for the authentic destiny of the German people. The rectoral address is, then, a solemn pledge before history in the name of the future of the German *Volk*. The result is a curious reciprocal relation between philosophy and National Socialism. On behalf of philosophy, Heidegger asserts the need to lead all others, including the Nazis, who in his view depend on philosophy for their justification. Having claimed the hegemony of the "movement" in virtue of his thought, from that standpoint Heidegger unhesitatingly makes a public commitment of his thought and all those dependent on it, by implication everyone, to National Socialism. Heidegger's speech exhibits a circular relation between philosophy and politics because philosophy grounds politics, to which it is unquestionably and unquestioningly committed.

Heidegger justifies his philosophical demand for the leadership of the Nazi movement through the relation he discerns between philosophy, science, the university, and the will of the people. He now invokes this relation in an enigmatic comment: "For the young and the youngest strength of the people [Denn die jung und jüngste Kraft des Volkes], which already reaches beyond us, *has* by now *decided* the matter."[173] This statement is ambiguous. It is probable that Heidegger is here referring to the students since throughout he has spoken as if their choice had already been made, as if they had sought out the professors to lead them and not conversely. He is also referring to the Nazi party. Heidegger became a member of the NSDAP on 1 May 1933, that is, before he became rector. With the exception of biologism, he evidently held all the views of the ordinary Nazi,[174] presumably including its proclaimed legitimacy to decide for the German people.

In general, the entire speech can be regarded as a public affirmation that the philosopher has rallied to the politics of Nazism on his own terms, namely with respect to the concerns and categories developed in his fundamental ontology. Throughout the address, Heidegger repeatedly stressed his conviction, founded in his own view of science, that the Nazi political undertaking requires the leadership of philosophers who are not themselves to be led. He indirectly reemphasizes the preeminent role he attributes to philosophy at the end of the speech. "But we fully understand the splendor and the greatness of this setting [dieses Aufbruchs] only when we carry within ourselves that profound and far-reaching thoughtfulness that gave ancient Greek wisdom the word: 'All that is great stands in the storm.' "[175]

His allusion to Plato here, in this crucial passage at the close of his talk, is significant for several reasons. Certainly, it calls attention to Heidegger's dependence throughout this speech on the quasi-Platonic view that philosophy founds politics. It also reinforces Heidegger's quasi-Platonic assertion that only a philosopher can lead the National Socialist revolution through the suggestion that only one who has understood the Platonic view can understand the present historical moment, with its possibility in the midst of extreme need to seize the occasion to realize the destiny of the German nation. Further, through an appropriate rendering of the passage cited, Heidegger now enlists Plato in support of his own view of the danger inherent in the present moment. It is, then, a matter of some concern that Heidegger, who was a competent Greek scholar, deliberately distorts the passage from Plato.[176]

Analysis of the rectoral address shows that efforts to portray Heidegger's interest in Nazism as superficial or transitory are refuted by the text. Heidegger's concern with National Socialism at this point is deep and later remains constant since it follows from a permanent part of his thought. Like most philosophical theories, Heidegger's thought later evolved, but the initial commitment to the concept of authenticity, which, in its plural form, underlies his insistence on the realization of the historical destiny of the German people, never changed. As passages from his later writings show, he never altered his basic commitment, following from a part of his thought that did not change, to the goal that apparently led him to Nazism in the first place, the realization in history of the destiny of German being, as a means to the authentic thought of Being.

This chapter has sought to understand Heidegger's Nazi turning in terms of factors external and internal to his thought. It has studied the stages of Heidegger's Nazi turning on the basis of his fundamental ontology to practice and then to National Socialism. I have argued that Heidegger's philosophical position is intrinsically political and have shown how Heidegger was led to practice on the basis of his thought and later was led to Nazism. I have further shown the presence throughout the rectoral speech of numerous concepts borrowed from Heidegger's fundamental ontology. Now I want to examine an important possible objection. One could concede that fundamental ontology is political and that it called for a practical turn but deny that in practice the political nature of Heidegger's thought called for a turn to Nazism. The point of the objection is to concede that it is not accidental that Heidegger turned to politics, but it is merely contingent that he turned to Nazism. It follows that his philosophy is not itself in question in his acceptance of National Socialism since he could have accepted another form of politics.

In my view, this objection is mistaken. There are various reasons for which Heidegger could have turned to another kind of political practice, such as the possibility that Nazism might not have existed. Once it is conceded that fundamental ontology in its very nature calls for a turn to politics, then it must be noted that Heidegger's theory has no intrinsic resources to prevent him from accepting either National Socialism or another similar theory. Fundamental ontology calls for completion in a turn from theory to political practice to bring about authentic Dasein, and, hence, an authentic thought of Being.[177] Authenticity depends on resoluteness on the part of one who sees beyond appearance into the essence of things, on one who is ready and able to choose for himself or herself and even for others. There is a kind of aristocratic authoritarianism built into Heidegger's theory of fundamental ontology which leads seamlessly to a politically antidemocratic political point of view. As in Plato's political theory, which is also antidemocratic, only the philosopher finally knows, and the philosopher's role is to decide for everyone.[178] Nazism might not have existed. Heidegger could have accepted another political practice than Nazism. But it was neither an accident that Nazism existed nor that he turned to it. For the same external factors that influenced the rise of Nazism and the development of his own thought also limited the kind of political choice he could reasonably accept. In sum, Heidegger's pursuit of Being, as he understood it, led to Nazism, and could in fact only lead either to this or another form of antidemocratic, authoritarian political practice. It is, then, no accident that Heidegger the philosopher of Being became Heidegger the Nazi, since Heidegger the philosopher and Heidegger the political activist are one and the same person.

3

The "Official" View and "Facts and Thoughts"

The rectoral address is a central document for the understanding of Heidegger's Nazism. It is a detailed, public statement at a moment when Heidegger, the newly elected rector, identified freely and boldly with a political movement that had only recently come to power and which many people, including Heidegger, regarded as opening the way to a brighter future for all Germans. It is further a revolutionary text, the text of a conservative revolutionary concerned to break with the immediate past and to renew a tradition interrupted by the defeat suffered by Germany in the First World War.

To begin with, the interpretation of Heidegger's speech was not controversial. The nature of the talk initially appeared clear to all commentators. There were disagreements about the wisdom of the message, but not about its nature. It was widely received as an explicit declaration of faith in Nazism, indeed as an effort to realize National Socialist goals within the university by numerous observers.[1] Heidegger's aim in his rectoral address only became controversial as a consequence of later events, in the course of which he resigned his position as rector, his relations to the Nazi party became strained, and Germany finally lost the Second World War. As a result of the German defeat, Heidegger was called to account for his actions as an activist member of the NSDAP. As part of his defense, he offered an account of his actions, including an interpretation of the rectoral address. As might be expected, Heidegger minimized the significance of his rectoral speech as well as other facets of his activity as a Nazi activist.

The "Official" View

I have interpreted Heidegger's turning from fundamental ontology to Nazism through the intrinsically political character of his thought. In my interpretation, Heidegger's political turn is squarely based on, and follows from, his philosophy. I discern an intrinsic link between his philosophical theory and his political practice. Heidegger also endorses an interpretation of his political action as deriving from his thought, for instance, in his acknowledgment that he was led to National Socialism by his conception of historicality,[2] in his admission that he regarded the Nazi rise to power as an opportune moment to seize the destiny of the German people,[3] and so on.

Now it is well known that theories are underdetermined by the facts on which they are based. The obvious consequence is that it is only rarely that factual material cannot be employed to support different, even incompatible, interpretations. It is, then, not surprising that the same material which I have adduced in support of my reading of the link between Heidegger's philosophical thought and political commitment is construed by others to provide a less damaging, more favorable reading of Heidegger's life and thought. Whereas I regard Heidegger's philosophy as ingredient in his politics, Heidegger's defenders are concerned to exonerate his thought from any significant role in his actions.

What I will call the "official" view is propagated not only by Heidegger but by some of his closest students. It is the view that, roughly speaking, there is no, or no important, link between Heidegger's philosophical position and National Socialism. It emerges in Heidegger's writings directly concerned with the rectoral period as well as in occasional hints scattered throughout his later corpus, and it is further developed and propagated by some of his closest followers in their own writings. This view was initially formulated by Heidegger himself at a time when he was threatened with loss of his relation to the university at the end of the war. Not surprisingly, it is intended to deny or at least to minimize a durable, profound, or even significant concern with National Socialism.

There is an interesting analogy between what I am calling the official view and Heidegger's later thought. His writing after *Being and Time* is largely a series of commentaries on that work, which is widely considered as his main philosophical contribution. There is an analogy between the efforts by Heidegger and certain of his followers after the fact to stress a peculiarly favorable interpretation of his life and thought and Heidegger's own effort to create a kind of Heideggerian orthodoxy. Like Marxism, which for more than a hundred years has subsisted on the claim of a privileged insight into the thought of the master thinker, so Heidegger's closest followers continue to dispute his "authentic" legacy through differing interpretations of his works and days. When all is said and done, the official view is vitally important to the orthodox followers of the master thinker, whose careers are inextricably linked to his, and who are, hence, concerned like the master to deny what can reasonably be denied and to limit the effect of what must be admitted. The aim in view that motivates both the master thinker and his disciples is finally the same: to save the phenomena, so to speak, by showing that however deplorable Heidegger's political engagement and actions might be, they have nothing, or nothing essential, to do with the master thinker's thought. Depending on the interpretation, it is possible to hold the master at fault with respect to his politics but not his thought, which, dissociated from him in a conceptual realm of its own, remains entirely unsullied by either time or circumstance.

The official view is not confined to Heidegger scholars only. An example of someone influenced by Heidegger, but not in any sense a Heidegger scholar, who also accepted the official view is provided by Jean-Paul Sartre, in his response to Lukács's critique of Heidegger's Nazism. In a polemical work, Lukács criticized Heidegger's connection to fascism and described Heidegger as a pre-fascist.[4] In response, Sartre objects to Lukács's supposed inability from an orthodox Marxist perspective to comprehend Heidegger because he simply will not read him; he will not make the effort to grasp the sentences one after the other. According to Sartre, who admits that he studied Heidegger's thought in Berlin in 1933 when Heidegger should have been at the summit of his "activism," "Heidegger has *never* been an 'activist'—at least not as he has expressed himself in his philosophical works."[5]

Sartre's view that Heidegger is not an "activist" is due, not to his own research into the matter, but rather to his uncritical acceptance of the "official" view of Heidegger's Nazism, which was already in evidence in the second half of the 1940s, significantly just around the time when Heidegger published the "Letter on Humanism." It is present in the first important discussion of Heidegger's Nazism in the pages of *Les Temps Modernes,* edited by Sartre. The discussion began with an important article by Karl Löwith, Heidegger's former student and later colleague. In response, Alphonse De Waelhens, the Belgian scholar of existentialism and phenomenology, immediately invoked two aspects of the "official" view: the insistence on a distinction in kind between Heidegger the philosopher and Heidegger the man; and what we can call the "expert defense," which consists in invoking the critic's alleged lack of sufficient expertise in Heidegger's thought.

In part, what I am calling the "official" view derives from a clement interpretation of the rectoral address, the text which, except for occasional hints, remained the only published statement directly confronting

Heidegger's Nazism from 1933 when it was delivered until his passing in 1976. Further elements of the "official" view have continued to emerge from Heidegger's *Nachlass,* including the appearance of the *Spiegel* interview immediately after his death and the publication in 1983 of the article from 1945. Since the official view of Heidegger's Nazism is partly based on his posthumous writings, the record is incomplete and still subject to change as further texts from his *Nachlass* appear. Unquestionably, the view of his Nazism and even of his entire later thought in the period after *Being and Time* has been altered by the recent publication, more than fifty years after its composition, of his important *Beiträge zur Philosophie (Vom Ereignis).*

Sartre's remark points to, but does not state, the "official" view. Oddly, there is no official presentation of the "official" view, which continues to inform the discussion. Although it has more than one version, it seems appropriate to illustrate it in the form favored by Hermann Heidegger, Heidegger's son and literary executor (*Nachlass-Verwalter*). Although not a philosopher, even in an extended sense, he is clearly a close follower and defender of his father's life and work; and he provides an average form of the "official" view in a clear, even transparent fashion.

The version of the "official" view favored by Hermann Heidegger is stated in an extremely brief foreword to a small work containing the rectoral address and Heidegger's 1945 article on his period as rector. In his foreword, Hermann Heidegger's comments are limited to these two texts only; but they suggest a proper way to approach Heidegger's Nazism in general. According to the son, his father's relation to Nazism, which was at most unimportant, has been largely misunderstood because of the misrepresentations of his father's rectoral address.

Hermann Heidegger makes this argument in a text of less than a page and a half. The text is divided into five paragraphs in which Hermann Heidegger describes the circumstances of the republication of these two texts. The statement of the "official" view is confined to the third and fourth paragraphs, which I will simply reproduce:

> Much has been said about the content of the speech that is false and untrue. From 1945 on down to the most recent past, even university professors have cited in their publications what were supposed to be statements from the Rectoral Address, which are not found there. The words "National Socialism" and "National Socialist" do not occur in this address; there is no mention of the "Führer," the "Chancellor of the Reich," or "Hitler."
>
> At the time, the title of the address alone made people listen more attentively. No doubt, Martin Heidegger was caught up in the mood that

seemed to promise a fresh start for the nation, as were also many of those who later became resistance fighters. He never denied his entanglements in the movement of the time. And to be sure, he made mistakes while rector. He did not deny his own inadequacies. But he was neither an uncritical fellow traveller, nor an active party member. From the very beginning he kept a clear distance from the party leadership. This showed itself, for example, in his prohibition of book burnings and of the posting of the "Jew Notice" in the university; in his appointment of deans, not one of whom was a National Socialist; and in that as long as he remained rector, he was able to keep the Jewish professors von Hevesy and Thannhauser at the University.[6]

Let us examine the son's narrative account of the supposed misrepresentations. In support of his interpretation, Hermann Heidegger offers two incompatible readings of his father's relation to Nazism. The first reading denies a link between Heidegger and Nazism. The second reading admits the link, which it then attempts to minimize.

Hermann Heidegger begins by denying Heidegger's Nazism. He asserts that even university professors have from 1945 until today cited passages in their writings which do not figure in this text. He then notes that in this text, we do not find any of the following words: National Socialism, *der Führer, der Reichskanzler,* or Hitler. The suggestion that Heidegger's view has been misrepresented by discussion of his rectoral address is strengthened by the further indication, in a passage preceding the one quoted, in which his son notes that the second edition of this speech was withdrawn from sale by the Nazi party, or NSDAP, after his father's resignation as rector.[7]

What is the intention of this paragraph? I believe that Hermann Heidegger intends for the reader to infer that since Heidegger does not refer directly in his speech either to Hitler or to Nazism, his speech cannot reasonably be construed as evidence that his speech is about National Socialism or that his thought led to Nazism. If there is nothing in the rectoral speech that identifies it as a statement of support for National Socialism, then there is obviously no reason to hold that fundamental ontology in fact led to Heidegger's Nazi turn. It follows that Heidegger's turning to a totalitarian form of political practice is, then, merely a contingent matter, unrelated to his philosophical theory, just one of those things, so to speak, but certainly not explicable on the basis of his philosophy, to which it may not even be related.

The text, which is meant to engender these inferences exonerating Heidegger, is remarkably vague. Since there is no indication of who cited what passages from this speech incorrectly, we cannot evaluate Hermann Heidegger's claim. The son is correct that the words listed do not occur in the text. We do not find the word *"Führer"* in the singular, but only in its plural form. But Hermann Heidegger's statement fails to consider a number of relevant issues, which we can put in the form of questions: How did the philosopher intend his speech to be understood? How was it understood? Was he misunderstood? There is no evidence that any of those who heard this talk, including Heidegger's followers or even representatives of official Nazism, ever doubted that his sibylline language referred to those items which, according to his son, he does not name, in fact precisely Hitler and the Nazi party.

The attempted linguistic defense, limited as it is, is inadequate to deny that Heidegger's thought was the conceptual basis of his political allegiance. Even Heidegger's son does not seem convinced by the suggestion that his father's speech has nothing directly to do with Nazism at all. In the next paragraph, he immediately supplements his implicit denial that the rectoral speech is evidence for Heidegger's turning to Nazism by admitting his father's implication in Nazi politics which he has just implicitly denied. His statement of Heidegger's involvement in National Socialist politics is interesting for several reasons, for instance in Hermann Heidegger's employment now of an indirect form of reference to Nazism—a form of reference whose significance he earlier disputes in the observation that neither Hitler nor National Socialism is directly named—through words which unmistakably refer to what he does not directly name.

He states that the title of the talk already caused one to prick up one's ears at that time. According to Hermann Heidegger, like many later resistance fighters his father was at that time caught up in the national mood of renewal (*Aufbruchstimmung*), a word that suggests the possibility of basic change. The comparison to "those who later became resistance fighters" suggests that Heidegger, too, was later part of the resistance to Nazism. Now employing the word "movement" (*Bewegung*), in line with frequent practice, to refer to Nazi party politics, which he does not directly name, he states that Heidegger never denied his temporary involvement (*vorübergehende Verstrickung*) in the so-called movement of the time. The son further admits that his father also certainly made mistakes as rector, which Heidegger never denied. But for the son, his father was never an uncritical fellow traveler nor an active party member. Hermann Heidegger sees his father's clear distance from the party in Heidegger's prevention of the book burning and of the hanging up of the *"Judenplakat,"* in his refusal to appoint only National Socialists, and in his efforts to retain such Jewish professors as Hevesy and Thannhauser.

The time is now long past in which one could simply deny that Heidegger had ever been a Nazi, that he had joined the Nazi party, that he had collaborated with it, that he had even believed in it. It is simply too late to deny rationally what is now part of the public record. At most, one can now only minimize or otherwise interpret what one can no longer deny as such. Perhaps for the reason that a simple denial cannot be maintained, in this paragraph Heidegger's son takes a more realistic line based on the admission of a minimal link between Heidegger and Nazism. Although still interested in reducing his father's involvement with National Socialism, he now admits a relation to Nazism which he seeks to minimize rather than to deny. In his grudging admission that his father did after all have a connection with Nazism, in fact that like everyone else he made mistakes during that period, something he did not deny, the son creates the impression of his father as a human being, with human frailties, who was for a short time only caught up with a dreadful situation and who accepted his errors.

This impression is misleading. Although Heidegger was caught up in Nazism, like numerous later resistance fighters, it does not follow that he was in fact a "resistance fighter" however conceived. Despite a number of hints in his writings that he later confronted Nazism, his own "resistance" to National Socialism is mainly limited to objections to its theoretical adequacy, particularly as a theory of Being. Although he collaborated with National Socialism, in part because he identified with its goals, in part no doubt also for opportunistic reasons, he never accepted it as a theory. There is, however, no evidence, nor does his son cite any, that Heidegger ever resisted such familiar Nazi excesses as the efforts to acquire world hegemony or to exterminate whole populations.

These remarks on Hermann Heidegger's account of Heidegger's Nazism can be summarized as follows: Hermann Heidegger illustrates two common forms of the "official" view of Heidegger's Nazism: on the one hand, an extreme form consisting in the denial of Heidegger's relation to National Socialism, for instance by denying that the rectoral speech in fact refers to this political movement; on the other hand, a more moderate form consisting in the denial of a more than minimal relation between Heidegger and Nazism. Common to these two variants of the "official" view is the claim that Heidegger's relation to Nazism was at most transitory and not centrally rooted in his thought. Heidegger's relation to Nazism is either denied or conceded, but a relation of Heidegger's thought to Nazism is denied.

This reading of Heidegger's relation to Nazism as merely contingent and, hence, unrelated to his thought draws support from two main sources. There is the understandable concern of those whose careers are based on Heidegger's thought to minimize or even to deny its role in his turn to National Socialism. This concern overlaps with Heidegger's own interest, which cannot be denied, in attempting to save his thought from being discredited by his Nazi turning. It is a matter of record that he was able to escape responsibility for his actions. For the most part, at least until the recent publications by Farias and Ott, Heidegger and his followers were able to deny a link between his philosophical thought and his politics, to carry on philosophical business as usual with only occasional attention to the outside world. One must simply concede that the official view of Heidegger's Nazism has been largely successful up to this point in avoiding, or at least minimizing, damage to Heidegger and his thought. At this late date, if the effort at damage control has come undone as the issue has finally escaped from the arid domain of professional philosophy and reached the wider public, it is because a few courageous writers were unwilling to participate in the ongoing whitewash of the relation between Heidegger's Nazism and his philosophy.[8]

"Facts and Thoughts"

The "official" view is rooted directly or indirectly in Heidegger's own efforts to help himself by presenting his own interpretation of the rectorate. His defense of his actions was developed in two later texts, at a time when his first enthusiasm for Nazism had inevitably been tempered by an awareness of the historical consequences to which it led: an article written in 1945,[9] but only published later, and the well-known *Spiegel* interview.

For historical reasons, there is no "natural" order in which to consider these two texts. Both the article and the interview were only published after Heidegger's death. The article appeared for the first time in 1983, some thirty-eight years after it was written, at the same time and in the same small volume as the republication of the rectoral address. The interview, which took place in 1966, was published only ten years later after Heidegger's death. It follows that the interview which took place more than twenty years after the article was written, in fact appeared in print considerably earlier. It contributed more than the article to shaping opinion about Heidegger. In fact, it is reasonable to assume that this was its intended task, that Heidegger intended his interview to shape the public view about his thought and himself after his passing, that he meant it to function as a kind of intellectual testament intended to "correct" the public record for generations to come. Otherwise, it is difficult to understand why he withheld publication until after his death. The aim of the article is different. Since the article is more technical and hence less accessible than the interview, it was probably not meant to shape public opinion in general. It is likely that Heidegger wrote it to influence the immediate situation in which he found himself, at a time in which he was obliged to answer for his actions before the military authorities immediately after the end of the Second World War.

It will be useful to concentrate on Heidegger's article since it is philosophically more substantive and less well known than the *Spiegel* interview. The rectoral speech has often been studied and the *Spiegel* interview is frequently mentioned, but to the best of my knowledge Heidegger's article on the rectorate has not yet been analyzed in detail. To begin with, it is helpful to place the article in historical context.[10] The French occupation, which began in the region of Freiburg on 25 April 1945, led to a process of denazification. As early as the beginning of May 1945, Heidegger's house was "confiscated" in virtue of his Nazi activity, which in practice meant that he and his family were required to share it with another family. Measures were further taken to confiscate his personal library. On 23 July 1945, Heidegger was obliged to appear before a commission composed of five professors. In his time of need, Heidegger turned to two people, Archbishop Conrad Gröber, who had helped to launch his academic career, and Karl Jaspers, his distinguished philosophical colleague and personal friend.[11] The commission, basing itself in part on a largely negative report submitted, in response to an invitation, by Jaspers, insisted on the incompatibility between Nazi doctrine and Heidegger's thought;[12] but it proposed in September 1945 that Heidegger be retired on pension with the right to teach.[13] The committee's report was submitted to the university senate, which took up the question on 17 October 1945. The verdict was that Heidegger was to be retired without the right to teach, and he was also forbidden to participate in any public way in the university. This decision was further made even more rigorous by the military authorities, who subsequently suppressed Heidegger's pension rights.

As could be expected, in order to defend himself Heidegger reacted against these measures as vigorously as possible. On 16 July he wrote to the *Oberbürgermeister* in order to protest the decisions to "confiscate" his house and his library. It has been pointed out that already in this letter we find the basic elements of the line of defense which Heidegger continued to maintain in numerous ways in a variety of later writings.[14] Heidegger's defense included claims that the actions taken against him amounted to discrimination against himself and his work since he never held office in the Nazi party and never was active in its various instances; that his work has constantly brought attention to the University of Freiburg and that he has constantly declined offers of positions elsewhere to remain in Freiburg; and that the actions taken against him were based on accusations whose content and origins were not known to him, and are of a type which so far have only been brought against important party functionaries, with whom he was neither in personal political contact either during or after his period as rector.

Unquestionably, Heidegger did bring attention to the University of Freiburg. He willingly chose to remain there when he received offers to go elsewhere.[15] The actions taken against him were not, however, based on anonymous accusations since the key document was the report, to which he had access, written by Karl Jaspers. In his report, Jaspers noted that:

— For personal reasons, as a friend of Heidegger, he would have preferred not to intervene.

— Heidegger's actions with respect to individuals were inconsistent, since he denounced Baumgarten as unworthy to be a National Socialist and as one who consorted with Jews, but helped his student Brock—who was in fact Jewish—emigrate to England.

— It is important that Heidegger, as Germany's most important thinker, be able to continue to write.

— Heidegger was one of the few German professors who actively collaborated with the Nazis.

— Heidegger is finally not a political person, but his reported change of heart in 1941 is meaningless since it would only have been meaningful immediately after 30 June 1934.

Jaspers recommended that Heidegger be offered a pension to continue his work, that he be suspended from teaching for several years, and that he be reinstated only after an inspection of his publications during that period and consideration of new academic conditions. In its report, based on Jaspers's recommendations, the commission stated:

Before the upheaval in 1933, philosopher Martin Heidegger lived in a fully unpolitical intellectual [geistigen] world, had, however, friendly relations (also through his sons) with the student movement of that period and certain literary leaders of the German youth, such as Ernst Jünger, who foresaw the end of the bourgeois capitalist period and the coming of a new German socialism. He expected from the National Socialist revolution a spiritual renewal of German life on a *völkisch* basis, [and] simultaneously, like many educated Germans, a reduction of social contradictions and a salvation of Western culture from the dangers of communism. He had no clear idea of the political-parliamentary antecedents which preceded the coming to power of the NSDAP, and he believed in the historical mission of Hitler who would bring about a basic political change.[16]

Both Jaspers and the commission, which acted on his report, dissociated Heidegger the thinker from Heidegger the man. Both described Heidegger as characterized by a lack of political insight and grave psychological and character flaws, in particular his effort to turn the Nazi rise to power to personal advantage, which he shared with Alfred Baeumler and Carl Schmitt. But both Jaspers and the commission sought to preserve Heidegger's philosophical achievement, which they regarded as untarnished by his turning to Nazism. Jaspers's own inability to perceive the extent of the link between Heidegger's acceptance of Nazism and his fundamental ontology is apparent in his congratulatory note to Heidegger after the talk, in which he praises Heidegger as someone who, unlike Nietzsche, will realize his philosophy in practice.[17] He differed in that respect from Croce, a more perceptive observer, who immediately grasped the significance of the connection between fundamental ontology and Nazism in his remark that Heidegger's action dishonored philosophy.[18]

It is in these difficult personal circumstances that Heidegger wrote his essay, "The Rectorate 1933/34: Facts and Thoughts." Our task now is to interpret Heidegger's text, intended to justify his actions as rector during a prior period at a moment when he has been called to account for that association. Heidegger undertakes to defend himself in an article slightly more than twenty pages long. In an obvious manner, more so than for the *Rektoratsrede,* the article from 1945 is indeed an occasional text, a document composed in the most extreme personal need, the kind of need which Heidegger in 1933 had previously attributed to the German people as a whole.

Like the rectoral address, this is more than an occasional text, although it is that as well. It offers the most important statement in Heidegger's corpus of his actions during the rectorate. Heidegger's analysis is embedded in a philosophical discussion that foreshadows the later evolution of his thought. Unlike the rectoral speech, which is mainly a philosophical argument elaborated on a significant occasion, his account of the rectorate is largely of a factual nature. The talk possesses a deliberately incantatory quality, which builds to a climax in the repeated invocation of history, fate, struggle, and the destiny of the German people in a time of need. In comparison, his account of the rectorate is more restrained, devoid of the "conceptual frenzy" that marked the speech. It is divided in an apparently arbitrary manner into three sections: an unnamed section that begins the article, followed by a long passage whose heading reads, "The aim and attitude of the rectorate are stated in the *Rektoratsrede* of May 1933," and ending in an account titled "The Time after the Rectorate."[19]

Heidegger is usually a self-assured writer, who confidently states his

view in an economical, apodictic manner. Uncharacteristically, his account of his rectorate is confused and confusing, with multiple repeti-
tions of the same or similar points within a single, short text.[20] Because
of the repetitious nature of the discussion, it is more than usually difficult to describe the relation among its various constituent parts. As a
guess, one can understand the articulation of the article as follows: the
first section, or introduction, provides a general orientation to the so-
called facts and Heidegger's thoughts about them; the second section
offers a more detailed consideration of specific points of the rectoral
address and the rectorate; and the last section indicates Heidegger's
view of the "discrimination" he suffered during the Nazi period, that is,
after his period as rector.

Since this is not a historical work, it is not necessary to consider the
historical accuracy of Heidegger's self-interpretation in detail. It is sufficient to indicate that the so-called factual material is controversial and
need not be accepted without scrutiny. Here a single, significant instance
will suffice to make this point. For instance, Heidegger claims that he
was not a party member and he only became one, as a matter of form,
after his first several weeks in office in order to respond to the perceived
interest of the university, although it was understood that he would not
be active in any way.[21]

This statement is important in the context of Heidegger's interpretation of the meaning one can attribute to his period as rector. Heidegger
does not deny that he was a member of the NSDAP; rather, he employs
a slight shift in the date of his adherence to suggest that his membership
was not voluntary, or not wholly voluntary, in order to minimize its
significance. The effect is to deny any concern with National Socialism as
such, although we have seen that the rectoral speech provides a wholly
different picture. On the contrary, it is known that, prior to becoming
rector, at a time when he was already actively involved in planning with
the Prussian *Kultusministerium,* Heidegger held that it would give other
colleagues a free hand to act against him were he to become a member
of the NSDAP.[22] And it is further known that he in fact became a party
member prior to his inauguration as rector.[23]

In defense of Heidegger, one could point out that he was not a professional historian or explain this divergence as due to his reliance on an
untrustworthy memory. Yet in the context of his effort to justify his
actions as rector, this and other such factual errors in this text, as well as
in other writings, tend to present a better case for Heidegger's side of
the story than is warranted by the facts. It is entirely plausible to infer
that Heidegger, who evidently carefully planned his decision to adhere
to the NSDAP, later exercised similar care to disguise the nature and
depth of this adherence, with respect to the original date and the entire

period after the rectorate. This is merely one instance of Heidegger's two-track approach in which he insists on the inner necessity of his thought while presenting a systematically misleading account of the Nazi turning in his thought.[24]

Heidegger begins his account, in the first section of his paper, by drawing a connection between four apparently disparate elements: his statement that he was unanimously elected rector despite his own hesitation to assume the job, his lack of relation to the Nazi party, his concern over whether the university would cooperate with him to discover and to shape its own essence, and the connection of the latter task with his inaugural address:

> In April 1933 I was elected rector by the unanimous vote of the plenum of the university. . . . I had no contact with the relevant government and party agencies, was myself neither a member of the party, nor had I been active politically in any way. Thus it was uncertain whether those at the center of political power would listen to me with respect to what to me seemed to be the necessary task [als Notwendigkeit und Aufgabe vorschwebte]. But just as uncertain was the extent to which the university would actively join me to discover and to shape its own essence in a more primordial manner. Already in my Inaugural Address [Antrittsrede], delivered in the summer of 1929, I had presented this task to the public.[25]

In his reference to the task of discovering and shaping the essence of the university, Heidegger in part names the central theme of the rectoral address. What he excludes is as significant as what he includes, because his defense of himself turns on this point. Heidegger's representation of his task as the defense of the essence of the university against all dangers is inaccurate in a deep, essential sense. His description of his task in the rectoral address differs from the main thrust of the talk, which is not the defense of the university as an end in itself but rather as a means to other ends of a political and philosophical nature. His aim in the speech is only incidentally the defense of the German university, or even the Greek idea of science, since his further goals include the coming to being of the German people as authentically German and, finally, the problem of Being that is the central theme in his position. Attention to the essence of the university differs fundamentally from attention to the essence of the university for a further purpose. In the first case, the defense of the university is an end in itself, whereas in the second case it is a means to another end or ends.[26] In his statement that he was concerned with the university as such, Heidegger by implication transforms what in the rectoral speech he presented as his concern with the university in order to realize the destiny of the German people and, I believe, his overall philosophical goal, into a simple defense of the German university against whatever threatened it from without. The result is a stunning, self-serving distortion of the main stated theme of the rectoral address: the affirmation that the German people wills itself to be itself—in a word, it assumes its own historical destiny—through the newly elected rector's assumption of the leadership of the "movement."

If this interpretation is accurate, we need to explain Heidegger's inaccurate depiction of his talk. A point made by Jaspers, the former psychiatrist, whose testimony proved most damaging in the deliberations of the committee, is relevant here. "He [i.e., Heidegger] does not perceive the depths of his earlier mistake, which is why there is no real change in him but rather a game of distortions and erasures."[27] Heidegger's discussion of the rectorate is an example of the evasive self-justification which Jaspers reports, and which is on display elsewhere in Heidegger's later efforts to shift responsibilty and to minimize his involvement in Nazism. In Jaspers's terminology, there is a game of distortions and erasures in evidence in the slight shift in language, but enormous shift in meaning, from Heidegger's statement—in the opening sentences of the *Rektoratsrede*—that he undertook to defend the essence of the university in order to realize the destiny of the German people to the later claim—in his article about the rectorate—that in fact he only undertook to defend the essence of the university.

The contrast between the rectoral address and Heidegger's discussion of this period is further apparent on a variety of levels. Heidegger's earlier formulation, in the speech, of what he refers to as a necessary task contradicts his later effort, in the article, to portray his earlier concern as limited to the defense of the university. It is plausible to argue for the defense of the university as a necessary task. It is less plausible, indeed odd, to refer, as he does in his later discussion, to this task as a necessity. In German the term "necessity" ("*Notwendigkeit*") derives from "necessary" ("*notwendig*"), which is roughly synonymous with such words as "*erforderlich*," "*unentberhrlich*," "*unvermeidlich*," "*zwangsläufig*," "*vorgeschrieben*," "*dringend*," "*unbedingt*." It refers not only to what is demanded, or not to be missed, but also to what is unavoidable, obligatory, foreordained, pressing, and unlimited. In German, a necessity is something that relates to fate or to destiny, precisely the task he described in his speech with respect to the German people, but which can scarcely be attributed to what he here describes as the defense of the university.

It is normal for Heidegger, in difficult circumstances, to take steps to save his philosophical work by dissociating it from his political activity. It would not be normal not to make this effort, not to use every means at his disposal to defend himself. Our role is to scrutinize the available historical and philosophical record with a view to determining whether

Heidegger's thought is compromised by his political actions. There is a distinction between the conclusion that his politics reflect on his thought and the determination of the accuracy of his interpretation of his thought and actions during the rectoral period. I have already argued that his thought is ingredient in his Nazi turning. His entire retrospective discussion of the rectorate is an effort to deny or to minimize the nature of his "political mistake" by subtly transforming what took place into something superficially similar, but in fact very different. A careful scrutiny of this text needs to determine whether it provides a faithful, or even an acceptable, reading of this situation and further to determine whether the interpretation provided is sufficient to refute the criticisms brought against his thought through the analysis of the rectoral talk.

Heidegger begins his defense by calling attention to his inaugural lecture, "What Is Metaphysics?"[28] This lecture, which was delivered in 1929, was later supplemented by an afterword added to the fourth edition in 1943 and by an introduction added to the fifth edition in 1949. Just as the writings after *Being and Time* often serve to interpret and reinterpret that work as Heidegger's view (and accordingly his view of *Being and Time*) changed, so the afterword and introduction Heidegger later added serve to interpret and reinterpret the inaugural lecture from a different, later perspective.

The lecture sketches Heidegger's understanding of metaphysics, his main theme, in a version close to the position of *Being and Time*.[29] Heidegger mentions the unfolding of the metaphysical inquiry, the elaboration of the question, and an answer to it.[30] In remarks on metaphysics, he develops a conception of nothing[31] in response to Leibniz's famous question: why is there something rather than nothing? In a way that recalls Kant, Heidegger maintains that metaphysics is a basic occurrence of Dasein and Dasein itself.[32] In the afterword, his view has progressed beyond philosophy toward thought in order to surpass metaphysics. He suggests that in thinking the ground of metaphysics, thought is no longer metaphysical.[33] He closes with a comparison between the thinker (*Denker*) and the poet (*Dichter*). For Heidegger, in saying the thinker names Being, and in naming the poet names the holy.[34] In the introduction, added still later, he provides a temporal framework for metaphysics, which he locates in a tradition running from Anaximander to Nietzsche, in which the nature of Being is hidden.[35]

The differences in the successive versions of Heidegger's inaugural lecture reflect the evolution of his thought. In a move indicating the philosophical roots of his political turn, in the article Heidegger now draws attention to a link between the initial version of the lecture and his rectoral address by citing the "introductory sentences" of his inaugural lecture.

We question, here and now, for ourselves. Our being (Dasein)—as members of a community of scientists, teachers, and students—is determined by science. What essential thing is happening to us from the very bottom of our being (Dasein), when science has become our passion? The fields of science lie far apart. They approach their subject matter in fundamentally different ways. Today this fragmented multiplicity of disciplines is held together only by the technical organization of universities and faculties, and retains some importance only because of the practical aims pursued by the different specialties. But the roots of the sciences in their essential ground have withered.[36]

He correctly states that his lecture was widely translated and that everyone knew that he then thought that the most pressing concern of the German university was to renew itself by withdrawing from its present concern with a pseudo-unity.

Everyone was in a position to know what I thought about the German university and what I considered its most pressing concern. It was to renew itself by returning to its essential ground, which is also the essential ground of the sciences; that is to say, by returning to the essence of truth itself instead of persisting in a technical organization-institutional pseudo-unity, it was to recover the primordial living unity that joins those who question and those who know.[37]

Obviously, the point of citing the passage from the inaugural lecture is to suggest a continuity between that lecture and the rectoral address at the small cost of admitting the philosophical dimension of the address itself. The aim is to suggest that the address is not political, because it, like the lecture, is focused on the defense of the university. The argument is, however, misleading. To begin with, the passage cited is not from the opening sentences, but rather constitutes the fifth paragraph of the lecture, which occurs on the second page of the text. It occurs in the course of a transition from metaphysics in general as a problem to Dasein which raises the problem of the nothingness named in Leibniz's question. The cited passage is incidental to the main theme of the lecture. It was, hence, unlikely to be generally known as Heidegger's position, even if a sharp-eyed reader would have noticed it. It was hardly likely to be known to everyone, since few people, with the exception of professional philosophers, and certainly few of the scientists to whom the lecture was delivered, were in a position to understand it.

The argument is further misleading in a deeper sense, since it exaggerates the continuity in order to hide the change that has taken place in Heidegger's thought in the intervening period. At some point after the lecture, a turning (*Kehre*) occurred in Heidegger's thought, including a move away from Dasein as the access to Being, a withdrawal from the transcendental philosophical approach employed by fundamental ontology, and even a withdrawal from philosophy. There is no hint of politics in the inaugural lecture. But politics is a main theme in the rectoral address. The unity of the university is not the main theme in either the lecture or the speech, but Heidegger misleadingly represents it as the main theme in both the lecture and the speech in his effort to defend himself.

Heidegger states that he hesitated to assume the rectorate since he knew that he would run into a conflict with the "new" and the "old," namely "political science" (*politische Wissenschaft*), based on a falsification of the essence of truth, and the tendency to advance a particular specialty in isolation from reflection on the essence of science.[38] Both points are Platonic in inspiration. His objection to the idea of a special science proceeding without reflection on the essence of science in general is an application of Husserl's quasi-Platonic objection to the supposed objectivism of the nonphilosophical sciences.[39] Heidegger earlier accepted this Husserlian point in *Being and Time* and in the speech. Husserl's view of objectivism follows Plato's well-known view that, as the science of sciences, philosophy grounds the other sciences and itself.[40] Here, Heidegger rejects the idea that a university should consist of separate departments whose relation to each other and to the implicit concept of science, the essence of the university, remains unthought.

The remarks about "political science" are more difficult to construe. Heidegger mentions "political science" on four occasions in this short essay, initially, as we have noted, in connection with the "new." He qualifies this comment in three later passages: in an assertion that "[i]t was never my intention to realize only party doctrines and to act in accord with the 'idea' of a 'political science,' "[41] in an observation that the talk rejects the idea of political science "proclaimed by National Socialism as a cruder version of Nietzsche's understanding of the essence of truth and knowledge,"[42] and again in a statement that "the ministry expressed ever more clearly the desire that the idea of 'political science' be taken far more seriously at the University of Freiburg than had so far happened."[43] The translator suggests in a footnote that Heidegger has in mind the politicization of science, in which truth is based in the *Volk*.

This suggestion is only partly correct. If Heidegger is indicating his opposition to the politicization of science, then his opposition is qualified by his admission that he never intended to realize *only* party doctrines. In this way, he admits that as rector he was also concerned to attain the goals of the party. The identification of a dual intention during the rectoral period helps to explain the curious duality in the rectoral speech where he insists both on the defense of science in the original sense and the link of the defense of science to the destiny of the German people.

On a deeper level, Heidegger supports "political science." The talk exhibits a form of Platonism in politics, according to which pure theory is practically relevant, indeed practically indispensable as the condition of the "just" state. Among other things, the rectoral speech is meant to recall that philosophy is the foundation of politics.[44] But if philosophy founds politics in a quasi-Platonic sense, then Heidegger cannot object to the politicization of philosophical science in general, but only to the way in which the National Socialists have carried this out. For the "Platonist" that he still was at the time of the rectoral address, pure theory is intrinsically political because it is practically relevant. He can only object to the transformation, or rather degradation, of theory to merely political ends, as in the discredited effort of Lyssenko in Marxist-Leninist biology or in the equally discredited idea of a Nazi physics. Yet Heidegger participated in an analogous endeavor. Certainly, his public acceptance of the *Führer* principle seems to indicate that at the time, for him the final arbiter of truth was Hitler, the German dictator.

Heidegger clearly rejects a vulgar, inauthentic form of "political science" in favor of the authentic variety. His opposition to the politicians and political scientists involved in the Nazi revolution has three aspects that need to be distinguished: To begin with, he opposes the attempted usurpation of the legitimate role of philosophy in politics, the same view that subtends his expressed desire to lead the leaders of the Nazi state. He further criticizes the scientific pretensions of a "science" which, from his reading of Greek thought, is not worthy of the name of philosophy. Finally, he is reacting against the crude, or vulgar, reading of Nietzsche proposed by Nazism, to which he opposes his own supposedly authentic interpretation.[45] On the contrary, a correct understanding of Nietzsche, adumbrated in Jünger, is invaluable for metaphysics and history.[46] If official Nazism depends on a crude version of Nietzsche, whose thought requires a deeper reading, then the critique of "political science" points beyond itself in the anticipation of an authentic form of National Socialism based on a more secure grasp of Nietzsche's position.

Heidegger admits only to assuming the rectorate as part of his "plan of founding the essence of the university in a primordial manner."[47] He offers three reasons for his decision:

(1) I saw in the movement [Bewegung] that had gained power the possibility of an inner recollection and renewal of the people and a path that would allow it to discover its historical vocation in the Western world. I believed that, renewing itself, the university might also be called to con-

tribute to this inner self-collection of the people, providing it with a measure [mass-gebend mitzuwirken].

(2) For this reason I saw in the rectorate an opportunity to lead all capable forces—regardless of party membership and party doctrine—back to this process of reflection and renewal and to strengthen and to secure the influence of these forces.

(3) In this manner I hoped to counter the advance of unsuited persons and the threatening hegemony of party apparatus and party doctrine.[48]

Heidegger here links together his perception of a historical opportunity he sought to seize, the way in which it could be realized through the rectorate, and the advantage to be gained by assuming the office of rector. This explanation is coherent; but it conflicts with the view that he became rector to defend the German university, and it fails to mention an essential point. Obviously, if Heidegger had a further political aim in mind, as he admits here, then his defense of the university is at most a piece in the puzzle but not the whole puzzle. His statement of his intentions here undermines his effort to distance himself from any political intentions through his desire to save higher education from disintegration. This noble intention, which all academics presumably share, should not be allowed to obscure Heidegger's political interest in assuming the rectorate. He fails, however, to mention his conviction, which he seems never to have abandoned, that the German people possesses a Western historical vocation that requires realization.[49] Significantly, his failure to mention this idea conceals a main link between his own view and Nazism: the shared belief that the unrealized essence of the German people would be realized through National Socialism. In revealing his belief in a *kairos* associated with Nazism and the university's part in it, he covers up an essential element: his continued adherence to the underlying idea which, from his perspective, brought Nazism and philosophy together.

Heidegger's remark that in assuming the rectorate he hoped to counter unsuited people, the party apparatus, and party doctrine requires a comment. He cannot simply mean that he was in favor of maintaining a certain level of quality in the university, since that would imply that he was concerned to differentiate gifted from ungifted Nazis. He also cannot simply mean that he was opposed to party doctrine in general or to the party apparatus as such. For he cooperated at least in part with that apparatus and willingly propagated its doctrine. Perhaps he means that he desired to maintain the ability of the university to determine itself. A reading of this kind is doubly persuasive. It fits comfortably with the idea of self-assertion in the title of the talk, which points to a refusal of any form of external direction of university affairs. It is further consistent with the broadly Platonic reading of the speech advanced here.

The more difficult question is why Heidegger believed that Germany was at a historical turning, why the time had come for philosophers to lead the state. The answer seems to lie in the evolution of his understanding of the *Seinsfrage* through his reading of Nietzsche and Jünger. Heidegger apparently not only believed with Plato that philosophy provided the ground of politics.[50] He further believed that his metaphysical perspective could see into history and included a capacity to discern the shape of the future, almost like a seer or prophet of Being. This conviction helps to explain some of the stranger passages in his corpus. For instance, in a request to the dean of the University of Freiburg to be relieved of all duties for the winter semester 1943/44 in order to carry out his research, Heidegger wrote: "The request I am making does not arise from a personal interest in the promotion of my own work, but from a knowledge of the historical limits of German philosophical thinking with regard to the future of the West."[51] Heidegger seems literally to have thought that the future of the West depended on the proper understanding of metaphysics, supposedly presented in his own thought. In other circumstances, someone who advanced such ideas would be a candidate for psychiatric treatment. It is a measure of the loss of perspective of contemporary philosophy that it accords such delusions serious consideration.

Heidegger hints at this understanding in his remarks on Nietzsche and Jünger. These remarks develop ideas barely sketched in the important lecture course, *An Introduction to Metaphysics,* delivered in 1935. Here, almost in passing, he suggests that, although misunderstood, Nietzsche is crucial to a grasp of the problem of Being. To grasp Nietzsche's view correctly, we need to unfold what is contained within it.[52] In a crucial passage, he then asserts a basic connection between the forgetfulness of Being, to which he holds that Nietzsche offers an essential clue, and the decline of nations and traditions:

> Is it the fault of Being that it is so involved? is it the fault of the word that it remains so empty? or are we to blame that with all our effort, with all our chasing after beings, we have fallen out of Being? And should we not say that the fault did not begin with us, or with our immediate or more remote ancestors, but lies in something that runs through Western history from the very beginning, a happening which the eyes of all the historians in the world will never perceive, but which nevertheless happens, which happened in the past and will happen in the future? What if it were possible that man, that nations in their greatest movements and traditions, are linked to Being and yet had long fallen out of Being, without knowing it, and that this was the most powerful and most central cause of their decline? (See *Sein und Zeit,* paragraph 38, in particular pp. 179f.).[53]

The references here to the early approach to the *Seinsfrage* in *Being and Time* and to Nietzsche show how Heidegger transformed his original analysis of the meaning of Being into an explanation of world history. We recall that he proposed an authentic theory of historicality (*Geschichtlichkeit*) in *Being and Time* in the context of his theory of Being.[54] As strange as it seems, Heidegger here extends what was earlier a philosophical analysis of the idea of history to the interpretation of historical events now and in the future.

His remarks here on Nietzsche further develop ideas raised in the inaugural lecture. Even in the amended version of the lecture, Nietzsche figures merely as an end point, a *terminus ad quem* of the metaphysical tradition begun by Anaximander. Heidegger now makes two further points. First, recalling his earlier reference in the talk to Nietzsche's statement that God is dead, he comments that this has nothing to do with atheism; rather, it indicates the loss of historical efficacy of the supersensible world, particularly the Christian God.[55]

Heidegger glosses this claim through further remarks, beginning with a reference to a lecture, delivered in 1943, concerning Nietzsche's statement.[56] This lecture was intended as an introduction to the topic of nihilism.[57] Heidegger now argues that the suggestion that God is dead and the reduction of value to will, or nihilism, can be understood only in terms of the will to power, in his view the central concept of Nietzsche's philosophy.[58] Nietzsche's insight is now said to provide a reflection beyond metaphysical thinking, that is, beyond the whole of Western metaphysics.[59] But Nietzsche deludes himself in thinking that this overturning of metaphysics is an overcoming of metaphysics, which merely recurs in his thought in a different fashion. "Nietzsche holds this overturning of metaphysics to be the overcoming of metaphysics. But every overturning of this kind remains only a self-deluding entanglement in the Same that has become unknowable."[60]

Second, Heidegger expands his view of how metaphysics enables us to understand politics through remarks on Ernst Jünger.[61] He states that he twice formed discussion groups (in 1932 and in 1939/40) to discuss Jünger's writings. He claims that these misunderstood writings offer a fundamental insight into Nietzsche's concept of metaphysics as a way to understand history, which is empirically confirmed, and which underlies the speech:

Together with my assistant Brock, I discussed these writings in a small circle and tried to show how they express a fundamental understanding of Nietzsche's metaphysics, in so far as the history and present of the Western world are seen and foreseen in the horizon of this metaphysics. Thinking from these writings and, still more essentially, from their foundations, we thought what was coming, that is to say, we attempted to counter it, as we confronted it. At the time many others also read these writings but together with many other interesting things that one also read, one laid them aside without comprehending their far-reaching import. Later, in the winter 1939/40, I discussed part of Jünger's book *The Worker* once more with a circle of colleagues; I learned how even then these thoughts still seemed strange and put people off, until "the facts" bore them out. What Ernst Jünger thinks with the thought of the rule and shape of the worker and sees in the light of this thought, is the universal rule of the will to power within history, now understood to embrace the planet. Today everything stands in this historical reality, no matter whether it is called communism, or fascism, or world democracy.[62]

The remarks on Jünger provide a crucial link between Heidegger's view of the rectorate and his interpretation of world history in terms of the *Seinsfrage*. We can reconstruct the chain of argument as follows. The problem of the meaning of Being yields a concept of authentic history (*Geschichtlichkeit*), including the interpretation of present and future history which are confirmed by experience. The argument rests on claims to grasp the views of Nietzsche and Jünger in an authentic manner. Nietzsche, who is misunderstood, provides an analysis of history as ruled by the will to power. Jünger, who is also misunderstood, sheds important light on Nietzsche through his view of the worker, which is empirically verified. Heidegger claimed to possess this seerlike insight during the rectorate since, as he states, "From the vantage point of this reality of the will to power I saw even then what *is*."[63]

The link Heidegger now proposes between metaphysics and history raises a series of issues about what he believed during the rectorate. With respect to the rectorate, there is a less obvious, more significant end in view. It is insufficient to paint the descent into the political arena from a Platonic angle of vision. Since Heidegger is moving now to reject Platonism in all its forms, to invoke it as a motivating factor during the rectorate would also be to deny that there was anything positive to begin with in the turn to real Nazism. Now this line of defense is not open to him if for no other reason than that he now believes that Nazism did not fail him but that Hitler and the other Nazis failed Nazism. He seems never to have regretted his adherence to National Socialism for the purpose of realizing the essence of the German people, or to further the understanding of Being, ends that he still accepts as valid. On the contrary, he recognizes—how could he deny it?—that this adherence has failed to produce the intended result. The "solution" is to attribute the attraction to politics to another factor of permanent value. If his political turn was motivated by metaphysics, then he can attribute the failure of his political insight, which is clear to him at the end of the war in the midst of the ruins of the Third Reich, to Being; and he can also defend the validity of his original concern with the destiny of the German nation as a valid concern.

The proposed shift from a concept of history, at the level of fundamental ontology, to the interpretation of history in terms of this concept raises the problem of the transition from theory to practice. Heidegger argues for this transition roughly as follows: Everything is now dominated by the will to power that holds sway in the space left through the withdrawal of Being, now present only in the mode of absence. Heidegger grounds his claim that everything stands in the historical reality of the will to power in the logically prior assertion that Being has somehow withdrawn. This is the deeper meaning of his reading of Nietzsche's proposition that God is dead. Beyond the claim about the loss of efficacy of the Christian God, Heidegger has in mind what he calls "the supersensible world," namely Being. For Heidegger, then, what has occurred and what will occur in the future is explicable on the basis of the withdrawal of Being, an "event" that in turn has in the past enabled and in the future will continue to enable the will to power to flourish unchecked. He expresses his reliance on this explanatory model in the form of two related questions about the past: "Had things been different [that is, if Being had not withdrawn so that everything is now subject to the will to power], would the First World War have been possible? And even more, had things been different, would the Second World War have been possible?"[64]

It is difficult to make a case for the relation Heidegger discerns between a withdrawal of Being, the will to power, and the occurrence of two world wars. Since we know no more about Being than about the thing-in-itself, claims for a link to its "withdrawal" cannot be based on direct knowledge, or experience, or anything other than an apparently "mystical insight" into what is. There is no reason to hold that the will to power flourishes because of the absence of Being since, apart from Heidegger's statement, there is no way to know the relation between Being and this Nietzschean concept. Even were it the case that Being had withdrawn, it is unclear how, otherwise than through the prophetic powers he now attributes to himself, Heidegger could possibly be aware of this occurrence. This assertion, then, appears to be nothing more than an *ad hoc* claim now made to explain such inconvenient "facts" as the evident failure of the rectorate and the turning to Nazism. It is important to note this rather obvious point since Heidegger's mystical insistence on the mythological event of the withdrawal of Being is a constant element in his later thought. And even if we grant Heidegger's claim, it is difficult to see how Heidegger can reasonably claim, other than in merely arbitrary fashion, that a withdrawal of Being is more significant for the Second than for the First World War.

Heidegger's proposed interpretation of movements as different as communism, fascism, and world democracy is vague in the extreme. These are obviously disparate political movements, each of which obeys a different intrinsic logic commanding its historical development. In theory, there is a clear interpretative advantage to be gained by considering the entire political spectrum in terms of a single explanatory factor. In practice, this approach is questionable since it is so general as to fail to explain the phenomena and fails to acknowledge what is different in the various political movements. It is intuitively obvious that an approach of such great generality—unable to recognize what separates communism, fascism, and democracy—cannot take the place of more concrete explanation.

Heidegger appeals to, but does not ground, the will to power as a central explanatory factor in the political domain. Even if this will exists and functions in the political arena, we need to know why it is more than one among a multitude of political determinants. It does not follow that if Nietzsche sheds light on metaphysics, he also sheds light on history. History and metaphysics are different since historical explanation, but not metaphysics, needs to respect pragmatic criteria. Theories of historical explanation should only be revised on pragmatic grounds to account, or to account better, for the observed phenomena. Now there are various traditional approaches to historical phenomena, including the appeal to demographic, economic, political, and social forms of explanation. Unless and until Heidegger can show that the will to power can usefully supersede such other explanatory models, the only reason to accept his favored view of the will to power is simple philosophical fiat. One can do so arbitrarily, but not on rational grounds.

Heidegger's substitution of a metaphysical problem for historical reality exemplifies the well-known philosophical tendency to substitute itself for the special sciences. This tendency follows from the old Platonic view that all the sciences derive their justification from philosophy, which further justifies itself. Without doubt, philosophy has an important secondary role to play in the clarification and critique of the basic concepts of the sciences. But it is a frequent error for philosophers to offer their "science" in place of the first-order disciplines. Heidegger's mistake lies in the dogmatic assertion that metaphysics, or his view of it, provides an adequate explanation of experience. It is possible that a philosophic concept is useful in a first-order discipline like history. It is also possible that such a concept is not relevant, or is weaker than the available explanatory frameworks. In any case, a determination of the significance of a second-order concept for a first-order discipline needs to be made within the first-order discipline itself since it cannot be made from within philosophy. In sum, a transition from theory to practice cannot be consummated within theory alone, prior to and apart from practice.

The explanatory framework which Heidegger introduces here figures prominently in his later thought. His later discussion of technology (*Technik*) presupposes the hegemony of the will to power in the void created by the withdrawal of Being.[65] His discussion is a transparent effort to read this aspect of his view, which arose only after the rectorate, backward into that period.

> Was there not enough reason and essential distress to think in primordial reflection towards a surpassing of the metaphysics of the will to power and that is to say, to begin a confrontation with Western thought by returning to its beginning? Was there not enough reason and essential distress, for the sake of such reflection on the spirit of the Western world, to awaken and to lead into battle [ins Feld zu führen] that place which was considered the seat of the cultivation of knowledge and insight—the German university?[66]

The passage cited provides a misleading reading of the nature of the so-called "battle" which Heidegger then desired to wage.[67] If we accept the rectoral speech as a faithful account of Heidegger's aims, then this comment provides an inaccurate account of Heidegger's intentions as rector. Further, the battle for science in the ancient Greek sense was not, as Heidegger earlier suggested, directed only to that end, nor, as he now adds, toward an overcoming of metaphysics, which was not then his goal. At the time, his effort was directed toward a renewal of metaphysics, since it is only later, with the deepening interest in Nietzsche, that he saw the need to overcome metaphysics. Finally, we have already noted that at the time Heidegger regarded the university as a means to an end, not as an end in itself.

His effort to relate the rectorate as a whole to what might have happened is less controversial. Heidegger here imagines what might have been if those in a position to do so had brought Nazism under control. "What would have happened and what would have been prevented, had, around 1933, all capable forces aroused themselves and joined in secret in order gradually to purify and moderate the 'movement' that had come to power?"[68] This transparent speculation about what might have been provides Heidegger with the opportunity to make several observations clearly intended to attenuate his personal responsibility.

To begin with, he admits that he failed to foresee what would later come to pass. This admission is significant since it is the basis of the effort later developed by Fédier, Heidegger's most orthodox French supporter at present, to argue that at the time of the rectorate no one could have foreseen what would later occur.[69] Heidegger's admission obviously contradicts his earlier assertion that he knew even then, namely during the rectorate, that everything can be interpreted as a function of the will to power. If he possessed a historical crystal ball during the rectorate, then he should have foreseen the future of Nazism. Since he admits that he did not foresee later developments, then either the will to power is insufficient to understand the entire range of political phenomena, despite Heidegger's explicit claim, or he did not have it available to him in 1933/34. In fact, both alternatives seem likely.

The speculation on what might have been suggests that had Heidegger's efforts been followed by others, the outcome might have been different. This is an adumbration of the idea that, after all, and in his own way, Heidegger was a "resistance fighter" against Nazism, perhaps even from the very beginning, or that his own relation to National Socialism was merely contingent. Now in view of the brutal nature of Nazism, there is no reason to believe that an attitude of the kind Heidegger describes ever could have been successful. There is no evident reason to credit Heidegger's rectorate as part of an effort to resist Nazism in more than the barest sense. It is known that Heidegger did oppose certain excesses, such as the posting of the "Jew notice."[70] But there is no indication, least of all in his talk, that he ever disagreed with the common end in view: the realization of the historical fate of the German people.

The suggestion that one could gradually moderate and purify Nazism is troubling. It implies that another, more moderate, even nicer form of National Socialism would be worthy of support, in fact an acceptable vehicle to realize political aims. This inference is suspect since Nazism in all its forms is at the very least unacceptable, certainly a paradigm of political evil. Through the implication that some form of National Socialism might be acceptable, Heidegger unwittingly opposes efforts by others to portray him as an unwilling participant, as later opposed to Nazism. He immediately undercuts this kind of reading when he writes that "first of all the positive possibilities that I then saw in the movement had to be underscored and affirmed in order to prepare for a gathering of all capable forces in a manner that would be grounded not only in the facts, but in what mattered."[71] It is difficult to understand what could be meant by a purified, moderate form of Nazism other than a purified, moderate form of evil.

The "Official" View and "Facts and Thoughts"

The portion of the discussion of the rectorate discussed so far serves to introduce the middle portion of the article, officially devoted to the rectoral talk. In the same way as Heidegger called for the "destruction" of the history of ontology in *Being and Time* in order to make out the claim for his interpretation of the meaning of Being, so Heidegger here undertakes to "destroy," to deconstruct, what otherwise appears evident in his speech. In the process, he sketches the main lines of what we have called the "official" view, intended to deny what can be denied, to reinterpret what cannot reasonably be denied in the most favorable light, and in general to preserve as much of his thought as possible from the taint arising from his Nazism.

Heidegger's deconstruction of his talk, his official reinterpretation of its stated purpose, has been largely successful in providing a more flattering reading of his life and work than they merit on the available evidence mainly because it has rarely been subjected to direct scrutiny. We need now to deconstruct Heidegger's deconstruction, his own effort to refute the rather obvious interpretation of the *Rektoratsrede* presented above. In this respect, my intention is to defend my interpretation of that text against Heidegger's own view of it, to defend a moderate reading of the talk as an effort to place philosophy in the service of Nazi politics against the rather more violent Heideggerian claim that this was not his intention at all.

Heidegger insists that "interpretation" means "to capture the Being of the entity despite its tendency to cover things up."[72] He maintains that an existential analysis constantly does violence to the claims of a so-called everyday interpretation. It will be necessary to do violence, not to Heidegger's speech, but to Heidegger's interpretation of it in order to bring out what is covered up in his text. The effort to do violence to Heidegger's auto-interpretation is designed to show that his reading provides a false appearance obscuring the essence of the text, which remains hidden.

Heidegger's reading of his talk is based on his view of interpretation. He remarks that for this text as with the spoken word, everything depends on something like interpretative goodwill as a precondition to the grasp of what is essential. "To be sure, in this case, as is the case with every spoken word, everything depends on the interpretation [Auslegung] and on the readiness to enter into what is essential and to get it into view."[73] This passage recalls Heidegger's well-known view that understanding projects possibilities, whose development Heidegger calls interpretation. For Heidegger, interpretation is never presuppositionless, but is always grounded in advance in a prior conception located in the fore-structure of the understanding, what Gadamer usefully calls a *Vorverständnis*.[74] According to Heidegger, the process of the development of an understanding is always the working out of a prior, incomplete grasp of the whole phenomenon in view.

Here, the reference to interpretation has a strategic value. In calling attention to his theory of interpretation at the beginning of the crucial section of the discussion, whose announced purpose is to show that the aims of the rectorate are expressed in the rectoral address, Heidegger is careful to present a favorable view of the matter. Since he holds that all interpretation consists in the development of an initial preconception, Heidegger is concerned to supply a global statement of his purpose to serve as a guide, as the conceptual horizon, of the discussion to follow. As he wants the reader to accept his interpretation, everything depends on the formulation of an acceptable prior conception as the basis for the further development of the initial, incomplete understanding.

Obviously, we need not uncritically accept Heidegger's proposed prior understanding of the rectorate. We need only accept it if it provides what one can roughly describe as a faithful account of the rectoral address. On a reasonable reading of this portion of the text, his argument consists of ten elements, including:

1. a statement of the aim of the *Rektoratsrede;*
2. a reinterpretation of the idea of battle in a supposedly authentically Greek sense;
3. a rejection of the obvious interpretation of the talk as inauthentic;
4. the assertion that official Nazism was displeased by the talk;
5. a statement of the tenuous nature of his relation to official Nazism;
6. a claim for the incompatibility between his view of the university and that of National Socialism;
7. a description of his decision to resign to protect the university;
8. an attribution of what occurred to metaphysics, which has become technology in the age of nihilism;
9. an acknowledgment of his conviction in the possibility represented by National Socialism;
10. an affirmation of the possibility to overcome nihilism through poetry.

These themes are main elements in Heidegger's defense through the simultaneous "destruction" of the obvious interpretation of his Nazism and the redescription of its main elements in order to conceal them within the "official" view of his relation to National Socialism. The fourth point is a purely factual matter, which falls to a historian. Point 5 has already been broached several times in the preceding discussion. Finally, the sixth point is a conclusion that either follows or fails to follow from the other points, and hence need not be addressed directly apart from the elements that compose the remainder of the argument. I turn now to the other points of Heidegger's defense.

A beginning can be made through scrutiny of Heidegger's view of the purpose of the talk, which he states on no less than three occasions. In successive paragraphs, he twice maintains, using the same term, that "the heart [Kernstück]" of the address is "the exposition [Darlegung] of the essence of knowing and science; the university is to be grounded on that essence; and on that ground it is to assert itself as German university"[75] and that it serves "the interpretation of the essence of knowing, science, and profession that is based on training in science."[76] In a third, later passage, he remarks, in a somewhat different description of his intent, that "the atmosphere of confusion" prevented him from carrying out "those efforts that were my sole concern and that had moved me to assume the office: reflection on the ethos that should govern the pursuit of knowledge and on the essence of teaching [die Besinnung auf die Wissenshaltung und auf das Wesen des Lehrens]."[77]

Heidegger's characterization of his intent in the speech requires scrutiny. A closer look reveals that instead of a single, univocal description, he proposes in fact three descriptions related through a kind of family resemblance. These three ways of depicting the essence of the speech are similar, but not identical. It is one thing to provide an exposition of the essence of science and learning in order to further the German university, for instance through its "self-assertion." It is something else to interpret the essence of knowing, science, and the profession to which it leads.

Since Heidegger claims to capture the essence in the initial description, then he can desire to ground (*gründen*) the university upon it. A description of the essence is apparently sufficient only for an explanation (*Erläuterung*). Presumably a statement of the essence captures, in Aristotelian language, what it is to be that thing, whereas an interpretation provides a description of that thing. By implication the essence is unique and admits of one exposition only, although there is presumably more than one possible interpretation of something. An exposition and a description of the essence coincide only if a description is univocal. But since different descriptions are possible, which do not coincide, obviously they do not describe the same essence in the same way. In short, different descriptions from different perspectives provide different views of what, in terms of the description, appears to be different.

The two descriptions of the heart of the matter as the essence that grounds and as an explanation present similar but subtly different views. The difference is greater with respect to the third description of the rectoral address as a meditation on the ethos of knowledge and the essence of teaching. The word translated here as the "ethos of knowledge" (*Wissenshaltung*) combines two terms that literally mean "the pose, posture, or attitude" and "knowledge," and that together signify "the attitude of knowledge." In his third description, Heidegger is primarily concerned with getting clear about the attitude one should take toward knowledge and the essence of teaching. What these three characterizations have in common is a certain average assertion that the talk is about the essence of science and knowledge as it concerns the university, which should be understood from this angle of vision.

Now "*Kernstück*," the word translated as "heart," is composed of two terms "*Stück*" and "*Kern*" meaning respectively "piece," "lot," "stretch," "distance," and so on, and "kernel," "core," and so on. The single, composite term can be rendered as the "central part" or "central portion" of the talk. Heidegger's claim, then, can be paraphrased as the assertion that the central portion of the speech is a meditation on the essence of knowing and science, and its relation to the university. Here we need to distinguish between an interpretation according to the letter and one according to the spirit.[78] As Kant complained, an interpretation can be literally correct with respect to the letter but fail to capture the spirit.

Heidegger's claim about the heart of his rectoral address is false with respect to its spirit but literally true. Heidegger is literally correct that the central portion of his talk concerns the essence of science and the German university. A passage on this topic occurs toward the middle of the talk. But his literal description of the *Rektoratsrede* does not describe it adequately; it fails to capture the spirit of a speech which it describes without regard to the context. The hidden motivation of this misdescription is not deeply buried. Since the rectoral speech was on the public record, it could not simply be denied. Heidegger's obvious intent, in a period when he is being called to account for his connection to Nazism, is to place it in a more favorable light than would otherwise be the case. For in calling attention to the meditation on knowing, science, and the university, he focuses on these topics to the exclusion of the surrounding remarks on the need to realize the destiny of the German nation through the Nazi state.[79]

It is important to be clear about the present claim. The main point is that in calling attention to the central part of the talk in a way that is literally true, Heidegger distorts its spirit. In effect, he takes the part for the whole by concentrating on the portion that occurs in the center of the talk, but which is eccentric to its main purpose. Hence, at the beginning of his defense, and despite his assertion of the importance of entering into the essential, of first getting the whole into view, Heidegger misleadingly substitutes the part for the whole in a way that covers up the whole by focusing on the part.

Heidegger's reading of his speech is an instance of inauthentic hermeneutics, of an interpretation in bad faith whose aim is to conceal what he knows. As soon as we see that, despite his statement in the first sentence of this section, Heidegger's strategy is not to enter into what is essential and to avoid getting it into view, it becomes easy to see that what he says about the so-called heart of his talk is literally true but false to the spirit of the speech. One must be less sanguine about his qualifying remarks concerning the two descriptions of the heart of the talk, which are untrue to the spirit of the speech and even literally untrue, at the very least a clear misreading intended to change the sense of the talk.

A prominent aspect of the *Rektoratsrede* was Heidegger's insistence on the three forms of service: labor, defense, and knowledge in relation to the community of the people, the honor and destiny of the nation among other peoples, and the spiritual mission of the German people.[80] In the talk, he further described them as equiprimordial.[81] Now the insistence on the equiprimordiality of the three forms of service obviously strains Heidegger's claim to have concerned himself merely with knowing, science, and the university. Perhaps for that reason, Heidegger now maintains, despite his explicit statements in the speech, that knowledge is prior to the other forms of service. For the future university is to be grounded on the essence of knowing and science which allows it to assert itself as a German university.[82] Here, Heidegger's chauvinism is apparent in the implied limitation of an authentic relation of the essence of knowing and science to the German university only. He seems to believe that at best this relation is intrinsically inauthentic elsewhere. Here and in other writings, Heidegger's chauvinism is evident in his repeated insistence on German philosophy as the sole legitimate heir of Greek thought. Every other form of philosophy is, then, inauthentic, by implication not worthy of the name.

After his remark on the future university, Heidegger immediately presents a revisionary interpetation obviously meant to qualify his claim in the rectoral address about the equiprimordiality of the three forms of service:

> Knowledge Service is named in third place, after Labor Service and Armed Service, not because it is subordinated to the former, but because knowing is what is authentic and highest, that unto which the essence of the university and therefore reflection gathers itself. As far as Labor Service, named in second place, is concerned, it may be permitted to remind the reader that long before 1933 this "service" grew out of the distress of the time and the will of the young, which gave it its shape. "Armed

Service," however, I mentioned neither in a militaristic, nor in an aggressive sense, but understood it as defense in time of need [als Wehr in der Notwehr gedacht].[83]

This statement betrays a visible unease. Heidegger's initial assertion that knowing is not subordinated to labor and defense is literally correct since they are equiprimordial, hence on the same level; but it is also false, since what is highest cannot be on the same level as anything else. In other words: either there was never an equiprimordiality, in which case knowing can be highest; or there was an equiprimordiality and knowing as a form of service is not higher than labor or defense. One should further be careful about the description of knowing as the highest since that emphasis runs counter to the effort, basic to Heidegger's fundamental ontology, to deconstruct the rationalistic emphasis in philosophy represented prominently by Descartes.[84] One should finally be hesitant about the description of knowing alone as authentic, since, then, nothing else, such as defense or work, can be authentic. In other words, and in Heidegger's terminology, it appears that only those engaged in knowing, by extension only members of the academy, are or possibly can be authentic. It is as if, in a strange version of the Platonic view that only philosophers can finally claim to know, Heidegger were to depict representatives of German philosophy as the only possible form of authentic human being.

Heidegger's reference to the historical origins of work service does not dispel the asymmetry between his depiction of the three pillars here and in the speech. For the explicit approval in the *Rektoratsrede* of the bond that binds into "the community of the people,"[85] he now substitutes a note as to how this form of service came about. But the most significant change is the effort to reinterpret, to deconstruct—in a word, to interpret away—his earlier understanding of defense. Unquestionably, Heidegger's present, literal comprehension of defense as defense in need-defense, perhaps more accurately defense in time of need, is meant to provide a reading of his intentions basically distinct from the Nazi military machine.

We recall that in his talk, Heidegger discussed armed service as a bond binding the student to "the honor and destiny of the nation" as a "readiness . . . to give all."[86] Heidegger's present effort to provide a different view of his understanding of defense occurs in two stages, including a description of the content of the talk and a reading of the term "battle." In the first stage, he proposes an elaborate, fourfold characterization of the content of the talk as:

(1) The grounding of the sciences in the experience of the essential region of their subject matter.

(2) The essence of truth as the letting be of what is, as it is.

(3) Preservation of the tradition that has handed down to us the beginning of our Western way of knowing in the Greek world. (Compare my two hour lecture course of the summer semester 1932: The Beginning of Western Philosophy.)

(4) In keeping with this, our responsibility as part of the Western world.[87]

Even a cursory glance at this list shows that its items are not equally relevant to the rectoral address. The first item is neither stressed in, nor consistent with, the quasi-Platonic thrust of the talk. At the time, Heidegger underscored the manner in which the various forms of knowledge are finally grounded in philosophy, for instance in his claim that all science is philosophy, from which it draws its strength and essence.[88] On the contrary, in his present post-Platonic phase he now insists that science grounds itself in its subject matter. The second item, the essence of truth as letting be, refers to a view of truth as disclosure already prominent in Heidegger's early work, but not central to the rectoral address.[89] The theme of the preservation of the Western view of science originating in ancient Greece, which Heidegger names in third place, is certainly a main current of the speech. This is also the case for the so-called responsibility as part of the Western world.

Heidegger offers the second stage of his reading of the concept of defense service in a detailed series of remarks on the term "battle" (*Kampf*). The relation of this term to Hitler's *Mein Kampf* in the immediate period leading up to the Second World War is difficult to overlook even now, and was even more obvious at the time. Heidegger's analysis develops a line of argument already broached in 1935, a mere two years after the rectoral address, in the lecture course published as *An Introduction to Metaphysics*. Here, Heidegger sketches the analysis of Heraclitus's fragment 53, which is the basis of his later attempt to "deconstruct" the word "battle." Already Heidegger argues that the word "*polemos*" means "conflict" in the sense of "*Aus-einander-setzung,*" literally "setting apart."[90]

Heidegger now makes use of his earlier analysis of "*polemos*" to draw attention from the clear link between "Kampf" and *Mein Kampf*.[91] Heidegger's remarks are obviously meant to deflect attention from the clear, but implicit, reference to Hitler—consistent with his overall effort in this text to minimize attention to his interest in National Socialism—through the simple expedient of reinterpreting the term "battle" to substitute another referent. This phase of the argument depends on an attempt to invoke an author's privileged access to his intentions. He insists that when he used the German term, he meant "battle" in a specifically Greek sense associated with Heraclitus's thought, in which the word "*polemos*" does not mean "battle." We can paraphrase the intent of the argument as an effort to show that despite the apparently ordinary manner in which he used "battle" in the rectoral address, in fact he meant by this word something other than "battle." The claim, then, is that on the testimony of the author we learn that on occasion he uses ordinary words in extraordinary ways that do not mean what they say. The presupposition of this kind of interpretation is that sense and reference can just be separated at will, since in any given instance a new sense and/or reference can be substituted without regard to the usual way of using the term. Carried to the extreme, the practice to which this argument refers would obviously render not only textual interpretation, but even communication, impossible.

Heidegger begins by saying that he understands "*episteme*" and "*aletheia*" in their Greek senses; and similarly "battle," too, is understood here in not just any way. "Battle" is thought in the sense of Heraclitus, fragment 53.[92] He then goes on to make two points, based on his revised reading of the word "*polemos*," or battle. To begin with he remarks that "*polemos*" should not be understood as "war" ("*Krieg*") but rather as "*eris*," or "strife" ("*Streit*"), in the sense of "confrontation" ("*Aus-einander-setzung*," Heidegger's emphasis). For Heidegger, one can also render "battle" ("*Kampf*") as "mutual recognition" ("*sich annerkennende Sichaussetzen*") and as "being-exposed" ("*Ausgesetztheit*").

This point is doubly difficult to accept. On the one hand, if Heidegger had had a specific Greek meaning in mind, it is at least odd that he did not specify his reference unless he meant intentionally to mislead. On the other hand, if he was thinking of Heraclitus's view of strife, then it is further odd to preserve the second, or alternative, meaning of "battle" as "mutual recognition." The presence of this second meaning of "struggle" undermines Heidegger's claim. It immediately calls to mind the well-known struggle for mutual recognition in the master-slave analysis which Hegel employs to understand the rise of self-consciousness within modern society.[93] The unexpected use of a Hegelian concept in this context, where Heidegger is pleading to be understood in terms of the hidden Greek roots of his thought, points to a different interpretation. For Heidegger's emphasis in the *Rektoratsrede* on the need for the German nation to struggle for the realization of its destiny is obviously more closely related to the struggle for mutual recognition, as Hegel depicts it, than to Heraclitus's supposed doctrine of *polemos* as *eris*.

Heidegger is, of course, aware that his interpretation is nonstandard. In the second stage of his argument, he protects himself against the more obvious reading of Heraclitus's concept of *polemos*, which he regards as a misinterpretation. "Not only should we not think *polemos* as war and, furthermore, appeal to the supposedly Heraclitean proposition 'War is the father of all things' to proclaim war and battle as the highest principle of all being and thus to offer a philosophical justification of the warlike."[94] The expression "war is the father of all things" is contained in the usual—for Heidegger, incorrect—rendering of Heraclitus's fragment 53. Heidegger insists that it would be a further error to provide a philosophical interpretation of the warlike (*das Kriegerische*). Not surprisingly, he says nothing about a philosophical justification of war, which he earlier offered in the rectoral address in his reference to Clausewitz.[95] He maintains that the essential meaning of "*polemos*" combines the terms "to show" and "to produce." "The essence of *polemos* lies in *deiknumai,* to show, and in *poiein,* to produce, as the Greeks say, to make-it-stand-out in open view. This is the sense of 'battle' thought philosophically, and what is said in the address is only thought philosophically."[96]

This argument is strained with respect to Heraclitus; it is even more strained in the context of an effort by Heidegger to minimize his association with National Socialism. Heidegger's revisionary interpretation of "*polemos*" turns on his claim of superior insight into the authentic meaning of the word. A standard reading of the Heraclitean passage in question renders this word as a so-called "metaphor for the dominance of change in the world."[97] Heidegger is entitled to read the term as he would like. But there is no reason to accept his reading as better than or even equal to the standard view. There is even less reason to accept Heidegger's present claim that he in fact was thinking of a specific interpretation of Heraclitus's doctrine of *polemos* when he employed the word "battle" in his speech. For all signs point to the more obvious association of "battle" with the struggle for German destiny, which on Heidegger's view of fate in *Being and Time* requires a battle, through Nazism— apparent in the unexpected use of the concept of "mutual recognition"—which is the main theme of the rectoral speech.

Heidegger's ineffective effort to "destroy" the obvious understanding of the term "battle" as meaning "battle" fails to convince. Heidegger's linc of argument is intrinsically flawed since the assertion about the rectoral speech is independent of his view of Heraclitus. On grounds of interpretative indeterminacy, we must reject the presupposition underlying Heidegger's remarks on Heraclitus, that is, that we can determine the correct interpretation of his or indeed any other position. What is the correct interpretation of Plato's *Republic*? We need only to formulate the question to see that it cannot be answered. In the present case, the attempt to interpret Heraclitus's position is further complicated by the enormous temporal distance, the uncertainty of the texts, and so on.

Even if Heidegger were correct about Heraclitus, he would not be entitled to draw the conclusion he does. It cannot be denied that Heidegger is the author of his own speech. But this fact does not give him interpretative privilege with respect to the reading of this text. He still needs to show the plausibility of his reading by comparison with other possible readings *in situ*. His ingenious reading of the word "*Kampf*" as "to show" and "to produce" is simply unconvincing alternatives for the passages in the *Rektoratsrede,* in which this word is more easily rendered in standard fashion as "battle" or "struggle."

Here, Heidegger's awareness that it is plausible to understand the speech as a proclamation of his faith in National Socialism and not as the defense of the university is a motivating factor in his effort to present a different interpretation. In the same way as he has argued with respect to a single word that "*Kampf*" in fact did not mean what it says, he now maintains that his address in general was not what it seemed to be, and that it was what it was not. His argument is based on the concept of reflection, which he sees as central to philosophy in the full sense of the term. The argument begins with a claim for philosophical reflection as the sole determinant of truth in the full sense. For Heidegger, the essence of the university cannot be determined on political or other grounds, distinct from reflection itself.

> From out of such reflection on the totality of the sciences, the university carries itself, by its own strength, unto its essential ground, a ground accessible only to the knowing that it cultivates. Its essence can therefore not be determined from some other place, from the standpoint of "politics" or of some other established goals [aus der "Politik" oder irgendeiner anderen Zwecksetzung].[98]

This is a version of the well-known Platonic doctrine that philosophy justifies the truth claims of all the sciences, including itself. But even in the rectoral address, Heidegger's quasi-Platonic insistence that philosophy founds politics was mitigated by other non-Platonic, even extraphilosophic concerns, in particular his basic commitment to German destiny in a time of need. For instance, in the initial paragraph of the speech, in a comment on the essence of the German university, he writes: "This essence, however, gains clarity, rank, and power only when first of all and at all times the leaders are themselves led—led by that unyielding spiritual mission that forces the fate of the German people to bear the stamp of its history."[99]

Heidegger applies his understanding of philosophy as determined by philosophical reflection only to the interpretation of the speech. For Heidegger, the very title of the address already indicates the role within it of genuine philosophical reflection. "In keeping with this fundamental conception and attitude [i.e., philosophical reflection] the address bears the title: 'The Self-Assertion [Selbstbehauptung] of the German University.' "[100] But this name was mainly misunderstood and covered up by the widespread failure to exercise genuine reflection in order to go beyond mere idle talk (*Gerede*). "Only a very few understood clearly what this title alone, taken by itself, meant in the year 1933, because only a few of those whom it concerned took the trouble to think through what is said, to do so clearly and without mystification, cutting through idle talk."[101]

This statement requires qualification. To begin with, the statement is unclear, since, as we have already noted, "self-assertion" can be understood in different ways. The claim is further doubtful since the "German university" obviously does not, did not, and could not assert itself, whatever the locution means in this context. Obviously, there is no German university as such, although there are German universities. The concept of the German university is an abstract designation for its constituent elements. Moreover, universities do not assert themselves nor can they do so, although individuals acting on their behalf can claim to act in this way. In the talk, Heidegger, newly elected as the rector of the University of Freiburg, acted on behalf of his own university as well as all other German institutions of higher learning. It is important to make these points, although they may seem obvious, since Heidegger complains that in the main he has been misunderstood.

As concerns his speech, Heidegger asserts that few have gone beyond idle talk. In *Being and Time,* this locution designates an inauthentic form of speech, as a form of the everyday being, or fallenness, of Dasein.[102] On this basis, Heidegger now claims that the most obvious way of understanding his speech is the product of an ordinary failure to think through the situation, due even to malevolence, in short the result of a lack of reflection which fails to penetrate to the essence of the phenomenon:

> One can excuse oneself from reflection and hold onto the seemingly obvious thought that here, a short time after National Socialism had seized power, a newly elected rector gives an address on the university, an address that "represents" ["vertritt"] "the" National Socialism ["den" Nationalsozialismus] and that is to say proclaims the idea of "political science," which, crudely, means: "True is what is good for the people." From this one concludes, and indeed rightly, that this betrays the essence of the German university in its very core and actively contributes to its destruction; for this reason the title should rather be: "The Self-Decapitation [Selbstenthauptung] of the German University."[103]

In this passage, Heidegger directly confronts the particular reading of his speech which is most dangerous for him. The comment on the view of truth as utility calls attention to a pragmatic approach, which Heidegger here attributes to a Nazi form of political science. Now in his fundamental ontology, he argued that the objects of experience are understood as they are in terms of the use to which they can be put. This is the point of his basic distinction between the readiness-to-hand and presence-to-hand.[104] In that sense, his early theory in *Being and Time* can fairly be understood as a transcendental form of pragmatism.[105] It is possible to read this objection as directed against his own earlier transcendental pragmatism as well as against an allegedly Nazi form of political science.

In retrospect, Heidegger's statement offers a remarkable anticipation of his persistent identification, present throughout his later writings, with a kind of ideal Nazism, distinguished from its real, Hitlerian form. By enclosing the words "represents" and "the" (as in "the" National Socialism) in quotation marks, Heidegger distances himself from a type of Nazism, namely that type which in fact existed and waged and lost the war, leading to his present predicament. In putting distance between himself and a variety of the genus, he is careful not to reject all types of Nazism. The extraordinary manner in which Heidegger here leaves open the door to further forms of National Socialism in the most obvious way only further undermines his effort to portray his rectoral talk as merely concerned with a defense of the German university.

Heidegger's attempt to refute the obvious, but supposedly superficial, reading of the rectoral address is unconvincing. He puts the problem as one of the representation of National Socialism. When formulated in this way, the claim is obviously ambiguous. As the rector of the university, Heidegger in fact represented National Socialism although he did not represent it as he thought he ought to, that is, as the leader entitled to lead the leaders, as the leader of the wider "movement." In sum, Heidegger simply fails to refute the obvious way of reading his speech as a claim to represent Nazism, and the failure of his effort inadvertently, but clearly, reveals his continued interest in a form of · Nazism "better" than the Hitlerian variety.

Heidegger goes on to observe that his address was understood neither by those to whom it was addressed nor by the Nazi party. He reports that Otto Wacker, the *Staatsminister für Unterricht und Kultus* in Baden, complained that the talk advanced a form of private National Socialism, not based on a concept of race, and that the rejection of "political science" was unacceptable. Wacker's reported reaction is certainly close to the mark. Heidegger did not explicitly base his talk on the concept of race, and he further mentioned neither Hitler nor the Nazi party.[106] But this is not in itself unusual. The decision to join a political party or to practice a religion is only rarely based on a total acceptance of the views in question. Moreover, there never was a Nazi credo, a set of minimal beliefs to which one needed to subscribe in order to be considered a Nazi in good standing. Like many other academics, Heidegger was unenthusiastic about the Nazi program of racial hatred. Since Heidegger never accepted, and presumably rejected, elements of the party program, such as its biologically based form of race hatred, it is correct to describe even the view in the rectoral address as a private form of National Socialism.[107] Heidegger further objects to the failure to consider what he had in mind for "the sake of the inner renewal of the university."[108] But this "failure" is to be expected if, as in the present case, attention was directed toward the realization of the Nazi program and toward the university only as it contributed to that end.

Heidegger devotes a paragraph to removing any suggestion of anti-Semitism. This issue is significant since it has often been argued that Heidegger not only was not a racist but was especially well disposed to his Jewish students.[109] Heidegger has been accused of[110] and defended against the charge of anti-Semitism.[111] He responds to this accusation by twice pointing out that he refused to post the so-called "Jew Notice" in the university.[112] Among Heidegger's defenders, the question of Heidegger's anti-Semitism is confused by related issues, such as the concern to differentiate anti-Semitism from anti-Judaism.[113] Recently, the efforts undertaken to protect Heidegger against this charge have been refuted through the publication of a previously unknown letter, written by Heidegger in 1929, that is, before the Nazis came to power, which clearly shows his anti-Semitism in his pointed rejection of the " 'Jewification' of the German spirit [Verjudung des deutschen Geistes]."[114] In the context of Heidegger's Nazism, the definitive refutation of the effort to protect Heidegger against the charge of anti-Semitism is important for what it tells us about Heidegger, who can no longer be protected against this accusation. It is further important since it effectively undermines the continued efforts of Heidegger's closest supporters to defend his life and thought through a supposedly deeper understanding of his position.

Heidegger's opposition to biologism is sometimes invoked to distance him from Nazism.[115] Yet the antibiologism which Heidegger shared with many other intellectuals is compatible with anti-Semitism and Nazism. Biologism was not as important to Nazism, at least until well after National Socialism came to power, as the traditional anti-Semitism strikingly present in, for instance, Luther's works[116] and even in speeches before the German Reichstag, or parliament.[117] There is a distinction between biologism and anti-Semitism. The Nazi view that only a member of the community (*Volksgenosse*), or someone with German blood, can be a citizen, promulgated as early as 1920, was made explicit in 1933 in the so-called "Aryan paragraph" (*Arierparagraph*). This defined "Aryans" as people with no Jewish ancestors and "non-Aryans" as those with at least one Jewish parent or grandparent.[118] Since the sole criterion for categorization as Aryan or non-Aryan was religion, not race, the anti-Semitism common among German academics, and espoused by Heidegger, is not antithetical to, but compatible with, Nazism.

Heidegger accords special attention to when and how he joined the Nazi party.[119] His aim is to show that he was only minimally interested in official Nazism. In this respect, he makes three points. First, he states that when he was already in office, it was called to his attention that the minister thought it important for rectors to belong to the party. Second, he accepted this invitation only on the explicit condition not to undertake any political activity. Third, as rector his membership remained *pro forma* only and he did not play any substantive role in the party.

This portion of the discussion represents at best a series of half-truths. It is false that Heidegger became a Nazi party member after he took office since it is known that he already belonged to the party at that time.[120] In fact, his sympathies for National Socialism go back at least to 1931, that is, before the Nazi party came to power.[121] It is also known that Heidegger voted for Hitler. Even sympathetic observers agree that he placed his hopes in Hitler in 1933.[122] It is further known that, even after his decision to resign as rector, Heidegger remained a party member until the end of the Second World War. It is fair to say that although Heidegger gave up his post as rector, there was never a break with official Nazism during this period.[123] In sum, despite his effort to minimize the relation to National Socialism, it is clear that Heidegger's interest in Nazism clearly antedated and survived his period as rector.[124]

Heidegger now turns to a description of the end of his rectorate. He describes his resignation as forced by an increasing pressure exerted on him to compromise his professional principles. He lists two instances, which he presents as threats to the university that arose in the second, or summer, semester of 1933. First, he says that it was made clear to him that the faculties required a National Socialist leadership, which entailed appointing deans based on political reliability as opposed to scholarship or teaching ability.[125] Second, he reports an effort, in accordance with the views of the medical, legal, and teaching professions, to divide the university into professional schools, which he viewed as threatening the unity and mode of academic training he favored.[126]

It is not clear why Heidegger resigned his position as rector. His description of his reaction to the twin dangers threatening the university is difficult to reconcile with his own claim to have assumed the rectorate only to protect the university. If he really desired to protect the university, then he had even more reason to remain as rector when the threat increased. Although we cannot discount Heidegger's genuine desire to bring about a form of university grounded in his understanding of Greek science, this factor alone is insufficient to explain his decision to resign. It has been suggested, in reference to Heidegger's determination to achieve power in the university, that the resignation was provoked by the violent elimination of Röhm and the SA leadership, Heidegger's supposed allies.[127] Heidegger's desire to achieve hegemony in the academy, illustrated in the rectoral talk by the quasi-Platonic claim to lead the leaders, is evident in the present text in two ways: the repeated rejection of "political science" and a comment in passing on Krieck's spreading influence in connection with the need to install a National Socialist leadership in the different faculties of the university.[128] It would be odd for Heidegger to object to the promotion of a National Socialist leadership in the university since as rector he ran the university, as its leader (*Führer*), according to the Nazi *Führerprinzip*. The objection to Krieck's spreading influence is plausible when we remember Heidegger's increasing dismay at Krieck's criticism of him.[129] But despite that dismay, Heidegger continued to collaborate with Krieck until September 1934, that is, even after he resigned as rector.[130] Still another reason is the evident indifference of official Nazism to philosophy in whole or in part. Although a number of philosophers, including Heidegger, made impressive efforts to achieve philosophical hegemony within National Socialism, the Nazis seemed rather unconcerned with philosophy in general.[131] The Nazi indifference to philosophy, of which Heidegger may only later have become aware, would have been difficult for him to accept since he took his own philosophical contribution with utmost seriousness, even to the point of insisting that without it Nazism could not be justified.

Heidegger presents his resignation as due to an incompatibility between his own and the Nazi view of the university and science, as well as between the National Socialist *Weltanschauung* and his own philosophy:

> In my meeting with the minister, who immediately accepted my resignation, it became clear that a discrepancy [Zwiespalt] separated the National Socialist conception of the university and science from my own, which could not be bridged. The minister declared that he did not want this opposition, which to be sure [wohl] rested on the incompatibility of my philosophy with the National Socialist *Weltanschauung,* to reach the public as a conflict between the University of Freiburg and the ministry.[132]

This description has an air of unreality. It is difficult to imagine a Nazi minister telling an important official about to tender his resignation that to do so would enable him to recover his freedom of action. Heidegger is correct to point to differences, or points of disagreement, between his and the Nazi views of the university and science. Such differences include the respective views of race, "political science," the quality of appointments, and perhaps the professionalization of the university. But these points of disagreement, some of which were already described in the rectoral address, were not new, and certainly did not come into being during Heidegger's short period as rector. Since these differences were in part already known to Heidegger and neither prevented his adherence to Nazism or his assumption of the rectorate, it is difficult to regard them as later motivating his resignation from the rectorate.

Heidegger traces the suggested incompatibility between his and the Nazi views of the university and science to the supposed incompatibility between his philosophy and the National Socialist "*Weltanschauung.*"[133] Heidegger's use of the term to characterize National Socialist thought recalls Husserl's attack on *Weltanschauungsphilosophie,* associated with Dilthey, and historicism as two forms of relativism, which leads to skepticism.[134] It points as well to Heidegger's rejection of the Nazi effort to develop a National Socialist *Weltanschauung* and even to reject philosophy in favor of a *Weltanschauung.*[135] In his application of this locution to the National Socialist view, Heidegger implies its inadequacy as a philosophy, the same point he made in the speech in his suggestion that it required genuine philosophical grounding;[136] and he further implies that it leads to skepticism and nihilism. Yet Heidegger overstates the degree of incompatibility between National Socialism and his own thought, since it was the area of agreement and not the disagreements which enabled Heidegger to turn to Nazism.

In the final part of this section, Heidegger reflects on the significance of his rectorate through a comment on its connection to modern science. This passage is important as a summary of his defense of his actions as rector and as an indication of the later evolution of his thought. "Unimportant as it is in itself, the case of the rectorate 1933–34 would seem to be a sign of the metaphysical state of the essence of science, a science that can no longer be influenced by attempts at its renewal, nor delayed in its essential transformation into technology [Technik]."[137] After noting that he only came to realize this afterwards, Heidegger refers to his 1938 lecture "The Age of the World Picture."[138] He then writes, in language that for the first time in this text directly recalls that of the rectoral address:

> The rectorate was an attempt to see in the "movement" that had come to power, beyond all its failings and crudities, something that reached much farther and that might some day bring about a gathering of what is German unto the historical essence of the West. In no way shall it be denied

that at the time I believed in such possibilities and for this reason renounced the thinker's most proper vocation in order to help realize them
in an official capacity.[139]

This reflection is obviously intended to place the rectorate within the
context of Heidegger's single-minded concern with ontology. For Heidegger, science is being ineluctably transformed into technology. This
view implies that Heidegger's failure can be imputed to the ontological
process itself, to Being, and not to his own failings, such as his failure to
perceive the nature of National Socialism, his mistaken evaluation of its
chances for success, his misunderstanding of the real possibility of leading the movement or reforming the university, and so on. Now the
implied shift in responsibility is plausible only if in fact there is a fated
transformation under way of science into technology. But it does not
follow that the ontological process, or metaphysics, or history is ineluc-ta-
ble because Heidegger "failed." It is plausible to consider his "failure"
as deriving from some rather more ordinary factors, such as a difference
of opinion between Heidegger, who represented Nazism in the university, and other Nazi officials about the nature of the university and
science, the increasing influence of Krieck, and so on. These are factors
unrelated to the supposed transformation of science into technology.

Heidegger's effort to attenuate his own responsibility rests on a doubtful thesis about the link between technology and science. Obviously,
there are different ways of understanding technology and its relation to
science. In Heidegger's model, what once was science in the Greek
sense gave birth to technology, which is in the process of devouring its
father. But this reduction of modern science to technology is an inaccurate description. Many forms of modern science are unimaginable without technology; but this is not true of modern science as such, which
cannot simply be reduced to technology. It is more accurate to say that
modern science and modern technology interact, although neither can
be reduced to, nor explained in terms of, the other.[140]

Heidegger's statement that in 1933 he believed that German destiny
could be realized through a turn to National Socialism is an accurate
account. It is entirely consistent with the spirit and letter of the rectoral
address and with the first element of his threefold consideration in assuming the rectorate.[141] But it is inconsistent with his repeated claim
elsewhere in this text that the heart of the rectoral speech is a concern
with the essence of science and knowing.[142] The result is to call attention
to a deep ambiguity in his overall aim in turning to Nazism. Here, Heidegger stresses his concern with the university as an end in itself; yet
study of the rectoral address clearly shows that in his speech his concern
with the university was subordinated to the destiny of the German *Volk;*

and he never tires of proclaiming that his single concern is finally the problem of Being.

Heidegger's remark on the rectorate suggests that science is metaphysical. His observation presupposes a standpoint "beyond" metaphysics. Heidegger ends his reflection on the rectorate with a comment on how to surpass metaphysics linked to the so-called turning (*Kehre*) of his later thought, including his transition from philosophy to thought, and indicating his growing attention to the importance of poetry.

> What is essential is that we are caught up in the consummation of nihilism, that God is "dead," and every time-space for the godhead covered up. The surmounting of nihilism nevertheless announces itself in German poetic thinking and singing.[143]

Heidegger's point is that, like science, all of modern life is caught up in the nihilism following from metaphysics—precisely the theme of his Nietzsche lectures—although a way beyond nihilism and, hence, metaphysics can be glimpsed in poetry.[144]

After the Rectorate

The shorter third, and final, section of the text bears the German title: "The Time after the Rectorate." It mainly concerns Heidegger's complaints about perceived professional slights after his resignation. He objects in passing to criticism voiced by Ernst Krieck, the Nazi pedagogue, and Alfred Baeumler, apart from Heidegger the most prominent German philosopher to identify publicly with Nazism. Heidegger complains as well that he was under surveillance and that his best students (Gadamer, Krüger, Bröcker) were kept back in their academic careers. He finally indicates unhappiness about the difficulty in publishing his writings and his exclusion from official German delegations to international philosophical congresses.

From a strictly philosophical perspective, this section is more historical and thus less interesting than the preceding ones. Four passages require comment. The first one is a remark Heidegger makes in passing about a philosophical meeting in Berlin to which neither he nor Jaspers was invited, but which apparently resulted in an attack on "existential philosophy." "In this case, too, as already during the rectorate, and notwithstanding the oppositions that divided them, my opponents demonstrated a strange willingness to ally themselves against everything by which they felt spiritually threatened and put into question."[145] This remark illustrates Heidegger's almost petulant view that he received insufficient attention, that he wasn't taken seriously enough.

Second, there is Heidegger's comment, also in passing, that he had no illusions about the possible consequences of his actions after he resigned from office.

> I had no illusions about the possible consequences of my resignation from office in the spring of 1934; after June 30 of the same year, these consequences became completely clear. Anyone who after that still assumed an administrative office in the university was in a position to know beyond the shadow of a doubt with whom he was bargaining.[146]

This passage is ambiguous. It might mean that after he resigned, for that reason Heidegger felt that he ran a personal risk, as was made clear with the physical elimination of Röhm and the S.A. leadership. Or it might conceivably mean that the realization of the kind of people with whom he was dealing led Heidegger to reassess his support for their common ends.

It is, however, unlikely that until 30 June 1934 Hitler's intentions were not clear. According to Fédier, the most unrelenting of Heidegger's defenders, the essence of Nazism was not clear until 1938.[147] Jaspers accepts the view that the Nazi intentions became clear only gradually, since he remarks in his report on Heidegger, where he doubts the extent of Heidegger's change of heart, that anything less than a radical turn away from Nazism after 30 June 1934 is of lesser worth.[148] But he remarks pertinently elsewhere that despite the lack of precise information, the general lines of Nazism, its lies, its criminality, were known to any one who desired to know.[149] In a letter to Jaspers, Heidegger admits that in 1933 and even earlier the "Jews and the left-wing politicians" already knew.[150] Indeed, somebody must have known since at the time Heidegger became rector in the spring of 1933, concentration camps were already being built in the region of Freiburg. It is absurd to maintain that Heidegger had not understood the main thrust of Nazism since Hitler had repeatedly made it perfectly clear in *Mein Kampf* and elsewhere. And Heidegger relied in part on this work, which he cited in his public praise of Schlageter as a kind of Nazi saint, as a hero in the sense identified in *Being and Time*.[151]

Third, there is a further remark on the significance of the rectorate, which Heidegger now describes in Nietzschean terms in a final effort to free himself from any responsibility. Whereas in the talk, he exalted the importance of the rectorate, he now demeans it as essentially meaningless. "Taken by itself, it [i.e., the rectorate] is as unimportant as the barren rooting in past attempts and measures taken, which in the context of the entire movement of the planetary will to power are so insignificant that they may not even be called tiny."[152] This description of the rectorate's significance is only apparently inconsistent with its earlier description through the supposed metaphysical transformation of science into technology. Common to both is Heidegger's conviction that the reign of metaphysics can be understood as ongoing development of the will to power whose most advanced form is the increasing encroachment of technology. Once again, it is difficult to overlook Heidegger's implicit self-exculpation in the face of the domination of what he now calls the planetary will to power.

Fourth, we can note the dark statement which ends the essay. "But these events, too, are only a fleeting appearance on waves of a movement of our history, of whose dimensions the Germans have as yet no inkling, even now that catastrophe has engulfed them."[153] Once again Heidegger makes the familiar, but unverifiable claim of superior insight into history, including the future, following from his basic distinction between authenticity and inauthenticity. This statement is further interesting for the obvious transformation of the revolutionary enthusiasm of the rectoral speech, where Heidegger thought he stood at a turning point in German history, into a kind of conceptual dark night of the soul where the real possibility for a radiant future has disappeared.

This chapter has been devoted to an examination of Heidegger's self-justificatory, indulgent interpretation of the *Rektoratsrede* in a time of personal need. Heidegger's defense consists in an effort to demonstrate that his rectoral address was directed toward the defense of the university with respect to knowing and science. Although this is literally true in part, it is insufficient as a description of the text as a whole, and false as an account of its spirit. For Heidegger's concerns with the university and with science as the rector, or educational *Führer,* of the University of Freiburg were means to other ends, including the grounding of Nazism in fundamental ontology; the realization of the Germans as German, the goal he shared with National Socialism; and further insight into Being.

The central insight that emerges from this inspection of Heidegger's self-interpretation of the rectoral address is the tension between his claim to be concerned only with the defense of the university and his continued stress on the destiny of the Germans and on Being. The latter concerns, which derive from *Being and Time,* remained constant throughout his later thought. We have already noted that Heidegger's remark that he did not renounce his thought in his effort, in an official capacity, to realize the essence of what is German, is significant.[154] This statement should be recognized as what it is, as a clear admission of a seamless web, a direct link, between his own thought, as he understood it, of the concept of authenticity applied to the Germans as a whole and his turn to Nazism as presenting a propitious moment, a *kairos,* to realize this goal.

"Ways to Discussion"

Heidegger's position later evolved, but it remained unchanged in important ways, including the concern with Being, the central theme in his thought early and late, and as concerns the authentic realization of the German people, based on his original concept of authenticity. An important statement of that point is available in a little-known, as yet untranslated text, published in 1937, that is, after the *Rektoratsrede* but before the essay about it. In his text, titled "Ways to Discussion," Heidegger ostensibly reexamines the Hegelian theme of the conditions of agreement between the French and the Germans.[155] He maintains that any agreement must be based on mutual respect, which he suggests can only come about through listening to each other and the courage for their "proper self-limitation [eigenen Bestimmung]."[156] In the second paragraph of this essay, he states his view of understanding among peoples in a description of the authenticity of a people, in a startling passage that requires full quotation:

Authentic [Echtes] understanding among peoples [Völker] begins and fulfills itself on one condition: this is in a creative reciprocal discussion leading to awareness concerning the historically shared past and present conditions. Through such awareness each of the peoples is brought back to what is ownmost to it [je Eigene] and grasps it with increased clarity and resoluteness [Entschiedenheit]. The ownmost in a people is its creativity [Schaffen], through which it grows into its historical mission [in seine geschichtliche Sendung hineinwächst] and so first comes to itself. The main feature [Grundzug] of its mission has been indicated for the historically cultured peoples in the present world situation [Weltstunde] as the rescue of the West [Rettung des Abendlandes]. Rescue here does not mean the simple maintenance of what is already present to hand [Vorhandenen], but rather signifies the originary, newly creating justification [Rechtfertigung] of its past and future history. Reciprocal understanding of neighbor peoples in their most ownmost means rather: for each the ownmost task [je eigene Aufgabe] is to know how to give oneself the necessity of this rescue. The knowledge concerning this necessity springs all the more from the experience of need, which arises with the innermost menace of the West, and from the power for an enlightening plan [Kraft zum verklärenden Entwurf] of the highest possibilities of Western man [abendländischen Daseins]. Just as the menace of the West drives toward a full uprooting and general disorder [Wirrnis], so, on the contrary, the will to the renewal from the ground up must be led through the final resolutions [Entscheidungen].[157]

This passage, composed after the rectorate, when Heidegger has returned to teaching, contradicts his description of the implicitly apolitical character of "a conversation of essential thinking with itself [Selbstgespräch des wesentlichen Denkens mit sich selbst]."[158] Although Heidegger gave up his rectorate, he continued to share the aim common to Nazism and his own thought—expressed here in Spenglerian terms, on the basis of his own view of authenticity—for the German people to realize itself in the future historical context. The mere fact that he here calls upon the French to do likewise in no sense alters the fact that he continues to mobilize the resources of his philosophy for an end in view which has not changed.

Heidegger clearly describes his view of the practical, hence political, role of so-called authentic philosophy. Unlike Hegel, who held a retrospective view of philosophy which looked back on what had already taken place, for Heidegger authentic philosophical knowledge is prospective, a form of anticipation for which the problem of theory and practice does not arise.

> By itself authentic philosophical knowledge [Wissen] is never the backward-looking addition to the most general representations on already known things, but rather the anticipatory opening through knowledge of the consistently hidden essence of things. And precisely in this way it is never necessary to make this knowledge immediately useful. It is effective only mediately in that philosophical awarenesss prepares new points of view and standards for all attitudes and resolutions [Entscheiden].[159]

Heidegger leaves no doubt here of the intrinsic purpose of authentic philosophy. In the midst of the social, political, and historical circumstances that were shortly to lead to the Second World War, he takes an aggressive view of the role of philosophy, strongly reminiscent of the early Marx's insistence on philosophy as tranforming the masses, as transforming the consciousness of the people.[160]

> If an authentic self-understanding is achieved in the basic philosophical position [in den philosophischen Grundstellung], if the power and the will for it can be correspondingly awakened, then the dominating knowledge [das herrschaftliche Wissen] rises to a new height and clarity. It prepares the way for the first time for a transformation of the peoples which is often invisible.[161]

This passage provides an important insight into Heidegger's adherence to Nazism as an ideal even after his resignation from the rectorate. Heidegger here relies on his conception of authenticity which he applies to philosophy and to the German *Volk*. He clearly insists on the revolutionary role of authentic philosophy in bringing about the realization of the true destiny of the German people.[162] If we accept Heidegger's assertion that his turn toward Nazism was motivated by the desire to realize German authenticity which he believed was made possible through National Socialism, then we can infer that his withdrawal from his official capacity does not represent an abandonment of his view of the revolutionary role of true philosophy or of the end in view; at most it represents an awareness that Nazism as it exists is ill adapted, in fact has failed, to achieve this goal.

We see the full significance of this point when we recall that in 1947, in the "Letter on Humanism," Heidegger suggested that in virtue of its inconsequential nature, after the so-called turning in his thought his view surpasses practice. "[T]hinking is a deed. But a deed that also surpasses all praxis. Thinking towers above action and production, not through the grandeur of its achievement and not as a consequence of its effect, but through the humbleness of its inconsequential accomplishment."[163] Is he saying that thinking is deeper than thought concerned with action and production? Is thinking inconsequential because, looking backward to the rectorate, it failed in its task? This is unclear. What is, however, clear is that this self-description of his thought is misleading since Heidegger never abandoned his attachment to Being, his concern with the realization of the destiny of the German people, and his stubborn conviction that his own thought has a key role in bringing about these ends. Heidegger's thought, even after his supposed turning beyond philosophy, was and remained political in this specific sense. Heidegger claimed to have assumed the rectorate in order to defend the university; but this was in fact merely a secondary end. For his deeper intention, as a close reading of the texts shows, was and remained the realization of the authentic essence of the German people and the furtherance of the thought of Being.

4

The History of Philosophy: Nietzsche and the History of Ontology

Provisional Results

The discussion has so far focused on the two texts most directly connected to Heidegger's turn to Nazism: the *Rektoratsrede* of 27 May 1933, in which the newly elected rector of the University of Freiburg publicly identified himself, the university he represented, and the German university in general with National Socialism; and the article from 1945, posthumously published only in 1983, in which Heidegger, personally beleaguered after the defeat of Germany, sought to distance himself from real National Socialism.

This inquiry into Heidegger's Nazism has taken seriously his statement that the hermeneutical process needs to defend against semblance and disguise—in a word, to snatch entities out of their hiddenness. I have scrutinized the *Rektoratsrede* and the 1945 essay with some care since these writings, particularly the latter, are more often mentioned than studied in detail. Study of these texts reveals that despite denials by some of Heidegger's staunchest defenders, and despite his refusal to accept certain elements of the heteroclite series of doctrines known as National Socialism, Heidegger identified, in fact deeply identified, with Nazism; but he later sought to mask this identification, in particular through the formulation of what I have called the "official" version of his relation to National Socialism, which was later developed and spread by his followers.

With respect to Heidegger's Nazism, the above discussion has demonstrated the following points *inter alia*.

— Heidegger turned to Nazism on the basis of his philosophical position.

— Heidegger's theory of Being, or fundamental ontology, includes a political dimension that can only lead to Nazism or something like Nazism—in short, a totalitarian political movement.

— Heidegger shared with National Socialism a common goal of the realization of the essence of the German *Volk.*

— Heidegger's concern with authentic human being, ingredient in the Nazi turning, is inseparable from his deeper interest in the problem of Being.

— Heidegger's stress on philosophy as the ground of politics is a further form of the Platonic view that philosophy is indispensable for the good life.

— In the context of his effort to realize the essence of the German *Volk,* Heidegger insisted on the defense of the university, in particular of science in the Greek sense and knowing.

— The defense of the university and of the Greek conception of science was an intermediate goal, not an end in itself, although he later portrayed it as the final end of his action as rector.

— Heidegger later sought to distance himself from National Socialism, in particular through an "official" explanation tending to deny what could be denied and to minimize what could not be denied in order to represent his philosophy as untainted by his politics.

— Heidegger's later claim that in 1933 he turned to National Socialism only in order to defend the university is indefensible; in fact, even as he seeks to deny an interest in Nazi politics, he continues to acknowledge that in 1933 he indeed believed that National Socialism represented a historic turning point in the destiny of the German nation.

— Heidegger's assumption of the rectorate also reflected his effort, like Krieck and Baeumler, to use the rise of National Socialism for his own personal advantage.

This list, which is not exhaustive, is helpful to focus the relation between Heidegger's thought and Nazism. Heidegger's relation to Nazism can be represented as a series of three turnings: a turning toward real National Socialism when he became rector of the University of Freiburg and attempted to found Nazi politics through his philosophy of Being; a second turning away from real Nazism when he resigned as rector; and a third, simultaneous turning toward an ideal form of Nazism. The first turning is based in his fundamental ontology. His theory of Being is intrinsically political, since it requires a turn to the political plane in order not only to comprehend, but to realize authenticity and, as a result, to further the grasp of Being. The second turning is a turning away from really existing Nazism for reasons that are not clear but that may well include Heidegger's tardy awareness of the evident failure of his effort to lead the leaders. During the period when he was rector, Heidegger went to considerable lengths to reform the university in order to bend it in the direction of Nazism. But in the end, he was not widely followed in this endeavor. It is a little as if, to vary the well-known fable, the king had no clothes on and he finally realized it. For although Heidegger sought to lead, few desired to follow him. The third turning is Heidegger's continued allegiance after the rectorate, not to Hitlerian National Socialism, which in reality did not measure up to Heidegger's idea of it, but its ideal form which Heidegger continued to favor.

This list indicates that Heidegger's relation to Nazism was founded in his philosophical thought, hence not a merely contingent occurrence due to his misperception of the political situation, lack of knowledge of the world, or uncritical acceptance of others' suggestions. It further indicates that, despite his withdrawal from the rectorate, he did not alter his conviction of the importance of National Socialism. Now this latter claim is controversial. As part of the effort at damage control, Heidegger and his followers have stressed that after the rectorate he withdraw into the isolation of the solitary thinker who continued to struggle with the thought of Being until the end of his life. It has typically been suggested, following Heidegger's own view of the matter, that his relation to Nazism was merely a transitory episode, a short and philosophically meaningless period that should not be exaggerated[1] and was in fact independent of his thought. Moreover, Heidegger has suggested, and his followers have affirmed, that in his later writings he came to grips with, in fact criticized, National Socialism.[2] We need, now, to address the question of how Heidegger's Nazism, whose existence can no longer be doubted, impacts on his later thought. Only in this way will it be possible to determine whether his later position is unaffected by his Nazism, or whether in his later writings he in fact confronts National Socialism, or, finally, whether he continues to maintain his interest in Nazism.

To make this determination, we will need to consider relevant portions of Heidegger's later writings. In a way, all of Heidegger's corpus is relevant since traces of the theme that concerns us here run throughout his thought from beginning to end. An example among many is Heidegger's recurrent opposition to any form of *Weltanschauungsphilosophie,* an objection he brings against National Socialism in the essay on the rectorate. The theme of the relation between philosophy and *Weltanschauung,* as well as further themes of university reform, prominent in the rectoral talk, and the relation of the theory of value to phenomenology, strongly criticized in 1935 in *An Introduction to Metaphysics* immediately after the rectorate,[3] are the three main topics of Heidegger's first lecture series in 1919.[4] In the motto he chose for the edition of his collected writings—*Wege, nicht Werke*—Heidegger justly emphasized the continual change of his thought. But there is an astonishing continuity in his position since the themes that initially attracted his attention are still there at the end.

In view of the size of Heidegger's corpus, it will be necessary to focus the discussion on those writings most relevant to the present discussion. Among his writings after the rectorate, in my view the most important texts for his later thought and for a grasp of his Nazism include his Nietzsche lectures, the recently published *Beiträge zur Philosophie,* and his essays on technology. If Heidegger later left Nazism behind, if he confronted National Socialism, this change will, or at least should, be visible in these texts. On the contrary, if Heidegger's turn away from real National Socialism were simultaneously a turn to an ideal form of Nazism, then it should be possible to point to passages in his writings which justify this reading of his later thought. In both cases, the time has come to go beyond unsubstantiated claims about what Heidegger may or may not have thought, what he may or may not have said, to examine the texts themselves as the final arbiter of the position without special pleading of any kind, in the same way as one would for any other thinker.

The *Rektoratsrede* and, to a lesser extent, Heidegger's discussion of the rectorate are exoteric writings, directed to the wider public and not specifically intended for the philosophical community. Heidegger's lectures on Nietzsche, his *Beiträge,* and the essays on technology, come under the heading of his esoteric writings, specifically directed to his students or to his philosophical peers, in which Heidegger sought to work out his own position. The task of this chapter is to carry the discussion of Heidegger's Nazism further in order to determine whether, and how, his own thought changed in the wake of his encounter with National Socialism, in particular the sense in which he comes to grips with Nazism in his later position. Heidegger suggests that his "first Hölderlin lecture" and his "Nietzsche lectures" were "a confrontation with National Socialism."[5] Following Heidegger, it has been claimed that from the moment of the lectures on Nietzsche "National Socialism ceases to become a historical recourse against errancy. It becomes, *in its idea and in its reality,* the most crepuscular form of errancy itself."[6] It has further been claimed that "with Nietzsche, Heidegger recognized the nihilism of real National Socialism."[7]

Heidegger's First Hölderlin
Lecture Series

The initial series of Hölderlin lectures are important in themselves and for a consideration of Heidegger's Nazism. They occurred in 1934/35, in close proximity to his resignation from the rectorate and immediately before the lecture series published under the title *An Introduction to Metaphysics*.[8] The first Hölderlin lecture series was later followed by two others, which have also been published, given in the winter semester of 1941/42 and in the summer semester of 1942.[9]

Heidegger's first series of Hölderlin lectures is titled *Hölderlin's Hymns Germania and the Rhine*.[10] Although there is a good deal of Hölderlin interpretation in this text, the lectures are mainly devoted to an appropriation of the poet for the purposes of Heidegger's own theory. Here in the wake of the rectoral address, and the failure of the rectorate, Heidegger turns to poetry several years before he embarks on a great cycle of Nietzsche lectures. Heidegger's discussion of Hölderlin has evoked sustained critical discussion.[11] Our concern here is less with the extent to which Heidegger contributes to Hölderlin scholarship than with the importance of his Hölderlin discussion for his own position. The immediate problem is to understand how poetry relates to Heidegger's evolving conception of the question of Being, which remains his central interest, and the effect of that turn to poetry on the relation between his thought and Nazism. We need to ask: does Heidegger free himself from, or loosen the ties to, National Socialism in the first cycle of Hölderlin lectures?

In order to understand Heidegger's use of Hölderlin, we need to characterize the point of development reached by Heidegger's thought in the immediately preceding period. Heidegger himself calls attention to the relation between the rectoral address and the inaugural lecture, "What Is Metaphysics?" As late as the inaugural lecture, Heidegger still maintained a version of the traditional view of philosophy as transcendental science. His increasingly overt turning toward Nietzsche was visible in the rectoral talk in his insistence on Nietzsche's proposition of the death of God and the idea of a confrontation with Western thought through a return to its beginnings. The consequence, which was played out in the Nietzsche lectures, the "Letter on Humanism," the *Beiträge zur Philosophie,* and other later writings, is the effort to move beyond philosophy.

This entire effort represents a strengthening of the antirationalist, even gnostic side of Heidegger's thought. Heidegger's original position combines rationalistic and antirationalist aspects. The rationalist thrust is evident in Heidegger's insistence in his writings through the period of the inaugural lecture on a version of the traditional view of philosophy as transcendental science. The incipient antirationalist side of his position is already evident in *Being and Time* in various ways, for instance in his insistence on the analysis of Dasein as prior to and apart from the various sciences (§ 10), in the antiscientific perspective of the work in general which Jaspers, for example, found objectionable,[12] in the abandonment of the Husserlian conception of transcendental truth, on which Heidegger insisted early in the book (§ 7) in favor of the view of truth as disclosure (§§ 44, 68), and in the idea of resoluteness (§ 74). The conceptions of truth as disclosure and resoluteness are basically antirational since there are no criteria to discern the correctness of either one.

The evolution of Heidegger's thought after *Being and Time* basically weakens its initial rationalistic side in favor of a growing antirationalism leading finally to the turn beyond the philosophical tradition. An antirationalist, quasi-gnostic side of Heidegger's thought is already evident in the rectoral address. It may even be directly related to Heidegger's mistaken identification of National Socialism as offering an occasion to seize the future realization of the Germans. Heidegger's perception of the advent of Nazism as a historical turning point depends on the ability to see into history. This is an application of the conception of truth as disclosure, a mainstay of Heidegger's position as early as *Being and Time*[13] and at least until the late essay, "The End of Philosophy and the Task of Thinking,"[14] to the interpretation of historical phenomena. As early as the rectoral talk, Heidegger claimed to use Nietzsche's thought, mediated by his own study of Jünger, literally to see into history, to grasp the essence of what is with respect to the present and future. In the wake of his coming turn away from philosophy to thought, Heidegger could no longer maintain this point in the same way. In his turn to poetry, specifically to Hölderlin, he maintained his antirationalist claim for insight into history and the future through a reference beyond the philosophical tradition.

Heidegger turns to Hölderlin's poetry as a source of extraphilosphical truth. His concern to appropriate Hölderlin's poetry for his effort to find truth in a realm beyond philosophy is apparent as early as the short "Preliminary Remark" (*Vorbemerkung*) preceding the first series of Hölderlin lectures. In this and other writings, Heidegger adopts the pose, based on his conception of authenticity, that readings of prior theories which differ from his own are inauthentic. He applies this claim to the interpretation of Hölderlin. For Heidegger, to misinterpret "Hölderlin and his Gods" is to reduce this "poet finally to ineffectualness [Wirkungslosigkeit]."[15] In approaching Hölderlin in this "historical"

manner, one misses the "essential," namely, that "he founded the beginning of another history, the history that begins with the struggle about
the decision on the coming or flight of God."[16]

Several words in this statement are suggestive, including "history,"
"God," "struggle," "beginning," and "decision." If we recall Heidegger's earlier attention, in the rectoral address, to Nietzsche's aphorism
about the death of God, as well as his remark in the *Spiegel* interview
that only a God can save us,[17] we can note Heidegger's stress on the need
to struggle concerning a decision about the future arrival or departure of
God. Here, Heidegger is preparing to use Hölderlin to forward his own
view of himself as a seer of Being, he who sees into the future, including
the possibility of the future of the Germans as German.

As the title of the lecture course suggests, it is divided into two parts,
each of which is ostensibly devoted to the analysis of a poem by the great
German poet. Taken as a whole, the discussion is very repetitive; Heidegger frequently returns to the same ideas, often in the same or closely
similar formulations. An example, among many, is the pathetic
statement—which in the wake of the rectorate has an autobiographical
ring—repeated several times, that we do not know who we are.[18] The
virtue of Heidegger's repeated treatment of the same, or similar, themes
is to accord them an almost pedagogical emphasis, appropriate for a
course, in order to permit the final view of a particular theme to emerge
gradually—by accretion, so to speak.

Heidegger insists that his aim is not to interpret Hölderlin but to
create a space for poetry in our historical being.[19] He understands his
task as surpassing metaphysics, hence implicitly going beyond philosophy itself, "in developing the question concerning the origin and basis of
Hölderlin's poetry as the poets of poets."[20] The reason for the concern
with Hölderlin's poetry, great as it is, is not a mere hermeneutics of
poetical texts. Hölderlin's poetry is important for reasons beyond its
mere poetic qualities, as providing a way to respond to the historical
situation, the situation in which, for Heidegger, the hour of our history
has struck.[21]

As is his fashion, Heidegger never directly argues his view, although
his writing is full of concealed arguments. We can reconstruct his view by
following along in the text. We do not know who we are, a point Heidegger repeatedly urges, in most striking fashion in the statement that "the
gods have flown, [and] who man is, we do not know."[22] Heidegger insists
that poetry can help us in our time of need. For Heidegger, poetry is a
way of literally making present a kind of saying of revelation,[23] both the
most harmless and the most fearful.[24] More to the point, Heidegger tells
us that the historical existence of peoples springs from poetry, from
which authentic philosophical knowledge derives as well, and that from

both follows the realization of the existence of a people as a people in the state, or politics. "We have already heard . . . that the historical existence of people, the rise, peak, and fall, spring from poetry and from this authentic knowledge in the philosophical sense, and from both the realization of the existence of a people as a people through the state—politics."[25]

For Heidegger, then, poetry is deeper than philosophy, which derives from it. A role earlier attributed to philosophy, namely the authentic gathering of the German *Volk,* is now displaced to poetry since philosophy depends on it. Consistent with his view that truth lies beyond philosophy, Heidegger now locates truth in poetry, which makes possible the historical repetition of the German heritage. Whereas before philosophy was shown to be political, now both poetry and philosophy are regarded as intrinsically political, since they lead to historical destiny in a political context. In the rectoral address, Heidegger presented a version of the Platonic idea that philosophy founds politics, but poetry was not a factor. Heidegger now attributes a fundamental political role to poetry. For Heidegger, poetry founds philosophy as its ultimate source, both are intrinsically political, and both are necessary for the Germans to finally be German in the full sense. What Heidegger in the rectoral address saw as the possibility for the realization of the German people through philosophy is now depicted as a realization finally dependent on poetry.

Heidegger develops his claim for poetry through a complex analysis of the relation between poetry on the one hand and Being, history, and a people on the other. For Heidegger, poetry gives (*stiftet*) Being. Or, as he also says, poetry is the most originary language of a people.[26] Heidegger expands this view slightly when he says that poetry is the basic framework of historical being and that language is the basic event of historical existence.[27] His point is that we literally are language or constituted by a discussion, but that poetry provides the most basic form of language in which our being as human beings is made available to us. The effect is to privilege poetry as a means to deliver us to ourselves—as beings defined through our use of language—from within the poetic dimension.

If this were the goal of Heidegger's view of poetry, it would not be very interesting. It would, in spite of his disclaimer, turn out to be a kind of romanticism preaching poetry as the source of who we are. Yet Heidegger is no mere romantic, although he is also that. In the rectoral address, he argued for philosophy as the condition of the gathering of the Germans in an authentic sense. Here, where poetry has taken on the role of philosophy, he makes a similar point with respect to poetry. The significance of poetry is that it captures the historical being of a people, its basic mood.[28] In fact, since "the fatherland" is Being, and the poet is the voice of Being, Heidegger concludes, in a passage that sounds suspiciously like Nazi propaganda, at a time when he has supposedly broken with Nazism, that through the poet the Being of the fatherland is experienced as the authentic and sole being.

> This [i.e., the fatherland] does not play the external role of a closely related case, in terms of which the passing away and coming to being in the passing away can be illuminated in an exemplary fashion; on the contrary, the Being of the fatherland [Seyn des Vaterlandes], that is, the historical existence of its people [des Volkes], is experienced as the authentic and sole Being, from which the basic orientation to beings in general arises and wins its structure [Gefüge].[29]

The upshot of the claim is that the authentic way of Being of the fatherland, hardly an innocent term in the midst of the Third Reich, is lodged nowhere else than in poetry. The simultaneous result is again to deny the legitimacy of official Nazism, this time in reference to poetry, and to point toward the achievement of the Nazi goal.

Heidegger further emphasizes Hölderlin's role, the link between Being and poetry, and the future-oriented nature of poetry itself. For Heidegger, Hölderlin is the giver of German being,[30] or again "As the poet of poets Hölderlin is the poet of the future German and the only one."[31] His claim to deliver the German destiny to the Germans, to enable them to become fully German by reclaiming their heritage, rests on the fact that he has presumably seen farther than other poets. But that he has been able to see into the future at all is not due to him alone. In a mystical remark, Heidegger maintains that the poet as seer is possible only because Being lets it happen, because Being opens itself to the poet. "Being permits poetry to emerge, in order in an originary way to find itself within it and hence in it in a closed manner [verschliessend] to open itself up as a secret."[32] Heidegger's point is that Being is the cause of its own manifestation in a guarded way within the framework of poetic language. Left unclear is how Heidegger could possibly be privy to the secret of Being. What is clear, however, is that Heidegger now holds that Being, which was earlier depicted as the theme of the discussion in *Being and Time,* as that which is common to entities, has now taken on the causal character of something that stands behind beings and lets them be, so to speak.

Heidegger's discussion culminates in a series of related claims about Hölderlin's poetry and the future of the Germans, not as Greeks, but as German. Despite Heidegger's attachment to Greek thought, for Heidegger Hölderlin represents the future of the Germans. "Hölderlin is not

Greece, but the future of the Germans."[33] Heidegger emphasizes, now reaffirming the fundamental character of his own philosophical concern before all else, that a historical people must necessarily base itself on Being. "Only a historical people [Volk] is really a people. It is only historical, however, if it occurs on the basis of the center of Being."[34] Referring now to the task of the historical destiny of the German *Volk,* Heidegger insists that the central and ownmost task for a people is to realize their national being (*das Nationelle*) as a nation. "In this struggle and only in it a historical people reaches its highest [level]."[35]

Heidegger's remarks on Hölderlin in the first cycle of Hölderlin lectures invite discussion on three levels: the contribution to Hölderlin scholarship; the displacment of his earlier view of philosophy in favor of poetry; and with respect to the link between his thought and Nazism. This is not the place to review Heidegger's contribution to the discussion of Hölderlin. We have already noted the significance of Heidegger's decision here to privilege poetry over philosophy as a source of truth. In this way, he rehabilitates poetry, in eclipse as a mere imitation of an imitation since Plato. For he rehabilitates the earlier Greek idea, criticized by Plato, for instance in both the *Ion* and the *Republic,* of the poet as inspired by and the interpreter of the gods, in Heidegger's case as offering the necessary hint to knowledge of Being.[36] Yet, as a result of the adoption of this conception of the power of inspiration, he abandons the traditional philosophical view, widely present in the philosophical tradition since Plato, as well as in Heidegger's own earlier position, that philosophy is the final, most adequate, in fact solely adequate source of truth.

For present purposes, the most important question is whether and how Heidegger's relation to National Socialism changes in this text. Heidegger's depiction of the first series of his Hölderlin lectures as a confrontation with Nazism is unwarranted. If we compare this text with the rectoral address, then the differences between their respective views of National Socialism are too slight to justify that conclusion. One obvious difference is a shift in emphasis consistent with the change from a public lecture on a ceremonial occasion in which Heidegger assumed the rectorate to a lecture course for students on the writings of a major German poet. Heidegger's repeated emphases in the talk on struggle, the leaders, and "political science" have no equivalent in the lecture course, although their omission here hardly seems decisive. Neither text directly mentions either Hitler or the Nazi party. In fact, Heidegger's claim in the rectoral address to lead the leaders, which is not repeated here, is clearly more antagonistic to National Socialism than the lack of reference in lecture course.

One of the difficulties in determining whether and how Heidegger later shifted his view of Nazism is the unclarity surrounding its original hold on his thought. It is possible that the attachment he earlier felt for Hitler began to fade or even vanished. But his link with National Socialism certainly surpassed whatever he may have felt for the person of Hitler. In the rectoral address as well as in later writings, including Heidegger's discussion of his rectorate and the *Spiegel* interview, he insists on the opportunity he then saw for the German people as German. This interest, even obsession, which he publicly expressed in the rectoral talk, is maintained in the initial series of Hölderlin lectures, which in this specific sense fully overlap with the rectoral address, for instance in Heidegger's insistence here on the realization of a people in a historical manner, on the idea that the hour of history has struck, on the need for a decision, on the assumption of destiny, on the extreme difficulty of the realization of national destiny, and so on.

If we take Heidegger at his word that his preoccupation with German destiny led him to Nazism, then there is no basis for his claim that his initial cycle of Hölderlin lectures represents a confrontation with National Socialism. With respect to the rectoral address, the most significant change lies in the means to the end, not the end itself. In the speech, Heidegger uncritically took a Platonic approach in grounding politics in philosophy in order to bring about the gathering of the Germans as German. Now, after the failure of his rectorate—which has not escaped Heidegger's notice—he still desires to attain the same end but now through a different means. Above all, he is clear that it no longer suffices to ground politics in philosophy. Philosophy still has a role to play, although its role is now indirect. The task of the philosopher is not to bring about the destiny of the German people directly, but to point to poetry, above all Hölderlin's poetry, as the means to realize that task.

For strategic reasons, as part of his effort to construct his own legend, to influence the reception of his life and thought, we can understand that Heidegger may have desired to portray his initial Hölderlin lectures as in fact coming to grips with Nazism. But the text, which does not support that interpretation, in fact reveals that he has not changed his mind about National Socialism or even about the shared concern to bring about German authenticity. He has merely changed his mind about the role of philosophy in bringing it about. It is false to claim that in the first series of Hölderlin lectures Heidegger either came to grips with, or weakened, his allegiance to this aim. At most, in the turn to poetry he came to grips with the failure of the rectorate, for his later writing, including the first Hölderlin lecture series, reveals a renewed determination to attain the same goal.

The History of Philosophy and the Nietzsche Lectures

There is no reason to believe that that Heidegger confronts National Socialism in his first cycle of Hölderlin lectures. There is no significant criticism of Nazism in these lectures; in fact, Heidegger here reaffirms his support for the historical gathering of the Germans, the very concern that is ingredient in his original Nazi turning. But perhaps Heidegger confronts National Socialism in his Nietzsche lectures. Heidegger's insistence that like the first Hölderlin lecture series, the Nietzsche lectures record his confrontation with National Socialism is accepted by a number of commentators. We need now to explore this claim in detail.

Heidegger's Nietzsche courses exhibit his approach to the history of philosophy. As a first step toward an appreciation of his reading of Nietzsche's thought, it is useful to characterize Heidegger's attitude toward prior philosophy. In general terms, Heidegger shares a form of the antihistorical bias, characteristic of the modern tradition, against the philosophical tradition. He is not biased against the history of philosophy as such, since he clearly borrows from it with great frequency in the process of working out his own thought. Yet in virtue of his approach to Being, in principle for Heidegger as for the majority of modern philosophers who maintain the separation between the history of philosophy and philosophy, the history of philosophy is a series of mistakes. The difference is that whereas most other thinkers reject the history of philosophy in general, at least initially Heidegger believes that he can return to certain insights in early Greek thought through his more limited rejection of the history of ontology since the early Greeks.

Most thinkers who devalue the history of philosophy simply do not know much about it. Examples are Descartes, Kant, and Husserl. Heidegger, who provides a stunning counterexample to the lack of historical knowledge typical of modern thinkers, is distinguished by his knowledge of the history of philosophy.[37] Like Hegel and few others in the modern period, Heidegger exhibits a truly comprehensive, encyclopedic grasp of the length and breadth of the philosophical tradition. Heidegger's unusual grasp of prior philosophy was apparent in *Being and Time,* which already exhibits a wide awareness of the history of philosophy from the pre-Socratics to the present. His interest in the history of philosophy is even more apparent in his later thought, which often takes the form of a series of commentaries on important philosophical predecessors, commentaries that Heidegger describes as an effort to dialogue with them on their own level.

Heidegger's knowledgeable approach to prior philosophy bears comparison with Hegel's. Heidegger explicitly credits Hegel with inventing the concept of the history of philosophy.[38] Hegel's discussion exhibits a profound grasp of the history of philosophy, but he is not a historian of philosophy if that implies a concern to study prior philosophy in independence of philosophy; and, for the same reason, neither is Heidegger. Yet Hegel and Heidegger differ radically in their respective approaches to the philosophic tradition. As concerns prior thought, Hegel's concern is epistemological whereas Heidegger's is ontological. Hegel considers prior thought from an epistemological perspective, as a unitary phenomenon composed of related efforts, which build upon earlier positions, in order finally to demonstrate the alleged unity of thought and being. From his ontological angle of vision, Heidegger maintains that the initial pre-Socratic insight into Being was later obscured and covered up by a turn away to another, mistaken approach, which continues to dominate the discussion of metaphysics until Hegel and Nietzsche. Heidegger's effort is directed toward a recovery of the initial pre-Socratic view of Being which supposedly lies hidden behind the later metaphysical tradition.

Hegel and Heidegger exhibit opposite attitudes to philosophy itself. Hegel is positively disposed toward the history of philosophy, which demonstrates ever greater progress in the study of the conditions of knowledge, and which finally reaches its traditional aim in his own theory. Heidegger holds that since the pre-Socratics philosophy has been engaged in a long, difficult, and finally meaningless metaphysical exercise. Heidegger's bleaker assessment that philosophy has historically failed to, and in fact cannot, realize its aim is widely shared by others in the modern tradition. In his later effort to move beyond philosophy, Heidegger came to accept a version of the view held in different but related ways by, among others, Wittgenstein, Kierkegaard, the Marxists, and Nietzsche—each of whom desired to surpass philosophy—that philosophy as such is inadequate to respond to its concerns. He further accepted a version of the Young Hegelian view that the philosophical tradition comes to an end in Hegel, which he restates as the claim that the history of metaphysics terminates in Nietzsche.[39]

Heidegger's thought is often understood in terms of figures in the historical tradition. Although he himself emphasizes his attachment to pre-Socratic thought, it is usual to classify his position in terms of possible sources in modern philosophy.[40] His historical interest developed in his early thought, even before *Being and Time.* His dissertation on the idea of judgment in psychologism, which concerned logic,[41] was followed in the second dissertation, or *Habilitationsschrift,* by a study of the categories and view of meaning of Duns Scotus.[42]

Heidegger's writings exhibit a wide acquaintance with prior philosophical thought. In no particular order, his corpus exhibits detailed study and knowledge of Parmenides, Anaximander, Heraclitus, Plato, Aristotle, Duns Scotus, Descartes, Kant, Schelling, and Nietzsche. His early concentration on ontological themes partly explains the nearly complete lack of attention to English-language writers, including all of Anglo-American analytic philosophy, and the relative inattention to such writers as Socrates, Fichte, Marx, Augustine, Thomas, and Husserl. Even Hegel, who is discussed often, is handled in a curiously incomplete manner, as if Heidegger were finally unable to come to grips with his thought.[43]

In general terms, inspection of Heidegger's writings reveals a progression from systematic discussion—presupposing extensive historical analysis, which is initially mainly absent—to less systematic, more historically oriented discussion. *Being and Time,* the main work of Heidegger's early period, is highly systematic, based on thorough knowledge of the history of philosophy, with the exception of English-language sources. In the English translation, the index of proper names contains eighty-two names, not a large number, mainly philosophers, as well as an occasional theologian, the New Testament, and so on. There are no references to English-language writers. But there are extensive references to a variety of important philosophers, including most prominently Aristotle, Augustine, Descartes, Dilthey, Hegel, Husserl, Kant, Parmenides, Plato, Scheler, Simmel, and Thomas. Other writers whose influence on Heidegger's position is significant, even decisive, are scarcely mentioned. These include Kierkegaard, whose thought certainly provides a basic influence on the formation of Heidegger's view of human being as Dasein,[44] Luther,[45] and perhaps Nietzsche.

Not surprisingly, since the view Heidegger expounds in this book is basically anti-Cartesian, it contains a detailed account and critique of Descartes's thought.[46] Heidegger further studies aspects of numerous other positions, such as Kant's refutation of idealism,[47] the relation of his own view of historicality to the theories of Dilthey and Yorck,[48] and Hegel's view of time and its relation to spirit.[49] In addition, there are numerous generalizations about the history of philosophy. An example is the assertion, as early as the first page of the work, that the view of Being put forward by Plato and Aristotle remained basically unchanged until Hegel.[50] Yet the historical interpretation underlying such interpretative generalizations is mainly absent in the work itself.

Although *Being and Time* mainly lacks specific historical analyses, Heidegger specifically indicates his view of the history of philosophy in his account of "The Task of Destroying the History of Ontology."[51] To provide for a radical new interpretation of Being as time, he desires to reappropriate the history of ontology in a way that frees, or makes available, possibilities that, in his opinion, have been covered up at least since the early Greeks. His aim is to take up the tradition but not to fall prey to it,[52] to prevent it from, in his words, blocking "our access to those promordial 'sources' from which the categories and concepts handed down to us have been in part quite genuinely drawn."[53] His ultimate goal is to interrogate the history of Being in order to return, beyond it, to the original experiences which determine it.

> We understand this task as one in which by taking *the question of Being as our clue,* we are to *destroy* the traditional content of ancient ontology until we arrive at those primordial experiences in which we achieved our first ways of determining the nature of Being—the ways which have guided us ever since.[54]

Heidegger's approach to the history of philosophy changes significantly in later writings. *The Basic Problems of Phenomenology,* the text of Heidegger's lecture course from spring semester 1927, the year in which *Being and Time* appeared, provides extensive historical interpretation within the systematic framework characteristic of Heidegger's position before the turning in his thought. *The Basic Problems of Phenomenology* takes up the central theme of the third section of part 1 of *Being and Time,* that is, the question concerning the meaning of Being through the demonstration that time is the horizon of all understanding of Being. According to the outline, the lecture course—it was organized as a book according to Heidegger's suggestions[55]—is divided into three main parts: a "phenomenological-critical discussion of several traditional theses about the meaning of Being in general," "the fundamental-ontological question about the meaning of Being in general," and "the scientific method of ontology and the idea of phenomenology."[56] In fact, the text of the course covers only the four chapters of the first part and the initial chapter of the second part. Roughly the last third of the work provides a purely systematic account of what Heidegger here calls "The fundamental ontological question of the meaning of Being in general." Roughly the first two-thirds of the book consists of a systematic treatment in detail of four traditional theses about Being.

Heidegger's systematic treatment of the different historical theses about Being is at least as comprehensive and relatively more detailed than the historical sections of *Being and Time.* He devotes fifty pages, for instance, to the analysis of Kant's thesis that being is not a real predicate in an analysis divided into three parts. The first part, devoted to "The Content of the Kantian Thesis," contains a detailed description of the Kantian exposition of his view in a precritical essay, "The Sole Possible Argument for a Demonstration of the Existence of God," and later in the two editions of the *Critique of Pure Reason*. The account of the Kantian thesis demonstrates a mastery of the relevant details, such as an effort to trace Kant's use of the term "reality" over Baumgarten to scholasticism,[57] a remark on the difference between Kant's conception of objective reality, and reality as elucidated,[58] and so on. The depth and breadth of Heidegger's approach to Kant's thesis is equaled by his treatment of the other historical theses he considers. Heidegger's other early writings often contain historical generalization, but among them this volume stands out in virtue of Heidegger's willingness to provide the historical analyses that underlie his sweeping judgments about prior thought.

Heidegger's inaugural lecture, "What Is Metaphysics?," delivered in 1929, is a systematic analysis nearly devoid of attention to the history of philosophy. In the same year, he published *Kant and the Problem of Metaphysics*, a work based on lectures presented in the fall semester of 1925 and at Davos in March 1929.[59] Heidegger's interpretation of Kant is a by-product of his work on the second part of *Being and Time*.[60] Beyond the specific discussion of the critical philosophy, this book is valuable for the light it sheds on Heidegger's approach to the history of philosophy.

There is a clear link between the book on Kant and *Being and Time*. In his proposed destruction of the history of ontology, Heidegger represents his own position as the completion of the intention animating Kant's critical philosophy. He states that Kant is his only predecessor, although for reasons intrinsic to his approach Kant was unable to complete his study of the link between time and the "I think," which ultimately, for Kant, did not even appear problematic.[61] Heidegger discerns the key to this problem in Kant's doctrine of the schematism. Heidegger argues for his interpretation through an exposition of selected parts of the critical philosophy, beginning with an effort to establish what he calls the problematic of temporality. He attributes Kant's inability to reach the "correct" result, for Heidegger's own view of the temporal nature of Being, to two reasons. First, Kant neglected the problem of Being, and the analysis of Dasein, to which he preferred the Cartesian position. Second, although he brought time into the subject, he took over the traditional view of time. Now although *Being and Time* established the problematic of temporality, it does not contain Heidegger's analysis of the Kantian doctrine of the schematism, which is provided in *Kant and the Problem of Metaphysics*. In that sense, independently of the light it casts on Kant's position, this book represents a vital, further link in the chain of Heidegger's effort to provide his view of Being as time with "true concreteness" through a destruction of the prior ontological tradition.[62]

In his study of Kant, Heidegger considers the critical philosophy as an incomplete anticipation of the problem of Being. He presents the *Cri-*

tique of Pure Reason as an effort to found metaphysics, which, accordingly, is revealed as a problem of fundamental ontology. The title of the Kant book, which is ambiguous, can be understood from two perspectives: as the question concerning being (*Seiende*) as such in its totality, and as an inquiry into the problem of metaphysics.[63] The discussion is divided into four main parts, including an analysis of the foundation of metaphysics, its carrying out, its originality, and its repetition.[64]

Any interpretation needs to reflect on its relation to what it interprets. This problem is especially acute in Heidegger's discussions of the history of philosophy since he never considers other views for their intrinsic merits, and always considers them in terms of his own project. Although his book sheds considerable light on Kant's position, it would be a mistake to read it merely as a study of Kant.[65] In the foreword to the translation, Thomas Langan, who closely follows Heidegger on this point, insists that the result is an "authentic Kantian commentary," in effect a model for all dialogue between thinkers, although he simply concedes that Heidegger is not concerned with what Kant meant or said.[66]

The very idea of a dialogue between thinkers is problematic since it is not clear what "commentary" means in this sense. The book, which documents an encounter of one powerful thinker with another, is not a dialogue, or at least not so in any simple sense because the encounter is clearly one-sided, a kind of monologue. Kant does not, and indeed could not, answer Heidegger either directly or through his writings since Heidegger makes no pretense at concentrating on what is either implicit or even explicit in the critical philosophy. And there is more than a hint that a commentary that concentrated on such matters would be inauthentic, by implication less valuable than one that did not.

Heidegger, who is aware of these issues, responds to them briefly in two places, which further illuminate his approach to the history of philosophy.[67] In the discussion of Kant's conception of the ground, he states that his work is concerned to bring out what Kant intended to say.[68] He points to a passage in which Kant talks about the need to go beyond what is said to the intention, and then adds that for this reason every interpretation is necessarily violent.[69] For Heidegger, a violent interpretation is not arbitrary since it is guided by a central insight, which is confirmed by its utility. "The directive idea itself is confirmed by its own power of illumination."[70] But this justification is unsatisfactory. In practice, it is obviously difficult to decide whether a given interpretation is in fact confirmed, since opinions will differ with respect to the significance of a given reading. It is further mistaken to believe that an interpretation that provides insight, and is, therefore, confirmed, is not merely arbitrary. An example, among many, is Kojève's justly celebrated, insightful, but demonstrably arbitrary reading of Hegel's *Phenomenology of Spirit*.[71]

As if unsatisfied by his remark on the limits of interpretation, Heidegger returns to the issue of violent textual interpretation in a new preface added to the second edition of the work. He notes that he has been correctly criticized for the violence of his interpretations. In response, he argues that, in the discussion of prior views, one must choose between two mutually exclusive alternatives: what he calls the method of historical philology, from whose perspective, by implication, the objections to his approach are justified; and what he calls an inquiry that is both historical and philosophical, whose aim is, in his words, "to set in motion a thoughtful dialogue between thinkers."[72]

Since in the second edition, Heidegger is willing to admit that some, but not all, interpretations are violent, his task becomes the justification of violent interpretations. At this point, he silently drops the claim to elicit the hidden aim of Kant's position. In fact, he no longer makes any claim to follow the text as written in any strict sense, since presumably that is the appanage of the philological approach which he rejects. The resultant views of violent textual interpretation are independent of each other. It could be the case that an interpretation captures the intent of a text even if, in practice, it would be difficult to agree on a claim to that effect; and it could also be the case that a given reading sets in motion a dialogue between two thinkers in Heidegger's sense although it demonstrably contradicts, or at least fails to grasp, the intention behind a particular text on a reasonable interpretation of it.

We can infer that Heidegger regards his study of the prior tradition as respecting the historical and philosophical, but not the philological, approach; we can further infer that Heidegger feels justified in ignoring such criteria as fidelity to the text and the intent of a thinker, what Kant would call the letter and spirit of a view, in order to bring about what he regards as dialogue.[73] The criterion, then, of the degree of success of Heidegger's dialogues with previous thinkers is not, and cannot be, the fidelity of his interpretations or even the extent of the light he throws on their positions, since he has in effect insulated his discussion against any evaluation in terms of its relation to the texts; the criterion lies wholly and solely in the way in which Heidegger is able to make use of a prior position in order to argue for and advance his own thought. It follows that, as Langan admits, what he regards as an authentic commentary and a model for dialogue between thinkers is in fact freed of all textual constraints, and, hence, merely arbitrary.

These remarks, added to the second edition of Heidegger's study of Kant, usefully indicate Heidegger's awareness, and attempted justification, of the problematic nature of his approach to the history of philosophy. Heidegger studies the history of philosophy increasingly in his later writings, although he only rarely reflects explicitly on his practice. Two exceptions occur in *An Introduction to Metaphysics*.[74] In a passage on the origin of philosophy among the Greeks, Heidegger remarks that being (*Seiende*) was called *physis*, which is usually translated as "nature," from the Latin *natura,* which means "to be born, birth."[75] Heidegger regards this displacement as neither innocent nor innocuous but rather as an instance of the general problem that in the translation from Greek into Latin the original Greek philosophical impulse was lost. All later philosophy is based on the translation of Greek thought into Latin, as a result of which philosophy has lost its original inspiration. This idea grounds Heidegger's persistent effort, through the interrogation of terms, to recover the earlier, allegedly "correct" meanings, which have supposedly been "covered" up in the later discussion, in order, as he says, "to skip over this whole process of deformation and decay and attempt to regain the unimpaired strength of language and words."[76]

The thesis underlying Heidegger's linguistic retrieval of philosophical insight is problematic. We cannot establish, and there is no reason to believe, that earlier is better, so to speak, that the so-called original meaning—even if it could be determined in a leap behind the tradition to its origins, which is highly doubtful—is in general closer to the truth of the matter, or more productive of philosophical insight. Even if translation often, even inevitably, results in a displacement of meaning, it does not follow that the result is a general loss of significant philosophical insight. To know how Aristotle employs the term *"ousia"* provides insight into his ontology; it provides insight into a correct view of ontology only if Aristotle's ontological view is correct. In principle, Heidegger's linguistic approach offers a way to retrieve elements of earlier views; but it cannot justify the claim that to retrieve earlier views is to retrieve the truth of the matter.

What I am calling Heidegger's attempted linguistic retrieval of original philosophical insight yields two views, both of which are problematic: the claim that there is an original insight that has somehow been covered up, and the related claim that what has been covered up can now be appropriately uncovered. These views are obviously independent of each other. It could turn out that there is an original philosophical insight that has later been covered up but which we cannot retrieve since we cannot determine the original, correct meanings of the words; it could further turn out that we can determine the original meanings of the words but no original philosophical insight is revealed; it could finally turn out, as Heidegger maintains, that to determine the original meanings of the words, by returning behind their subsequent linguistic displacement, enables us to grasp original philosophical insight.

Now ordinarily translation provides the way to recover a meaning in a language that has later changed, either through intralinguistic translation, in which we consult a manual, dictionary, or lexicon of some kind to determine, say, how an English word was earlier expressed, for instance in Middle English or even in Anglo-Saxon, or through interlinguistic translation, such as through the use of a Greek-English lexicon to determine the meaning of a Greek term. In recent years, translation has come under attack as in principle arbitrary.[77] In virtue of his claim that a linguistic displacement has occurred in the translation of the original texts, Heidegger cannot rely on any later discussions. But if he needs in each case to determine the so-called original meaning without appealing to the available scholarly apparatus, he must find a way to guard against the charge of mere arbitrariness.

Heidegger attends to this problem in the course of a second, lengthy passage from the same work on the relation of thought to being in early Greek philosophy. He concedes that his interpretation must appear as an "arbitrary distortion"[78] with respect to the prevailing types of interpretation. He further concedes that he is correctly accused of reading in what cannot be exactly determined. But, he asks rhetorically:

> Which interpretation is the true one, the one which simply takes over a perspective into which it has fallen, because this perspective, this line of sight, presents itself as familiar and self-evident; or the interpretation which questions the customary perspective from top to bottom, because conceivably—and indeed actually—this line of sight does not lead to what is in need of being seen.[79]

No doubt it is always useful, and sometimes unavoidable, to examine critically what we think we know, to scrutinize the habitual as a possible source of error. But it does not follow that, this having been done, the resultant textual interpretation avoids, or that Heidegger avoids, new forms of error, such as reading into the texts what one wishes to find there, which he here refers to as "what is in need of being seen."

Even in Heidegger's most systematic writings, such as *Being and Time,* the history of philosophy, especially the history of ontology, is never far from his mind. In the long period after this work, Heidegger directly considers historical themes with increasing frequency. This relative change in emphasis can be illustrated in various ways. For instance, the three collections of essays Heidegger published between 1950 and 1967 are largely concerned with historical topics.[80] A better index is furnished by Heidegger's lecture courses from 1923 on, namely volumes 27–55 inclusive in his collected works, now being published. Of these twenty-eight volumes, nine are devoted to systematic and nineteen to historical topics. It follows that Heidegger gave rather more attention to historical themes than to systematic ones in his lectures, although the proportion was inverted in his published writings. Now if we take Heidegger's 1935 lecture course as a fictitious dividing point, we note a clear change in the relative attention to historical subjects around this point. Prior to 1935, there are a total of eleven lecture courses, including four on systematic and seven on historical questions. After 1935, there are fifteen lecture courses, including one or at most one and a half on systematic issues;[81] but all the rest concern historical topics. Hence, there is not only an increasing, but even a predominant, concern with historical matters after 1935, at least in the lecture courses.

Heidegger's Nietzsche Lectures

Partly because of Heidegger's concern with the history of ontology, Heidegger was increasingly concerned with Nietzsche after 1935. Heidegger's increased interest in Nietzsche's thought is apparent in an enumeration of the historical topics Heidegger treats in his lecture courses after 1935. There is one course each on Kant, Parmenides, and Heraclitus. There are two each on Schelling and Hölderlin. But no fewer than six are devoted to Nietzsche.[82] Hence, one can infer that starting in 1935 he devoted a very large fraction of his work in the classroom to direct study of Nietzsche's thought.[83] This inference is further strengthened by inspection of Heidegger's publishing during this period, which includes several articles directly concerned with Nietzsche's thought,[84] as well as two large volumes on Nietzsche quarried by Heidegger from his lecture courses.[85]

Heidegger, of course, was not the only thinker interested in Nietzsche, who almost immediately became exceedingly influential after his death in 1900. According to David Krell, Nietzsche was a literary phenomenon whose thought was widely seen, by those who came to maturity in the First World War, as correctly predicting the ruin of Germany.[86] Peter Gay points to widespread instances of Nietzsche's literary influence during the Weimar Republic, including his impact on Aby Warburg, the founder of the Warburg Institute, who took Nietzsche, Burckhardt, and Usener as his models; the circle around the poet Stefan George, which was attracted to Nietzsche, especially in the work by Ernst Bertram, for his celebration of Hölderlin; and Thomas Mann, who admired Nietzsche as well as Wagner and Schopenhauer, each of whom influenced *Buddenbrooks*.[87] Others associated with the George-Kreis who wrote on Nietzsche include Ernst Gundolf and Kurt Hildebrandt.[88]

Nietzsche's philosophical impact was considerable. In 1901, Wilhelm Windelband, the neo-Kantian historian of philosophy, still thought of him as a poet.[89] A long stream of others discussed Nietzsche as a philosopher. With Goethe, Oswald Spengler considered Nietzsche as one of his two models.[90] As early as 1902, the Kantian Hans Vahinger published a book on Nietzsche, which was followed in 1911 by a chapter in his main work.[91] In 1907, the sociologist and neo-Kantian philosopher Simmel brought out a study of Schopenhauer and Nietzsche.[92] In fact, there was so much attention to Nietzsche in the discussion at this time that one can even differentiate between cultural, life-philosophical, and existential approaches to his thought.[93] Still a fourth approach is represented by the interest in the relation of Nietzsche and Christianity.[94]

Heidegger's relation to Nietzsche is complex.[95] There are at least six ways in which Nietzsche functions in Heidegger's thought, including (1) the constitution of Heidegger's own original position; (2) Heidegger's desire to contribute to knowledge of Nietzsche's thought through collaboration on the critical edition and the interpretation of Nietzsche's position; (3) within the framework of the study of the history of ontology, as a subset of the history of the philosophical tradition; (4) in the transition from the first beginning to the other beginning through the turning in the *Beiträge* and other writings, hence as a link between the early fundamental ontology and the later critique of technology; (5) as part of Heidegger's defense of his claim to philosophical hegemony within the Third Reich, through the refutation of other readings of Nietzsche; and (6) in Heidegger's claimed confrontation with National Socialism.

It is easier to document the role played by Nietzsche's thought in Weimar culture and National Socialism than in the constitution and later evolution of Heidegger's position. When Nietzsche began to exert a pull on Heidegger's thought is a matter of debate. As early as 1960, Gadamer suggested that Heidegger's true predecessor in raising the problem of Being against the whole direction of the Western tradition is Nietzsche. For Gadamer, the aim of raising Nietzsche's criticism of the Platonic tradition to the level of the tradition, of confronting Western metaphysics on its own level, is already implicit in *Being and Time,* even if Heidegger only realized this afterward.[96] Other observers tend to place the turn to Nietzsche after the development of fundamental ontology. Although Heidegger attended Rickert's lectures on Nietzsche, for Pöggeler Nietzsche's influence on Heidegger only becomes decisive in 1929–1930.[97] Arguing against Pöggeler, Krell dates the concern with Nietzsche to Heidegger's student days in 1909–1914 and sees traces of Nietzsche's influence in Heidegger's early thought, prior to *Being and Time,* including the *Habilitationsschrift* and the subsequent *venia legendi* lecture.[98] Nietzsche is mentioned three times in *Being and Time.*[99] Taminiaux has recently used Heidegger's extensive reference to Nietzsche's "Second Untimely Meditation" to argue that of all those to whom Heidegger refers in this work, Nietzsche is the only earlier thinker whose position he seeks to make his own.[100] These writers do not differ about whether Nietzsche influenced *Being and Time;* rather they differ with respect to the extent of that influence. There seems to be a clear link between Nietzsche's distinction between the overman, or superman, and ordinary mortals, for instance in *Beyond Good and Evil,* and Heidegger's canonical distinction in *Being and Time* between authenticity and inauthenticity. Heidegger's increasing interest in Nietzsche's thought after *Being and Time* is based on his conviction of its importance for his own position. Between 1927 and 1935, when the Nietzsche lectures began, Nietzsche's influence on Heidegger's thought quickly assumes major proportions. Nietzsche is already present in an important way in Heidegger's rectoral address. Here, in his habitual rhetorical style, Heidegger asks what if Nietzsche is right that God is dead.[101] In the article on the rectorate, he insists on the significance of Jünger in providing access to Nietzsche's thought, which in turn offers the possibility to think and even to foresee the history and present of the Western world in terms of metaphysics.[102] Nietzsche's precise impact on the constitution of Heidegger's fundamental ontology is unclear; but in 1935, it is clear that Heidegger had come to see his metaphysical task as gaining a true grasp of Nietzsche and of fully developing Nietzsche's thought.[103]

This conviction underlies Heidegger's collaboration with the Nietzsche Archives in the preparation of a new version of Nietzsche's collected works and his own reading of Nietzsche's thought. According to Marion Heinz, Heidegger was already in contact with the archives in the late 1920s.[104] He became a member of the editorial board in May 1934. Along with H. J. Frank and Alfred Rosenberg, head of the Amt Rosenberg, he took part in a commission charged with publishing a critical edition of Nietzsche's work and letters. From a letter to Leutheusser dated 26 December 1942 it is clear that he was further active in the preparation of the new edition of the *Will to Power (Der Wille zur Macht).* It seems that he visited the archives twice a year during the period 1936–1938 as a member of the editorial commission. It is further known that in the preparation of his lectures on Nietzsche, he consulted Karl Schlechta, the editor of Nietzsche's collected works. It is not clear what his relation to the archives was after 1939. Heidegger did not participate in the meetings in 1941. The same letter to Leutheusser indicates that he resigned from the commission. It seems that Heidegger justified his decision in terms of the dispute in 1938 between the Nietzsche Archives and the *Reichsschriftumskammer,* which rejected the first volume of the new edition of the collected works, from which it withdrew its support. There is extant a notification by the office, on which Heidegger wrote by hand: "This was to be expected: afterward work in common with the commission impossible; only work for Nietzsche's works—in independence from the edition."[105]

Heidegger's interest in Nietzsche's thought continued after he ended his collaboration with the Nietzsche Archives. His attention to Nietzsche is the main example of his effort to "dialogue" with another thinker on his own level in order to bring out what the latter supposedly wanted to, but could not, say, and to carry the discussion further than the point at which it was left. This "dialogue" is carried out at enormous length over a period of years, first explicitly—out loud, so to speak—in a series of lectures and articles, and then later in silent form, after the Nietzsche lectures, in many of Heidegger's later writings. We have already noted this "dialogue" in the Nietzsche lectures given between 1936 and 1940, in the lecture course planned but not given in the academic year 1941/42, and in several articles. Significantly, Nietzsche is still prominent in Heidegger's lecture course in the first semester of the academic year 1951/52, when he was permitted to resume teaching.[106] But Nietzsche is not discussed explicitly in the spring semester of this same lecture course. After the early 1950s, Nietzsche recedes into the background as an explicit theme, but what Heidegger learned from this encounter continued to shape his own thought in the years ahead.

To appreciate Heidegger's discussion of Nietzsche, it is useful to contrast it with his discussion of Descartes and Kant. In theory, Heidegger's treatment of thinkers after the pre-Socratics—that is, after what he discerns as the early turn away from the original, correct approach to Being—should be negative, although in practice this is not always the case. Heidegger's treatment of prior thinkers is sometimes less strict than his simple bivalent framework requires. Heidegger himself suggests that his attitude toward the past is not simply negative. "But to bury the past in its nullity is not the purpose of this destruction; its aim is *positive;* its negative function remains unexpressed and indirect."[107] The criterion for Heidegger's specific attitude seems to reside in his conviction about the utility of a given position for his own purposes.

The often positive aspect of Heidegger's reaction to other thinkers is entirely lacking in his reading of Descartes. Simply stated, Heidegger consistently treats Descartes in a wholly negative manner, as the arch-villain of the philosophical tale. His negative approach toward Descartes is already in evidence in *Being and Time* in the passage on the destruction of the history of ontology. Here, Heidegger argues that in the Middle Ages, Greek ontology becomes a fixed body of doctrine that is transmitted by Suarez, Descartes, and others, in basically unchanged fashion in later thought up to and including Hegel.[108] Descartes plays a key role in the transmission of an unexamined doctrine in the form of an ontology irreconcilably different from Heidegger's own view, based on the ontological difference. "In Descartes we find the most extreme tendency toward such an ontology of the 'world,' with, indeed, a counter-orientation toward the *res cogitans*—which does not coincide with Dasein either ontically or ontologically."[109] A similarly negative attitude toward Descartes and Cartesian thought is maintained in later writings, for instance in Heidegger's rejection of all forms of the humanist, anthropological approach.[110]

The discussion of Kant is more complex. On a superficial level, the treatment is equally negative, as in the suggestion that, except for the omission of an ontology of Dasein, Kant merely took over the Cartesian ontology in dogmatic fashion.[111] Yet Heidegger's reading of Kant's position is finally more nuanced. Heidegger discusses the critical philosophy on four occasions in *Being and Time*, with respect to the concept of time, the problem of Being, the refutation of idealism, and the transcendental unity of apperception.

(1) In an early reference to temporality, Heidegger indicates that the establishment of this problematic, the task of the second division of the book, will show that Kant took over the Cartesian view dogmatically, and hence neglected the problem of Being and the analysis of Dasein. The result was that Kant's concept of the schematism did not penetrate to the central ontological problem.[112] The implicit suggestion that Kant's approach can be carried beyond Kant is worked out in Heidegger's study of the relation between the critical philosophy and metaphysics. In an obvious departure from the more usual epistemological readings, Heidegger interprets Kant's position as an incomplete effort to lay the foundation of metaphysics which, through an appropriate repetition, can be completed.[113]

(2) In a discussion of the concept of "world" in Descartes and Kant, Heidegger maintains that the latter's rejection of being as a real predicate is an uncritical restatement of the problematical Cartesian view in a manner indicative of a failure to master the basic problem of Being.[114] This same claim is formulated in a more graceful but conceptually equivalent manner in the more detailed treatment of the Kantian thesis in the parallel lecture course.[115] For Heidegger, Kant's analysis fails because it lacks an explicit theory of Dasein.[116] In a later passage, Heidegger explicitly suggests that under appropriate conditions Kant's approach can be salvaged for the problem of Being. Here, Heidegger remarks that the four theses examined in this book, including Kant's, represent aspects of a unity toward which he is striving through their examination. "The four theses formulate only externally and still covertly the systematic unity of the basic ontological problems, toward

which we are groping by way of the preparatory discussion of the theses."[117]

(3) Heidegger further analyzes Kant's Refutation of Idealism as an example of Dasein's supposed tendency to bury "the external world" before proving its existence.[118] He maintains that Kant's alleged confusions manifest Dasein's falling and resultant comprehension of the "world" as mere presence-at-hand. Although he claims that the neglect of the existential analytic of Dasein impedes the establishment of the phenomenological problematic, he concedes the partial validity of each of the various approaches to the "problem of reality."[119]

(4) Heidegger studies Kant's transcendental unity of apperception under the heading of the self. He objects to Kant's view as an ontologically inappropriate description of the self in terms appropriate for a *res cogitans,* as something always present-to-hand.[120] He insists against Kant that the self is not a being-in-the-world in this sense. According to Heidegger, the self can finally only be discerned through the phenomenon of care, or the authentic potentiality for being one's self.[121]

In *Being and Time,* the central thread of Heidegger's treatment of Kant is the claim to carry Kant's position beyond the point at which it was left to its intended conclusion. Heidegger believes that Kant's theory lacks an analysis of Being and of Dasein, and hence fails to achieve its goal; and he further believes that his own analysis of Dasein enables us to see the critical philosophy as valuable for the problem of metaphysics. In this respect, there is a limited analogy between Heidegger's view of Kant and Sartre's view of Marx.[122] Both are concerned with the completion, through an aspect supposedly supplied by his own thought, of an important but supposedly incomplete theory. The difference is that whereas Sartre holds that Marxism is unsurpassable as the philosophy of our time, Heidegger holds only that the critical philosophy is at best an incomplete anticipation of his own.

There is a significant difference in Heidegger's treatments of Kant and Nietzsche. With respect to Kant, Heidegger points to the critical philosophy as solidly ensconced within, and, for that reason, limited by, the philosophical tradition, which it uncritically accepts. Heidegger believes that this dogmatic acceptance of the prior tradition is the reason why Kant is unable to carry out the intrinsic aims of his thought. Even if Heidegger applauds Kant's intentions, he finally rejects the critical philosophy as a whole. With respect to Nietzsche, Heidegger applauds the effort as a whole, which he does not reject. To a degree unlike that of any thinker since the pre-Socratics, Heidegger thinks of Nietzsche as anticipating in incomplete form his own thought as he later came to understand it.

There is, of course, ample precedent for the idea that a later theory takes up the central theme of and completes an earlier position. Heidegger's relation to Nietzsche partially resembles Hegel's relation to Kant. Like Fichte and Schelling, the young Hegel accepted the intent of Kant's position as basically correct. Hegel held that there was only one system of philosophy; and he regarded the views of Fichte and Schelling as further modifications of the critical philosophy.[123] Hegel's position is an effort to develop the Kantian speculative insight in accord with the spirit, but not the letter of the Kantian philosophy.[124] Similarly, in Nietzsche Heidegger finds a concern with two basic characteristics of his own thought: the problem of Being, and the revolt against the Platonic tradition following from this problem. Just as in his own position Hegel thinks with Kant against Kant, so in his own position Heidegger thinks with Nietzsche against Nietzsche in order to complete the proposed revolt against the Platonic tradition. Now Hegel's thought literally took form in his debate with Kant and such "Kantians" as Fichte and Schelling. Despite Heidegger's awareness of Nietzsche, his original position was already in place before he entered into "dialogue" with Nietzsche. For Heidegger, Nietzsche's importance does not lie in the constitution of his own thought; it lies rather in the later evolution of the original position. In fact, it would be an exaggeration to claim that, despite Nietzsche's influence on Heidegger's thought, Heidegger was ever, even for a brief period, a true disciple of Nietzsche. As for Hölderlin and the other writers he studies, Heidegger is never a disciple in any obvious sense, and always attuned to the possibility of using another body of thought for his own.

Beyond his strict contribution to Nietzsche scholarship, or work for Nietzsche's works, Heidegger's Nietzsche discussion has a triple function in his thought: to assert his own role in German philosophy by refuting other extant readings, to contribute to his own study of the history of ontology, and further to develop his analysis of Being. Like other philosophers, Heidegger was constantly concerned with the struggle for influence in the university, especially the German academy. In the Third Reich, this struggle was circumscribed by two additional factors: the normal academic disagreements concerning Nietzsche's thought, and the relation between Nietzsche and National Socialism.

Nietzsche functioned during the Third Reich for both political and philosophical goals. Baeumler points to a parallel in the views of Nietzsche and Hitler.[125] Enge, who was the head of the Nietzsche Archives in Weimar, stated that he owed "the interpretation and evaluation of the Hitler movement to the study of Nietzschean ideas concerning blood and the decline of cultures and my own observation of social phenomena."[126] Algermissen insists on the concern of both Hitler and Mussolini with Nietzsche.[127] Mussolini published and lectured on Nietzsche, and understood fascism as the realization of Nietzsche's thought. When he was twenty, Mussolini published an article on Nietzsche, in which he wrote: "In order to attain the ideal picked out by Nietzsche a new type of free spirit must arise, spirits which are hardened by war, and loneliness, and in great danger, spirits which will free us from love of our neighbor."[128] On 29 July 1933, his fiftieth birthday, the Nietzsche Archives sent him the following telegram:

> To the most masterful son of Zarathustra, of whom Nietzsche dreamed, the genial awakener of the aristocratic values of Nietzsche's spirit, the Nietzsche Archives sends on his fiftieth birthday a telegram, in testimony, that he is faithful to the master's work and has consciously come to grips with it.[129]

And on 26 May 1934 Mussolini held a two-and-a-half-hour speech in the Italian parliament in which he took up Nietzsche's slogan from Zarathustra: "War first only makes a man, as childbearing a women."[130] Hitler also thought of his political work as the realization of Nietzsche's aims. Even before 1933, he visited Weimar often. In 1938, he paid for a temple to be erected to Nietzsche's memory. In August 1943, he sent his friend Mussolini a specially printed collection of Nietzsche's complete writings. And the Nietzsche Archives reciprocated the attention in its ceremonial presentation to him of Nietzsche's *Stockdegen*.

In the Third Reich, both pre-Nazi and Nazi thinkers were concerned with Nietzsche's thought. Klages, who is a transitional figure, published a work on Nietzsche's psychology.[131] Baeumler studied Nietzsche as philosopher and politician.[132] Nietzsche's appropriation by Nazi thinkers for their own purposes is well known but not well studied.[133] Two exceptions are provided by Lukács and Stackelberg. Lukács devotes a long chapter to Nietzsche as a leading irrationalist in the so-called imperialist period in the context of his lengthy study of the rise of irrationalism from the later Schelling and Kierkegaard to Hitler.[134] For Lukács, fascism is the logical successor of vitalism, which draws the conclusions of the work of Nietzsche and Dilthey.[135] Nietzsche is present in the background in Stackelberg's balanced account of the road from *Volk* theory to Nazism,[136] but he is entirely absent in Cassirer's study of the state.[137]

We have already noted that Nietzsche was widely discussed in Germany starting even before 1900. In his review of sixty years of the Nietzsche discussion, Löwith describes no fewer than twelve important interpretations identified with the names of L. Andreas-Salomé, O. Ewald, G. Simmel, Bertram, Ch. Andler, Klages, A. Baeumler, E. Emmerich, Th. Maulnier, K. Jaspers, L. Giesz, and Heidegger.[138] If we except Giesz, who wrote after this period, in entering into the field of

Nietzsche interpretation Heidegger joined battle with no less than ten rivals, eight of whom wrote in German.

In his lectures, Heidegger was most concerned with the approaches of Jaspers and Baeumler, but for different reasons. Jaspers was an anti-Nazi, an important philosopher, an existentialist whose thought in part resembled Heidegger's, and a personal friend, to whom Heidegger unavailingly turned for support in a time of need. Baeumler was an unoriginal thinker, a Nietzsche specialist, but not a philosophical rival in any real sense. Jaspers reports that C. Schmitt, Heidegger, and Baeumler were three very different professors, each of whom sought to reach the peak of the National Socialist movement.[139] It is known that Baeumler, one of the first professors appointed by the Nazis, was linked to Alfred Rosenberg even before they came to power in National Socialism. Beginning in the summer semester of 1933, Baeumler was Professor for Political Pedagogy in the University of Berlin. Heidegger knew Baeumler well from the Nietzsche discussion. At the beginning of the Third Reich, in 1933, Heidegger collaborated with both Baeumler and Krieck, although in each case, as early as the end of that year or the beginning of the next year the relationship had been transformed into open opposition, even something approaching hate.[140] Baeumler remained close to Rosenberg and National Socialism in general after Heidegger's resignation as rector.

Heidegger's Reading of *The Will to Power*

Heidegger's discussion of Nietzsche is mainly centered on a complex interpretation of *The Will to Power*.[141] This work has come down to us as a series of notes Nietzsche composed in the period 1883–1888. Heidegger's Nietzsche lecture courses present Heidegger's reading of Nietzsche's long-projected, finally unwritten work. The series of lecture courses is composed of two volumes in the version Heidegger worked over for publication,[142] and of four volumes in the English translation of selected portions of the lecture courses, which also incorporates other material.[143] For present purposes, I will rely on the English translation, which I will supplement, as necessary, with references to the reworked, published version and to the original lectures. Heidegger's lecture courses on Nietzsche covered five semesters. At present, only two of the five lecture courses as originally given have been published.[144]

Heidegger indicates his overall aim in a series of programmatic statements in the first volume, containing material from the first lecture course. For Heidegger, Nietzsche is misinterpreted as a poet-philosopher or as a philosopher of life.[145] Like those students of Plato concerned to interpret Plato's thought through his unwritten texts, Heidegger holds that Nietzsche's main philosophical contribution lies in the text he did not write.[146] Heidegger points out that the work was planned over many years but never written; and he further points out that it was intended to name "the basic character of all beings."[147] He regards this book as Nietzsche's chief contribution, the work in which Nietzsche decisively confronts all earlier Western thought. Heidegger believes that the confrontation with Nietzsche has not yet begun and its conditions have not yet even been realized. For Heidegger, then, Nietzsche marks the end of Western metaphysics and the beginning of another question of the truth of Being.[148] He sums up this very large claim about the main doctrines in Nietzsche's position in hyperbolic language and melodramatic fashion:

> Now, if we do not thoughtfully formulate our inquiry in such a way that it is capable of grasping in a unified way the doctrines of the eternal return of the same and will to power, and these two doctrines in their most intrinsic coherence as revaluation, and if we do not go on to comprehend this fundamental formulation as one which is also necessary in the course of Western metaphysics, then we will never grasp Nietzsche's philosophy. And we will comprehend nothing of the twentieth century and of centuries to come, nothing of our own metaphysical task.[149]

This passage does not demonstrate any of Heidegger's claims about Nietzsche's thought. Rather, it deflects attention from Heidegger's specific claims through a gigantic assertion about the importance of Nietzsche's position for philosophy, for history, even for all human being. This passage provides a reaffirmation of Heidegger's pretense, familiar since the rectoral address, to be able to interpret the present and even the future through Nietzsche's metaphysics. Now we have also seen that he makes a similar assertion in his discussion of Hölderlin. Perhaps, then, the basic idea is less the utility of a given body of thought to comprehend all of history, including what is yet to come, than Heidegger's attribution to himself, in his description of his ability to grasp what will yet be, of a clearly prophetic, magical power, supported by no analysis at all, to see into time. The general idea is that a close scrutiny of the writings of a major thinker or poet—and it doesn't seem to matter which it is—is an adequate substitute for a crystal ball in the interpretation of the future.

In the crucial fourth chapter, Heidegger turns to the content of *The Will to Power* in order to demonstrate the claimed unity of Nietzsche's position. This chapter has a dual function in Heidegger's discussion: to present Heidegger's interpretation of what he regards as Nietzsche's crucially important but misunderstood position, and to rule out a supposedly incorrect reading of Nietzsche's view. As the title to the chapter makes clear, Heidegger's own reading is centered on Nietzsche's doctrines of the eternal return of the same and the will to power. He notes that at present the prevalent interpretation does away with the doctrine of the eternal return of the same and, hence, excludes a fruitful grasp of Nietzsche's metaphysics.[150]

Two issues, which arise in the fourth chapter and should immediately be addressed, are Heidegger's unusual approach to the contemporary discussion of Nietzsche's thought and the relation of his interpretation to the Nazi reading of Nietzsche. Heidegger himself introduces the issue of his use of other interpretations. Early in his initial lecture course on Nietzsche, he states that he will not refer to the massive Nietzsche literature since none of it can help his endeavor.[151] We are meant to understand that his own approach is so distinctive as to set aside all other discussion of Nietzsche's thought, which need not be taken into account. This is a version of his conceit, on frequent display in his interpretation of prior philosophical views, that only his own readings are authentic. In place of the secondary literature, he recommends "the courage and perseverance" to read Nietzsche's own writings.[152]

Heidegger's stress on the need to study Nietzsche in preference to writings about Nietzsche is good advice on the premise that in most cases it is preferable to read the original texts rather than the discussion about them. Yet Heidegger's remark is misconstrued as implying that Heidegger in fact abstracted from the Nietzsche literature in the development of his own reading of Nietzsche's thought. His Nietzsche lectures contain occasional remarks on other interpretations; and he unexpectedly devotes a chapter in part to the available Nietzsche literature, with special attention to the writings of Jaspers and Baeumler,[153] which he treats as examples of an incorrect way to understand the doctrine of the eternal return of the same.[154]

The relatively circumspect treatment of Baeumler, an insignificant thinker, is probably due to his status as a well-known Nietzsche specialist, whose general interpretation of *The Will to Power* Heidegger apparently made the basis of his own. Certainly, when Heidegger's lectures were worked over for publication well after the end of the Second World War, Heidegger had nothing more to fear from Baeumler's close connections to the Nazi party.[155] Heidegger objects to Baeumler's interpretation of Nietzsche on three grounds: Baeumler's assertion that the idea of eternal recurrence expresses a personal "religious" conviction; Baeumler's claim that both the doctrines of the eternal return of the same and the will to power cannot be correct on pain of contradiction; and finally the link drawn between the former doctrine and Heraclitus's thought.[156]

In response, Heidegger makes the following points.[157] He denies the correctness of Baeumler's reading of Heraclitus. He uncharacteristically states that even if there is a contradiction, that is merely a demand to think a difficult thought, which cannot therefore be assimilated to religion. And he adds, plausibly in view of Baeumler's role as a professor of political pedagogy, that the latter rejects the importance of the concept of the eternal recurrence for Nietzsche's position on political grounds.[158]

Baeumler's interpretation of Nietzsche is less important than Jaspers's. Jaspers is widely regarded as a significant philosophical thinker, and his reading of Nietzsche's thought, and its relation to Heidegger's, has attracted attention.[159] Heidegger's remarks on Jaspers are briefer, but more pointed.[160] In comparison with Baeumler, Heidegger believes that Jaspers has a better grasp of the function of the idea of the eternal return in Nietzsche's thought. Yet Heidegger complains that Jaspers fails to bring the idea of the eternal recurrence in contact with the grounding question (*Grundfrage*) of Western philosophy, which is Heidegger's basic philosophical concern. Heidegger attributes this failure to Jaspers's view that there is "no truth or conceptual import in philosophy," in effect that philosophy is impossible, which causes him to underestimate the vital importance of Nietzsche's idea.[161] It is, then, interesting to note that Jaspers believed not only that Heidegger did not understand science in his fundamental ontology but that Heidegger's theory was no more than a modern form of gnosticism and of magic.[162]

Jaspers's stature, unlike Baeumler's, as a worthy philosophical adversary explains Heidegger's unease at Jaspers's supposed rejection in general of the possibility of philosophy; it perhaps also explains the unusually sharp remark on Jaspers in a passage omitted from the lectures as reworked for publication, now available in the publication of the original lectures. In a passage in a postface, entitled "The Falsification of Nietzsche's Philosophy up to Now," Heidegger writes: "The greatest falsification—if one finds all and each in his [reading] and makes the 'so well as also' into a principle, and utilizes the whole only as existential clarification [Erhellung] and as 'psychological phenomenon.' Jaspers!"[163]

Heidegger's rapid remarks on Baeumler and Jaspers, and occasional comments on other Nietzsche interpreters,[164] do not constitute an adequate response to the large and varied Nietzsche literature of the time. Heidegger's treatment of the available lines of interpretation is overly selective. On balance, it is obvious that he fails to accord satisfactory attention either to the Nietzsche discussion as a whole—with which he may not have been deeply familiar and which he proposes merely to bracket—or even to the views of Baeumler and Jaspers. Heidegger's account of Jaspers's views of Nietzsche, which he acknowledges as philosophically more significant, is especially brief, schematic, and, hence, unsatisfactory. But the insufficiency of Heidegger's hasty account of Nietzsche readings that he regarded as competing with his own is not due to his inability to discuss matters in more detail. Rather, it is probable that for Heidegger the approaches of Baeumler and Jaspers to Nietzsche were merely instances of the contemporary juggling with "transmitted concepts" which, being uncritical, failed to come to grips with ontology on a fundamental level.[165] Heidegger probably thought that it was sufficient to keep open the possibility of his own, "deeper" interpretation of Nietzsche by calling in question those among the available approaches which tended to close off the lines of inquiry he intended to pursue.

The relation of Heidegger's interpretation of *The Will to Power* to Nazi interpretations of this work is important. It has been suggested that Heidegger's reading of Nietzsche prevented Nietzsche's incorporation into the Nazi pantheon.[166] Yet Heidegger's overall approach to Nietzsche is redolent of the Nazi line, including his preference for *The Will to Power* as the height of Nietzsche's art and his treatment of it as a systematic analysis. According to Walter Kaufmann, the two main false readings of the book are both due to Nietzsche's sister, Elisabeth Förster-Nietzsche: the view that it represents Nietzsche's crowning achievement, prominently represented by Baeumler; and the contrary view that the work is not worth reading at all, due to Karl Schlechta.[167] Baeumler formulates his view succinctly:

> *The Will to Power* is Nietzsche's philosophical *magnum opus*. All the basic results of his thinking are brought together in this book. The aversion of its author against systematizers should not prevent us from calling this work a system. Nietzsche only objected to the artificial, logically conclusive form of spinning out systems [Systembauerei]. For he well knew that all true philosophical thought is internally systematic, namely, it has a creative central point, which defines and supports the whole. Nietzsche is a systematic thinker in this sense as Heraclitus is, or Anaximander, whose systematic spirit we recognize from a single sentence that remains extant.[168]

Heidegger's reading of *The Will to Power* can be regarded as developing Baeumler's approach with respect to his own theory of Being. Since Nietzsche completed five books in his last active year, 1888, and another two in the two immediately preceding years, a case needs to be made that this particular work represents the key to Nietzsche's position.[169] Heidegger not only insists without apparent reason on *The Will to Power* as the peak of Nietzsche's thought, but further appears to adopt a version of the Nazi reading of that work in his approach to Nietzsche. It is, then, difficult to regard Heidegger's Nietzsche interpretation as "saving

Nietzsche from a Nazi distortion," whatever that phrase means, since Heidegger uncritically takes over Baeumler's variant of the Nazi view of *The Will to Power* as the basis of his own.

Heidegger's Nietzsche lectures occur at a crucial moment in his evolution, when he is in the process of making a transition from fundamental ontology to a new version of his position, supposedly beyond philosophy. Heidegger's view is always labile, but particularly so during this period. In virtue of the unstable nature of Heidegger's thought at this time, his attitude toward Nietzsche is deeply ambivalent. As he does for other views, in the lectures Heidegger studies Nietzsche's thought within the context of the history of ontology. For Heidegger, Nietzsche's "system" is the source of a radically new thesis about Being which, in its novelty, returns back behind the tradition to the early Greek thought of Being.

Heidegger's position evolves between *Being and Time* and the lectures on Nietzsche. Yet the modifications—which are reflected in such important intervening texts as the work on Kant or *An Introduction to Metaphysics*—remain, or at least mainly remain, within the overall framework of fundamental ontology. Heidegger's familiar claim that previous thought merely incompletely adumbrates his own, illustrated in his study of Kant, is still present, although to a lesser degree in his lecture course on metaphysics, in such themes as the so-called fault of Being,[170] the unique philosophical status of the Greek and German languages,[171] repetition,[172] grounding,[173] and so on. But there is also a beginning displacement, evident in the emergence of new themes—some of which receive a considerable development in later writings, and which seem to surpass the conceptual armature of fundamental ontology in the direction of something new—such as the uneasy position of Europe between Russia and America,[174] the full unfolding of Nietzsche's thought,[175] and *techne* as neither art nor technology.[176]

In the Nietzsche lectures, Heidegger's position transgresses fundamental ontology, however understood, to something beyond it. Heidegger's view of the importance of an unfolding of Nietzsche's thought dominates his Nietzsche lectures, where Nietzsche functions as a further development of the original thought of Being and as a transition toward a new form of the original thought. These lectures reflect both a residual permanence and an incipient change in Heidegger's position, the coexistence of the original position, as it developed in the interval between its formulation and these lectures, and the transition to another view, closely based on, but different from, its predecessor, toward which Heidegger moves through what, for want of a better word, is a displacement.

Both the continued presence of the original view and the slow transition to the new form of the original theory, or the new theory that will arise out of the original position, are visible in the crucial fourth chapter of the initial lecture series where Heidegger comes to grips with other interpretations and begins to state the outlines of his own reading of Nietzsche's thought. Not surprisingly, since Nietzsche functions here to complete the original framework and to point toward a new one, this chapter can be read from either of two angles of vision: from the philosophical perspective of the history of ontology, or as pointing beyond that history to a new form of thought purportedly beyond philosophy.

Here, Heidegger indicates the link between his reading of Nietzsche and the history of ontology. He begins the chapter by reformulating in other words the statement with which the previous chapter ends, cited above, about the unity of Nietzsche's position and its importance for present times and for the centuries yet to come. For Heidegger, the term "will to power" names what is basic to any being. He then introduces an important distinction between the supposedly first, essential question of philosophy and its final preliminary question (*Vorfrage*). Nietzsche's doctrine, Heidegger says, answers the final preliminary question but not the first, essential question. To ground this assertion, Heidegger maintains that here, at the end of Western philosophy, the decisive query is not the basic character of beings, but that of Being itself, the meaning of Being.

> The expression "will to power" designates the basic character of beings; any being which is, insofar as it is, is will to power. The expression stipulates the character that beings have as beings. But that is not at all an answer to the first question of philosophy, its proper question; rather, it answers only the final preliminary question. For anyone who at the end of Western philosophy can and must still question philosophically, the decisive question is no longer merely "What basic character do beings manifest?" but "What is this 'Being' itself?" The decisive question is that of "the meaning of Being," not merely that of the Being of beings.[177]

This passage is helpful to an appreciation of the later development of the Nietzsche lectures and their significance for Heidegger's thought. It is evident from the distinction between the first essential question and the final preliminary question that Heidegger is continuing to operate within the wider context of the fundamental ontology developed in *Being and Time*. Heidegger signals his intention here to demonstrate the unity of Nietzsche's thought through an appropriate reading of its basic concepts, precisely that unity which he has claimed but not so far demonstrated. At this point he further advances a thesis not present in *Being and Time* in his observation that we have now arrived at the end of Western philosophy. This new thesis is not a change in the basic position;

it is rather a description of the philosophical tradition as a whole from the perspective of fundamental ontology, whose consequences have now become clearer to Heidegger in his reflection on the position developed in *Being and Time.* In restating the view advanced in his fundamental ontology according to which the important question is not the nature of beings but the meaning of Being in general, he associates Nietzsche with his basic question. The result is to call attention to a relation between fundamental ontology and Nietzsche's position which was not present, or at least not clearly present, in *Being and Time,* and which has perhaps only become apparent to Heidegger in the years after he composed this book. Heidegger now depicts Nietzsche as responding not to the question itself but to a condition for its response, which, in turn, opens the way to a possible response to the basic question of all philosophy, a response that has supposedly become possible only now at the end of the Western philosophical tradition.

The history of ontology belongs to a negative approach to the previous discussion of metaphysics intended to free the ground for a positive appropriation of a hidden insight from early Greek thought. The justification of the negative moment of the projected destruction of ontology was to make possible a positive reappropriation of ancient doctrine, which has been covered up in the subsequent but erroneous discussion of Being. In principle, Nietzsche belongs to this discussion as the author of a theory of Being that must be taken into account in any effort to destroy the history of ontology. Since Nietzsche's most important contribution to this history occurs in a book that was never written, Heidegger's effort to destroy the history of ontology requires him to treat as history, and hence in the past, something which literally never took place. In that sense, his discussion is nothing more than a mythical interpretation of a mythical treatise.

From within the perspective of fundamental ontology, and through the interpretation of Nietzsche's unfinished, in fact unwritten, study, a putative masterpiece, Heidegger sees Nietzsche's key contribution to the history of ontology as the conception of the will to power. He insists that Nietzsche's other interpreters, say, Baeumler and Jaspers, have not grasped the importance of this doctrine. For Heidegger, Nietzsche's doctrine is a definitive response to the question of the being of beings as beings. Since Heidegger interprets "will to power" as meaning "the eternal recurrence of the same,"[178] he objects to the reading of this concept presupposed in the usual association of Nietzsche with Heraclitus.

As a view of the being of beings as beings, Nietzsche's conception of ontology addresses a specific issue which, for that reason, does not respond to Heidegger's own, more general concern with the meaning of Being. A concern with truth occupies an increasingly central position in

Heidegger's later thought, including the *Beiträge*. He states that "meaning" is what makes it possible that "Being in general can become manifest as such and can come into truth."[179] But Nietzsche's view must not be ignored, since it is essential to respond to the question of Being preceding the question with which Heidegger is concerned, and so make an answer to the latter question possible. Even if Nietzsche's ontological view falls short of Heidegger's, for Heidegger it nonetheless surpasses all other views, which he stigmatizes collectively as a mere playing with concepts. "What is proffered today as ontology has nothing to do with the question of Being proper; it is a very learned and very astute analysis of transmitted concepts which plays them off, one against the other."[180]

Heidegger argues for the importance of Nietzsche's thought of Being against the background of Western philosophy. In reference to Heraclitus, he maintains that becoming is grounded in Being. According to Heidegger, through the idea of eternal recurrence Nietzsche returns behind the later tradition to the Greek beginnings of Western thought. He believes that Nietzsche takes up the beginnings of Western philosophy in the customary manner, despite his otherwise original grasp of pre-Socratic thought. Nietzsche's view is revolutionary, Heidegger maintains, not because it overturns another, but rather because it uncovers what has previously been covered up. Heidegger now attributes to Nietzsche the thought of the essence of time.

> Thinking Being, will to power, as eternal return, means thinking Being as Time. Nietzsche thinks that thought but does not think it as the *question* of Being and Time. Plato and Aristotle also think that thought when they conceive Being as *ousia* (presence), but just as little as Nietzsche do they think it as a question.[181]

Heidegger's discussion of Nietzsche's ontological view collapses an important distinction, which Heidegger apparently overlooks. There is a difference between thinking the being of beings as beings as the will to power and the thought of Being as time. For Heidegger, the view of the being of beings as beings as the will to power is a usual but mistaken approach to ontology repeated erroneously throughout the metaphysical tradition. On the contrary, the thought of Being as time is the view which Heidegger opposes to the metaphysical tradition, and which he wants to recover in pre-Socratic thought. It is the view which he prepares in the entire second division of *Being and Time* and to which he alludes in later writings. His view of the relation of time to Being is clearly expressed at the outset of his lengthy account of "Dasein and Temporality": "Within the horizon of time the projection of a meaning of Being in general can be accomplished."[182]

Heidegger reads the "idea of the will to power as eternal recurrence" to mean the "inner character of beings, that is, the basic character of anything insofar as it is," what he refers to as the "final preliminary question," and as "the idea of Being as time." The latter is, of course, an idea which Heidegger also "finds" in Plato and Aristotle, and which Nietzsche "rediscovers." For Heidegger, the idea of Being as time is no longer that of the final preliminary question. This idea, hence, goes beyond beings as beings to address at least implicitly the question of the meaning of Being—not, as Heidegger says, to the book in which this question is raised, but to its question.

In sum, Nietzsche's thought of Being is important for Heidegger's concern with the history of ontology for at least four reasons. First, it provides the definitive account of the being of beings as beings. Second, it raises the thought of Being as time. Third, it points to the problem that occupies Heidegger in *Being and Time* and in all his subsequent writings, to which he alludes here in terms of the question of the meaning of Being. Fourth, it closes the circle of the ontological tradition in returning to the early idea of being which was later covered up and which Nietzsche helps to uncover through his metaphysical revolution. In a word, with respect to the history of ontology, Nietzsche stands out as "destroying" the received approach. He offers a different view that "solves" the final preliminary question and calls attention to, but does not pose, the basic question. Nietzsche's thought of being differs from the views of previous thinkers, such as Descartes, Kant, and even Hegel, thinkers whom Heidegger regards as having dogmatically repeated the usual but erroneous view of being, which they fail to examine and merely restate. Only Nietzsche opens the way to a new thought of being, which Heidegger regards as a very old thought present in early Greek philosophy.

We have reviewed the way in which Heidegger considers Nietzsche's thought of being, against the history of ontology, within the framework of fundamental ontology. But we can also read the same passage, from a different angle of vision, as opening the way, through study of Nietzsche's thought, to a version of Heidegger's position lying beyond fundamental ontology. This reading is suggested by Hcidcggcr in many places in his lectures on Nietzsche, for instance in an appendix to the first volume of the lectures, added in May 1937 but not taken up in the version reworked for publication. Here, in a comment on Nietzsche as a transitional figure, he notes that the transition leads to a new beginning: "A transition [Ein Übergang], the transitions [Übergänge] introduce a second beginning."[183] Heidegger further brings in a number of distinctions discussed in detail in the *Beiträge,* at which he was at work from 1936 to 1938, that is, during the period of the Nietzsche lectures, including the concepts of *Grundfrage* and *Leitfrage, Gefüge,* and so on, all of which relate to his conception of the other beginning.[184]

This passage in the fourth chapter offers a series of hints that separately and together point to the way in which Heidegger made use of his Nietzsche lectures in the evolution of his position beyond its original formulation and subsequent development to another, later form. So against the view that a revolutionary merely destroys, Heidegger maintains that as a revolutionary Nietzsche reveals what lay concealed. With respect to Nietzsche's activity, he writes: "But what is essential in the revolutionary is not the overturning [Umwendung] as such; it is rather that in overturning he brings to light what is decisive and essential."[185] The fruit of Nietzsche's revolutionary activity is his thought of being, namely, his thought of being as time. But like Plato and Aristotle, who also had this thought, Nietzsche failed to think it as the question of Being and time, that is, he failed to anticipate Heidegger's thought.[186]

This characterization of Nietzsche as a philosophical revolutionary who does not merely destroy is as interesting for what it does not say as for what it says. Unlike his remarks on Descartes, Kant, and all other modern thinkers, Heidegger does not depict Nietzsche as someone who simply perpetuates a traditional but erroneous view of being. In Heidegger's remarks, Nietzsche is promoted to the level of the twin pillars of the Greek tradition, outshining all other thinkers in modern philosophy, whose thought dogmatically continues what since the time of the Greeks has no longer been thought. Nietzsche's limitation is that he fails to question what calls for a question, namely the view of Being as time. In that sense, despite the positive import of his philosophical revolution, like Plato, Aristotle, and all others he falls below the level of *Being and Time.*

Heidegger is convinced that despite the limitations of Nietzsche's system, Nietzsche's thought of being is decisive and necessary. Since Heidegger collaborated with others on the critical edition in order to improve on the available versions of Nietzsche's texts, we know that he was not satisfied with the editions already available. He correctly points out that we cannot know how Nietzsche would have modified the work we possess had he been able to complete it. He further maintains that we possess the presuppositions to think Nietzsche's authentic philosophical thought.[187] Once again, Heidegger distinguishes between a so-called genuine interpreter and the crowd of uninformed readers, in practice all others who are supposedly unable to grasp Nietzsche's authentic philosophical thought (*Nietzsches eigentliches philosophisches Denken*), or at least are unable really to think it.

How is one to think Nietzsche's thought? For Heidegger, it is not sufficient merely to follow the aphorisms in the order in which they are disposed, since, as he concedes, the order is arbitrary; this is only possible by thinking through the movement of the thought of the questioning of the authentic questioning (*Denkbewegung des Fragens der eigentlichen Fragen heraus*). In this way Heidegger promises to accomplish two crucially important tasks. First, he intends to hear Nietzsche himself, something which, he implies, no one else has so far been able to do. This implication follows from the conjunction of a pair of claims already mentioned: that with respect to ontology Nietzsche towers above anyone else since Plato and Aristotle, and that contemporary ontological thought is quite literally worthless. Second, Heidegger does not merely want to hear Nietzsche. For he does not intend merely to receive another position in passive fashion, even that of Nietzsche; and his goal is not to learn the nature of Nietzsche's thought for itself. Rather, he wants to hear Nietzsche's thought of being in a critical way in virtue of his own conviction that it is essential to Western philosophy. "Still, in all this what remains decisive is to hear Nietzsche himself; to inquire with him and through him *and therefore at the same time against him,* but *for* the one single innermost matter that is common to Western philosophy."[188]

Nietzsche's thought enabled Heidegger to progress beyond his own initial view in a later development which is more than another form of fundamental ontology. The result, paradoxically, is not to go beyond metaphysics to nonmetaphysics, since Heidegger cannot abandon metaphysics in his abandonment of philosophy.[189] If he did, then he would have to admit the nonphilosophical status of early Greek thought, whose importance never changes in his eyes. Like Kant, who desired to leave behind bad metaphysics at the same time as he specified the condition of metaphysics to come as a science,[190] Heidegger intends to throw off the bad metaphysics which he sees as pervading the Platonic tradition, and philosophy itself, which he identifies with bad metaphysics, in order, finally, to build correctly on pre-Socratic thought to grasp Being as such in what can only be authentic metaphysics.

Heidegger's and Nietzsche's respective contributions can be assessed in terms of what Heidegger here refers to as the innermost matter (*innerste Sache*) of Western philosophy. Heidegger insists that Nietzsche ends metaphysics, and attributes to him a special status as the last metaphysical thinker. Yet he explicitly denies that Nietzsche fulfills metaphysics, for instance by bringing it to a close or successfully completing the metaphysical quest.[191] To see this point, to comprehend that with Nietzsche the metaphysical discussion has in a sense come to a limit, is to move beyond that limit and toward the completion of metaphysics. But to do so is also to move beyond the position of *Being and Time* where, depending on one's reading of this text, Nietzsche was either absent or not explicitly appreciated. Since Nietzsche brings this philosophical movement to an end, since his thought stands at the outer reaches of Western metaphysics, it also stands beyond it as a theory that points beyond the limits and indicates the direction to be taken.

The shift in Heidegger's position enabling him to grasp the dimensions of Nietzsche's contribution is an integral part of the evolution of his own thought. Heidegger regards his own contribution to Nietzsche scholarship as twofold. On the one hand, we have noted that Heidegger literally believes that unlike others he can not only listen to but even hear Nietzsche.[192] This mystical faith in his own hermeneutic capacity should be illustrated by his capacity to think through Nietzsche's problem, which is not the same as simply reading the aphorisms. In that sense, Heidegger means to suggest that he understands not only the letter but the spirit of a position which has so far escaped its other readers. But there is no basis to evaluate Heidegger's claim to be the authentic interpreter of Nietzsche's thought, and it is even unclear—just as it is unclear in respect to Kant's position—what an authentic reading would look like.

On the other hand, Heidegger holds that he can and must continue the process of unfolding Nietzsche's thought beyond the point at which Nietzsche left it, by thinking it through with and against Nietzsche in order to unfold it against its letter, even against Nietzsche's understanding of its spirit. In the same way as Hegel believed that he could think Kant's revolution in philosophy through to the end and complete the Platonic tradition, Heidegger believes that he can think Nietzsche's system through to the end and complete the pre-Platonic thought of Being beyond Platonism in order to respond to the innermost philosophical task. In this respect, there is an exact analogy between Hegel's dependence on Kant and that of Heidegger on Nietzsche: in both cases the former desired to complete the latter's position in a way perhaps foreign to its spirit, and certainly foreign to its letter, but without which it cannot be grasped and could not initially have been formulated.

The impact of Nietzsche on Heidegger's thought is not exhausted by the Nietzsche lectures. Heidegger's later thought continues to unfold his perceptions of the consequences of Nietzsche's position, as he reads it, in the effort to move decisively beyond the Western tradition in the authentic thought of Being. In this effort, Heidegger depicts Nietzsche from two angles of vision: as one who closes the Western discussion of metaphysics by returning to an earlier view, and as one who in the closing opens another era of authentic ontology.[193] Through the dialogue with Nietzsche in his later thought, Heidegger extends his initial rejection of modern philosophy to englobe Platonism in all its forms and, to the extent that fundamental ontology is insufficiently radical, his own earlier thought as well.

A measure of the change in Heidegger's position with respect to his earlier writings lies in the various themes he studies in his discussion of Nietzsche's thought. Often these are themes not present in his earlier writings, or not present in the same way, or which take on a different role in later writings. These themes, which Heidegger in every case associates with Nietzsche, include the will to power, the eternal return of the same, and revaluation—the three basic ideas Heidegger identifies in Nietzsche's thought—as well as nihilism and the reversal, or turning. The result is a change of emphasis and, in at least one case, that of the turning, the emergence of an important new idea.

Further Discussion of Heidegger's Nietzsche Lectures

Heidegger's views of Nietzsche have attracted attention in a specialized literature. As in the case of any original text, it is difficult, perhaps not possible, to provide more than an incomplete idea in a summary.[194] Since we are concerned here with Heidegger's Nazism, a few very brief remarks will suffice to delineate some main themes of his lectures on Nietzsche.[195]

We have already noted that early in the initial lecture series Heidegger twice asserts the unity of Nietzsche's basic concepts of the eternal return of the same and the will to power in the transvaluation (*Umwertung*) of all previous values. The first volume is divided into three large discussions concerning "The Will to Power as Art," "The Eternal Return of the Same," and "The Will to Power as Knowledge." In the account of "The Will to Power as Art" Heidegger brings together his interest in the link between art and truth and his concern with Nietzsche's position.[196] He presents Nietzsche's view as an inverted Platonism, culminating in a relation between the will to power as art, and as a way to understand the unity of Being and becoming.

> Art as will to semblance is the supreme configuration of will to power. But the latter, as the basic character of beings, as the essence of reality, is in itself that Bcing which wills itself by willing to be Becoming. In that way through the will to power Nietzsche attempts to think the original unity of the ancient opposition of Being and Becoming. Being, as permanence, is to let Becoming be a Becoming. The origin of the thought of "eternal recurrence" is thereby indicated.[197]

Heidegger regards the eternal return of the same, which he discusses in a lengthy section, as Nietzsche's basic metaphysical position. He sees this concept as a confrontation with the Platonic-Christian mode of thought characeric of the Western tradition. The discussion culminates in three points. First, Nietzsche's idea constitutes the end of metaphysics.[198] Second, Nietzsche's effort to eliminate the fundamentally Platonic position through its inversion in his own system fails, and in fact confirms Platonism.[199] Third, Nietzsche's failure, at the end of metaphysics, to go beyond it can function as the opening to transcending it if we adopt a questioning attitude toward his guiding question: what is Being?[200] In other words, we can use Nietzsche's effort to transcend Western thought, by thinking with him and against him, to carry out what he meant to accomplish.

The account of "The Will to Power as Knowledge" occupies the last part of the first volume. Here, from the vantage point of his view of Nietzsche as the last metaphysical thinker, Heidegger explores Nietzsche's idea of truth as an "illusion." He interprets Nietzsche's doctrine of the return as pointing to a view of truth based on value, related to correctness.[201] In the same way as he refused to accept Nazi biologism, Heidegger refuses the appellation of "biologism" for Nietzsche's thought,[202] although he maintains that in Nietzsche's system correctness refers ultimately to life itself.[203] From an epistemological point of view, Heidegger regards Nietzsche as favoring permanence over change in the idea of the eternal return of the same, which finally refers to life.[204]

The second volume contains seven smaller accounts of the "The Eternal Return of the Same and the Will to Power," "European Nihilism," "Nietzsche's Metaphysics," "The Ontological-Historical Definition of Nihilism," "Metaphysics as the History of Being," "Sketches of the History of Being as Metaphysics," and "Memory in Metaphysics." The most important passage, which takes up roughly half of the second volume, concerns the topic of European nihilism.[205] Heidegger's discussion here of nihilism is neither unprecedented nor even unusual. To the best of my knowledge, this theme is not discussed in his corpus, or at least not discussed under that title, prior to the Nietzsche lectures. But nihilism was a frequent topic in the German-language discussion of the period.[206] The theme is further anticipated in Heidegger's earlier writings under the heading of nothing (*das Nichts*).

The idea of nothing is discussed by Heidegger in several early texts. In *Being and Time,* in a remark on authenticity and inauthenticity Heidegger describes inauthenticity as not nothing but as average;[207] and in a later passage, he states that nothing functions as that in the face of which we are anxious.[208] Here, nothing is related to value, as values that can be realized in authentic comportment, that can fail to be realized in inauthenticity, and that can be definitively lost in death. Heidegger brings out another dimension of nothing in "What Is Metaphysics?" by reemphasizing the relation to human being and adding an explicit link to

metaphysics. In the inaugural lecture, nothing, which science has supposedly failed to analyze, becomes an explicit theme. According to Heidegger, "Da-sein" literally means "being held out into the nothing."[209] Nothing here is presented as transcendence, or the Being beyond beings, as
the nihilation of nothing that is human being.[210] Heidegger goes on to
claim that when we reflect on nothing, it leads to the metaphysical
question of the meaning of Being.[211]

Heidegger's discussion of nothing continues his earlier reflections on
this theme. In *Being and Time,* he was concerned with the individual and
with falling as a basic kind of being that belongs to everydayness, or
inauthentic Dasein. A similar concern is visible in the rectoral address,
where Heidegger mentions Nietzsche's statement that God is dead and
asks about the consequences for science in the Greek sense given the
abandonment of today's man in the midst of beings.[212] In the Nietzsche
lectures, he provides a historical interpretation of Nietzsche's view as a
determination of a fall away from Being as such. He further refers to a
passage in *Being and Time,* in which falling is described relative to the
potentiality for being-in-the-world.[213]

In *An Introduction to Metaphysics,* Heidegger brings together his
prior analyses of nothing in relation to value and metaphysics in an
explicit meditation on history from Nietzsche's perspective. He now
provides what can only be regarded as a mythical explanation of the
source of fallenness through an equally mythical happening. In an important passage, which largely anticipates the discussion of nihilism in the
Nietzsche lectures, he writes:

> And should we not say that the fault did not begin with us, or with our
> immediate or more remote ancestors, but lies in something that runs
> through Western history from the very beginning, a happening [ein
> Geschehnis] which the eyes of all the historians in the world will never
> perceive, but which nevertheless happens, which happened in the past and
> will happen in the future? What if it were possible that man, that nations
> in the greatest movements and traditions, are linked to Being and yet had
> long fallen out of Being, without knowing it, and that this was the most
> powerful and most central cause of their decline?[214]

In comparison with earlier discussion of this theme, the account in the
course on metaphysics differs in the dual emphasis on an event linking
metaphysics to history and on a grasp of that event in respect to Nietzsche's thought. Nietzsche is said to be important in that he alone has
grasped the fall away from Being which supposedly determines all of
Western history and which is now manifested in the decline due to the
fall out of Being. This same decline is visible in Europe's being pinched
between Russia and America, in the rise of modern technology, and in

the spiritual decline affecting Germany, that most metaphysical of nations, which needs to realize its vocation through an authentic renewal
of the fundamental question of metaphysics.[215] Once again, Heidegger is
merely stating his obviously mystical belief in the salvific power of a
renewal of philosophy for the future history of the world.

Heidegger believes that the importance of Nietzsche's insight into
history goes beyond merely getting metaphysics right after several thousand years. This new understanding means that we can now make another beginning, a beginning beyond the old beginning which will not
merely be a continuation of what has previously occurred. "To ask:
'How does it stand with being?' means nothing less than to capture, to
repeat, the beginning of our historical-spiritual existence, in order to
transform it into the other beginning."[216] All of these themes, including
metaphysics, technology, modernity, are now decisively linked by Heidegger to his understanding of the unfolding of Nietzsche's thought with
respect to the decisive event described as the fall away from Being.

The discussion of nihilism in the lectures on Nietzsche records Heidegger's effort, in a lectures series given in 1940, to come to grips with the
fall away from Being. In comparison with his earlier writings, his Nietzsche lectures innovate through a detailed study of Nietzsche's grasp of
this so far unnamed but fateful event, the introduction of a partially
novel terminology to refer to the event and its consequences, and the
statement in allusive fashion of the outlines of the position he began to
develop in the *Beiträge* in the period immediately preceding this lecture
course.

The term "nihilism" occurs in previous writers, but Heidegger believes that Nietzsche uses it in a different way to designate a phenomenon he was the first to identify. For Heidegger, Nietzsche concentrates
the meaning of the concept in the statement "God is dead," interpreted
as the loss by the "Christian God," or the "transcendent" in general, of
any meaning for beings and for human being.

> Nietzsche uses nihilism as the name for the historical movement that he
> was the first to recognize and that already governed the previous century
> while defining the century to come, the movement whose essential inter-
> pretation he concentrates in the terse sentence "God is dead." That is to
> say, the "Christian God" has lost His position over beings and over the
> determination of man.[217]

Heidegger now argues for a connection between an ongoing event in
which the transcendent loses its sway and the history of ontology. If
Nietzsche's metaphysics is the fulfillment of Western metaphysics, then
we can only confront the former if we confront the latter.[218] In *Being and*

Time, the history of ontology was the series of incorrect views which, through their dogmatic reproduction, continue to dominate the metaphysical tradition deprived of access to the original Greek insight into Being. Here, the history of ontology is revealed as coextensive with the ongoing process of the loss of transcendence symbolized by the death of the "Christian God."

> Nihilism is that historical process whereby the dominance of the "transcendent" becomes null and void, so that all being loses its worth and meaning. Nihilism is the history of being itself, through which the death of the Christian God comes slowly but inexorably to light. In his recognition of the ongoing process of nihilism, the history of being, and metaphysics itself, has come to an end.[219]

But since history continues, the task at present is to reflect on the significance of the end of metaphysics as symbolized by the statement of the death of God.

> The end of metaphysics discloses itself as the collapse of the reign of the transcendent and the "ideal" that sprang from it. But the end of metaphysics does not mean the cessation of history. It is the beginning of a serious concern with that "event" [Ereignis]: "God is dead."[220]

Heidegger makes a number of further points to indicate the significance of nihilism for his own thought. His remarks on Nietzsche's relation to Descartes reflect an acute embarassment. This is an illustration of Heidegger's arbitrary, often violent reading of views in the philosophical tradition to follow his prior explanatory framework instead of adapting his framework to the views. Since Heidegger's view of Being depends on the rejection of Descartes, in virtue of his conviction of Nietzsche's importance it cannot be that Nietzsche accepts the Cartesian philosophy. Heidegger provides a strained, unconvincing effort to demonstrate that Nietzsche only seems to accept the Cartesian theory since he fails to grasp it. Although Heidegger concedes that Nietzsche adopts Descartes's fundamental philosophical position,[221] that Nietzsche is in fact admittedly rigorously committed to the Cartesian concept of subjectivity,[222] Heidegger nevertheless maintains that Nietzsche holds a different view,[223] since Nietzsche misunderstands the relation of his own view to the Cartesian view.[224]

Heidegger ends his discussion of nihilism with a reaffirmation of the significance of Nietzsche's insight. As in the rectoral address, he maintains that Nietzsche's metaphysical view is insightful for the present historical period. Heidegger here attempts a transition from the thought of Being to a characterization of social being. Unlike Sartre, who held that Marxism is the philosophy of our time, Heidegger believes that this age is defined by Nietzsche's metaphysics.[225] The leading characteristic of this period is an indifference to the true thought of Being, which has given way to a worldview (*Weltananschauung*) concerned with beings as opposed to Being, the decline of metaphysics in the legitimate sense of the term, and the increasing dominion over beings.

In Heidegger's terminology, "worldview" is antithetical to metaphysics in the true sense since through the conjunction of ideas and values the essence of Being, even the distinction between Being and beings, has been lost. For Heidegger, contemporary metaphysics has become a meaningless echo of true metaphysics. The rise of the dominion over beings has only been rendered possible by the emergence of the concept of the worldview at the end of metaphysics. But this result is not due to human being; rather, according to Heidegger it is due to Being itself, which is the cause of the history of being and, as a result, of human history. In the last paragraph, Heidegger writes:

> The age of the fulfillment of metaphysics—which we descry when we think through the basic features of Nietzsche's metaphysics—prompts us to consider to what extent we first find ourselves in the history of being. It also prompts us to consider—prior to this—the extent to which we must experience history as the release [Loslassung] of being into machination [Machenschaft], a release that Being itself sends, so as to allow its truth to become essential for man out of man's belonging to Being.[226]

Heidegger's Nietzsche Lectures and the Turning (*Kehre*)

Heidegger's stress on the historical importance of a mythical withdrawal of Being provides insight into two further themes: the relation of the Nietzsche lectures to the *Beiträge,* and the important but obscure concept of the turning in his thought. The central concept of the *Beiträge* is the concept of the event (*Ereignis*). Now the German language has a number of words which mean "event," including *"Erlebnis," "Geschehnis,"* and *"Ereignis."* It has been suggested that in writings prior to the first series of Nietzsche lectures, Heidegger routinely employs the word *"Geschehnis"* to refer the so-called crucial event of Western history.[227] In the crucial passage in the discussion of metaphysics, cited above, in both the published version and in the original lecture course Heidegger uses the word *"Geschehnis"* to designate the event which Nietzsche was allegedly the first to perceive,[228] whereas in parallel passages referring to the "death of God" in the rewritten and original lecture versions of the Nietzsche course he employs the term *"Ere-*

ignis."[229] In writings after this period, he consistently reserves "*Ereignis*" to designate the particular historical event and he utilizes "*Geschehnis*" to refer indiscriminately to other events.

Heidegger's change in terminological emphasis is accompanied by a conceptual alteration of his position, which undergoes a transformation or deepening, but not a rupture, in the so-called turning in his thought. After a passing reference in the "Letter on Humanism," the difficult concept of the turning (*Kehre*) came to dominate discussion of the relation between the earlier and later phases of Heidegger's thought.[230] The concept of a turning is well-known in German thought, for instance in Marx's obscure suggestion that his own theory can be regarded as the inversion (*Umkehrung*) of Hegel's idealism.[231] Marx's suggestion, which has been seen as fundamental to an interpretation of his position by generations of students, implies that his position grows out of a fundamental transformation of, but not a break with, Hegel's position. Heidegger employs the concept of the turning in order to suggest an analogous transformation in his view, whose later form develops in a fundamentally new way, but does not fully leave behind, his earlier thought. In a comment on *Being and Time,* Heidegger remarks that his standpoint is not changed, but deepened;[232] and in another comment on Sartre he remarks that the latter reverses or inverts (*umkehrt*) the traditional order in the relation of essence and existence.[233]

The German language is particularly rich in etymologically related terms to express the idea of turning and related concepts. There is a clear etymological link between "*Kehre*" and "*Umkehrung*" through "*Umkehr.*" "*Umkehrung*" can be rendered as "overturning," "reversal," "conversion," or "inversion," whereas "*Kehre*" means a "turn" or "bend." Both are further related to "*Umdrehung,*" that is, "turning" or "revolution." In the first series of Nietzsche lectures, Heidegger mentions the idea of an *Umkehrung* in a number of places, in particular the early chapter on *The Will to Power* and in a later chapter concerning truth in Platonism and positivism.[234] In the former, Heidegger describes Nietzsche's nihilism as a countermovement to nihilism within nihilism. Nietzsche's procedure, he maintains, is a constant reversal (*ständiges Umkehren*).[235] In the discussion of Nietzsche's philosophy as an *Umkehrung* of Platonism, he remarks on the need to change the order so that the *Umdrehung,* or turning around, will become a *Herausdrehung* from Platonism, or twisting free.[236] But a turning (*Drehung*) is not necessarily a reversal (*Umkehrung*), as he later reminds us; it can rather be a kind of penetration (*Eindrehen*).[237]

Heidegger thinks of Nietzsche as attempting a turning within nihilism in order to overturn and go beyond Platonism. It is, then, reasonable to see in this concept an earlier version of Heidegger's own later effort, through a turning, to progress beyond his own earlier thought, Nietzsche, Platonism, and metaphysics.[238] Both the idea and the date of the turning are controversial. It is possible that there is not a single turning, an isolated event, but rather several turnings, or types of turning, in Heidegger's thought. This way of reading the turning is plausible since even the most labile positions do not change suddenly or in discontinuous fashion, but rather undergo shifts in emphasis over time. If this is the case, then the term "turning" does not designate a single event, such as a sudden shift or a break, but rather refers to the process of the evolution of Heidegger's position from the original phenomenological ontology, with its stress on a transcendental analysis of the problem of Being in terms of Dasein, to a later, nontranscendental analysis of this problem which no longer depends on Dasein.

It is unclear why the turning, or turnings, took place. The process may have been set in motion by a renewed encounter with Nietzsche, more precisely through the growing awareness, which can be traced through the texts, of the importance of the idea manifested in the slogan "God is dead," which finally gives rise to the extensive meditation on nihilism. If we accept this hypothesis, then we can plausibly understand the turning as a number of related elements in Heidegger's position arising out of his meditation on the supposed withdrawal of Being, through Nietzsche's insight, over a period of years beginning no later than the early 1930s.[239]

One precipitating factor seems to have been Heidegger's later realization that later philosophy did not simply fall away from Being, leading to the emergence of an inauthentic metaphysics. There is, hence, a reversal in Heidegger's understanding of the concept of falling, which in *Being and Time* was ascribed to Dasein's inauthenticity, or failure to choose itself authentically, but which is later ascribed to the mythical event in which Being withdraws. If this is the case, then the turning in Heidegger's thought represents his effort to think what is no longer, or at least no longer primarily, a suppposed infidelity to Being, but what he later comes to see merely as the hand that Being has dealt us.

In general, we can discern at least the following features as constitutive of the turning in his thought. First, there is a turn away from Dasein to Being, since Being, not Dasein, is the source of its own occultation. This explains the eclipse of Dasein, or the analysis of Dasein, and the later disinterest in authenticity, elements that are no longer relevant to the thought of Being. Second, there is the new focus on the loss of the thought of Being as an event due to Being itself. Although *Being and Time* pointed toward the thought of Being as time, it turns out that the problem of the meaning of Being needed to be rethought in terms of an initial event which, in a sense, creates the problem. Third, there is a turn to Nietzsche since he alone, on Heidegger's view, has recognized the primordial event which since the beginning determines Western history and Western metaphysics. This explains the realignment of Heidegger's fundamental ontology after 1935, perhaps even before, as an attempt to unroll the consequences of Nietzsche's thought of Being. Fourth, there is a decision to deepen the earlier approach, which is no longer tenable, or at least not tenable as originally understood. When Heidegger says that we need to recapture or to repeat the beginning of our historical epoch in order to transform it into another beginning, it is significant that he characterizes such repetition as "anything but an improved continuation with the old methods of what has been up to now."[240] In this sense, the celebrated turning, or the turn to another beginning, represents an effort to push the questioning back to a deeper level, to begin again on a prior remove, finally once and for all to make a true beginning. It is the desire to make a deeper, truer, in fact finally true beginning which is manifest in the detailed effort in the *Beiträge* to think another beginning from the perspective of the so-called event.

Fifth, there is a political turn that does not precede but follows from the turning in Heidegger's thought. In the lecture course on metaphysics, after he resigned as rector and severed his official connection to National Socialism, Heidegger repeats his call to follow the political lead of metaphysics in order to undo, if not for the world, at least with respect to Germany, the ravages supposedly wrought by the withdrawal of Being in the mythical event. His effort to lead the leaders is, and is seen by him as, an attempt to seize the propitious moment in which this supposedly most metaphysical nation can arrest its decline and assume its historical destiny. Heidegger reemphasizes this point in his statement of the necessity for Germany to act on behalf of itself and the history of the West in order to avoid catastrophe through decisive action.

> All this implies that this nation, as a historical nation, must move itself and thereby the history of the West beyond the center of their future happening [Geschehens] and into the primordial realm of the power of Being. If the great decision [Entscheidung] regarding Europe is not to bring annihilation, that decision must be made in terms of new spiritual energies unfolding historically from out of the center.[241]

Yet this statement after the rectoral period does not record a new or even a substantially different conviction; rather it restates in almost equivalent language a familiar view, a muted echo of the essential message of the rectoral addresss, a conviction Heidegger continues to hold, and which he expressed in his speech noting the importance of Nietzsche's slogan "God is dead" and calling for the realization of German destiny. There is an obvious continuity between Heidegger's claim in the rectoral address to lead the leaders, to realize the ends which he shares with Nazism, and the statement in the lectures on metaphysics of the need for decisive action to realize German destiny. In both cases, the call for action, for the translation of metaphysics into politics, follows from a turning in Heidegger's thought based on his reading of Nietzsche's slogan.

The Nietzsche Lectures and Nazism

The turning in Heidegger's thought was not a single event, but a series of transformations of which he only later became aware. Among the turnings, there is Heidegger's political turning, on the basis of his understanding of metaphysics, to National Socialism. But perhaps there is also another turning, or at least another part to the turning, such as a turning against National Socialism? The view that Heidegger later turned against Nazism has often been expressed by Heidegger and his followers. In a remark on his lecture course from 1944/45, Heidegger states that his Nietzsche lectures were a confrontation with Nazism. In reference to his lectures on "Poetizing and Thinking," he writes: "This was in a certain sense a continuation of my Nietzsche lectures, that is to say, a confrontation [Auseinandersetzung] with National Socialism."[242]

The view that Heidegger later turned against the "movement" is widely accepted by Heidegger's followers. For instance, Arendt locates a turn against Nazism between the first and second volume of the Nietzsche lectures, in which Heidegger purportedly comes to grips with "his brief past in the Nazi movement."[243] Aubenque affirms that in 1935 Heidegger tried to save an internal truth of National Socialism but that beginning in 1936 in the Nietzsche lectures he rejected Nazism as a possibility.[244] Krell states imprecisely that in lectures and seminars after 1934 Heidegger began to criticize the Nazi ideology of *Blut und Boden* more and more openly.[245] For Vietta, Heidegger's analysis of Nietzsche's view of nihilism constitutes a recognition of the intrinsic nihilism of Nazism.[246]

In order to determine whether Heidegger confronted National Socialism in his Nietzsche lecture series, it is useful to note some of the differences between the lectures from this period as given and as prepared by Heidegger for publication. Examination of the text shows that in the published versions Heidegger sought to conceal his reliance on Nietzsche's concept of nihilism in order to draw political conclusions. So in the lectures on Schelling in the spring semester of 1936, immediately prior to the Nietzsche lectures that began that fall, in the context of a remark on knowledge Heidegger suddenly interjects a statement to the effect that the efforts of Hitler and Mussolini to react against nihilism were determined by Nietzsche:

> It is known in this respect that Mussolini as well as Hitler, both men who in different ways in Europe have introduced contrary movements concerning the political shape of the nation and of the people, are again in different ways essentially limited by Nietzsche, although it is not the case that in this way the authentic metaphysical region of Nietzschean thought immediately received its value.[247]

Since it was known that both Mussolini and Hitler were interested in Nietzsche, the interest of the omitted passage is that Heidegger here signals that both were in fact determined by what they failed fully to comprehend. And in the first series of Nietzsche lectures, again in a passage omitted in the version revised for publication, Heidegger once more insists on the importance of his evocation of Nietzsche's slogan in the rectoral address: " 'God is dead' is not an atheistic proposition, but rather the formula for the basic experience of the event [des Ereignisses] of Western history. I consciously put this statement in my *Rektoratsrede* of 1933."[248] Here, Heidegger correctly emphasizes the continuity between his attitude toward Nietzsche both during and after his service as rector of the University of Freiburg.

One can admit the existence of a controversy with National Socialism in the Nietzsche lectures but deny that Heidegger here turns against Nazism. Obviously, a disagreement on one point is compatible with agreement, even a large measure of agreement, on other points. Those who follow Heidegger's description of the Nietzsche lectures as a controversy with National Socialism need to answer two questions: what is the nature of the controversy with National Socialism within the Nietzsche lectures? In what sense does it constitute a turning against Nazism? It is difficult to evaluate Krell's imprecise statement since it does not refer to a specific passage or text. Arendt's claim is not sustained by the inspection of the texts. Even were there a shift in tone, as she claims, between the first and second volumes of the Nietzsche lectures, it would follow neither that the second volume represented a confrontation with Nietzsche[249] nor that Heidegger here severed his connection with Nazism.

In different ways, Aubenque briefly and Vietta in more detail both correctly point to Heidegger's controversy with Nietzsche and National Socialism; but both incorrectly conclude from the existence of an objection to the metaphysical acumen of Nazism, a complaint about it as theory, that Heidegger rejects Nazism as politics or its political goals. The controversy with Nietzsche, mentioned above, includes related critiques of such topics as his supposedly confused view of values, his allegedly unsatisfactory effort to come to grips with Platonism from which he is said to fail to escape, his questionable understanding of his relation to the Cartesian philosophy, and so on.[250] But a critique of Nietzsche, or even of Nazism as a theory or theoretical entity, is not the same thing as a rejection of the political aspect of National Socialism.

In the rectoral address, Nazism is never named, although the reference to it is unmistakable. To the best of my knowledge, in the Nietzsche lectures National Socialism is never directly named and hence never overtly criticized. But Heidegger does criticize Nazism as an approach to Being, and more obliquely as a political movement that springs from an incorrect form of metaphysics. The controversy with National Socialism is perhaps most evident in brief remarks at the end of the long discussion of nihilism, where Heidegger opposes so-called authentic metaphysics, which rests upon the ontological difference, to an inauthentic metaphysics, or worldview. If the statement about the worldview is an allusion to National Socialism, then Heidegger's statement that "dominion over beings can develop only with the beginning of the fulfillment of metaphysics" is a veiled description of the way in which Nazism has become possible in the age defined by Nietzsche's metaphysics.[251] Heidegger's objection, then, is that as a mere worldview National Socialism represents an inauthentic metaphysics, which must be rejected. In this way, Heidegger distances himself from every inauthentic form of metaphysics, including National Socialism, supposedly thrown up by nihilism.

It is probable that Heidegger here rejects Nazism as a theory of Being. Yet he does not object to the political consequences of National Socialism. A political rejection of National Socialism would only follow if he believed that a metaphysically bad theory is, in virtue of that fact, politically unacceptable. In my view there are two reasons to refuse this interpretation. First, although when Heidegger accepted the rectorship he allied himself with National Socialism as the *Führer* of the university, he never accepted the political hegemony of Nazism. Heidegger's refusal of Nazi political leadership is clear in his determined argument in the rectoral speech from a Platonic perspective that philosophy, not "political science," must lead the state. Second, in the rectoral address, in the lectures on metaphysics, in the lectures on Nietzsche, and in all his later writings, Heidegger maintains the goal, which he shares with Nazism: the realization of the destiny of the German *Volk*.

In sum, in his critique of National Socialism Heidegger apparently rejects its mistaken interpretation of Being. Yet he does not distance himself here or, to the best of my knowledge, anywhere else in the Nietzsche lectures or in other writings on the history of philosophy from political Nazism as such. In the limited sense that he criticizes National

Socialism as a theory of Being, Heidegger is correct to claim that his Nietzsche lectures represent a confrontation with Nazism; but the confrontation is mainly limited to Nazism as a form of metaphysics in the age of nihilism. It is obviously incorrect to interpret this limited confrontation with Nietzsche or with the metaphysical capacity of National Socialism as a turn against Nazism. There is nothing in the texts to show that Heidegger's turning is a turning against the political consequences of Nazism and even less to show that it is a turning against Nazism as such. In fact, since Heidegger apparently never accepted official, or real, Nazism with which he colloborated, and to which he belonged as an official member of the Nazi party, it would indeed have been difficult for him later to turn against it.

5

Nazism and the *Beiträge*
zur Philosophie

Heidegger's *Beiträge*

The single most important text for the relation between Heidegger's later position and his Nazism is a still little-known, recently published treatise composed in the period immediately following the rectorate: *Contributions to Philosophy* (*On the Event*) (*Beiträge zur Philosophie (Vom Ereignis)*). The *Beiträge*, one of Heidegger's most difficult but most important works, is a highly technical philosophical study, unlike the semipopular texts and lectures so far considered.

In turning to the *Beiträge*, we enter uncharted territory. The speech and the essay we have studied above are available in English translation; they are at least well known and often mentioned, and the speech although not the essay has often been discussed. Although the Hölderlin lectures are not yet translated, Heidegger's Nietzsche lectures are available in English; the worked-over German version has been in the bookstores for many years, and the original lectures are now being published. With the exception of a few colleagues who possessed copies of the original manuscript, the *Beiträge* is not well known, even to the large circle of Heidegger enthusiasts. It was published only in January 1989. It is at present untranslated, and is still rarely mentioned outside of the circle of Heidegger specialists.[1]

Any discussion of the *Beiträge* must face difficulties specific to this unfinished, difficult text. The *Beiträge* is the only major Heideggerian work that has not yet been discussed in detail in the enormous Heidegger secondary literature. In writing about a work, especially one that is not well known, there is a natural tendency to cite passages, in fact to cite with more than usual frequency, in order in this way to make the work available to the scholarly public. This is useful in order to acquaint the reader with this difficult, little-known text as much as possible in Heidegger's own words. Yet even to write about this work requires one to undertake the perilous effort, which cannot be successful, in Kant's words a *vergeblich Versuch,* to put into standard English or at least into English a treatise that is scarcely in German, at least as measured by standard German. We do not possess a standard philosophical vocabulary to render Heidegger's difficult terminology in this work, unusually difficult even by Heideggerian standards. The difficulty in presenting Heidegger's thought in the *Beiträge* begins with the crucial term "*Ereignis,*" the master word of Heidegger's later thought, which, in the absence of received practice, I shall arbitrarily translate here as "event."[2] Since there is as yet no translation of the work as a whole or even any agreed-on way to render key terms, the passages cited will be rendered in literal fashion, with closer attention to meaning than to English style.

Although Heidegger is never an easy thinker, the *Beiträge* is especially difficult to comprehend. It is as if Heidegger, who in the wake of *Being and Time* increasingly thought of himself as the most important thinker of modern times, perhaps since the pre-Socratics, were forced here, in the wake of the failure of the rectorate, to come to grips with himself and his philosophy in the midst of a Nazi Germany heading rapidly toward a world war. There is a sense of urgency and confusion in this text, a feeling of the embarrassment of thought before the present day and history, a palpable confusion, present in none of Heidegger's other writings. There is an existential dimension in this text, equally present in the rectoral address, but with none of the self-confidence, conceptual hubris, even overweening pride evident in the speech.

Important philosophical works resist easy summary. It is not possible to describe the *Beiträge* in simple fashion since the thought it contains is of extraordinary complexity. As this text has only recently been published, there is no standard, or even well-known, way to understand it, so that any reading literally has to forge its own route. In the absence of guidelines, or extensive prior discussion against which to react, with respect to the *Beiträge* this chapter will concern itself with two tasks: a general description of some main lines of this difficult text, as a sort of first effort to relate it to Heidegger's corpus, without which a more detailed discussion would be literally out of context;[3] and a more specific scrutiny of its connection to Heidegger's Nazism.

In view of its recent appearance, it is both easy and difficult to write about this text. It is easy to do so since the *Beiträge* has only recently appeared. Accordingly, there is almost no discussion that needs to be taken into account. It is for that reason also difficult to write about, since there is no well-traveled path to follow; and, with a single exception, there is not even a well-developed view of the precise relation of this work to the question of Heidegger's Nazism. In order to prepare for an analysis of the link of this book to National Socialism, it will be useful to provide some general remarks about the treatise.

The text of the book was handwritten by Heidegger during the period 1936–1938 and transcribed by his brother, Fritz Heidegger, in typewritten form.[4] The original manuscript, which was compared by Heidegger with the typescript prepared by his brother, is described by the editor as consisting of 933 handwritten pages, mainly of the size known as DIN A5.[5] It appeared for the first time in 1989, in the year of Heidegger's hundredth anniversary, as volume 65 of his collected works, in a version edited by Friedrich-Wilhelm von Herrmann.[6] The whole is divided into eight parts and 281 numbered paragraphs of uneven length.

The *Beiträge* is obviously unfinished.[7] Although much of the work is rather polished, even complete, there are numerous passages that lack final form. These include discussions embedded within other discussions, and even "sentences" that lack verbs.[8] The terminology is particularly laborious: many words are written in hyphenated form, presumably in order to indicate their etymologies; Being is no longer written as *Sein* but now appears as *Seyn,* and Dasein occurs as Da-sein; and there are numerous neologisms that render translation even more perilous than usual.[9] The reading is unusually difficult, even by Heideggerian standards. Although the parts of the book cohere internally, they do not form a single whole, and the overall line of argument is difficult to determine.

Little about the published book is clear, perhaps including the proper ordering of its parts. In a handwritten note, dated 8 May 1939, Heidegger complains that the discussion of Being, the second part of the typewritten manuscript, is not at its proper place and indicates that his manuscript requires another revision.[10] The editor reports that he placed the discussion titled "Das Seyn," at the end of the published version.[11] He justifies this decision through the remark that Heidegger renumbered the pages in such a way as to suggest this reordering of the manuscript. But a revision is more than a change in the numbering of the pages or the ordering of the parts of the work which Heidegger carried out. It is an open question whether a finished, or even a further-revised, manuscript would have presented its constituent elements in the same or a different order.

In part because the book has so recently been published, there is little literature and even little agreement about it. Pöggeler—for many years, one of the few to have a manuscript of the text—has always believed that it is Heidegger's *Hauptwerk*.[12] This opinion was quickly contested by others after the work appeared. In response to Pöggeler, Alexander Schwan characterizes the *Beiträge* as Heidegger's second great philosophical work.[13] He insists that it refutes Farias's thesis that Heidegger remained a convinced National Socialist.[14] For Schwan, the *Beiträge* indicates a clear withdrawal from the interrelation of philosophy and politics in 1933.[15] Schwan maintains that the *Beiträge* does not lead to a criticism of National Socialism but to a renunciation of practice.[16] Von Herrmann, who takes a weaker line, describes the *Beiträge* as merely one of Heidegger's main works.[17] Vietta regards this book as Heidegger's most important *Hauptwerk* after *Being and Time,* a view that continues to give primacy to the early study of fundamental ontology.[18] He makes extensive use of this text to examine what he describes as Heidegger's critique of National Socialism and technology.[19] More recently, Pöggeler has insisted that the *Beiträge* presents a sharp critique of National Socialism, as well as liberalism and Bolshevism.[20] Thomä states without elaboration that the *Beiträge* continues Heidegger's critique of Nazism as it exists.[21] On the contrary, Tertulian maintains that in the *Beiträge* Heidegger manipulates the history of ontology in order to conceal fascist political goals.[22]

Obviously, this book is not only a key document in Heidegger's position; it is also a key document for a grasp of Heidegger's comprehension of Nazism after the rectorate. For this reason, the *Beiträge* is itself caught up in the political struggle now under way. It opposes defenders of Heidegger's life and thought, who for generations have resisted full access to the Heidegger Archives and sought to prevent the appearance of damaging material, and those who are less concerned to defend Heidegger than to uncover the truth. This political struggle concerns the *Beiträge* in three ways. First, and most obviously, there is the scholarly interpretation of the text itself, the kind of hermeneutical struggle that occurs in any learned enterprise. Second, there is the prior problem of the establishment of the text, the object of interpretation, the determination of what is available for scrutiny. It is, then, a matter of some concern that a question has been raised about the completeness of the present published version of this text.[23] It is fair to say that the text we now have is probably incomplete, and we do not know what has been omitted from it. Obviously, it is important to have a full version of the text on which to base an informed judgment, and just as obviously, that is probably not the case at present. Third, there is the present struggle, unusual in scholarly circles, recently under way between those who control the ongoing edition of Heidegger's collected writings in German and the American publishers to find a translator acceptable to both parties to render this text into English. In view of the political stakes, and the history of Heidegger scholarship, in which even noted scholars are frequently personally implicated in sustaining a particular interpretation, one can anticipate efforts to control even the wording of politically sensitive passages in the English translation.

Interpretation of the *Beiträge*

The approach in *Being and Time* to the problem of the meaning of Being through Dasein is later transformed through a turning (*Kehre*), or reversal, announced in the "Letter on Humanism," in which everything is reversed, through a new thinking which abandons subjectivity.[24] Heidegger describes his new thinking as "no longer philosophy, because it thinks more originally than metaphysics—a name identical to philosophy."[25] The precise nature of the turning in Heidegger's thought is a matter of scholarly dispute.[26] Yet it is clear that the *Beiträge* belongs to an effort to make a new beginning, to effect a transition from philosophy to the so-called new thinking—in short, through questioning in another track, which will arise from the transition from that followed by Western thought.[27]

A feature of Heidegger's consistent emphasis on the problem of Being and his later turn away from subjectivity is a change in his view of truth. Following Heidegger's suggestion that his book must be understood in terms of his notes from his lectures (*Vorlesungen*), von Herrmann points to Heidegger's lectures from the 1930s, particularly the volume titled *Basic Question of Philosophy: Selected "Problems" of "Logic"* (*Grundfragen der Philosophie: Ausgewählte 'Probleme' der 'Logik'*) from the fall semester of 1937/38, above all the appendix (*Anhang*) under the title "From the First Draft" ("Aus dem ersten Entwurf").[28] For von Herrmann, the relation between these two texts centers around the theme of truth as disclosure.

This suggestion is supported by Heidegger's repeated mention in the *Beiträge* of two lectures (*Vorträge*) concerning truth from this period: "On The Essence of Truth" ("Das Wesen der Wahrheit") and "The Origin of the Work of Art" ("Die Ursprung des Kunstwerkes"). In *Being and Time,* Heidegger proposed an ontological view of truth as both objective and subjective. He insisted on the objective component of truth in his claim that a true assertion signifies the essence of the object. "To say that an assertion '*is true*' signifies that it uncovers the entity as it is in itself."[29] He stressed the subjective component of truth through his conception of Dasein, as in the assertion "that truth, in the most primordial sense, is Dasein's disclosedness, to which the uncoveredness of entities belongs."[30] Here, Heidegger carried his emphasis on the subjective component of truth to great lengths, for instance in the claim that truth only is as long as there is Dasein,[31] so that Newton's laws literally were neither true nor false prior to Newton, through whom the laws became true.[32]

In his later writing, consistent with the deemphasis of Dasein, and the decentering of the subject, Heidegger turns away from the subjective element while continuing to stress a view of truth as disclosure. Now he depicts truth as the disclosure that reveals an aspect of what still lies concealed. "Philosophical thinking is gentle disclosure that does not renounce the concealment of being as a whole."[33] In the *Beiträge* he carries this view still further by underscoring the event of that which is to be disclosed. So in the one-page section preceding the work, he stresses the verbs "to occur" or "to happen" ("*ereignen*"), as in the "event" ("*Ereignis*"). This stress preserves a clear etymological link to Heidegger's earlier insistence on the ownmost (*eigen*) as the basis of authenticity (*Eigentlichkeit*).[34]

The passage preceding the book is mainly devoted to comments on its subtitle: "Concerning the Event" ("Vom Ereignis").[35] For Heidegger, in the historical period (*Zeitalter*) of the transition from metaphysics to the historical thought of Being (*das seynsgeschichtliche Denken*)[36] one needs to think the truth of Being from out of a more basic approach. This suggests his intention to differentiate between an earlier metaphysical, and a later, post-metaphysical period, characterized by a new form of thought, different in kind from its predecessors, and based on a historical perspective lacking in metaphysics. The new form of thought, in the post-metaphysical period toward which, in Heidegger's opinion, we are now tending, will be historical in a way that earlier thought was not.

> Future thought is a thought-*process,* through which the as yet in general hidden realm of the becoming of the essence [Wesung—literally, essencing] of Being passes and so is first illuminated [gelichtet] and reached in its ownmost character of an event [in seinem eigensten Ereignischarakter].[37]

Heidegger makes it clear that he regards his new approach as breaking with the past, perhaps including his own past, in a way that carries forward his earlier basic insights. It is no longer a case, he points out, of expounding something objective, but of hewing to (*übereignet*) the event. The result is an essential change in the concept of human being from that of a rational animal to that of Da-sein. Pointing now to his subtitle, he writes: "From the event occurs [ereignet] a thoughtlike-saying listening to Being and in the word 'of' ['des'] Being."[38]

As the title suggests, the entire work is concerned with the theme of

Ereignis. The book is divided into eight sections, whose connection remains unclear: The Preliminary Glance (Der Vorblick), The Trace (Der Anklang), The Handing Over (Das Zuspiel), The Jump (Der Sprung), The Ground (Die Gründung), To-come (Die Zu-künftigen), The Last God (Der letzte Gott), and Being (Das Seyn). Being, which was earlier written in the modern German manner as *Sein*, is now written as *Seyn*, presumably in order to set off the new beginning from the first beginning.[39] The unfinished, repetitive, even obsessive character of the work can be indicated by the fact that in the first section, which is divided into forty-nine numbered paragraphs, no fewer than five bear the title "Vom Ereignis"[40] and two others are titled "Das Ereignis."[41] In addition, in this same section there are ten paragraphs concerning beginning thought (*das anfängliche Denken*)[42] and seven about the decision (*Entscheidung*).[43] A similar situation is repeated in the other parts of the work.

Despite its unsystematic nature, the *Beiträge* has a rich, almost polyphonic, fugue-like character.[44] It is without doubt a key text for a grasp of the thought of the later Heidegger. To the best of my knowledge, without exception all of the themes that later emerge in Heidegger's writings are sounded here. These include the overcoming of metaphysics, the rejection of Platonism, the critique of modernity, the interpretation of Nietzsche, Hölderlin and poetry, the turning (*die Kehre*), the last god, thought as distinguished from philosophy, the enframing (*das Gestell*), the critique of technology, silence, nihilism, *Gelassenheit,* and so on. Accordingly, this text plays a double role: as a key mediating link between the early and late phases of Heidegger's position, and as a key indication of the interrelation of the many motifs that emerge in his later thought.

Important insights are scattered throughout the work. An example is the perhaps untranslatable description of *Machenschaft* as "[d]er Bezug der Unbezüglichkeit," roughly "the relation of that which is beyond relation," which aids in understanding the perhaps equally untranslatable concept of enframing (*das Gestell*).[45] Another instance is the repeated reference to the difficult idea of the turning (*die Kehre*), which Heidegger mentions on virtually every second page, for example when he writes:

> The event has its innermost happening [Geschehen] and its widest scope [Ausgriff] in the turning. The turning that comes to be in the event is the hidden ground of all others, subordinated, with respect to their provenance, dark, easily taken as "final" turnings, [geometrical] circles [Zirkel] and circles [Kreise].[46]

The importance Heidegger attaches to the concept of the turning is apparent in his further remark that only future history will tell whether the insight thus gained into the hiddenmost events will remain open or be closed forever to human being.[47]

Since Heidegger here rejects system, and since his discussion is not systematic, it cannot be described in a systematic manner without doing violence to it, without distorting its antisystematic character. The nature of the work as a whole can be indicated through selective commentary on some themes raised in the first section, in the lengthy "Preliminary Glance."[48] Since this section comprises about a fifth of the entire book, and functions as its introduction, it is reasonable to treat it as a preface, not only to this particular work but also to Heidegger's later thought in general.

As the *Beiträge* belongs to the transition to the other beginning, we can expect Heidegger to be critical of even the most refined instances of the first beginning. His remark that "[t]he time of 'systems' is past"[49] suggests that earlier "systems" were never fully systematic and that, to the extent that he himself earlier adopted this aim, he was mistaken. In his pursuit of the distinction between the two forms of thought, he differentiates (1) the question of Being (*Seinsfrage*), or the basic question (*Grundfrage*) as concerns the truth of Being conceived from a new, historical point of view, and (2) the prior philosophical question concerning beings, now designated as the leading question (*Leitfrage*).[50] There is a suggestion that fundamental ontology, which was still determined by the leading question, was insufficiently radical, since it had failed to penetrate beyond the later tradition to its roots.

The other beginning, like the first approach, can only be stated in language. Heidegger maintains that the thoughtful saying of the other beginning is a pointing out (*Weisung*) but not a teaching (*Lehre*).[51] He stresses the difficulty of his new thought in an odd, pathetic statement, which may also have a political resonance: "No one understands what 'I' am *thinking* here."[52] If we note that here as elsewhere, Heidegger intends his thought literally to see into the present and future, we can understand this remark as another indication that Heidegger feels that his work is not being accorded the respect that is its due since it is literally misunderstood. Since Heidegger still intends to grasp the possibility of the historical gathering of the German *Volk* through his position, there is a political cast to his remark.

Another constant in Heidegger's thought, despite change in his position, is his continued interest in Being. Heidegger reaffirms the ontological continuity in his thought by insisting that the question concerning the "meaning" of Being in *Being and Time,* "in short, concerning the *truth of Being,* is and remains *my* question, in fact counts as the *really only one* [denn sie gilt ja dem *Einzigsten*]."[53] Since in his initial Hölderlin lectures, Heidegger has in the meantime turned to poetry as a fundamental source of truth, he now signals a turn away from transcendental phenomenology toward the supposedly peculiar ability of the poet to respond to this question.[54]

Heidegger differentiates his new thought from the initial thought, or transcendental phenomenological ontology, which thinks Being as presence out of the presencing. "The thought of Being as event is the beginning thought, which as a controversy with the first beginning prepares the way for it."[55] His new thought, hence, does not break with, but rather goes behind, and founds, or deepens, the initial thought. For Heidegger, his new thought depends in part on a concept of history which is not a region of beings but a glance in the essencing (*Wesung*) of Being itself.[56] The result is to distinguish between his own earlier effort to grasp the Being of beings, stated at length in *Being and Time,* and the effort begun here to grasp Being directly. The new approach requires a reconceptualization of the basic concepts of the first approach, which cannot simply be taken up unaltered in the new thought. For instance, care, which was earlier described as "[t]he totality of Being-in-the-world,"[57] is now conceived, in difficult terminology, as the anticipatory resoluteness to the truth of Being as well as the apprehension in the there.[58]

If the first beginning was philosophical, then the other beginning presumably reaches backward beyond philosophy. Heidegger addresses the question of how the new thought relates to philosophy in a series of remarks. "Philosophy as self-reflection [Selbst-besinnung] in the indicated way is first realizable [vollziehbar] as the beginning thought of the other beginning."[59] The new beginning, while no longer philosophy, is intended, then, to realize philosophy. One thinks of other such claims, for instance the well-known Marxist view that Marxism is the realization on the plane of science of the aims of philosophy.[60]

As the Marxists frequently do with respect to Marxism, Heidegger stresses in various ways that his proposed new beginning is not philosophy. "In the region of the other beginning there is neither 'ontology' nor in general 'metaphysics.' "[61] There is no ontology, since the leading question does not circumscribe any domain; and there is no metaphysics since the new thought no longer takes its departure from beings present to hand, as in the Cartesian position, or known objects, as in idealism. In a further return to the question of system, now linked to an implicit rejection of Cartesianism, he observes that this theme can only be raised from within a tradition dominated by mathematical thought. "This thought and the order based on it remains outside the question of whether it belongs to a system or not. 'System' is only possible in the wake of the dominance of mathematical thought (in the wide sense of the term)."[62] Obviously, then, although Heidegger need not abandon conceptual rigor, he cannot present the new phase of his thought in systematic form; in his view, the very idea of system arises only within a deficient form of metaphysics.

The result is an essential clarification of the *Seinsfrage* that continues to preoccupy Heidegger. In terms of his distinction between the old *Leitfrage* and the new *Grundfrage,* he remarks:

> The *leading question* defined from the Greeks until Nietzsche the same approach to the question concerning "Being." The clearest and greatest example for the unity of this tradition [Überlieferung] is Hegel's *Logic.* On the contrary, for the basic question Being is not an answer and a region of an answer, but the most questionable [Frag-würdigste].[63]

It is not the answering of the question of Being but the widening of the questioning, the awakening and the clarification of the *power* of the question (*Fragekraft*) in respect to this question, which still only springs from need and the upswing of Being-there (*Da-seins*).[64] The result, according to Heidegger, is the repetition of what must occur ever more decisively since the end of metaphysics is neither a "teaching" nor a "system" but rather "must become the authentic history and consequently the most hidden."[65]

Heidegger insists that the truth of Being which this thought captures is identical with the essence of Being.

> This truth of being is certainly not different from Being, but is rather its ownmost essence [eigenstes Wesen]; and therefore it lies in the history of Being, whether this truth gives itself [verschenkt] or fails to give itself [verweigert]; and so first authentically brings the unfathomable [das Abgründige] into its history.[66]

He sees this new thought as successful where "theory of knowledge" fails. "The 'theory of knowledge' is, however, only the form of the lack of awareness [Ratlosigkeit] of modern metaphysics with respect to itself."[67] This conclusion follows from his view, itself a further form of his idea of truth as disclosure, that the essential identification of truth and Being is available only to his new thought. "The truth of Being is the Being of truth."[68]

The *Beiträge* is a major text in the transition of Heidegger's thought from its original beginning to another beginning. Now our concern in this chapter is not with the later evolution of Heidegger's thought as such; it is rather limited to the significance of this evolution for his

Nazism. Accordingly, I have sought briefly to describe some main themes of the *Beiträge* in order to provide a context to consider its relation to Heidegger's Nazism. My limited aim was not to provide a full, or even an adequate, discussion of this work—a difficult task for any important philosophical treatise, especially so for this rich, complex, but unsystematic work—but rather to set the stage for a determination of whether, as has been claimed, in the *Beiträge* Heidegger confronts Nazism.

Nazism and the *Beiträge*

It is difficult to address the theme of Heidegger's relation to Nazism in the *Beiträge* for several reasons. Material relevant for an evaluation of this theme is not confined to a single passage or a single portion of the work, which it traverses from the beginning to the end, from the initial comments, such as Heidegger's remark, cited above, that he is not understood—which anticipates his later assertions in the 1945 article on the rectorate that the rectoral address was not understood—to his suggestion in the final paragraph of the book that speech is grounded in silence.[69] It follows that this theme is intimately bound up with, hence inseparable from, the work as a whole.

Naturally, Heidegger's relation to Nazism in the wake of the resignation as rector and the abandonment of transcendental phenomenology can no longer be precisely the same. In particular, Heidegger can no longer strive for personal privilege within the academy through his position as philosophical *Führer* of the University of Freiburg nor can he continue to legitimate Nazism on the basis of fundamental ontology, which he has now given up. Yet Heidegger's relation to Nazism exhibits a remarkable continuity between the exoteric public statements in the rectoral speech and the esoteric "postphilosophic" view on display in the *Beiträge*.

The description of of the rectoral address as representing a kind of "private National Socialism,"[70] to which Heidegger objects in the article on the rectorate, correctly characterizes his view of Nazism in the *Beiträge*. Here, he criticizes its real form as an incorrect means to an end even as he continues to accept the end in view, for which he again proposes a "philosophical" means. Although he no longer offers his fundamental ontology in order to lead the leaders, he neither abandons the relation of "philosophy" to politics nor turns away from Nazism. He no longer proposes to ground National Socialism in fundamental ontology, yet he continues to insist on his "philosophy," in this case his new thought to attain the end in view shared with Nazism: the destiny of the

German people. The relevant difference is that Heidegger's new beginning is no longer understood as a sufficient means to a political end,
which it is intended to achieve only indirectly, through the justification
of the prophetic role of great German poetry. In other words, although
Heidegger's position changes, and although he abandons philosophy for
thought beyond philosophy, he does not abandon, in fact he specifically
maintains, the political role of his thought of Being.

The recurrence of Heidegger's stress on the Germans as German at
this late date in his thought is not less, but even more, troubling than
before. In his early thought, beyond any strictly political sympathy with
Nazism, Heidegger was pushed in this direction by fundamental ontology that insisted on Dasein, above all its authentic form, as the way to an
authentic thought of Being. As a result of the turning, and the decentering of the subject, in this work, Heidegger has already moved
away from the analysis of Dasein as the clue to Being toward a view of
Being as self-disclosing. It follows that Heidegger's continued insistence
now as before on the *Volk* is doubly significant. On the one hand, it
presumably indicates that his effort to decenter subjectivity is only incompletely carried out, since this concept continues to recur in his
thought. On the other hand, to the extent that the ongoing concern with
Being has been uncoupled from Dasein, it clearly shows the persistence
of a political preference for the aim shared with Nazism.

Heidegger's continued acceptance of this political goal, which motivates all his writings after the rectoral address, is not incompatible with
criticism of real National Socialism. To grasp Heidegger's criticism of
National Socialism, it is useful to recall that his thought is limited
throughout his corpus to the problem of Being. Heidegger's continued
concern with Being literally prevented him from coming to grips with or
even understanding the nature of Nazism as Nazism, which he seems to
have regarded as an insufficient form of modern metaphysics, in patent
disregard of its effects on human being.

In the *Beiträge,* Heidegger's critical remarks about National Socialism
are easily overlooked for several reasons. First, in keeping with his
concern with Being, the critique of National Socialism is strictly ontological in character and in that respect is unlike other, more standard discussions. It is fair to say that no one unfamiliar with Heidegger's thought
would even recognize that it contained reservations about Nazism. His
rare critical remarks on Nazism in this and other writings invariably
concern its supposed insufficiency as a theory of Being. Here as elsewhere, Heidegger is chillingly insensitive to the significance of Nazism
for human being. For instance, in the most direct comment on Nazi
ideology in this work, in the context of a remark on "blood and race" as

the "bearers of history," Heidegger is primarily concerned with the defense of his own earlier distinction between history and historicality, that is, with an adequate concept of history.[71]

Second, the critical remarks directed to National Socialism are always secondary to Heidegger's main concern in this treatise, which is to sketch the outlines of the other beginning. In the *Beiträge*, Heidegger's reservations about Nazism are intrinsic to his new theoretical posture, the rejection of the insufficient radicality of his first beginning, which he now regards as a continuation of the metaphysical movement from Anaximander to Nietzsche. He is, then, critical of his own earlier fundamental ontology as well as National Socialism and other views as well, all of which from his perspective remain committed to an approach from which he now seeks to free himself. Since Heidegger's criticism of National Socialism is of the same generic type as that which he routinely brings against anything associated with modern metaphysics, his objections to Nazism in no sense grasp its essential nature.

Third, in keeping with the antisystematic character of Heidegger's later thought, there is no single systematic statement of his objections to National Socialism anywhere in his writings, least of all in the present work. In part, the unsystematic nature of his criticism is no doubt due to the resolute rejection of system in this text and in his later writings. In part it may also be due to his inability to confront directly the consequences of his earlier identification with Nazism on the basis of his thought.[72]

Heidegger's specific objections to Nazism in the *Beiträge* are consistent with the evolution of his position since *Being and Time*. In *An Introduction to Metaphysics* he continued the turn to Nietzsche begun in the rectoral address, and he reaffirmed the significance of Nazism and sketched aspects of what later became the critique of technology. In "Wege zur Aussprache," he emphasized his interest in the realization of the ownmost being of the Germans even as he criticized Descartes in order to comprehend the metaphysical essence of technology. In "The Age of the World Picture"—originally given as a lecture about the time Heidegger stopped working on the *Beiträge*—he criticized modern science and the so-called philosophy of the worldview, or *Weltanschauungsphilosophie,* and included a critical remark in passing on National Socialism.[73] All of these elements now appear in the *Beiträge,* where Heidegger criticizes National Socialism as illustrating the worldview correlated with the rise of technology in the age of metaphysics, a worldview which he intends to surpass through a turn to the other beginning.

In the *Beiträge,* Heidegger's reservations with respect to the theory of National Socialism are dispersed virtually throughout the work. They appear in passages concerning such varied themes as metaphysics, technology, *Weltanschauungsphilosophie,* nihilism, the *Volk,* and, perhaps more surprisingly in the treatment of transcendental philosophy, the cult of personality, various forms of religion, and silence. Now it is not easy to describe a series of remarks which the author did not choose to restate as a single connected discussion. It would be a mistake to provide them with a systematic format when Heidegger now rejects this approach for reasons intrinsic to his position. The alternative, to be employed here, is to survey a selection of the ways Heidegger is critical of National Socialism in this work.

The *Volk*

The discussion of Heidegger's relation to Nazism so far has exposed a triple turning, centered in Heidegger's acceptance of the National Socialist conception of the realization of the Germans as German, based in German *Volk* ideology, both for its own sake and for his concern with Being. The triple turning is manifest in Heidegger's turn toward real Nazism in his assumption of the rectorate, his turn away from it when he resigned his post as rector, and his turn toward an ideal form of National Socialism. The fundamental thread that binds together the three political turnings in Heidegger's thought, the concern with the *Volk,* is prominent in the rectoral address and recurs after the rectorate in the initial lecture series on Hölderlin and in the Nietzsche lectures. It is a recurrent theme throughout the *Beiträge.* Attention to Heidegger's remarks on the *Volk* will offer insight into his supposed confrontation in this work with National Socialism. It is reasonable to suppose that if Heidegger desired to break with, or even to distance himself from, Nazism in the period after the rectorate, his desire would be evident in his treatment of the *Volk* throughout the book. At the same time, through the inspection of these passages, we will gain further insight into Heidegger's position in this work.

The following survey of Heidegger's account of the *Volk* in the *Beiträge* does not aim at completeness; it is intended to provide no more than a representative sample of how he uses this concept. In the *Beiträge,* Heidegger discusses, or at least alludes in passing to, the *Volk* in numerous passages throughout the work. Taken together, these passages provide an indication of his view of Nazism during a period in which he is in the process of fundamentally revising his thought in the wake of the failure of his rectorate. A typical instance of Heidegger's rejection of National Socialism as a theory occurs in a remark on *Volk* ideology in a passage on *Ereignis,* the main theme of the book, where he objects to the idea of a worldview.

We have already noted that Heidegger is critical of the idea of the philosophy of the worldview, or *Weltanschauungsphilosophie,* as early as his initial lecture series, as well as in his review of Jaspers's *Psychology of World Views* (*Psychologie der Weltanschauungen*).[74] In *Being and Time,* Heidegger does not discuss the concept of the worldview, to which he returns in his lectures on *The Basic Problems of Phenomenology.* Here, he notes that a worldview is a coherent set of beliefs arising in relation to a particular individual at a given time, but not a theory as such; and he follows Husserl in arguing for a difference in kind between philosophy and a worldview. "If philosophy is the scientific construction of a worldview, then the distinction between 'scientific philosophy' and 'philosophy as worldview' vanishes."[75]

In the *Beiträge,* in his "postphilosophical" phase, from the vantage point of the other beginning Heidegger criticizes National Socialism as a mere *Weltanschauung* like Christianity or liberalism.[76] According to Heidegger, both the Christian view of transcendence and its denial in terms of the *Volk* as the aim of history are forms of liberalism (*Liberalismus*). He further maintains that what today appears under the heading of a "worldview" is an alloy formed of varying parts of Christianity, *Volk-Ideen,* and culture (*Kultur*). His objection, which is not clearly formulated, seems to be that a worldview of any kind presupposes that one already essentially knows what a person is, in terms of which the transcendent has meaning; but, on the contrary, it is only in terms of the transcendent that we can know beings, including human being.

> As different as these "worldviews" are, and although they openly or covertly oppose each other—if the sending into the undecided [Sichumtreiben im Unentschiedenen] can still be named a battle—they all agree, without knowing or ruing it, that human being is posited as that which one essentially knows, as a being [Seiende], as that in respect of which and from which every "transcendence" is defined and accordingly as that which hence must first define the human being. But this has been made basically impossible since the human being is already grasped as definable, instead of defining it in terms of something else, which must be dis-placed [ver-rückt] from the previous determination, in order in the first place that the initially definable may be defined.[77]

Heidegger objects to the definition of the transcendent in terms of human being since he holds that human being must be understood in terms of Being in general; but the requirement to do so is concealed by the forgetfulness of Being. "Or is there the possibility that this displacement [Verrückung] comes over man? Certainly. And this is the need of the forgetfulness of being."[78] Heidegger maintains that the awakening of this need is the initial displacement of man into what he calls the between, characterized as an openness, that is, an openness in which Being occurs.

> This "betweenness" ["Zwischen"] is, however, not a transcendence with respect to man, but on the contrary is the openness [jenes Offene], to which man as the founder and *Wahrer* belongs, in that he as Da-sein occurs [er-eignet] is from being itself [vom Seyn selbst], which does not essence [west] otherwise than as occurrence.[79]

In light of Heidegger's concern with *Ereignis* as the dominant theme of the other beginning, we can paraphrase his muted objection to *Volk* ideas as well as his own form of the first beginning as follows: Any explanation of the transcendent from an immanent perspective overlooks the fact that the immanent is explicable only in terms of the transcendent in the same way as Being in general is the "ground" of beings. One must, then, reject any form of the "anthropological" approach to ontology, such as the Cartesian position, the approach to Being in terms of Dasein featured by his own fundamental ontology, or a philosophy based on a worldview, or even the assumption of the *Volk* as the goal of history. Note, however, that Heidegger's continued interest in the *Volk* is compatible with his own rejection of its teleological claim since, from his ontological angle of vision, the end in view is not the *Volk* but Being.

Heidegger is not more critical of the *Volk* approach in this and other passages because his main concern does not lie in the rejection of National Socialism as such, but rather in the transition from the first to the other beginning. There is another example in Heidegger's lengthy analysis of the concept of decision at the end of the first section of the book. Heidegger's discussion here suggests his continued concern with the realization of the destiny of the German people, the theme so prominent in the *Rektoratsrede*. In a passage on the "decision," Heidegger emphasizes a point made at the beginning of the initial Hölderlin lecture series:[80] the decision is either for history or for its loss.[81] According to Heidegger, there is a commission to carry out the innermost need arising out of the abandonment of Being. This decision occurs through the so-called gift or the staying away from that which is designated as the future directed.

> *How does the decision occur?* Through the *gift* [*Geschenk*] or the staying away [den Ausbleib] from the excellently symbolized [jener ausgezeichneten Gezeichneten], which we call "the future-directed" ["die Zukünftigen"] in contradistinction to the many kinds of as you please and unrelenting later considerations [Späteren], which have nothing more ahead and nothing more behind themselves.[82]

Heidegger provides a list of five forms of *Gezeichneten*. The fourth form includes individuals, namely, the few and the many, understood not numerically but in terms of their symbolic function. In a manner similar to Sartre's later view, Heidegger describes this form as possessing a hidden agreement (*Einverständnis*) which, for historical reasons, can suddenly appear, thereby causing individuals suddenly to become a *Volk*.[83] In the fifth point, Heidegger affirms that the *Volk* is defined by the uniqueness of Being, whose task it is to ground. "This people [Dieses Volk] is in its origin and definition only according to the one-time occurrence [Einzigkeit] of Being itself, whose truth it must ground in a single place [in einer einzigen Stätte] in a single moment [in einem einzigen Augenblick]."[84] Here, Heidegger repeats his revolutionary view of the *Volk* that comes together in a propitious historical moment. With respect to the rectoral address, an important difference is that Heidegger is no longer interested in the destiny of the *Volk* for itself, but as a way to ground Being. In this way, he obliquely suggests that his turn toward Nazism was not only intended to bring about a gathering of the Germans as German, hence, not only for the perverse humanism whose highest form is National Socialism. Rather, his Nazi turning is also, perhaps above all, for the purpose of realizing his own authentic thought of Being.

Another reference to the *Volk* occurs in one of Heidegger's numerous remarks on the so-called abandonment of Being (*Seinsverlassenheit*). In a section on a supposedly enduring problem, he suggests that this phenomenon corresponds to the prevalent understanding of Being, which fulfills and hides its forgetfulness.[85] Attention to such traits as generality and contemporaneity concern beings, but not Being as such. According to Heidegger, the ground of the historical uprooting of Being is due to Being itself, which withdraws before beings.

> The innermost ground of the historical uprooting is essential, grounded in the essence of Being [im Wesen des Seyns gründender]: Being [Seyn] withdraws before being [dem Seienden] and it is hence then as "being" ["seiend"] and even as "in the process of being" ["seiender"] that it lets itself appear [erscheinen lässt].[86]

Heidegger offers a list of no fewer than sixteen ways in which the forgetfulness of Being announces itself (*sich meldet*).[87] The first form of the forgetfulness of Being is a decided insensitivity to the ambiguous character of the essential.

> The *full insensitivity with respect to the ambiguous* [das völlige Unempfindlichkeit gegen das Vieldeutige] in that which is regarded as essential. Ambiguity occasions [bewirkt] the powerlessness and the displeasure

concerning an effective decision. For instance, whatever "*Volk*" means: the social, the racist, the lower [das Niedere] and the below [das Untere], the national, the remaining [das Bleibende]; for instance, whatever is called "godly" [göttlich].[88]

In a word, Heidegger here is objecting to the dogmatic, theoretically insensitive character of Nazism, apparent in its insensitivity to the manifold forms of *Seyn* as *Seiende*.[89] In sum, Heidegger is unhappy that the National Socialists are unaware of his own ontological difference. What is surprising is that Heidegger should be either surprised or dismayed to learn that the Nazis were less than fully absorbed, were in fact uninterested, in his own approach to Being, in the same way that they were also uninterested in the effort of Rosenberg, the well-known Nazi "philosopher," to bring about a profound spiritual renewal.[90] Heidegger's objection reveals, then, an astonishing lack of awareness of the nature of Nazism.

There is another remark on the *Volk* in a passage on "The Occurrence [Das Erlebnis] and 'Anthropology.' "[91] Here, Heidegger affirms that "anthropology" has today become the center of the scholasticism of the worldview (*Weltanschauungsscholastik*). He restates his rejection of the approach to Being from a person-centered perspective, before remarking that the differences between the various forms of the anthropological approach are insignificant; for the significant question is whether one attempts a transition to another beginning or desires to continue the Platonic tradition.

> The anthropological hairstyle [Frisur—i.e., the particular type], whether Enlightenment-moral, or psychological-scientific, or social scientific-personalistic, or Christian, or folk-political [politisch-völkische], is all the same: the question, that is, whether it questions [erfragt] about another beginning, or whether one continues to insist on the decline under way since Plato, which is only still possible if one talks oneself into taking one's lack of awareness as the overcoming [Überwindung] of the tradition [Überlieferung—literally, what is handed down].[92]

This passage is mainly significant for Heidegger's insistence that the anthropological perspective, which he earlier connected to the influence of Descartes, is in fact rooted in the Platonic tradition itself.[93] In this way, he extends his earlier objections to Descartes to the origins of philosophy in the Greek tradition. Once again, it is clear that his objection to the *Volk* approach lies in its supposed theoretical indebtedness to the first beginning illustrated by Platonic philosophy.

We find several further references to the *Volk* in a discussion of nihilism as the absence of ends in Nietzsche's ateleological sense.[94] We

have already noted that one of Heidegger's favorite hermeneutical strategies is to assert that he and he alone comprehends a particular position
or body of thought. In the article on the rectorate, he made this claim
with respect to Jünger's position. Here, Heidegger remarks that Nietzsche's view of nihilism has still not been understood. For Heidegger, the
moral and idealistic interpretations of this concept are preliminary since
nihilism must be comprehended as the result of the abandonment of
Being. He holds that it is a sign of the incomprehension of Nietzsche to
consider Nietzsche's "teaching" of "nihilism" as a form of cultural psychology. Since there is a refusal to acknowledge the lack of goals, one
"has" goals again.

> Then, the insightful reflection runs about as follows: what would we come
> to if this were true or would become true? And one does not imagine that
> *even this reflection,* that is, the attitude and conduct toward being [zum
> Seienden], is the authentic nihilism. And hence one suddenly "has" goals
> again, even if it is only rather a *means* for the establishment [Ziel-
> aufrichtung] and observance [Verfolgung] of goals: for instance, the
> *Volk.*[95]

Once again, the *Volk* view is invoked as an illustration of the refusal to
accept his own view of thought beyond philosophy.

In still another critique of Cartesianism, Heidegger comments on the
Volk in a passage on "The abandonment of Being and 'science.' "[96] For
Heidegger, science is unable to understand the essence of Being. The
abandonment of Being follows from the interpretation of the being of
beings (*Seiendheit des Seienden*), the main theme of thought. In modernity, truth has been sought in the form of certainty with respect to
beings, particularly in the realm of science (*Wissenschaft*). In order to
progress toward the other beginning, we need to reflect on modern
science. In a clear rejection of the concept of a ground associated with
Cartesian foundationalism, he writes:

> Every kind of theoretico-scientific (transcendental) grounding [Grund-
> legung] has therefore become as impossible as an "attribution of mean-
> ing" ["Sinngebung"] which assigns a *Volk*-political [völkisch-political] or
> any other anthropological determination of goals [Zwecksetzung] to the
> present at hand [vorhandenen] and accordingly essentially [Wesens-
> bestand] unmodifiable science and its operation [Betrieb].[97]

Heidegger's point is that henceforth any form of foundationalism is
impossible since foundationalism as such presupposes a concept of science as grounded in a ground that is not a ground. The idea of a *Volk*
worldview figures here, in a restatement of Husserl's view of objectiv-

ism, as a deficient form of science which is not reflective about its own conditions.

The conception of the *Volk* recurs in incidental fashion in one of the longest sections of the *Beiträge*. This section follows a short paragraph on the Greek conception of the idea (*Idea*),[98] which Heidegger regards as an interpretation of truth leading to the entire later interpretation of being (*Seiendheit*) as objectivity (*Gegenständlichkeit*). For Heidegger, it is only from the vantage point of the other beginning that the question of the original meaning of the concept of truth can be raised. He develops this point in a detailed reflection on "The Idea, Platonism, and Idealism,"[99] which is curiously divided into different subsections. This section contains a lengthy, untitled meditation in twenty-seven numbered points, which is interrupted between points 14 and 15 by two smaller passages: a short discussion, in ten points, titled "Hegel's concept of the idea and the first possibility of a philosophical history of philosophy from its first beginnings"; followed by a shorter discussion, composed of four points, called "What belongs to the concept of 'idealism.' "

Throughout the *Beiträge,* as part of his transition to the other beginning Heidegger rejects Platonism in all its forms. In this section, he criticizes its occurrence in contemporary thought. In point 21, he identifies six clusters of contemporary Platonism: "ontology," which presumably means any ontological approach concerned with being (*Seiende*) as opposed to being as such (*Seyn*); all teachings concerning "values" or "meaning" concerning "ideas" and ideals; as well as views that deny them, such as positivism and biologism; all types of "life" philosophy (*"Lebens"-philosophie*), such as Dilthey's view; various combinations of the preceding; and Nietzsche's view, which, in its concern to transform Platonism, falls back into it.[100]

Heidegger immediately amplifies his understanding of Nietzsche's understanding of Platonism in the next point. Here, the concept of the *Volk* appears in Heidegger's rejection of still another form of worldview, in what he calls Platonism for the people. Returning now to a theme present since the rectoral address, Heidegger argues that philosophy provides the key to history. For Heidegger, Nietzsche is the first to have understood the key role and importance of Platonism for the history of the West. "On the other hand, Nietzsche is the one who for the first time recognized the key role (*Schlüsselstellung*) of Plato and the importance of Platonism for the history of the West (the rise of nihilism)."[101] Heidegger credits Nietzsche with grasping the significance of Plato between the pre-Platonic and post-Platonic moments, although he objects that Nietzsche mistakenly understood pre-Platonic thought in a Platonic way and not in terms of itself. Now invoking his own turn to the other beginning, Heidegger attributes Nietzsche's mistake to a supposed failure to recognize the *Leitfrage* as such and to complete the transition to the *Grundfrage*. In essence, then, Heidegger finds that Nietzsche is guilty of failing to anticipate the evolution of Heidegger's later position. Heidegger then remarks: "But it is even more important that Nietzsche detected Platonism in its hiddenmost forms: Christianity and its *Verweltlichungen* are everywhere 'Platonism for the people' ['Platonismus fürs Volk']."[102]

There is a further reference to the *Volk* in a passage on various aspects of Da-sein.[103] The precise relation between human being and Dasein is difficult to determine. In *Being and Time* and subsequent writings, Heidegger sometimes clearly identifies human being and Dasein, or uses the terms as near synonyms, and sometimes appears to differentiate between them. Distinguishing here between human being (*der Mensch*) and Da-sein, understood as existence, Heidegger suggests that the man is grounded in existence.[104] He describes human being as one who is needed by Being for the "essencing" of the truth of Being.[105] In this sense, human being plays a role in Heidegger's view of Being similar to its role in some versions of Christian theology. Turning now to Dasein and the people in another short paragraph, Heidegger remarks that the essence of a people can only be understood in terms of Da-sein, and then adds that the people can never be a goal or aim as in the *Volk* worldview or in commerce.

> *The essence of the people* [*des Volkes*] can only be understood from Da-sein and this means at the same time that the *Volk* can never be a goal or aim, and that such an opinion is only a *Volk*-type extension [völkische Ausweitung] of the "liberal" thought-of-the-"I" [des "liberalen" "Ich"-gedankens] and of the commercial view of the maintenance of "life."[106]

Heidegger's assertion here that a *Volk* can be understood only in terms of Da-sein is an extension of the claim that Da-sein grounds human being. Heidegger's insistence that a people can never be an aim or goal is consistent with the rejection of teleological thought in the other beginning.

Heidegger's objection to a *Volk*-extension of "liberalism" and of a "commercial" approach to life, which is clearly limited to the way in which the concept of the *Volk* is formulated, is not directed against the conception as such. In the remainder of the passage, he reformulates this conception through a quasi-Platonic view of insight possessed by only some members of the group. For Heidegger, who here draws on his earlier discussion of the concept of mood,[107] the essence of a people lies in its voice understood, not as arising in a natural way, but only occasionally and in the few.

But the essence of the people is its "voice" [Stimme]. This *voice* does *not*, however, speak, in a so-called immediate flood [Erguss] of the common, natural, undistorted, and uneducated "person" [unverbildeten und ungebildeten "Mannes"]. Then this chosen witness [Denn dieser so angerufene Zeuge] is already very distorted and no longer moves in the originary relation to being [zum Seienden]. The "voice" of the people speaks seldom and only in the few [in Wenigen], if it [i.e., the voice] can be brought to sound [zum Klingen].[108]

If the "voice" of the people does not speak through everyone, but only through the few, and the latter are not associated with National Socialism or other forms of "liberalism," then this passage can be read as a further form of Heidegger's quasi-Platonic view in the rectoral address that finally only the philosopher can secure the good life for the people. Heidegger's continued faith in the supposedly exceptional, indeed unique, capacity of philosophers to discern political truth is inconsistent with his concern in the *Beiträge* to reject Platonism in all its forms. His insistence on the superior insight of the selected few, even as mediated through Nietzsche, a constant feature of all his later thought, including the discussion of technology, is clearly quasi-Platonic.

The short, sixth section of the book, devoted to what is to come, prepares the way for another short discussion concerning "The Last God."[109] In the sixth section, there are two consecutive paragraphs concerning the *Volk*.[110] From the perspective of the other beginning, Heidegger describes the "last god," a theme that later recurs in the *Spiegel* interview, as beyond all reckoning, hence, beyond such terms, associated with the first beginning, as "monotheism," "pantheism," or "atheism."[111] The language of the discussion of what is to come recalls that of such writers as Nietzsche and Spengler. In Nietzschean terminology, Heidegger evokes future beings (*die Zukünftigen*) as slow and long-listening founders of the essence of truth.[112] In Spenglerian terms, he describes "the hour of the fall of the West," interpreted philosophically, but not politically, as the end of the age of metaphysics.[113] Once again, Heidegger insists on his mystical pretense, a steady theme in his thought after the rectoral address, to interpret the present and future through his superior insight into metaphysics.

In his remarks on "The essence of the people and Da-sein," Heidegger returns to his conviction that only the few can provide a people with its identity.[114] For Heidegger, who here makes use of a notion of plural authenticity originally mentioned in *Being and Time*,[115] a people only is one when it receives its unifying idea and so returns to Being. In this way, a people bypasses the danger of merely turning on its own axis, or of falling prey to the false god of one's unlimitedness. Heidegger maintains that the idea that unifies a people can only be discovered through those who listen silently, that is, by those who are the true ground of the Being of these beings.

> A *Volk* is only a *Volk* if it receives its history through the discovery of its god, through the god, which, through history, compels it in a direction [hinwegzwingt] and so places it back in being [es so in das Seiende zurückstellt]. Only then does it avoid the danger of turning only on its own axis [um sich selber zu kreisen] and that which is only a condition of its maintenance, falsely honoring its unlimited [zu seinem unbedingten zu vergötzen]. But how can it [i.e., a *Volk*] find the god otherwise than if those who *seek* silently *for* it and as these seekers even apparently [sogar dem Anschein nach] must oppose the *still not volkhafte "Volk"*! However, these seekers must be themselves first; they are to be prepared as being [seiende]. What is Da-sein other than as the *ground* [*Gründung*] of the being of *these* beings, of the future beings of the last god.[116]

Heidegger now sums up his view of this relation in a single sentence describing the essence of the people as grounded in the historicity of those who seek to listen from their relation of belonging to the last god. "The essence of the people is grounded in the historicality of those listening to *themselves* [*Sichgehörenden*] *on the basis of* [*aus*] the relation of belonging to the god."[117]

This passage provides another clear indication of Heidegger's refusal to accept the hegemony of National Socialism and his assertion of the practical significance of his thought in bringing about the future of the Germans, both constant features in his writings beginning with the rectoral address. Heidegger's remark on the need to oppose the still not *volkhafte "Volk"* is difficult to construe. By placing the term *"Volk"* in quotation marks, he points out that it is not yet a *Volk* in his sense, since it has not yet been unified in an authentic manner around its own essence. If this passage refers to the German people, then Heidegger is disputing the success of National Socialism as far as bringing about the historical realization of the essence of the *Volk* is concerned. Here, in other language, Heidegger reaffirms his intimate conviction that the "philosopher" is the essential link for the authentic gathering of the German people. This passage provides a qualified restatement, from a point "beyond" philosophy, of the ancient Platonic claim that finally only a philosopher, only one attuned to the problem of Being in general, can lead the German people with respect to its own destiny.

With respect to Platonism and his own earlier writings, here the relevant difference is Heidegger's effort to combine his insistence on the political import of his own theory with his acknowledgment of modern nihilism. In light of Heidegger's conviction that nihilism follows from

Nietzsche's statement that God is dead, we can regard Heidegger's view of the last god, to be discovered by the philosopher, as a necessary political corrective, as a way to provide a new sense of direction to society. For Heidegger as for Nietzsche, the essence of the people is grounded in the few exceptional human beings. Like Kant, who held that the philosopher is the lawgiver of human reason,[118] Heidegger apparently believed that only a "philosopher" could provide a new sense of direction in the age of nihilism. For only a thinker, one who meditates in silence, can discern the last god.

Heidegger continues this line of argument in the next paragraph, entitled "Da-sein and the future beings of the last god."[119] This passage provides a transition to his account of the last god. Now further developing his mythological account, he describes this imaginary concept as a kind of historical vademecum at the beginning of a new history beyond history. For Heidegger, the last god will introduce a series of contradictions as paths which, when followed by the people, will lead it back to its essence and enable it to create its own history. "This god will set up the simplest, but farthest contradictions [Gegensätze] over his *Volk* as the paths over which they wander outward in order to find its essence again and to exhaust the moment of its history [und den Augenblick seiner Geschichte auszuschöpfen]."[120] The concept of the last god functions here as an organizing principle to enable a people to find and to realize its essence within history. Heidegger's conception of history beyond history echoes Marx's well-known view of the distinction between prehistory and history in the human sense, which only begins in and through the transition from capitalism to communism.[121] If we distinguish between authentic and inauthentic forms of history, as correlated to the essential and distorted forms of a *Volk,* then Heidegger's point is that in the other beginning, through its relation to the last god, the people will finally reach historical authenticity. Once again, the philosopher appears as the one who points the way to an authentic historical realization of the essence of the *Volk.*

The final comment on the *Volk* we will mention occurs appropriately in the last part of the book, in the discussion of Being in general (*das Seyn*) in a passage on being (*das Seiende*).[122] Once again Heidegger offers a description of an inauthentic people, whose lack of authenticity he indicates by enclosing *Volk* in quotation marks. This passage follows an earlier discussion of being (*Seiende*) and calculation in which Heidegger maintains that a result of the drive to master the environment in quantitative terms is the loss of the relation to being (*Seiende*).[123] In his following remarks on being (*das Seiende*), he unsystematically examines different aspects of the phenomenon.

Heidegger's comment on the *Volk* in this context is interesting for the link he identifies between Greek thought and German romanticism. Ever attentive to Greek thought, Heidegger asserts that "nature" ("*Natur*") is a debased form of the Greek "*physis*" and then raises the idea of a theoretical reformulation of Goethe's ideas of "earth" and "life." For Heidegger, a rooting around (*Wühlen*) in the irrational is required to complete the modern period. He remarks that Romanticism has not yet reached its end, since it still seeks an "unclarification" (*Verklärung*) of being (*Seiende*) which it opposes to other views. He maintains that the resultant lack of clarification manifests the effort to renew culture that is uprooted from the people. "The historical renovation of 'culture' is invited to this raising up [Verklärung] and its uprooting is practiced in the '*Volk*' [im '*Volk*' betrieben] and striven to communicate it to everyone."[124]

The *Volk* and Silence (*Schweigen*)

This chapter has considered the evolution of Heidegger's Nazism in that huge, as yet only partially explored continent known as the *Beiträge zur Philosophie*. To test the claim that Heidegger here breaks with, or at least distances himself from, National Socialism,[125] we have examined Heidegger's scattered remarks throughout the work on the concept of the *Volk*. Consideration of his Nazism in terms of this concept is justified by its central role in the amorphous series of doctrines collectively known as the National Socialist worldview and in his own turn to Nazism. It is reasonable to suppose that any turn away from Nazism would be visible in his treatment of this concept.

Heidegger's criticism of National Socialism in the *Beiträge* is based on a perspective that is astonishingly foreign to that revolutionary movement. Whatever else Nazism was, it was mainly, centrally concerned with the practical problem of world domination. On the contrary, here as elsewhere Heidegger considers Nazism from his own theoretical vantage point, in terms of the criterion of a theory of Being. In the few instances where Heidegger objects to Nazism, it is invariably because of its supposed failure, as a form of worldview, to achieve full theoretical status through a transition to the other beginning that he sketches in this book. Heidegger does not reject National Socialism as such in this work, and certainly not because of the practical consequences to which it led; rather he objects to it for its theoretical deficiencies from his ontological vantage point, for its supposed failure to provide an adequate theory of Being.

The *Beiträge* is indispensable to comprehend the interrelation between Heidegger's Nazism and the evolution of his position in the period after the rectorate. With respect to National Socialism, Heidegger's other beginning is continuous with his earlier thought in three main ways. First, there is a further stress on the destiny of the German people which remains to be realized in history, a commitment that Heidegger continues to share with National Socialism. Second, now as before, Heidegger holds that what he earlier stigmatized as "political science" and still rejects as a mere worldview is inadequate to achieve its end in view. In a word, although Heidegger accepts the Nazi goal, which was ingredient in his turn toward National Socialism, he continues to reject Nazism as an adequate means to that end. Third, in the *Beiträge* Heidegger reaffirms the point made in rectoral address: the German people need finally to be led to their destiny by Heidegger's thought since it cannot realize itself as German through National Socialism. The difference, of course, is that in the meantime Heidegger's thought has evolved beyond philosophy to the other beginning, in virtue of which Heidegger has come to believe that "philosophy" cannot lead directly to the gathering of the German as German. It can only point to that goal whose realization lies through the turn to poetry, in particular to the thought of Hölderlin.

In sum, Heidegger's thought has changed, but its relation to German destiny remains unchanged. Heidegger remains convinced of his own messianic role in bringing about the destiny of the German people within history. Further, he remains convinced that Nazism is not finally conducive to that shared end. In his later thought, Heidegger does not reject a political role for "philosophy," for his new thought beyond the Platonic tradition, although he rejects philosophy. Even in his rejection of Platonism, Heidegger retains his confidence—characteristic of the hubris often restated since Plato by others, and perhaps characteristic of philosophy itself—that the thought of a philosopher, in Heidegger's view the view of thinker of Being, is a necessary condition of the good life.

Heidegger's critique of Nazism in this work cannot be denied, although its extremely limited extent should be stressed. Here, his objection to National Socialism is always limited to its failure as a theory of Being. Heidegger's failure to object to the political consequences of the Nazi worldview is significant, since it suggests an incapacity of his thought—that is, the thought of a great thinker, in the opinion of some observers the most important thinker of this century—to grasp the political specificity of National Socialism. It is an error to hold that after the rectorate Heidegger breaks with Nazism on a political plane. Even in the rectoral address, his commitment to National Socialism was tempered by his refusal of the hegemony of politics, which he intended to found in philosophy. In the *Beiträge* his view has not changed, since he continues to accept the point he has always shared with Nazism: insistence on the authentic gathering of the Germans.

We can end this chapter with a comment about Heidegger's silence.[126] It is well known that in his writings, Heidegger never publicly spoke to the problem of the Holocaust, about which he remained silent. The *Beiträge* suggests an interesting reason for this attitude, for Heidegger's failure to assume the moral consequences of his commitment to a worldview whose well-known excesses have been decried by history.[127] In *Being and Time,* Heidegger in passing describes silence (*Schweigen*) and hearing as possibilities of discursive speech.[128] He characterizes the possibility of authentic silence in genuine discourse, as distinguished from mere silence.[129] In the discussion of conscience, he maintains that the call of conscience is silence.[130] In the initial cycle of Hölderlin lectures, immediately after the rectorate, he modifies this view in maintaining that we are a conversation, which means as well that we are silence.[131] He further inverts the relation between silence as a form of speech and speech in order to ground speech in silence.[132] Heidegger exploits this revision of his view of silence in his discussion of Nietzsche. Here, he states that the highest form of saying lies in being silent (*verschweigen*) about what must be said; the saying of thought is being silent (*ein Erschweigen*).[133] Heidegger's revised understanding of silence suggests that to be silent is not only possible in an authentic manner; in fact, silence is the most authentic form of speech. In a word, to be an authentic person requires that one in effect be silent.[134]

Heidegger raises the theme of silence in two places in the *Beiträge*. In a pair of passages in the first part, he examines the silence (*Erschweigung*) of Being in general as a *Sigetik*.[135] This term is a neologism coined by Heidegger, formed from the Greek "*sigao*," whose infinitive form means "to be silent or still, to keep silence."[136] Heidegger uses this term to refer to those who still think according to a "logic" used to fit what is thought into compartments. His point is that this "logic," which belongs to the first beginning, is inadequate to grasp the *Ereignis*, which is the theme of the other beginning. In this sense, one can say that Being in general is silent with respect to the thinking effort to depict it. Heidegger returns to the theme of silence in the last paragraph of the book, in a comment on the origin of speech.[137] Now following the revised understanding of silence announced in the initial Hölderlin lectures, he maintains that speech is grounded in silence. According to Heidegger, silence is the measure, since it first provides the standard. "Speech is grounded in silence. Silence is the hiddenmost holding to the measure [verborgenste Mass-halten]. It holds the measure [Mass], in that it first provides the standards [Maßstäbe]."[138]

This passage in the *Beiträge* suggests an interesting philosophical explanation for Heidegger's later silence, unrelated to personal psychological weakness, or moral insufficiency, or the effort to preserve one's honor. On the basis of this text, we can infer that in the face of the mere chatter of supposedly inauthentic beings, Heidegger kept silent at least in part on philosophical grounds, for the reason that to do so is supposedly to engage in an authentic form of genuine discourse, to maintain the standards of rigorous thought based upon silence.

Heidegger's idea of silence should be put in perspective. His point differs from Wittgenstein's view that one should be silent about what cannot be expressed in speech.[139] Heidegger is not willing to take a skeptical stance, for instance by asserting that one should say nothing about what one cannot know. Rather, Heidegger's revised doctrine of silence—a view which, like its original formulation, is presented without any effort to justify the change—is intended to point to silence as the highest level of speech. The modification is, however, significant, even "convenient" in the present context, after the failure of the rectorate. For this revised view of silence provides Heidegger with a reason, rooted in his thought, to remain silent in an authentic manner, to refuse on philosophical grounds to say anything, anything at all, to decline in virtue of his theory to take a public position on the Holocaust, on Nazism, or on his view of Nazism. But one must wonder whether a form of thought can be authentic or even rigorous if this means to remain silent before the Holocaust whose central meaning it can neither express nor grasp.

6

Nazism and Technology

The *Spiegel* Interview, Technology, and Nazism

In the context of the present inquiry, Heidegger's view of technology is important because of claims that it functions as a critique of National Socialism. Heidegger's conception of technology has received extensive attention.[1] The focus of the present discussion is not this conception as such, which has already been studied in the literature, but rather its relation to his Nazism. Yet it is not possible to analyze the connection between Heidegger's view of technology and his Nazism unless we understand his conception of technology. Accordingly, this chapter will need to devote substantial attention to an analysis of Heidegger's complex interpretation of technology.

The link between Heidegger's view of technology and Nazism is controversial. With a single exception, most observers consider Heidegger's view of technology as indicating his distance from National Socialism.[2] Heidegger himself calls attention to the relation of his theory of technology to Nazism in the well-known *Spiegel* interview. Heidegger's *Spiegel* interview is more significant than its designation as an interview suggests. It was not the result of a simple meeting with a journalist, but the product of careful planning, whose text was later worked over before publication. The interview records Heidegger's largely successful effort to influence the way in which his person and thought would be regarded after his death. Now the single most important theme of this interview consists in Heidegger's comments on the theme of technology which emerges in his later thought. It is, then, useful to examine the text of his interview as an initial indication of the relation between his view of technology and his Nazism.

Heidegger's interview with *Der Spiegel* offers a simplified but not inaccurate access to his difficult theory of technology. In the course of the interview, Heidegger makes a series of points about technology, which are clearly related to his later thought:

1. His understanding of technology changed from the early idea of the confrontation between human being and planetary technology, in his lecture course on metaphysics, to the later idea of enframing (*Gestell*).[3] Enframing is roughly a conception of horizon, as the limits within which something occurs. For Heidegger, the limit of modernity is technology.

2. The force of global technology as a factor in determining history can scarcely be overestimated.[4] This is a further form of the view, which emerges in Heidegger's later thought, that human being is powerless before Being.

3. At present, he is unconvinced that democracy is adequate as a political system in a technological age.[5] Heidegger here draws the political consequence of his later conception of Being as the real historical agent.

4. Human being is unable to master or to respond adequately to the essence of technology.[6] This idea is the corollary of the view that ultimate agency is lodged in Being.

5. The age of technology has brought forward a series of technological relationships in which man is uprooted from his tradition and his home.[7] Heidegger here returns to a form of his idea of authenticity, which he later develops in the direction of an authentic form of life.[8]

6. Metaphysical thinking, which ends in Nietzsche, is unable adequately to think technology.[9]

7. The essence of technology lies in the concept of enframing.[10] This is an indication of how Heidegger understands technology.

8. The situation of human being with respect to technology is not one of fate and it is possible to prepare for a reversal (*Umkehr*).[11] Heidegger holds out in this way the prospect of emerging from the hegemony of technology. This signals a residual role for thought beyond philosophy.

9. National Socialism was moving in the direction of reacting against technology although it fell short of the goal.[12] Heidegger

now disputes the view that Nazism was itself a simple manifestation of technology, or only that, since he insists that Nazism
intended to react against the hegemony of modern technology.

10. We can prepare to counteract technology, although only a god
can save us, through a new appropriation of the European tradition in which thinking transforms thinking.[13] This is a further
formulation of Heidegger's conviction that after the death of
God, which Nietzsche has announced, after the end of the old
mythology, we require a new mythology.

There is a clear connection between Heidegger's Nazism and his approach to technology. Heidegger describes his theory of technology as
an effort to go further down the road traveled by National Socialism,
understood as an initial but intrinsically insufficient effort to come to
grips with the problem of technology.[14] Numerous commentators have
insisted on the role of technology in Nazism, in particular on the integral
way in which it furthered Nazi genocide.[15] Heidegger takes a completely
different, in fact opposite line. For Heidegger, National Socialism opposes the rule of technology; but in virtue of its supposed incapacity to
think, Nazism is unable to break away from it.[16] Heidegger presents his
own thought as an improvement on the "inadequate" effort of Nazi
thinkers to face technology. In answer to a question raised during the
interview, Heidegger states:

> It seems to me that you are taking technology too absolutely. I do not
> see the situation of man in the world of global technology as a fate which
> cannot be escaped or unravelled. On the contrary, I see the task of
> thought to consist in helping man in general, within the limits allotted to
> thought, to achieve an adequate relationship to the essence of technol-
> ogy. National Socialism, to be sure, moved in this direction. But those
> people were far too limited in their thinking to acquire an explicit rela-
> tionship to what is really happening today and has been underway for
> three centuries.[17]

Here, in his own way, Heidegger is signaling, as clearly as he can—
candidly, and accurately—that his theory of technology is meant to
carry out the ideas which the National Socialists were too limited to
develop through a theory of technology with political consequences.
What does it mean, in the era of technology, to achieve an adequate
relationship to the essence of technology, an explicit relationship to what
is happening today and has been under way for three centuries? One
thing it means is to confront modernity. Now in the period after *Being
and Time,* most explicitly in the Nietzsche lectures, Heidegger came to

understand his own thought of Being as confronting modernity, and the rule over beings, in the name of Being. Nazism, too, he tells us in this passage, made a similar attempt, although it fell short in its inability—which Heidegger criticizes in a variety of texts, such as the Nietzsche lectures and the *Beiträge*—to think Being authentically. Now part of the authentic thought of Being is authentic human being, or Dasein, as the vantage point from which to comprehend Being. Authentic human being is what Heidegger since the rectoral address has in view through the idea of the historical realization of the Germans as German. Although Heidegger has undertaken to deconstrust subjectivity in order to consider Being without Dasein, in another sense Dasein is still central to his thought in his concern with resistance to the loss of tradition and of the place to dwell.

If this is correct, we can anticipate that Heidegger's theory of technology, which he intends as a carrying out of the confrontation of technology which the Nazis were too crude to perform, continues to share the insistence on the authentic gathering of the *Volk*. Like his theory of Being, the theory of technology which derives from the theory of Being is intrinsically political, where politics is directed toward the authenticity of the Germans and, beyond the Germans, toward knowledge of Being. To miss this point, to understand his theory of technology merely as an analysis of technology, even more precisely as a scrutiny of the essence of technology, is simply to miss the central thrust of Heidegger's view.

I have brought together Heidegger's remarks on technology in his interview in the form of a connected argument. Taken together, these remarks yield an informal sketch of Heidegger's later understanding of technology as an all-encompassing, global phenomenon, beyond the control of human being, including the metaphysical form of thought said to end in Nietzsche; these comments further provide an insight into Heidegger's insistence that the spell of technology can be broken, or reversed, by a form of thought, such as Heidegger's, different from metaphysics, which goes further than National Socialism in order to reappropriate the Western tradition in a new way.

According to Heidegger, a reversal can only come about through a thorough rethinking of the Western tradition. He states that

> it is my conviction that a reversal can be prepared only in the same place in the world where the modern technological world originated, and that it cannot happen because of any takeover by Zen-Buddhism or any other Eastern experiences of the world. There is need for a rethinking which is to be carried out with the help of the European tradition and of a new appropriation of that tradition. Thinking itself can be transformed only by a thinking which has the same origin and calling.[18]

The view of technology sketched in Heidegger's interview, and which only appears in Heidegger's later work, has an obvious connection to his preceding writings. Ideas that reappear now in this extension of his position include the concern with Being, the supposed incapacity of ordinary thought to comprehend the "situation," the claimed need to break with the metaphysical tradition which purportedly draws to a close with Nietzsche, the reference to fate, the alleged connection between nihilism and technology, and Heidegger's suggestion that he intends to carry further the effort begun, but not completed, by National Socialism. Since the roots of Heidegger's concept of technology lie deep within his earlier writings, we will need to consider its emergence within the position as a whole before we turn to its mature form. A grasp of Heidegger's understanding of technology will enable us to envisage its relation to his Nazism.

On the Background of
Heidegger's View of Technology

To begin with, it is useful to recall in outline the development of the theme of technology in Heidegger's position. This theme is not explicit in his early philosophy and only becomes explicit after the turning in his thought as a by-product of his attention to nihilism. Technology is not an important theme in *Being and Time*. To the best of my knowledge, the only explicit mention of technology is in a single sentence in § 69, in the course of a lengthy discussion of "The Temporality of Being-in-the-World and the Problem of the Transcendence of the World." In part b of this paragraph, clumsily titled "The Temporal Meaning of the Way in Which Circumspective Concern Becomes Modified into the Theoretical Discovery of the Present-at-Hand Within-the-World," Heidegger writes: "Reading off the measurements which result from an experiment often requires a complicated 'technical' set-up for the experimental design."[19]

Yet if not the theory of technology, at least the basic conceptual framework from which it will emerge is already in place as early as *Being and Time*. So in the famous discussion of equipment from a clearly pragmatic angle of vision, Heidegger draws the well-known distinction between readiness-to-hand (*Zuhandenheit*) and presence-to-hand (*Vorhandenheit*). He then writes, in a reference to what nature is in itself:

> Here, however, "Nature" is not to be understood as that which is just present-at-hand, nor as the *power of Nature*. The wood is a forest of timber, the mountain a quarry of rock; the river is water-power, the wind is wind "in the sails." As the "environment" is discovered, the "Nature" thus discovered is encountered too. If its kind of Being as ready-to-hand is

disregarded, this "Nature" itself can be discovered and defined simply in its pure presence-to-hand. But when this happens the Nature which "stirs and strives," which assails us and enthralls us as landscape, remains hidden. The botanists' plans are not the flowers of the hedgerow; the "source" which the geographer establishes for a river is not the "springhead in the dale."[20]

In this passage, Heidegger, who does not yet possess a developed concept of technology, presents the dark side which, he believes, technology tends to hide or to cover up. To see this point, we need to dig a little deeper than the official concern in this paragraph with the relative priority between presence-to-hand and readiness-to-hand which defines entities "ontologico-categorially."[21] For Heidegger, the initial access to entities is solely in terms of an "in order to" structure, through a possible use to which they can be put. It follows, then, that a pragmatic intention structures the world and its contents as they are revealed to us. If the way in which we turn to the world structures what we find there, by implication the particular structure we impart to the world removes from it certain aspects that cannot be found because they are literally rendered invisible by the kind of utilitarian perspective one adopts, or even the utilitarian perspective itself. This is the deeper meaning of Heidegger's remark, in the passage cited, that beyond the botanists' plants and the geographers' river there are the flowers of the hedgerow and the springhead in the dale. Heidegger's point, then, is that at the same time as modern technology, illustrated in such sciences as botany and geography, reveals a world called into being by different forms of technological perspective, it also tends to hide or to occult another, more "natural" world.

This passage, which is not yet a theory of technology, points toward the need for an explanation of how, under circumstances associated with nihilism, technology itself, in principle meant to improve life, works against the realization of that aim. In Heidegger's succeeding writings, the theory of technology gradually emerges until he focuses on it directly. This topic is already on his mind in the lecture course on metaphysics. Here, in the context of his meditation on metaphysics, he interprets the Greek root of the German word often rendered as technology ("*Technik*") against the background of the ancient Greek tradition.

In a remark on the relation of "*physis*" and "*techne,*" he translates the latter as denoting neither art nor technology but knowledge. By "knowledge" he understands "the ability to plan and to organize freely, or to master institutions."[22] Heidegger later amplifies his understanding of *techne* as knowledge in the context of a lengthy discussion of Sophocles' *Antigone*. In an interpretation of the word "*deinon,*" he employs the term *"Machenschaft,"* from *"machanoen,"* to describe "the power, the powerful, in which the action of the violent one moves," to refer to the "machination . . . entrusted to him."[23] If we take Heidegger's comments on *techne* as adumbrating his later doctrine of technology, we can perceive in this remark a foreshadowing of what he regards as the essential passivity of human being with respect to a violent phenomenon not under human control. If knowledge requires effective transparency, or control, then such knowledge is accompanied by a constitutive opacity, or lack of control.

Heidegger amplifies the manner in which *techne* as knowledge presupposes an active aspect in further comments on the link between *techne* and art. For Heidegger, knowledge is not mere observation, but involves a looking beyond what is given at any time. He further stresses the forward-looking, prospective aspect of *techne* by noting that it is the Greek term for art, which allows the emergence of what is concealed, which, then, realizes, which accomplishes in the form of an entity.

> Because art in a pre-eminent sense stabilizes and manifests Being in the work as an entity, it may be regarded as the ability, pure and simple, to accomplish, to put-into-the-work [ins-Werk-setzen], as *techne*. This accomplishment is a manifesting realization [Erwirken] of being *in* the entity.[24]

But if Being manifests itself in technological production, then the human role is overshadowed by that which so to speak makes use of it. Technology is not, or is not only, the employment of a means to reach an end in view; technology, as in the Greek sense of art, is the revealing of what reveals itself through technology in independence of us.[25]

In later writings composed during the 1930s, Heidegger begins to develop various aspects of his view of technology. In the *Beiträge,* through the concept of machination Heidegger emphasizes the relation of technology to calculability and to the modern period. For Heidegger, calculation originally becomes possible through the application of scientifically grounded mathematical technique.[26] Yet in Heidegger's eyes, technology is at best a mixed blessing. Heidegger stresses its negative aspect in a later remark, in a protest against the way in which the familiar insistence on the expansion of technology, in the rise of mere number, of simple gigantism, brings about a transformation of human being.[27]

Heidegger finds the origins of modern technology in early Greek philosophy. In a remark about Plato, Heidegger attributes the difficulties of modernity to the central figure in the Western philosophical tradition. On the basis of a concept of *techne,* Plato's supposed preference for entities, mere beings, made possible the rise of modern technology, whose result is seen in an alleged forgetfulness of Being and a supposed denial of history.[28] In this way, Heidegger establishes to his satisfaction that modern technology, and by implication the whole modern period, is only possible because of the turn away from an authentic comprehension of Being. The double consequence of Heidegger's analysis is to forge a metaphysical link between the question of Being and technology, and to uncover a metaphysical ground to oppose technology and modernity. Heidegger's disparaging comment on Plato is consistent with Heidegger's later effort to reject metaphysics and philosophy for another form of thought beyond philosophy. It points to the deep connection between Heidegger's view of technology and his rejection of all metaphysics since the pre-Socratics.

The connection of technology with modernity and metaphysics, to which Heidegger alludes in the *Beiträge,* is strengthened in subsequent writings. In an important essay on representation, Heidegger insists on the link between technology and modern science while seeming to distance himself from his earlier claim about the relation of calculation and technique. Heidegger now maintains that technology is as important as modern science, since it is an autonomous domain; but technology cannot be understood as an application of a mathematical form of physical science.

> One of the essential phenomena of the modern age is its science. A phenomenon of no less importance is machine technology. We must not, however, misinterpet that technology as the mere application of modern mathematical physical science to praxis. Machine technology is itself an autonomous transformation of praxis, a type of transformation wherein praxis first demands the employment of mathematical physical science. Machine technology remains up to now the most visible outgrowth of the essence of modern technology, which is identical with the essence of modern metaphysics.[29]

This passage uncovers an important new aspect of technology, which is now revealed as the ground of modernity and, for that reason, as the continuation of the metaphysical turn away from an authentic grasp of Being. For Heidegger, metaphysics grounds an age by giving it a specific viewpoint, and ours is the age of technology. Modern technology, which is so far most visible in so-called machine technology, is modern metaphysics. Since Heidegger also holds that the metaphysical tradition carries with it a false understanding of Being, modern technology is a phenomenon that we need to surpass if we are to return to a true metaphysics. The technological conquest of the world, produced through the appearance of the gigantic, and the attachment to quantity, although perhaps a special kind of greatness, only signifies a metaphysical decline.

Heidegger further contributes to his nascent view of technology in a brief passage in the "Letter on Humanism." The passage begins with a meditation on homelessness, which he sees as resulting from the turning away from Being by beings. For Heidegger, homelessness is becoming the destiny of the world (*Weltschicksal*).[30] He sees Marx's concept of alienation as the analysis of a phenomenon due to, and covered up by, metaphysics. From Heidegger's perspective, Marx's specific contribution lies in his understanding of the relation of alienation to history, an insight so far unmatched by later thinkers who fail to enter into dialogue with him, which is possible only if one grasps the essence of materialism.[31]

These claims require careful consideration. It is unclear that Heidegger has avoided the danger of facile statements about materialism, about which he warns us. His assertion that no one has so far been able to dialogue with Marx in virtue of the inability to think history is possibly accurate for Husserl but more questionable for Sartre.[32] One must also question Heidegger's dogmatic assumption of the Marxist myth that Marx's position is fairly described as materialism.[33]

Heidegger's basic claim is that in order to think history, we must think Being in the authentic sense. His remarks on technology, meant to support his stress on the priority of the question of Being, reveal the importance he attaches to this phenomenon. Heidegger insists that the essence of materialism, the position he attributes to Marx, is concealed in technology. The result is in effect to reverse what he, following the standard Marxist reading of Marx, understands as Marx's effort to think technology through "materialism," that is, as an outgrowth of the concentration of capital in modern society. Since Heidegger believes that technology can only be understood in terms of the forgotten history of Being, Marx's position, although deeper than others, is nonetheless superficial when measured by this standard. In this way, Heidegger transforms Marx's question concerning the nature of modern life, which Marx studies in terms of the institution of private property and human being, into his own question concerning Being.

Heidegger argues for his rival theory of Being as the key to modern society by drawing a link between technology and the contemporary historical moment. For Heidegger, technology is a mode of the manifestation of the truth of Being in the ancient Greek sense; through technology, the history of metaphysics appears. From Heidegger's perspective, technology is merely the visible aspect of metaphysics. Now making a difficult transition from technology as a manifestation of Being to political doctrines, he asserts that the latter as well derive from Being. The problem is that thought, which is determined by Being, is inadequate either to grasp Being or to conceptualize the present historical moment. Metaphysics cannot think the present era, in which it is the dominant mode of thought. Heidegger's assertion that politics depends on Being is further important for an understanding of his turning toward Nazism. If ontology leads to politics, as Heidegger now maintains, then it is reasonable to suppose, as the discussion has previously shown, that his view of Being could also induce a political turning, including a turning to Nazi politics.

In an important passage that ties together different themes of his overall position with his concept of technology, Heidegger writes:

> The essence of materialism is concealed in the essence of technology, about which much has been written but little has been thought. Technology is in its essence a destiny within the history of Being and of the truth of Being, a truth that lies in oblivion. For technology does not go back to the *techne* of the Greeks in name only but derives historically and essentially from *techne* as a mode of *aletheuein,* a mode, that is, of rendering beings manifest. As a form of truth technology is grounded in the history of metaphysics, which is itself distinctive and up to now the only perceptible phase of the history of Being. No matter which of the various positions one chooses to adopt toward the doctrines of communism and to their foundation, from the point of view of the history of Being it is certain that an elemental experience of what is world-historical speaks out in it. Whoever takes "communism" only as a "party" or a *"Weltanschauung"* is thinking too shallowly, just as those who by the term "Americanism" mean, and mean derogatorily, nothing more than a particular lifestyle. The danger into which Europe as it has hitherto existed is ever more clearly forced consists presumably in the fact above all that its thinking—once its glory—is falling behind in the essential course of a dawning world destiny which nevertheless in the basic traits of its essential provenance remains European by definition. No metaphysics, whether idealistic, materialistic, or Christian, can in accord with its essence, and surely not in its own attempts to explicate itself, "get a hold on" this destiny yet, and that means thoughtfully to reach and gather together what in the fullest sense of Being now is.[34]

This passage is important for several reasons. First, Heidegger indicates that a theory of technology needs to take a historical approach. He credits Marx's view as an advanced example of this approach. Second, he stresses, as he did in *Being and Time,* that history can only be thought in terms of Being. Third, from this perspective, Heidegger maintains that a theory of technology which explains the phenomenon of technology in terms of modern society and not conversely is unacceptable. The result is to maintain his insistence, consistent in his works, on the primacy of the question of Being. Fourth, he insists on the inseparable link between technology and metaphysics or the history of ontology. In this way, Heidegger signals his intention to utilize his concern with Being as the crucial insight to understand technology. Fifth, he brings out the fateful consequence of the understanding of technology in the escape from homelessness which afflicts modern man and the return to Being from the forgetfulness of Being. This is again a signal that, despite the later effort to decenter subjectivity, Heidegger still maintains the emphasis, present as early as *Being and Time,* on the link between Being and authenticity.

A Note on Technology and Heidegger's Wider Position

So far we have been considering the genesis of Heidegger's understanding of technology in a series of texts in which it is at most an occasional theme. This is not the same as an analysis of the view of technology within Heidegger's wider position. Although there is an occasional reference to technology in earlier writings, this theme only engages Heidegger's attention in a central way after the onset of the turning in his thought, a process already under way at the time of the rectoral address. The date in question is obviously important. If the turn to Nazism is prior to the turning in his thought, then, for strategic reasons concerning the defense of Heidegger's thought, it is convenient to depict the turning as a turning against Nazism.[35] If the turning occurs before or during the rectoral period, then this claim is no longer plausible.

The complex evolution of Heidegger's position known collectively as the turning requires an understanding of the way that, for Heidegger, the decline of the thought of Being is linked to the rise of a form of society which not only turns away from, but actually impedes, a comprehension of Being. We can spell this point out as follows: One of the consequences of the turning is that Heidegger to his satisfaction establishes a connection between a mythical event at the onset of Western history and the decline of authentic metaphysics. For Heidegger, Nietzsche's contribution is to identify the ongoing phenomenon of nihilism which Heidegger reads as the turn away from Being. Heidegger goes beyond Nietzsche in order to maintain that modernity itself, more precisely the modern concern with entities, is both a symptom of and contributes to the occultation of Being. From the perspective of the turning in his thought, Heidegger understands the rise of technology as the essence of modernity following from the withdrawal of Being. In sum, the turning in Heidegger's thought requires a further turn to a theory of modernity which can only turn out to be a further consequence of his basic concern with Being.

If the turn to technology is a further aspect of the lengthy turning in Heidegger's thought, we can understand the specific influences that shaped his conception of technology and its relatively late emergence as integrally related to his wider position. The turning occurs in part during Heidegger's effort to come to grips with Nietzsche, during Heidegger's effort to evolve a new mythology in the new space created by Nietzsche's nihilism, the idea following from Nietzsche's proclamation that God is dead. Accordingly, we can expect Nietzsche to influence Heidegger's concept of technology as well. We can further expect the concept of technology to assume its mature form only after a point when Heidegger himself becomes aware, and publicly acknowledges, that a process of development is taking place in his position—namely in the "Letter on Humanism"—and begins to consider how to carry that process forward. An understanding of technology is not important in the initial form of the position, which features an abstract analysis of Being as time unrelated to a specific historical context; but it is important, indeed essential, for the revised version of the position which comprehends the problem of Being as a function of a specific historical event, which in turn requires an analysis of the present historical period.

Influences on Heidegger's View of Technology

Heidegger's pessimistic assessment of technology echoes a disillusionment about technological advances widely felt by others as well.[36] A deep unease about the relation between technology and philosophy surfaced early in the nineteenth century, in the wake of Hegel's system. In the middle of the century (1857), in a well-known study of Hegel, Haym complained that the time for system was past since the very bases of physical and spiritual life were in the process of being transformed by the triumph of technology.

> Hegel's system and its hegemony was after the brilliant period of our classical poetry the last great and universal manifestation on the purely spiritual plane which our fatherland has produced. Nothing like that has occurred since that time. In fact, much to the contrary. We find ourselves for the moment in a great and almost universal shipwreck of the spiritual and of belief in spirit in general. Let us look at the most recent facts of naked truth! An unprecedented and simply decisive change has taken place. This is no longer a time for system, no longer a time for poetry or philosophy. This is instead a time in which, thanks to the great technical discoveries of this century, matter seems to have come alive. The most basic underpinnings of our physical and our spiritual life are being ripped apart and transformed by this triumph of technology [Technik].[37]

Nor was the distrust of technology confined merely to nineteenth-century thinkers. In 1931, toward the close of the Weimar Republic, Jaspers, who typically insisted on the importance of science, spoke for many others in evoking the threats posed by technology and the machine, as well as tensions between technical organization and existence.[38]

The breadth of Heidegger's reading means that his conception of technology could have been influenced by any number of writers. Here, it will suffice to mention merely Nietzsche, Jünger, and Spengler. Heidegger's interest in Nietzsche precedes, in fact necessarily precedes, Heidegger's theory of technology, which presupposes his reading of Nietzsche's view of nihilism. There is a natural progression in Heidegger's thought from his attraction to Nietzsche's idea that God is dead, to the nihilism it supposedly signifies, and the relation of nihilism to technology. Between the rectoral address, where he stressed the nihilistic implications of the alleged death of God, and the final series of lectures on Nietzsche, Heidegger's understanding of nihilism changed radically. The relative optimism present when he became rector was later transformed into a bleak pessimism about the possibility of surpassing what Heidegger, in the rectoral address, describes as "the forsakenness of modern man in the midst of what is."[39]

A darker understanding of nihilism emerged during Heidegger's lectures on Nietzche. Heidegger's theory of technology relates the technological phenomenon to nihilism. If the decisive step is the connection between nihilism and technology, it is not surprising that Heidegger only worked out his theory of technology when he possessed his reading of nihilism.

When Heidegger staked his claim to the hegemony of Nazism, he thought that in order to rescue modern man it would be sufficient to resurrect the authentic Greek idea of science in the ontological form of his fundamental ontology. At the time, he believed there was a single common solution to rescue modern man and to defend the university from the encroachment of, or the threat posed by, the so-called "Christian-theological interpretation of the world and the mathematical-technological thinking of the modern age."[40] Several years later, at the close of the Nietzsche lectures, Heidegger no longer thought that it was possible to cast off nihilism with ease, if at all. Heidegger turns toward technology to formulate an aspect of his increasingly pessimistic reading of the pervasive and persistent nature of nihilism that surrounds us.

In an important passage at the close of the Nietzsche lectures series, Heidegger points briefly to his understanding of the connection between nihilism and modern technology. For Heidegger, the mythical event of the withdrawal of Being results in the ongoing nihilism perceived only by Nietzsche. Heidegger diagnoses the result of nihilism within the traditional binary framework of theory and practice. On the theoretical level, there is a decline of the thought of Being manifest in what passes for metaphysics and in the theory of the worldview. On the practical level, there is a disappearance of the distinction between Being as such and beings manifest in the concern to rule over beings. For Heidegger, technology can be understood as the extension of the rule of human beings over beings, which occurs in the space created by the turn away from Being. He insists that with the completion of metaphysics and the decline of the thought of Being, technology flourishes as never before. "This is the basis of the fact that complete, unlimited, undisturbed and confused hegemony over being [Seiende] can develop only with the beginning of the fulfillment of metaphysics."[41]

Ernst Jünger's influence on Heidegger's conception of technology, which has been studied in the secondary literature,[42] is visible in a number of Heidegger's texts. We have already noted more than once that in his discussion of the rectorate Heidegger invokes Jünger as a mediator in order to understand the past and present in terms of Nietzsche's metaphysics.[43] Heidegger confirms this point in his article "Zur Seinsfrage"— originally intended as a contribution to a festschrift for Jünger on his sixtieth birthday—where further he credits Jünger with a description of European nihilism in the period after the First World War.[44] Heidegger specifically acknowledges the debt of his own thought on technology to Jünger's success, not in describing an already known phenomenon, but in making available "a new reality."[45]

Jünger described the so-called new reality in his book, *The Worker: Hegemony and Form* (*Der Arbeiter: Herrschaft und Gestalt*).[46] This book was originally published in 1932, several months before the National Socialists seized power in the beginning of 1933. In the foreword to the first edition, Jünger describes his intention, in quasi-phenomenological terms, as an effort to describe the form of the worker, beyond party perspectives and beyond theory. Jünger perceived a new reality, in which the worker actively determined history and a changed world.[47] In the foreword to the second edition, more than thirty years later, looking backward, Jünger described his work as an effort to find a way to understand the present at a moment when the forces of change have clearly signaled the advent of a new period.[48] He further insisted that if the main actors had acted according to the principles he sketched, much could have been avoided, even the use of armed force.[49]

Jünger's book reads like a kind of mad Spinozism in which determinism is freedom and the worker is free in submitting to a centrally organized dictatorship. The work is written in a tedious style and is certainly tedious to read. It mainly consists of a series of statements which, since they rarely develop to the stage of argumentation, are difficult to summarize. Jünger develops his idea of the worker in opposition to bourgeois liberalism and, to a lesser degree, to Marxism.[50] Jünger's principal theme is the overwhelming importance of the worker as the key to a new form of society. He describes the *Führer* as the first soldier or first worker, and he further suggests that the contract is to be replaced by an organization along the lines of an army.[51] Accepting an organic theory of the state, popular among conservative thinkers, Jünger maintains that rule and service are one and the same.[52] Glorifying the importance of the worker, he asserts that the rise of the worker signifies the rise of the new Germany.[53] For Jünger, the possibility of reaching a deeper, richer, more fruitful world lies in an awareness of the superiority of the worker over the citizen (*Bürger*).[54] On his view, the task of the worker is to show a total engagement (*die totale Mobilmachung*), which is the will to submit to total dictatorship.[55] Jünger further stresses the emphasis on obedience in his claim that the demand for freedom is at the same time a demand for work.[56]

Jünger's book is intellectually very weak, difficult to take seriously, worthy of consideration here only because of its impact on Heidegger. It is hard to imagine that a thinker of any importance, much less someone often classified as one of the great thinkers of our time, could be influenced by the work of an intrinsically insignificant writer such as Jünger, much less form a group to devote considerable time to the study of his "thought." Heidegger is generous in crediting Jünger's influence on his own theory, although Heidegger appears to owe more inspiration than insight to Jünger's work.

The article Heidegger contributed to Jünger's festschrift is an occasion to rethink some aspects of his view of Being in reference to Jünger's writings. In his article, Heidegger concentrates his attention on Jünger's understanding of nihilism in relation to work (*Arbeit*). Heidegger simply denies that we emerge from nihilism when we become aware of it.[57] For Heidegger, the fulfillment of nihilism is not its end, but rather its beginning.[58] Heidegger assimilates Jünger's problem to his own by comparing the work in which the form of the worker receives its meaning to the Being of beings.[59] We are meant to understand Jünger's view of technology as following from the mobilization of the world through the form of the worker—which Heidegger further reads as offering insight into the newly emerging metaphysics of the will to power—as basically connected to the problem of Being. Heidegger further links the question of how one emerges from nihilism with the question of how one knows Being. He suggests that the overcoming of metaphysics lies in getting over, or in recovering from (*Verwindung*), it, roughly in turning one's back on the problem;[60] and he equates this result with the healing of the forgetfulness of Being (*Seinsvergessenheit*).[61]

The third influence on Heidegger's comprehension of technology is Oswald Spengler. Heidegger's interest in Spengler, which has not often been studied in detail, is significant in the genesis of his thought.[62] Heidegger lectured on Spengler as early as 1920.[63] His repeated references to Spengler in his early lecture courses in Freiburg have been interpreted as one of the factors impelling Heidegger to transform his interest in individual authenticity in *Being and Time* to the authenticity of the *Volk* in his turn toward Nazism.[64] Spengler's concern with technology, already apparent in his well-known account of the decline of the West, is more sharply focused in his study of the connection between human being and technology.[65]

Heidegger's concern with Spengler can in part be attributed to a shared pessimism widely felt in German circles at the end of the First World War, just prior to the onset of the Weimar Republic. We have already noted that Spenglerian themes resonate throughout the rectoral address.[66] Such themes include the concern that Germany become the subject of history, the claim to understand the present and to foresee the future, the conception of the present as fraught with danger, German destiny as decisive for world history, and so on. Spengler's influence is equally obvious in Heidegger's theory of technology. A short list of themes concerning technology which Heidegger shares with Spengler would include at least the following: the relation between technology and the destiny of human being; the link between technology, culture, and history; the analysis of technology in terms of the concept of the instrument; the idea of struggle, including technological struggle, as ennobling; care as future-directed; the conviction that we have now arrived at a historical turning point, within which technology is a main component; and a condemnation of our enslavement by machines and technology. With respect to technology, the main difference between Heidegger and Spengler lies in Heidegger's resolutely antianthropological perspective, the result of his insistence on the question of Being and later move away from Dasein. For this reason, Heidegger declines to follow Spengler's generally anthropological perspective, apparent in Spengler's concern to study technology and the decline of the West in general in terms of the historical origins of man.[67]

Consideration of the influences on the formation of Heidegger's understanding of technology yields three results. First, here and elsewhere in his position Heidegger borrows, and, if necessary, rethinks, ideas that were in the air at the time. This in turn suggests the usefulness of knowledge of the immediate intellectual context for an understanding of Heidegger's thought. Second, it has been noted that Heidegger's view of technology emerges as a result of his long discussion of Nietzsche's view of nihilism. Third, we see that his understanding of technology is derived from—or inscribed, so to speak, within—the framework of his pursuit of the question of Being. Technology is not a phenomenon Heidegger studies for itself, because of his concern with technological problems, or through an interest in the ongoing discussion concerning them. For Heidegger is never interested in technology as such, and always interested in it only against the background of his obsessive concern with Being.

Heidegger's Mature Theory of Technology

A discussion of the origin and influences on Heidegger's understanding of technology would be incomplete without an account of his mature view of technology. Now there is no single major text in which Heidegger develops his mature conception of the technological phenomenon. Rather, there are a number of works of varying size in which technology is a theme. These texts culminate in a four-lecture cycle, titled "Insight into What Is," given at the end of 1949 and repeated in 1950.[68] Of these lectures, one remains unpublished and nearly inaccessible.[69] A second one, which is published and available in English translation, is only minimally connected to the problem of technology.[70] Both of the remaining lectures are directly concerned with technology.[71] Both address the same, or similar material in related ways and both are from the same period. Since Heidegger subsequently reworked his discussion of "The Question concerning Technology," since it is more substantial, and since it concerns the "essence" of technology, it is representative of his mature understanding of technology.

The essay to which we now turn is difficult, even in comparison with Heidegger's other writings. For whatever reason, Heidegger's considerable capacity to communicate his meaning seems suddenly to have been bracketed, placed in parentheses as it were. He has further not been helped by a translation into English which is often even odder than Heidegger's frequently odd German text.[72] This is especially regrettable since Heidegger's thought, which normally depends on the analysis of language, is even more than usually dependent on etymological commentary in this essay.

One difficulty in presenting Heidegger's theory of technology is that it seems to follow squarely from his claims about the German language. We can start to describe his view by pointing to the parallel between this essay and Heidegger's persistent concern with the problem of Being. As in *Being and Time,* where he inquires into the meaning of Being, so in this essay he raises the question of the meaning of technology, or more precisely its essence. Here, after his turn away from the philosophical tradition, he claims to understand "essence" in a supposedly nonmetaphysical sense. For Heidegger, the essence of technology is different from technology and not itself something technological.[73] This assertion depends on his understanding of "essence." Heidegger clarifies his understanding of "essence" and the essence of technology by pointing to the Latin words "*quidditas*" and "*genus.*" "Essence," or we can say the essence of essence, is something which, to reproduce his own terminology, endures, holds sway, administers itself, develops and decays. In this connection, he calls attention to the etymological relation of the term "essence" ("*Wesen*") to the verb "*währen*" and to Goethe's use of the "mysterious" word "*fortwähren.*"[74] Perhaps what he has in mind is the distinction between something that just is, for instance a fixed property, and the Aristotelian concept of *energeia,* which denotes that which not only is but is also in act.[75]

Heidegger's strategy is to insist that an approach to technology that is not squarely based on Being—in a word, any approach other than his own—falls short of the phenomenon. Heidegger does not deny that technology is partly instrumental, although he denies that instrumentality is central to it. For Heidegger, everyone "knows" the "instrumental or anthropological statements about technology," that is, that technology is a means to an end and a human activity.[76] Whether or not everyone believes these statements to be true, certainly some observers, for instance Spengler, accept roughly this approach.[77] For Heidegger, the usual instrumental or anthropological conception of technology picks out something true about technology but misses its essence, which is neither instrumental nor anthropological. His solution is to address the noninstrumental, nonanthropological aspect of technology through a reflection on a concept which, in his view, is presupposed by both instrumental and noninstrumental, or essential, views of technology.

Heidegger's reflection links technology to teleology and, through teleology, to a Greek view of causality. Since he holds that ends and means relate to causality,[78] he attempts to show the noninstrumental essence of technology through a discussion of causality, as illustrated by Aristotle's familiar fourfold analysis. If technology results from human intentional actions, then it is normal enough to interpret it teleologically. Since Heidegger maintains an antianthropological angle of vision, he cannot invoke a human form of teleology. His solution is to invoke a conception of Being as the final agent. Since *Being and Time,* Heidegger has consistently argued that Being is what is sought by human being as the central concern and central question of human existence. Heidegger now supplements his quasi-Aristotelian view of Being as what is sought with a causal analysis of Being as causally active, as the real historical subject, based on the Aristotelian conception of causality.

Heidegger begins by pointing out that there is no corresponding

Greek word for what has become known as causality. Heidegger interprets the corresponding Greek concept as ways of responsibility (*Verschulden*) for bringing something into appearance, of letting something come forward as present (*An-Wesen*).[79] By deliberately employing a term incorporating the German for "essence" ("*Wesen*"), he smuggles his own conception of truth as disclosure into his reading of the ancient Greek view of causality. Heidegger goes on to maintain that the process of rendering present, or presencing, transfers from concealment to unconcealment within what he designates as the revealing (*das Entbergen*). Since for Heidegger, revealing corresponds to what the Greeks called *aletheia,* his analysis leads to his familiar view of truth as disclosure.

We can summarize Heidegger's complex line of reasoning as follows. Technology, which is mainly understood instrumentally, is not only instrumental in nature. An analysis of the original Greek concept of causality, understood as a means of bringing into presence, suggests that the Greeks understood "causality" as "a revealing in general, or disclosure." Since disclosure is another name for truth, technology cannot be understood in an essential manner as instrumental; for it is essentially concerned with revealing, or truth. "Technology is therefore no mere means. Technology is a way of revealing."[80] It follows that the essence of technology does not consist in instrumentality since technology is a form of disclosure, or manifestation of truth.

We have been following Heidegger's teleological analysis of technology as a form of disclosure. Now this point is not tangential, but central, to Heidegger's view of technology. In order to tie the phenomenon of technology to the problem of Being, he needs to demonstrate that technology is the form in which Being manifests itself. The stakes are high since he needs to find a way to maintain his claim, central to his thought since *Being and Time,* that the problem of Being is prior to all other concerns. In order to make out this assertion, Heidegger must be able to develop a theory of technology on the basis of his theory of Being. The assimilation of technology to disclosure is intended to bring the phenomenon of technology within the orbit of his conception of Being.

The structure of the argument is clear, impressive, but finally unconvincing. Heidegger's analysis falters on a crucial point. His demonstration that technology is not merely instrumental rests on the analogy he invokes between the supposedly original meaning of causality in ancient Greek thought and modern technology. Now it is unclear that Heidegger's linguistic analysis of the meaning of the corresponding Greek term is correct. But if, for purposes of discussion, we grant that Heidegger has correctly captured the original meaning of the Greek idea of causality, it does not follow that his ancient Greek model essentially or even accurately describes modern technology. In the absence of an explicit justification of this analogy, which Heidegger does not provide, we need not grant Heidegger's point, central to his analysis, that technology is a mode of disclosure. Although Heidegger might be correct, nothing he says about modern technology justifies this crucial inference.

In the remainder of his essay, Heidegger supposes this crucial, but undemonstrated, assertion: technology is essentially concerned with truth as a way of revealing. To begin with, he relies on the Greek etymology of the word "technology" (*"Technik"*) to make two points. First, *techne* belongs to *poiesis* as a mode of bringing forth (*Her-vor-bringen*). Here, Heidegger follows Aristotle's own discussion of the relation between *techne* and *poiesis*. Second, in ancient Greek thought *techne* is linked with *episteme* as a mode of knowledge. In effect, Heidegger conflates two different forms of knowledge, namely *episteme,* or science, and *techne,* or art. The basic difference, which is spelled out in Aristotle's discussion,[81] is roughly that between knowing how and knowing that. For Aristotle, only knowing in the full sense, either *episteme* or *sophia,* could be understood as a disclosure of an essence. In Aristotle's position, *techne* falls under the heading of practical theory, which does not reveal an essence. Following his earlier, pragmatic analysis of readiness-to-hand in *Being and Time*, Heidegger, however, insists that *techne,* and, hence, technology, concern the disclosure of essences. From this line of reasoning, based on the interpretation of the way the term *"techne"* figures in Greek philosophy, Heidegger again reaches the conclusion that technology is a mode of revealing, hence essentially associated with truth.[82]

The obvious objection is that Heidegger's view of *techne* is not descriptive of technology in the modern epoch. Heidegger concedes that his conclusion only partially applies to modern technology. He maintains that modern technology, which is also a revealing, is further characterized as a challenging (*Herausfordern*). For Heidegger, modern technology specifically differs from its earlier forms in its formulation of unreasonable demands placed on our surrounding world. The unreasonable nature of the requirements put upon nature lie in the concern to extract and to store energy.

> The revealing that rules in modern technology is a challenge which puts to nature the unreasonable demand [das Ansinnen] that it supply energy that can be extracted and stored. But does this not hold true for the old windmill as well? No. Its sails do indeed turn in the wind; they are left entirely to the wind's blowing. But the windmill does not unlock energy from the air currents in order to store it.[83]

Heidegger understands this demand put to nature as disclosing, exposing, and as perpetuating itself in a further series of demands.

> This putting upon [Stellen], put to the energy of nature, is a promotion [Fördern] in a two-fold manner. It promotes [fördert] in that it unlocks and exposes. Yet that demanding is always itself directed toward demanding something else, i.e., driving forward to the maximum utility at the least expense.[84]

Heidegger's sketch here of modern technology as consisting in an unlimited series of demands for energy put to nature calls for two comments. First, this view recalls the passage cited above from *Being and Time,* in which Heidegger calls attention to the idea of accepting nature as it is, as allowing nature to show itself, so to speak. Both passages seem to indicate a kind of vague ecological consciousness manifest in the assertion that our demands put to nature are unreasonable. We are meant to infer that when nature is required to respond to us on our terms only, something is covered up or at least left hidden.[85]

Second, there is an equally vague recognition that modern technology is linked to a self-perpetuating economic process that feeds on human beings and the entire surrounding world, as described, say, by Marx. Now Heidegger does not here or elsewhere endorse an economic interpretation of the modern world. In fact, he obviously cannot invoke this form of explanation since it runs counter to his reliance on Being as the ultimate explanatory factor. But equally obviously, the description of modern technology as an open-ended effort to extract and to store energy from nature is not meaningful in itself; it is meaningful only in the context of the self-perpetuating, increasing demands for ever-expanding economic activity typical of modern industrialized society.

Heidegger develops his view of technology as a form of disclosure by introducing Aristotelian concepts of potentiality and agency. Following Aristotle, he maintains that when disclosure occurs, a potentiality is actualized. He employs the term *"Bestand"*—the past participle of *"bestehen,"* meaning "to be permanent, or to persist"—to designate the potentiality to be actualized, more precisely to refer to the way in which what is concealed becomes unconcealed, or becomes present (*an-west*).[86] He further invokes the specific conception of agency contained in his teleological view of technology as disclosure to assert the difficult point that human being, which provides the necessary avenue for disclosure, for instance in conceiving, acting, or doing this or that, does not itself control the process of disclosure. "But man does not have control over unconcealment itself, in which at any given time the real shows itself or withdraws."[87]

Heidegger's appeal to a transhuman form of agency is not in itself novel. There is considerable precedent for this kind of explanation, not only in theology, but virtually throughout the philosophical tradition— in modern German thought, in Hegel's concept of the absolute and Marx's idea of capital. Like Marx, who turns to capital to explain modern industrial society, including technology, Heidegger also relies on a transhuman explanatory principle to ground modern technology. If there is a transhuman causality at work, then human being is not the subject, or agent of the process, or at best human being possesses limited agency only. Heidegger obscurely expresses this point when he writes that "modern technology as an ordering revealing, is, then, no merely human doing."[88]

If technology is not a human doing, then Heidegger must describe the agent of the process. He characterizes the essence, but not the agent of technology under the heading "enframing [Gestell]." Heidegger deliberately uses this word, which ordinarily means "a piece of apparatus," in a nonstandard way to designate "the essence of technology."[89] We recall Heidegger's insistence that technology is a form of disclosure, or revealing of what is to be revealed. We further recall his conviction that the essence of technology is not itself technological. He now relates both points to his conception of enframing as the essence of technology in a formulation that seems more complex than what it means to say. "Enframing means the collection of that demanding that puts upon man, i.e. challenges him, to disclose the real, in the mode of ordering, as potential. Enframing means that way of disclosing which obtains [waltet] in the essence of modern technology and which is nothing technological."[90]

Heidegger's view of essence appears to conflate essence with the causal interpretation of agency he favors in this essay. An essence is what it is to be something, whereas a causal agent is a principle that is the source of an event. For instance, a match may cause a fire in a specific set of circumstances, but it is essential to the match to be able to burn, whether or not it causes a fire in something else. Heidegger, who fails to observe this distinction, employs his conception of enframing, which he identifies as the essence of technology, as a causal agent. If human being is not responsible for technology, it must be enframing that puts the so-called unreasonable demand to nature to yield energy that can be stored. And it must be enframing that reveals truth in the process of disclosure that transcends the instrumental aspect of modern technology.

For Heidegger, science depends on technology and not conversely. An obvious objection to Heidegger's analysis follows from the fact that modern science, for instance, mathematical physics, is some two centuries older than modern technology. It is natural to believe, as has often been believed, that modern technology is dependent upon the rise of modern science, and hence to be explained in that way. Heidegger responds that modern natural science does not prepare the way to technology, but only to modern technology. He maintains that in physics the so-called demanding disclosure that typifies technology already rules, so that physics is merely the messenger, so to say, of enframing. For Heidegger, it only appears that modern physics makes modern technology possible since the essence of modern technology has long been hidden. He sums up his claim that modern technology must be understood through enframing, not through modern science, as follows:

> Because the essence of modern technology lies in enframing, modern technology must employ exact physical science. In this way, the deceptive illusion arises that modern technology might be applied natural science. This illusion can assert itself only as long as neither the essential origin of modern science nor the essence of modern technology is sufficiently found out.[91]

Heidegger obviously intends to defend his view that technology derives from Being. His defense consists of the unsupported statement that enframing, which he regards as the essence of technology, was manifest in physics before it became manifest in modern technology. Now it follows that it is illusory to regard modern technology as applied science only if one accepts Heidegger's assertion about enframing as true without supporting evidence. Heidegger's analysis is further questionable since it is unclear that modern science, which frequently makes use of technology, is essentially technological. Although technology plays an important role in modern science, there are exceptions, types of theoretical physics, say, which do not depend on technology. Heidegger's point is, hence, not descriptive of modern science as a whole; at best, it applies to part of modern science only. In sum, we may refuse to accept Heidegger's suggestion, through remarks on the Greek concept of causality, that enframing is the essence of technology. We should refuse to accept Heidegger's assertion that modern science depends on technology since he does not argue this point and it is apparently false.

Heidegger is apparently convinced that he has met the challenge posed by the widespread interpretations of technology as instrumental and as applied science. In the remainder of his essay, he repeats material already presented and further discusses his conception of enframing through connections drawn to destiny, danger, and art. The link to destiny recalls Heidegger's remarks in *Being and Time,* to which we have frequently referred, on fate (*Schicksal*) and destiny (*Geschick*). Heidegger returns to the notion of destiny in a series of remarks on the connection between enframing and disclosure. The first step is the comment, following from the idea of enframing as a revealing, that the essence of technology brings man on the way to disclosure. This leads to the second step, contained in the further comment that "to bring on the way" ("*auf einen Weg bringen*") is equivalent to the locution "to send" ("*schicken*"). On this fragile, linguistic basis, Heidegger describes destiny as a collective sending. "We shall call that collective sending [versammelde Schicken] which first sends man upon this way of revealing *destiny.*"[92]

Heidegger links destiny to history, production, and disclosure. He maintains that we understand the essence of history in terms of destiny. Or, as he also says, it is through the sending (*geschickliches*) that it becomes historical (*geschichtlich*).[93] He further describes destiny as a bringing forth (*Her-vor-bringen*) or producing, that is, as poetic, where "poetic" is understood in terms of the Greek "*poiesis.*" And he maintains that the destiny of disclosure rules man and not conversely, although he denies—using another word for destiny or fate (*Verhängnis*)—that this is a compulsion (*Zwang*). For Heidegger, who now distantly echoes his conception of freedom as submission to authority in the rectoral address, freedom is unrelated to will in any way. He insists that one becomes free in belonging to the area of destiny as someone who listens (*ein Hörender*) not as someone who obeys (*ein Höriger*). Since revealing is a process of concealment, he also says that freedom rules over the free in the sense of what is lit up (*Gelichteten*)—even perhaps illuminated—or disclosed (*Entborgenen*).

Heidegger's remarks on the connection between enframing and destiny are based on his impressive capacity—some would say his abuse of the language—to draw attention to linguistic analogies. The etymological similarities he notices between sending (*Schicken*), destiny (*Geschick*) and history (*Geschichte*) are a slender reed upon which to connect technology and these other phenomena. If history is a collective happening, it does not follow that history can be understood as reflecting human destiny in the Heideggerian sense of the term. One must further question the interpretation of destiny as poetic. This inference follows only if the possibilities that a person or a people might desire to incarnate or take on are firmly located in the past, as Heidegger maintains. Yet tradition as such is not necessarily desirable, and, hence, worthy of repetition; only some traditions are.

Finally, the description of human freedom on display in the role of the listener is a qualified restatement of Heidegger's view of Dasein as concerned with the meaning of Being. Although enframing is related to destiny, it is not akin to *moira* in the Greek sense, as something which could not be otherwise. Heidegger rejects the idea of technology as fate "where 'fate' means the inevitableness of an unalterable course."[94] Heidegger is concerned to keep open the possibility that a qualified observer—perhaps even a philosopher who has now gone beyond philosophy, such as Heidegger—can free us from technology. Once again, he affirms a quasi-Platonic view of philosophy, in this case his post-metaphysical thought, as the condition of true politics. His clear aim is to preserve a social role for his new thinking which is no longer philosophy. But his account of human freedom in the face of technology need not be accepted. For Heidegger does not justify his insight, which he rather seems to "deduce" from his prior theory.

The remark on danger is associated with the possibility of freedom from technology. Heidegger develops this point through further consideration of the idea of disclosure. Returning to his claim that the essence of technology is enframing, he notes that disclosure imposes a choice between what is disclosed and what is not disclosed and hence remains hidden. For Heidegger, the choice between these possibilities endangers human being with respect to destiny. In his view, as destiny disclosure is itself danger. "The destiny of disclosure is not any form [of danger] but *the* danger."[95] Heidegger makes a determined effort to convince us that he is concerned not only with types of danger but with danger itself in a series of examples. One form of danger lies in the possible misinterpretation of what is disclosed, or revealed. Examples of this phenomenon are said to include the reductive interpretation of God as an efficient cause, as in the concept of the God of the philosophers supposedly prevalent in theology; and the possibility, in an apparent reference to modern science, that in the midst of correct determinations "the true withdraws from the correct."[96]

For Heidegger, who now introduces a distinction between forms of danger, the destiny of disclosure is danger as such; but the destiny that obtains in enframing is the supreme danger. Heidegger believes that the so-called supreme danger manifests itself in two ways: through human demands addressed to nature, and in the delusion that everywhere human being encounters only human being. As concerns enframing, Heidegger obscurely holds that when a person puts demands to nature, one fails to see that it is the person who is being addressed. This remark is a reformulation of Heidegger's earlier point in *Being and Time,* that in putting demands to nature we fail to attend to nature and cannot perceive what our very demand occults. The statement that we fail to grasp that it is the person who is being addressed is a further statement of Heidegger's conviction that Dasein is defined by its concern with Being. It is also a hint that by coming to grips with technology, the authentic gathering of the German people may occur. In that case, the obscurely expressed danger, on which Heidegger insists in this essay, is nothing more than the possibility that people, particularly the German people, will fail to realize the Nazi goal. If this reading is correct, then through his attention to the danger of disclosure Heidegger is insisting again on the point central to the rectoral address: only if he leads the leaders will it be possible to bring about an authentic gathering of the German *Volk*. For even at this late date, after he has turned against philosophy, Heidegger, who thinks of himself as possessing insight even into the future, continues to believe in the political destiny of his view of Being; for his post-metaphysical thought is the only way to realize German authenticity.

Heidegger sees danger as following from the mysterious concept of enframing. He maintains that it is enframing that shunts man into the kind of revealing that derives from making demands to nature and which, he believes, conceals other types of disclosure, even the disclosure of truth. It follows that it is not technology but rather its essence that is the danger. "Destiny, that sends to ordering, is the most extreme danger. Technology is not dangerous. There is no demonry of technology; on the contrary, there is the mystery of its essence. As a destiny of disclosure, the essence of technology is the danger."[97] Heidegger's point, consistent with his objection, is that metaphysics, namely an inauthentic thought of Being, blocks access to the thought of Being. Since for Heidegger technology prolongs metaphysics, then its essence impedes access to Being. Because an authentic view of Being is the prerequisite for authentic human being, the consequence is to prevent the manifest German destiny.

Heidegger regards the danger as great but not as irremediable. In a reference to Hölderlin, he maintains that danger and what he calls the saving power are entwined. In order to expound the sense in which technology harbors a so-called saving power, Heidegger interprets the verb "to save" ("*retten*") in a causal sense, consistent with his analysis of the Greek notion of causality, to mean "to cause the essence to appear."[98] Heidegger's reading of "to save" is consistent with an interpretation of the entire essay and Heidegger's theory of technology as part of a continuing concern with German destiny, in the present case through overcoming the danger of technology. We are meant to infer that the essence of technology, which is itself a great danger, has within itself the possibility of disclosing its essence. But we still need to understand the term "essence." Turning now to the usual senses of the term, Heidegger maintains that enframing is not the essence of technology if that means something like "a common genus," since it is rather a way of disclosure. For Heidegger, it is technology itself which demands that we think the concept of essence in another manner.

On this basis, Heidegger considers anew the concept of essence which the Greeks already understood as permanence. Like the Greeks, Heidegger also stresses permanence, since what he calls essencing

(*Wesende*) endures. In this respect, he invokes the idea of an initial
agency in order to grasp permanence as relative to that which is itself its
source and so to speak atemporally permanent. In a passage difficult to
render into English and to interpret, which Heidegger italicizes in order
to stress its importance, he writes: "*Only the granted endures [das
Gewährte währt]. The initially enduring out of the early [period] is the
granting [das Gewährende].*"[99] Heidegger may have nothing more obscure in mind than his familiar idea that the destiny of the *Volk* is
permanently present as a possibility to be seized within history through
appropriate insight. We are familiar with his insistence that human being
cannot seize its own possibility by itself since the capacity to do so must
in effect be granted by a suprahuman agent, presumably Being, which is
responsible for the historical process. In this way, Heidegger can maintain that the original granting, in respect to which enframing comes to
be, also sends along with it a so-called saving power within technology
itself. The result, once again, is to cast himself, as the one who understands technology, in the familiar, quasi-Platonic role of the thinker
indispensable to the good life.

Heidegger's interpretation of technology as either a danger or a sign
of salvation lies in the link he seeks to establish between technology and
Being, his main concern, and the role now attributed to Being as a
causal agent. The danger derives from the turn away from Being, in
which technology prolongs bad metaphysics. His positive point is that if
only we will turn back to Being, technology can be overcome. On this
basis, it is easy to infer that the saving power will in the first instance be
due to the thinker who finally is not led astray but has insight into Being,
namely Heidegger himself. Although technology tends mainly to turn us
toward the formulation of ever new demands to be put to nature, we can
break through the fascination due to the instrumental approach to technology to seize its essence.

> Everything, then, depends upon this: that we ponder this arising and that,
> recollecting, we watch over it. How can this happen? Above all through
> our catching sight of what comes to presence in technology, instead of
> merely staring at the technological. So long as we represent technology as
> an instrument, we remain held fast in the will to master it. We press on
> past the essence of technology.[100]

There is a possible tension between Heidegger's quasi-Platonic insistence on the decisive character of philosophic insight and his anti-
Cartesian rejection of an anthropological approach to technology. Heidegger is careful not to accord too much weight to insight into technology in order to preserve the claim that technology is not a human doing

and hence not under human control. To do so would, to overstate the case for his grasp of technology, even the possibility to grasp it, only undercut his own view that technology follows from the turn away from Being. He notes that the essence of technology is ambiguous, since it is associated with danger and with the so-called saving power. He states that the question concerning technology, formulated in the title of his essay, is the question concerning the event (*Ereignis*) of revealing and concealing in which truth appears. In this way, he maintains, we are not yet saved, although by facing danger hope grows. "Might there then be granted a beginning disclosure, a saving in its initial appearance [zum ersten Scheinen] in the midst of danger, which in the age of technology rather hides than shows?"[101]

This passage suggests a vague sense of hope, just as Kant invoked the postulates of God and immortality to entertain the possibility of happiness as following from moral action.[102] Heidegger immediately moves to dispel any false optimism by a series of remarks on the Greek concept of art suggested by "*techne,*" the root of the word "technology." He utilizes his conviction of the superiority of Greece over modernity to suggest an alternative view of technology. According to Heidegger, in ancient Greece art served to manifest the true as the beautiful, as a form of disclosure. Once again rejecting any velleity of human agency, he states that we cannot now tell "whether art may again be granted this highest possibility of its essence,"[103] namely the capacity of revealing truth, presumably insight into Being useful for human being. Since human being is not the final agent, it cannot itself effect the return to the original sense of art. At best, it can reflect on the nontechnological essence of technology from the basis of art concerned with truth, precisely the stance Heidegger takes in this essay.

We can summarize the main lines of Heidegger's mature understanding of technology as follows. His approach to technology follows from his concern with Being, in particular through application of his theory of truth as disclosure. His view is marked by a fourfold rejection of technology as a human doing, as instrumental, as applied science, or as a form of progress. (1) To begin with, Heidegger rejects the anthropological approach to technology since in his view technology derives from Being and not from human being. (2) Heidegger also rejects the widespread views of modern technology as essentially instrumental on the grounds that technology is not only instrumental; rather, it is connected with the appearance of truth, hence, with problem of Being. (3) Heidegger further rejects the interpretation of technology as applied science on the grounds that modern science presupposes the essence of technology. (4) Finally, Heidegger rejects the idea that modern technology represents progress. On the contrary, modern technology is fundamentally dangerous because it has turned away from the manifestation of truth which was the function of the Greek view of art. Heidegger holds that technology induces a particular way of relating to the world revealed under this perspective which simultaneously conceals it in other ways.

Toward Criticism of Heidegger's View of Technology

Heidegger's theory of technology is primarily interesting as an extension of his theory of Being. But if it is only secondarily a theory of technology, we need to ask whether his understanding of technology needs to be taken seriously. To put the question somewhat differently: is Heidegger's view of technology important only, or mainly, in order to understand the later evolution of his theory of Being? or is it also important, even central, to any grasp of modern technology? This question has added significance in view of the claim that much in Heidegger's writings has begun to pale, perhaps even to seem mythological, but his view of technology deserves to be taken most seriously, to be seen as the most powerful part of his corpus, where everything comes together.[104]

In my view, the interest in Heidegger's theory of technology can only lie in an effort to elaborate an antianthropological conception of modern technology, but not in any insight into specific technological phenomena. The early Heidegger insists on the importance of the analysis of concrete phenomena, but one will look in vain in his writings for a detailed discussion of specific technological issues, such as the inventions of the weight-driven clock, paper, or gunpowder. Despite his early quasi-Husserlian emphasis on the concrete, Heidegger simply fails to engage the discussion of technology in a specific manner.

Heidegger's attention to the link between modern technology and its earlier anticipation in ancient Greece and his awareness that technology limits, or tends to exclude, certain possibilities are important points worth developing. With respect to ancient Greece, unfortunately Heidegger seems more interested in how ancient Greek thought understood the etymological root of "technology" than in the link between historically different technological stages. In his essay, he has nothing at all to say about ancient machines and other earlier forms of technology. In comparison, his essay falls below the level of *Being and Time,* where, for instance, he repeatedly mentions the relation between clocks and time.[105] Here he further omits any discussion of other technological stages, for instance the technologies of ancient Egypt or ancient China. The result is a severely foreshortened view that fails to reflect the proper role of ancient Greek technology among other important predecessors of medieval and modern technological developments. As concerns the relation between modern and ancient Greek technology, Heidegger is perhaps misled by an imperfect analogy between philosophy and technology. It is plausible to hold that modern philosophy emerges from its origins in the Greek philosophical tradition since the Western form of philosophy arises in the Platonic tradition. But it is not plausible to maintain that technology as we know it arises within, or can be understood in terms of, ancient Greek technology, which was only one of the important sources of modern technology.

Heidegger is correct in saying that a commitment to technology tends to divert attention from what is not technologically useful. Yet he seems unaware that even the decision to listen to nature in a supposedly nonviolent manner consists in imposing an interpretative framework upon it. It is not the case that the alternative consists in a choice between a technological explanatory matrix or none at all since to decide for the latter is to effect a choice. Although it might be desirable to comprehend nature without violence, this is clearly not possible if to do so requires one to abandon any structure of interpretation. Heidegger's own interpretative structure is clearly evident in his constant recourse to the categories of Being.

Heidegger's suggestion of a form of the Greek concept of art as an alternative to modern technology is unsatisfactory. The obvious objection is that technology is not art. Although art on occasion relies on forms of technology, for instance in the casting necessary to create a bronze statue, types of art entirely dispense with technology of any kind, such as drawing in the sand on a beach. Further, Heidegger gives no indication that he has ever considered the obvious social cost necessary to realize his idea of technology. To return to something like the Greek view that Heidegger favors would require the abandonment of more familiar forms of technology, which are deeply embedded in modern industrial society. Since the capacities to feed and clothe the population depend on modern technology, were one to take seriously Heidegger's technological vision, were one to attempt to put it into practice, modern life as we know it would have to be abandoned. There is something very utopian about such an idea.

The main defect of Heidegger's theory of technology lies in his arbitrary, unjustified assumption of a particular theory of agency as its basis. The problem of agency, or subjectivity, is an important philosophical theme. The part of the modern philosophical tradition stemming from Descartes can be understood as an ongoing effort to comprehend the subject, initially as a kind of epistemological placeholder, an ultimately bare posit, such as the Cartesian cogito or the Kantian transcendental unity of apperception, and later as a social being in the views of Fichte, Hegel, and Marx. Heidegger's nonanthropological analysis of technology differs in a fundamental way from the average interpretation of technology, whether as instrumental or applied science, which presupposes that technology yields to an anthropological approach. In his early thought, Heidegger utilizes the concept of Being as a pole of attraction, much as the Aristotelian God, which acts in that it is desired. In his later thought, Heidegger rethinks Being as an event (*Ereignis*) acting upon us, for instance as sending or granting various capacities to art, technology, and so on.

Heidegger's extension of his theory of Being to the phenomenon of technology is problematic. A line of argument acceptable within the context of his thought of Being is not necessarily acceptable when considered on its own merits. Even if, for purposes of argument, we grant the correctness of Heidegger's later view of Being against the background of his position, and the correctness of his extension of his view of Being as a theory of technology, it does not follow that we need accept his view of technology. Heidegger "derives" his understanding of technology from his understanding of Being, but he provides no reason to accept his view of technology as such. The view of Being as agent which follows from the evolution of his position is not supported by his analysis of technology. To put the same point differently: Heidegger holds that phenomenology is concerned with disclosing what is concealed; unfortunately, Heidegger does not disclose his transhuman concept of Being as agent within, but rather imposes it upon, technology.

Heidegger's arbitrary conception of agency leads to a number of difficulties in his understanding of technology. First, there is an evident inability to differentiate forms of technology. A theory of technology must be able to distinguish among different forms of technology. There are obvious differences between the horse-drawn plow and the tractor, the spear and the atom bomb, the abacus and the computer, the movable-type printing press and the linotype machine, and so on. Each pair illustrates the difference between an earlier and a later way to perform the same or similar tasks. In each case, later technology builds on and improves the performance of earlier types of technology. The chronologically later kinds of technology in these examples are also technologically more sophisticated and, in that sense, technologically more advanced. Since Heidegger apparently condemns modern technology as such, he does not, and in fact is unable to, introduce such routine distinctions. But such distinctions are not merely a useless finesse; they are rather necessary in order to make a choice of the means as a function of the end in view.

Second, his nonanthropological interpretation of technology is problematic. Heidegger's claim does not follow from a critique of the rival view or views, which he simply rejects in virtue of his prior commitment to Being as the ultimate explanatory factor. A prior commitment helps to explain why Heidegger analyzes technology as he does, but it does not justify his analysis. In order to make out his nonanthropological technological view, Heidegger needs to supplement his analysis, for instance through a demonstration that the anthropological and nonanthropological approaches exhaust the possible ways to understand technology, an indication of the basic flaws leading to a rejection of the so-called anthropological approach, or an argument in favor of his own rival view. It is not sufficient to point out that Heidegger's theory successfully accounts for the transhuman agency exhibited by technology unless it can be shown that technology has a transhuman dimension, something Heidegger merely asserts but does not demonstrate.

Third, Heidegger exaggerates the differences between theories of technology which differ not in kind, but in degree only. A reference to Heidegger's and non-Heideggerian readings of technology as respectively authentic and inauthentic reflects his conviction that the exclusive authenticity of his own approach is guaranteed by its link to Being. Yet Heideggerian and non-Heideggerian views of technology are not mutually exclusive, but overlap. An example is the status of Marx's theory, which Heidegger praises for its concern with history while criticizing its purported failure to subordinate the essence of materialism to the history of being.[106] Now Marx's position is a form of philosophical anthropology that can be understood as an analysis of technological society in terms of a theory of capital formation.[107] Marx's theory of modern society in part relies on the anthropological perspective of human activity, and in part relies on a transpersonal concept of capital as the agent of capitalism.[108] Since Marx's position combines both human and transhuman concepts of agency, Heidegger is incorrect to regard his own appeal to a transhuman form of agency as an exclusive alternative to other views of technology.

Fourth, there is the weakness of Heidegger's effort to show the plausibility of his interpretation of technology as a form of disclosure. Heidegger simply does not demonstrate that technology is more than instrumental; he rather "deduces" that this must be the case from his prior commitment to Being. According to Heidegger's line, if technology depends on Being, then it must be that it discloses that which, according to Heidegger, sends it. Heidegger's only argument that technology is a form of disclosure rests on the fragile link provided by the etymology of the term, in order to draw connections between art (*techne*), technology (*Technik*), destiny (*Geschick*), history (*Geschichte*), and sending (*Schickung*).

Heidegger's use of etymology is arbitrary and unjustified. It is not obvious why he could not have used the same play of etymologies to draw connections between technology (*Technik*), the science of technology (*Technologie*), and reason (*logos*) as well as chic (*schick*), chicness (*Schickheit*) and the quality of being chic (*Schicklichkeit*). If etymology is the clue to truth, then there are no obvious limits at all to it since Heidegger is at perfect liberty to make the words say what he wants to find in them. The example, already discussed, of his "deconstructive" reading of battle, or *Kampf,* as *polemos,* and then as *eris,* exemplifies the manner in which the skillful use of a willful form of etymology can lead from a to b no matter how a and b are chosen. Like Humpty Dumpty in *Through the Looking Glass,* Heidegger employs his willful form of etymology as if the relevant question were less the truth of the words than who is to be master. Heidegger is aware of this problem, of the frequent accusation of reading things into texts and, by extension, reading the words in order to confirm his predetermined view.[109] But his position has no way to respond to this objection.

Heidegger's argument rests on an unwarranted assumption that etymological relations between words further disclose relations of reference. Obviously, words refer beyond themselves to what they designate. Etymological analysis is sufficient to establish a connection between words, but it is insufficient to establish a connection between their designations. It does not follow because the etymology of "technology" yields "*techne,*" the Greek word for art, that technology was once a form of disclosure of the truth or that modern technology ought to become a form of art in the Greek sense. Even if we grant, for purposes of argument, that the ancient Greek concept of art designated by "*techne*" referred to disclosure, it does not follow that the earlier view is true and the later view is false unless one also assumes that what is older is also correct. An etymological connection based on meaning says nothing at all about a possible relation based on reference.

Fifth, Heidegger's understanding of technology is overly abstract. Technology presupposes a multiply determined environment, with social, political, historical, and other components. Heidegger offers us a theory of technology as such. But there is no technology in general; there are only instantiations of forms of technology, such as those required to produce steam engines, lasers, supersonic airplanes, and so on. Technological achievements need to be grasped in the wider context in which they arise. One does not need to be a technological nominalist to hold that if anything like a general theory of technology is possible, it can only be based on the concrete analysis of specific technological forms. Heidegger is concerned with the history of ontology, but he is apparently unconcerned with the historical manifestation of technological being.

Sixth, Heidegger provides an inadequate analysis of the relation of technology and applied science. In response to the tendency to interpret technology as applied science, Heidegger asserts that applied science already depends on technology. Certainly, modern science makes use of modern technology. Biological research requires a centrifuge just as the study of microparticles requires some form of particle accelerator or astronomy various types of telescopes. Yet it follows that modern science presupposes the concealed essence of technology only if enframing is the essence of technology and if it is concealed. These are points that Heidegger asserts but does not demonstrate. Further, modern technology is largely dependent on applied science, which utilizes ideas borrowed from so-called pure science in practical ways, such as the theory of relativity, whose formulation is partially responsible for thermonuclear devices as well as the harnessing of the atom in order to generate electricity.

Seventh, Heidegger's understanding of technology is incompatible with a commitment to democracy, democratic values, and what is called the democratic way of life. Heidegger reminds us of this consequence in both word and deed: in his statement, quoted above, that he is not convinced that democracy is the best political system; and in his turning in the early 1930s to National Socialism, a main example of political totalitarianism. Democracy is problematic, but at this late date it is still the best political means to attain and to defend the goal of human freedom. Other thinkers have rejected democracy, most notably in Plato's embrace of the concept of aristocratic government.[110] But there is a significant difference. Plato rejects the democratic type of government on the basis of a commitment to the state as a whole, hence to human being. Yet Heidegger rejects democracy because of his commitment to Being, but not to human being, also manifest in his nonanthropological theory of technology. Heidegger's antimetaphysical theory of technology is by definition antidemocratic; it presupposes as a leading characteristic the rejection of the anthropological viewpoint that is the foundation of democracy.

The ethical implications of Heidegger's view of technology are perhaps less visible but even more important than the political ones. There is a continuous line of argument leading from the Enlightenment commitment to reason to the insistence on responsibility as the condition of morality, which peaks in Kant's ethical theory.[111] When Heidegger attributes ultimate causal authority to Being, he clearly reverses the Enlightenment view that through the exercise of reason human being can attain dominion over the world and itself. In the final analysis, if Heidegger is correct, human actions depend on the gift of Being, hence on a suprahuman form of agency. Heidegger's insistence on Being as the final causal agent signals an abandonment of the idea of ethical responsibility. If responsibility presupposes autonomy, and autonomy presupposes freedom, then to embrace Being as the ultimate explanatory principle is tantamount to casting off the idea of ethical responsibility, the possibility of any moral accountability whatsoever.

Heidegger's rejection of the idea of responsibility other than through the commitment to Being is incompatible with the assumption of personal moral accountability. This consequence, which follows rigorously from his position, calls for two comments. First, it in part explains his failure ever to take a public position on the well-known atrocities perpetrated by the Nazi movement to which he turned. If one's ontological analysis does not support the concept of personal responsibility, then one does not need to react on the personal level to what, from Heidegger's perspective, can be attributed to Being. Second, Heidegger's rejection of personal responsiblity in his later thought denies a fundamental tenet of his own earlier position. In *Being and Time*, Heidegger maintained that authenticity required a resolute choice of oneself. But if choice depends on Being, then in the final analysis, as Heidegger clearly saw, the only choice is the choice for or against Being.

Technology and Heidegger's Nazism

The discussion of the origins and nature of Heidegger's theory of technology provides the background necessary to grasp its relation to his Nazism. One observer has seen Heidegger's inability to come to grips with Nazism as deriving from his view of technology.[112] But others, Heidegger's defenders, while aware of these passages and others as well, have accepted as correct his own statements that he broke with National Socialism in 1934 and that his later thought, in particular his analysis of technology, represents his effort come to grips with National Socialism. One qualified observer maintains that Heidegger's break in 1934 with his political engagement was total, and further maintains that Heidegger's thought around the period of the *Beiträge* was already in opposition and contradiction to Nazism.[113] Another observer even regards Heidegger's critique of technology as following from his critique of Nazism.[114]

The view that Heidegger broke with politics in general or Nazism in particular through his view of technology is not supported by an examination of the texts. As in his other writings, Heidegger's criticism of National Socialism as a theory is balanced by visible sympathy for its political goal, construed narrowly as the gathering of the Germans as German. The *Spiegel* interview clearly records Heidegger's conviction that the Nazi effort to confront technology was in principle correct, although the Nazis were too unsophisticated to carry it out. Heidegger's suggestion that his own view of technology can be understood as an extension of the National Socialist effort to confront this phenomenon has been amply supported by examination of Heidegger's "The Question concerning Technology."

Heidegger's suggestion in the *Spiegel* interview that the Nazis were correct to confront the hegemony of modern technology was not an isolated comment in his corpus. A similar passage, among the most controversial in his entire corpus, occurs in his lecture course on metaphysics. The lecture course in which the remark occurs was originally given in 1935 and was published in altered form in 1953. Heidegger's comment is embedded in a longer remark about values, in which he characteristically criticizes any approach to philosophy in terms of the concept of value before turning to the philosophy of National Socialism. His comment, which was reproduced in the version of the lecture course which appeared in 1953, gave rise to a well-known polemic, which can be briefly summarized as follows.[115] Prior to publication, Heidegger was advised to change the passage in question.[116] After the revised version of the lecture course appeared, Heidegger was attacked by Habermas[117] and was defended by Lewalter.[118] In a letter to the editor, Heidegger uncharacteristically defended himself and claimed, contrary to fact, that the passage had not been altered.[119] He repeated this claim in a letter to S. Zemach,[120] and again in the *Spiegel* interview.[121]

According to Petra Jaeger, the editor of Heidegger's *Introduction to Metaphysics*, the original text probably contained still another sentence, which Heidegger omitted in the revised version.[122] The initial version is unavailable and, hence, unverifiable, since the page of the manuscript containing this passage is missing in the Heidegger Archives. In the revised version, presumably modified in order to obscure his continued attachment to an ideal form of Nazism, Heidegger seems to have altered the passage in two ways: in the substitution of "movement" for "N.S.," which might perhaps lead one to think that he had some other movement in mind; and in the addition of the passage in parentheses to indicate the continuity between technology and National Socialism, which one qualified observer reads as imparting a negative cast to the concept of greatness.[123] The revised passage reads

The works that are being peddled about nowadays as the philosophy of National Socialism but have nothing whatever to do with the inner truth and greatness of this movement (namely the encounter between global technology and modern man)—have all been written by men fishing in the troubled waters of "values" and "totalities.[124]

The revised version of this passage is singularly important for an understanding of Heidegger's Nazism after the rectorate, including its link to his theory of technology. Here, with great clarity, in 1953, well after the end of the Second World War, at a point when Heidegger, who has returned to teaching, no longer has anything to fear from the Nazis or anyone else, he states his appreciation for the supposedly misunderstood essence of National Socialism, in virtue of the so-called movement's important effort to confront global technology. Heidegger publicly affirms his conviction in Nazism, not the real Nazism of Adolf Hitler, but an ideal kind that has not yet been and still might occur. Heidegger's remark is not a strategic claim, an effort to curry favor, to protect himself or his family, but in all probability a sincere statement of his conviction. We are already familiar with Heidegger's frequent assertions, common in claims of orthodoxy, with respect to the views of Kant, Nietzsche, and Jünger, that only he, Heidegger, has understood them. Here, he makes a similar claim with respect to Nazism. For Heidegger evidently thought of himself as the only "orthodox" Nazi, as the only one able to understand the essence of National Socialism.

This passage further stresses the connection, later emphasized in the *Spiegel* interview, between Heidegger's Nazism and his theory of technology. As in the interview, here as well, Heidegger insists on the importance of National Socialism in confronting the rule of technology. Heidegger's statement in 1953 is fully consistent with the later statement in the *Spiegel* interview in 1966. In both instances, he underlines his conviction that National Socialism is a valuable, but finally incomplete, effort to counter the effects of modern technology. Although his view of technology later changed, his appreciation of Nazism's role remained constant. It is, then, appropriate to consider Heidegger's theory of technology as a revised, reworked, better formulation of the unsuccessful Nazi effort, as Heidegger understands it, to free us from the rule of technology.

In the accounts of Heidegger's Nietzsche lectures and the *Beiträge,* it was possible to point to passages in which he criticized the failures of Nazism regarded as an ontological theory. To the best of my knowledge there is nothing in the public record to suggest that Heidegger was at all sensitive to the human suffering wreaked by Nazism, in fact sensitive to human beings in more than an abstract sense. The best that Vietta, currently the staunchest German defender of Heidegger, can do is to point to a diary entry by Heribert Heinrichs recording a discussion in which Heidegger supposedly described Hitler as "the robber and criminal of this century"—certainly a mild judgment in view of the enormity of the evidence—and further claimed to have totally revised his own view of National Socialism after 1938.[125] Yet the available evidence contradicts this view, since Heidegger's own writings after that date reveal a continued sympathy for National Socialism, namely for the Nazi effort to confront technology, and a lack of concern for the crimes committed by the Nazis.

Heidegger's failure to denounce, or even to acknowledge, Nazi practice can be interpreted as an oblique resistance to the practical consequences of his theoretical commitment. He was obviously unwilling to acknowledge the failure of his turn to Nazism, not for mere psychological reasons, but on good philosophical grounds; for his turn to Nazism was grounded in his own theory of Being, which he never abandoned. For the same reason, he was also unwilling to abandon National Socialism, or at least an ideal form of it, because of his continued interest in certain points where his thought converged with Nazism, including the coming to be of the Germans as German and the confrontation with technology. Heidegger's insensitivity to the effects of Nazism in practice is coupled, then, with a residual theoretical enthusiasm for a form of Nazism in theory.

In Heidegger's writings on technology, at least two passages indicate a striking insensitivity to human suffering. Heidegger, who understood technology as a form of disclosure, was careful to conceal and not to reveal some of his most deeply held views about the technological process. There is a passage in the original version of Heidegger's essay, "The Question concerning Technology," which originated as a lecture in 1949 under the title "Enframing" but which was altered in the version published in 1954.[126] In the version published during Heidegger's lifetime, the text, which was clearly changed to conceal an earlier formulation, retains only seven words in the translation, five in the revised text: "Agriculture is now the mechanized food industry."[127] This banal point hardly reveals the startling claim embedded in the original manuscript, which only became available some seven years after Heidegger's death. The original passage reads as follows: "Agriculture is now a mechanised food industry, in essence the same as the manufacturing of corpses in gas chambers and extermination camps, the same as the blockade and starvation of nations, the same as the production of hydrogen bombs."[128]

From a strictly Heideggerian point of view, this passage is literally correct, since he maintains that all of modernity suffers from the turn away from Being which leads to the hegemony of technology. Yet this passage is disturbing, in part because of Heidegger's manifest insensitivity, in a period when he emphasizes the *Ereignis,* to the most catastrophic moral *Ereignis* of our time: the Holocaust. Heidegger, who is sensitive to Being, is startlingly insensitive to human being. There is further a manifest conceptual mistake in simply considering all forms of technology as indistinguishably alike. For Heidegger has failed to consider, and certainly failed to comprehend, the relation of technology to the event of the Holocaust: the unparalleled way in which all available technological resources were harnessed, and new ones were invented, specifically to commit genocide. No amount of liberal handwringing at this late date should be allowed to obscure Heidegger's incapacity, not only to respond to, but even to comprehend, the Holocaust through his theory of technology.[129] His theory, hence, fails the test of experience.

Another passage occurs in a still unpublished lecture on technology, delivered in 1949. The manuscript reads:

> Hundreds of thousands die en masse. Do they die? They succumb. They are done in. Do they die? They become mere quanta, items in an inventory in the business of manufacturing corpses. Do they die? They are liquidated inconspicuously in extermination camps. And even apart from that, right now millions of impoverished people are perishing from hunger in China.
>
> But to die is to endure death in its essence. To be able to die means to be capable of this endurance. We are capable of this only if the essence of death makes our own essence possible.[130]

Heidegger's obvious insensitivity to the suffering wrought by the Second World War is also exhibited in another context, in a letter to Herbert Marcuse. Marcuse, Heidegger's former doctoral student, as a Jew early emigrated to escape persecution by the Nazis. He later corresponded with Heidegger about Heidegger's role in National Socialism. In answer to a letter from Marcuse, dated 20 January 1948, Heidegger replied in part:

> To the severe and justified reproaches formulated "over a regime that has exterminated millions of Jews, that has made terror a norm and that transformed everything connected to the concepts of spirit, freedom, and truth into its opposite," I can only add that instead of the "Jews" one should put the "East Germans," and that is even more the case for one of the Allied Powers, with the difference that everything that has happened since 1945 is known to all the world, while the bloody terror of the Nazis in reality was kept secret from the German people.[131]

This chapter has examined the link between Heidegger's Nazism and his view of technology. Heidegger's supporters have suggested that Heidegger confronted Nazism through his theory of technology, or even that his theory of technology arises out of his confrontation with Nazism. Study of Heidegger's texts presents a different, darker picture of Heidegger, a thinker stubbornly committed to the metaphysical racism he shared with Nazism and to a revised version of the supposed Nazi effort to oppose technology. Heidegger's theory of technology is, then, not a confrontation with Nazism but a confrontation with technology from a Nazi perspective. Heidegger's theory of technology only extends, but does not free him from, his concern with National Socialism.

The account of Heidegger's conception of technology closes the second phase of this discussion. The initial phase considered Heidegger's turning to National Socialism on the basis of his philosophical thought. The second phase discussed Heidegger's understanding of the rectorate and the later evolution of Heidegger's position as philosophy and beyond philosophy in relation to Nazism. Heidegger's defenders maintain that in his Nietzsche lectures, in the *Beiträge,* or in his writings on technology, he confronted Nazism. Yet inspection of Heidegger's texts shows that although Heidegger did criticize National Socialism as an unsatisfactory theory of Being, the same criterion he brought against philosophical positions, such as Kant's and Descartes's, he did not criticize its political practice. Study of the texts has further shown Heidegger's continued acceptance of certain aspects of National Socialism, such as its supposed insight into technology. Heidegger continued as well to maintain his steadfast conviction in the metaphysical racism he shared with both the real and ideal forms of National Socialism. Now the effort to defend Heidegger, above all his thought, has mainly been conducted in abstraction from Heidegger's texts, which inconveniently tend to undermine efforts to defend Heidegger's life and thought. In the third and final phase of the discussion, we need to examine the Heidegger reception itself.

The French Reception of Heidegger's Nazism

Heidegger's relation to Nazism raises questions on two distinct levels. On the one hand, there is the theme, analyzed in preceding chapters, of what Heidegger did and thought, and how that relates to his own thought, initially in his philosophical phase, to his fundamental ontology, and later in his so-called post-philosophical phase, to his new thinking. Heidegger's Nazism is obviously central for an appreciation of his position. One of the aims of this essay is to show that a distinction can no longer be clearly drawn between Heidegger's "philosophy" and his Nazism, for the two are deeply intertwined. On the other hand, there is a further theme—parasitic, so to speak, on the preceding one—concerning the reception of Heidegger's Nazism. Since the philosophical tradition consists in the ongoing effort to understand and to evaluate the available philosophical positions, it is important to address the manner in which scholars have attempted to come to grips with the complex series of problems posed by Heidegger's Nazism.

Reception of Heidegger's Nazism

The reception of Heidegger's Nazism is a part of the continuing reception of his thought in an enormous and rapidly growing literature. The reception of Heidegger's Nazism, although not always under that name, has been under way for several decades, at least since the 1930s[1] Heidegger was sympathetic to Nazism before he became a member of the NSDAP. If we date Heidegger's Nazism from his official adherence to the Nazi party, then its reception began in the reaction in newspaper reports and by his philosophical colleagues to his rectoral address in May 1933.[2]

From the beginning, the reaction to Heidegger's Nazism was sharply divided between those who condemned the association of philosophy and Nazism and those who were able to perceive something good even in the turn to the clearest example of absolute evil in our time. Among the earliest reactions by colleagues, we have already noted Croce's complaint that Heidegger dishonored philosophy in the rectoral address[3] and Jaspers's congratulatory note to Heidegger on receipt of the text of the speech.[4] These were isolated reactions. The first philosophical debate between representatives of different views of Heidegger's Nazism began only about a decade and a half later, in the second half of the 1940s in the pages of the French intellectual journal *Les Temps Modernes*.[5] In the main, the debate has often been as heated as it was uninformed. The uninformed nature of the debate is due to the successful efforts of determined Heidegger enthusiasts even now to exclude material, important for an informed judgment, from public and even scholarly access. The first study of the available information was provided in 1960 by Guido Schneeberger in a bibliography, whose appendixes attracted attention.[6] Two years later Schneeberger published a reader of relevant materials.[7] In both instances, he was forced to publish his works privately in order to escape the restrictions of German copyright law with respect to material for which he could not receive permission to publish.

Until recently the reception of Heidegger's Nazism developed in a largely desultory fashion, attracting little attention, with occasional bursts of activity. Significantly, as late as the mid-1970s, in a detailed study of Heidegger's political thought, an observer could state that only three books required mention.[8] Although the reception of Heidegger's Nazism was never as tranquil as ordinary scholarly debate, it was burst asunder, literally transformed, by two publications in the late 1980s: Farias's resolute effort under difficult conditions finally to study Heidegger's Nazism in a wider historical context,[9] and Ott's historically more careful but even more damning effort toward a Heidegger biography.[10] Farias's book served as a catalyst for a strident debate virtually across western Europe, which now gives signs of spreading, in more scholarly, less virulent form, to the United States.[11] It is a measure of the subversive character of Farias's assault on the Heideggerian establishment that although he lives and teaches in Germany, he was only finally able to publish his book in France.

In the multiple phases of the discussion of Heidegger and politics, the controversy in France stands out for several reasons, including its extension over some four decades, the passion with which it has been conducted, the sense of importance it has been accorded, and the degree of attention it has aroused. It further stands out for the clear way in which the lines have been drawn, unusual in scholarly debate, for or against Heidegger. At present, the main defense of Heidegger, as well as the main attack, are both being waged within the limits of the French-language discussion of his thought. For this reason, the French discussion of Heidegger's Nazism provides the outstanding example of how later philosophers have confronted the multiple problems posed by the Nazism of one of the main philosophical thinkers of this century. Accordingly, the aim of this chapter is to come to grips, not with the French reception of Heidegger,[12] but with the more limited topic of the French reception of Heidegger's Nazism.[13] In view of the scope of the French discussion, major stress will be placed on an understanding of the significance of the main lines of the controversy as distinguished from an encyclopedic presentation of all the material.[14]

The Master Thinker in French Philosophy

In order to understand the particular, indeed peculiar, nature of the French reception of Heidegger, it is helpful to provide a brief characterization of the French intellectual context, above all French philosophy. Philosophy in general is not given to rapid changes, since it often takes centuries for problems to be formulated, for ideas to attain wide appeal, for shifts in emphasis to occur. Just the opposite is the case in French thought as viewed on a certain level. In the last two decades, an exceedingly short period by philosophical standards, French philosophy has considered and later discarded options proposed by structuralism, post-structuralism, the *nouveaux philosophes,* hermeneutics, existentialism, semiology, postmodernism, and so on. There is obviously no guarantee that the latest mode on the scene, deconstruction, which is better known and more influential in the United States than in France, will survive, or survive more than the proverbial fifteen minutes during which each of us will supposedly be famous.[15]

The rapid pace in which the various aspects of French thought come into being and pass away suggests that French philosophy—which gave rise to the postmodernist theory according to which there is no ground, no overarching single tale that locates all its variants—in itself is postmodernist.[16] One could easily infer from what by philosophical standards seems to be the nearly instantaneous rise and fall of competing points of view that, to parody Yeats, things have indeed fallen apart since the center does not hold, in fact fails even to exist.[17] But these appearances are indeed deceiving since to a perhaps unsuspected extent there is an intellectual center in French intellectual life, which underlies and makes possible the profusion and confusion of swirling ideas only in its various manifestations.

France is not alone in possessing an intellectual *noumenon*. Another example is the increasingly precarious dominance of analytic thought in Anglo-American philosophical circles, which has begun now to loosen through the realization of some of its main practitioners that it was no longer possible, or even productive, to continue to exclude other forms of thought.[18] For different reasons, a similar phenomenon can be observed in eastern Europe, where the long political hegemony of Marxist orthodoxy has clearly given way to philosophical *perestroika,* in Soviet philosophy and elsewhere in eastern Europe.[19]

Although French thought may seem to be the philosophical analogue of the Maoist injunction to let a hundred flowers bloom, from a historical point of view it has long been dependent on a single main component. After the French Revolution, which in principle guaranteed fundamental rights, including religious rights, to all, France remained, and still remains, a mainly Roman Catholic country;[20] to a scarcely lesser extent French thought has been dominated over several hundred years by forms of Cartesianism.[21] It is hard to imagine and difficult to describe the extent of Descartes's influence on French intellectual life, which descends even to the level of a correctly written paper, the so-called *dissertation,* in the *lycée.* It is not without reason that Sartre has been called the last of the Cartesians and Merleau-Ponty, his younger colleague, has been hailed as the first non-Cartesian French philosopher. For in France over the course of several hundred years, Descartes has played the role of the master philosopher, *le maître penseur,* whose thought furnished the central organizing principle of all intellectual life.

In the period since the 1930s the two main philosophical developments in French thought, namely the attention to Hegel and then to Heidegger, can both be explained with respect to the dominant Cartesianism. The introduction of Hegel in France has been aptly, although not entirely accurately, traced to the influence of Alexandre Kojève's famous seminar on the *Phenomenology* during the late 1930s.[22] Although a brilliant thinker in his own right, a major star in the philosophical firmament, and indeed critical of Descartes, Hegel is also in numerous ways a neo-Cartesian, who perpetuates the well-known Cartesian concerns with certainty, truth in the traditional philosophical sense, metaphysics, first philosophy, and so on.[23] The importance of Hegel's influence on French thought in this century should not hide the extent to which, in reacting against Hegel as the *maître du jeu,* the master of the game, later French thinkers were reacting through Hegel to the continued influence of Descartes.[24] This reaction is in part prolonged in the more recent turn to Heidegger, a notorious anti-Cartesian.

Roughly since 1945, and increasingly in recent years, French thought has been increasingly dominated by Heidegger.[25] To understand the turn to Heidegger in French philosophy, two factors are important. First, there is Heidegger's well-known anti-Cartesianism, which conveniently meshes with the continued reaction against the father of French philosophy, in a form of conceptual parricide stretching over more than three centuries. Heidegger's thought is inseparable from its anti-Cartesian bias, which only grows deeper in his later turn away from Dasein in part in order to expunge any residual Cartesianism.[26] Heidegger's attempt to dismantle modern metaphysics resembles French philosophy itself. The introduction of his thought within the French context as part of the reaction against Hegel, or rather the French form of Marxist Hegelianism, only showed the persistence of the difficult effort to throw off the Cartesian background.

Second, there is the more immediate antihumanist reaction to the prevailing left-wing Marxist, humanist form of French Marxism, associated with such writers as Kojève in the first place, as well as at various times Camus, Nizan, Sartre, Merleau-Ponty, Garaudy, Foucault, perhaps Lévi-Strauss, Barthes, and others, which bothered, in fact offended, those concerned to maintain the traditional French value-system. Heidegger's self-proclaimed antihumanism, in fact an effort to found a new humanism surpassing the old variety, provided a convenient way to throw off the yoke of Hegel's influence, which to many seemed merely a stand-in for Marxism, including its political dimension.

Jean Beaufret later played a main rôle, but at least initially Jean-Paul Sartre was mainly responsible for creating the French fascination with Heidegger. Sartre's *Being and Nothingness,* which was doubly dependent on both Hegel and Heidegger, focused attention on both thinkers during the Second World War, reinforcing the interest in Hegel and turning attention to Heidegger. Sartre's dual interest in Heidegger and Hegel was seen by many as problematic. The form of Hegelianism current in France, to which Sartre also subscribed, was a left-wing Marxist humanism pioneered by Kojève. Heidegger's own self-described antihumanism was, to begin with, perceived as humanism, particularly in the extensive discussion of Dasein in *Being and Time.* Heidegger's thought was in part seen as a necessary course correction to what, certainly from a Roman Catholic religious point of view, was perceived as a form of antihumanism associated with Sartre's atheistic form of existentialism.[27] The point is that although Heidegger left the seminary and later the church, and his link to Nazism was not an expression of humanism in any ordinary sense, his thought was perceived as a *moindre mal,* a lesser evil, by those appalled by Sartre's own form of existentialist humanism.

What is the extent of Heidegger's influence in French philosophy?

There is a measure of truth in Heidegger's famous *boutade* that when the French begin to think, they think in German.[28] To an important extent Heidegger's thought now forms the horizon of French philosophy. The dominance of Heidegger in French philosophy can be illustrated by the startling fact, certainly unprecedented in any other country with a major role in the Western philosophical tradition, that at the present time the three main younger scholars of Aristotle (Rémi Brague), Descartes (Jean-Luc Marion), and Hegel (Dominique Janicaud) in France can all be described either as Heideggerians or as basically influenced by Heidegger's thought. French Heideggerianism is a flourishing industry, perhaps the most important contemporary source of studies of Heidegger's thought in the world today. Within France, Heidegger's influence has in the meantime penetrated in other directions as well. It is no exaggeration to say that at present Heidegger and Heidegger alone is the dominant influence, the master thinker of French philosophy, and that his thought is the context in which it takes shape and which limits its extent. It is, then, no wonder that in the recent resurgence of controversy about Heidegger's link to Nazism, French philosophy has tended to equate the attack on Heidegger with an attack on French philosophy.

Origins of the French Discussion of Heidegger's Politics

This incomplete account of the source and extent of Heidegger's influence in French philosophy is intended to make possible a closer look at the French discussion of Heidegger's Nazism. This complex discussion, which is still under way, has so far unfolded in three separate moments, or waves. These include a short, initial debate (1946–1948) shortly after the end of the Second World War, in which the topic was examined in a cursory manner; a rapid revival of the same debate in the mid-1960s after, indeed partly as a result of, the publication of certain documents calling attention to Heidegger's Nazism; and more recently in the direct, ongoing reaction to the publication in French translation of the Spanish manuscript of Farias's already classic study.

Even before we examine the debate on Heidegger and Nazism in France, we can note in passing three significant features that distinguish it from other portions of a discussion that has by now largely exceeded the limits of a single country or language. First, there is a certain well-known parochialism, long characteristic of French thought of all kinds, which traditionally proceeds as if it formed the entire conceptual universe whose center and nearly sole focus was Paris. Just as, with selected exceptions, French thinkers are mainly, even cheerfully, unaware of non-French forms of thought, so the debate on Heidegger's relation to

National Socialism has largely occurred without consideration of the discussion under way elsewhere. To be sure, there are occasional references to Hugo Ott, the Freiburg historian, or to Otto Pöggeler, the author of an influential study of Heidegger's thought; but for the most part, to a degree unusual in the ever-smaller cultural world, the French debate concerns mainly, often only, itself.[29]

Second, in contrast with the widespread French cultural and political xenophobia, we can note that a number of the most important participants in the French debate on Heidegger's relation to National Socialism are either foreign-born French, or not French at all, for example, Farias, Weil, Löwith, Tertulian, Lukács. This extra-French influence, which has throughout tended to calm and to refocus an often wildly passionate, occasionally irrational debate, was present even at the beginning.

Third, there is a particular philosophical focus due to the contingent fact that until several years ago, when a pirated translation of *Being and Time* was published, only the first half of the book was available in French. Even access to this part of the text was severely restricted by the dependence on a single, strategic Heideggerian essay as the way into fundamental ontology.[30] The French reception of Heidegger has for many years been focused through Heidegger's "Letter on Humanism." This text is Heidegger's response to a letter addressed to him on 10 November 1946 by Jean Beaufret, the French philosopher, who later became the main figure in the introduction of Heidegger's thought in France, a tireless proselytizer for the Heideggerian point of view. Heidegger replied to Beaufret's letter in December 1946 and then reworked his response for publication.

The resultant text is both philosophical and strategic in character. Although this text is a serious philosophical study, it is also a masterly effort by Heidegger to attract attention to his thought in a neighboring country at a time when he was seriously beleaguered in his native Germany. As an open letter to a figure on the French philosophical scene at a time when Heidegger was in eclipse because of his association with the Nazi regime, there was an obvious strategic value to the claim that there had been a turning (*Kehre*) in his position, by implication a turning away from his earlier view which was also a turning away from Nazism. Understood in this way, the concept of the turning appears as a tacit, even graceful admission of an earlier complicity, combined with a suggestion of a fresh start, untainted by earlier transgressions, and a suggestion to provide a reasonable alternative to Sartre, a perhaps objectionable French guru. These are all characteristics that quickly raised Heidegger's stock in French intellectual thought and may even have been calculated to do so. Significantly, although at the time Heidegger had already moved far from his original position, his "Letter on Humanism" has been described by a French commentator as the best introduction to *Being and Time.*[31]

In other texts from his later writings, Heidegger continues to insist on the uniqueness of the Germans; but not by accident in the "Letter on Humanism" Heidegger opposes nationalism of any kind as metaphysically anthropological and subjective.[32] His stated opposition here to biologism, a doctrine to which Heidegger seems never to have subscribed, limits the dimensions of Heidegger's admitted political error.[33] Heidegger's opposition here to Sartrean existentialism and humanism of all sorts as metaphysical[34] is balanced by his careful description of his alternative as the only one able to think "the humanity of man," as an attempt to "think the essence of man more primordially" in order to restore its original sense, and as a view that "in no way implies a defense of the inhuman but rather opens other vistas."[35] Heidegger's depiction of his form of nonmetaphysical humanism as more meaningful than its better-known alternative is clearly stated: "To think the truth of Being at the same time means to think the humanity of *homo humanus.* What counts is *humanitas* in the service of the truth of Being, but without humanism in the metaphysical sense."[36]

The fact that, for contingent reasons, the French reading of Heidegger has largely proceeded from an antimetaphysical humanist focus explains the relative ease with which Heidegger displaced not only Sartre but Hegel as well in French thought and the violent reaction to the appearance of Farias's book. Beyond his status as an important thinker, Heidegger's implicit claim to be a true humanist smoothed the way for the displacement of views frequently regarded as either antihumanistic or associated with antihumanism. The shocking revelation that what many had long regarded as essentially humanism in the deepest sense was possibly no more than a false appearance is basic to the French reaction to recent revelations about Heidegger's politics. It is, then, not by chance, that the French discussion of Heidegger's political thought has been so heated since the debate revolves around the essentially political question of whether, as Heidegger and his followers claim, Heidegger's position is a new antimetaphysical humanism or whether, on the contrary, as others have held, it is a metaphysical form of racism, based on a durable commitment to the superiority of the German people.

In France, the intellectual debate on Heidegger's Nazism began in the pages of *Les Temps Modernes,* one of the best-known French intellectual journals. This journal was founded by Sartre and his colleagues when France was liberated from the Nazis and later edited by him for many years. The early existentialist Sartre is well-known as the author of the view, which to some, including the later Sartre, appeared to ignore the constraints of real life, that we are always and essentially radically free. The initial phase of the debate, which includes texts by Karl Löwith, Alfred de Towarnicki, Eric Weil, Alphonse De Waelhens, and Maurice de Gandillac, is preceded by an editorial note. Here, immediately prior to the publication of the famous "Letter on Humanism," an unnamed editor, in all probability Sartre, draws a comparison between Heidegger and Hegel. Just as the latter's later thought led him to compromise with Prussia, so Heidegger the man and Heidegger the political actor are one and the same; and his political choice follows from his existential thought. In the same way as an analysis of Hegel's position removes any suspicion with respect to dialectical thought, the writer suggests that a similar analysis will do the same for Heidegger, in fact will demonstrate that an existential view of politics is at the antipodes of Nazism.[37]

The First Wave

The initial phase of the French discussion comprises no fewer than three subphases, including articles by Karl Löwith, Maurice de Gandillac, and Alfred de Towarnicki, followed some time later by articles by Eric Weil and Alphonse De Waehlens, and ending with responses by Löwith and De Waelhens. Gandillac, who was apparently the first French philosopher to come in contact with Heidegger after the war, went on to an important career as a professor at the Sorbonne. Löwith is a former student, later colleague of Heidegger, who spent the war in exile. He is well-known for his own work as well as for an interesting study of Heidegger which attempted to understand why and how Heidegger achieved such philosophical importance.[38] Weil, a Jew who was the assistant of Cassirer, himself a Jew, early emigrated to France where he achieved prominence as an original thinker, above all for an important analysis of philosophical categories.[39] De Waelhens was a well-known Belgian scholar of phenomenology and existentialism, the author of important studies of Heidegger, Husserl, Merleau-Ponty, and others. Towarnicki is a journalist who is still active.

Here as in the later debate, it is instructive to regard the discussion as a series of dialectically interrelated analyses of the same phenomenon from diverse points of view. Both Gandillac and Towarnicki embroider various themes of the "official" view of Heidegger's Nazism, due finally to Heidegger himself. Gandillac provides a short account of a visit to Heidegger's home which from the present perspective makes two interesting points.[40] On the one hand, he presents with sympathy Heidegger's view that Hitlerism was the historic manifestation of a so-called structural disease of human being as such. It is significant, since Heidegger later insists on the misunderstood essence of Nazism, that in Gandillac's account he refuses to incriminate the fall of the Germanic community, whose true sense of liberty he still desires to awaken. On the other hand, several times in the article we are told that Heidegger was seduced like a child by the exterior aspects of Hitlerism, that he was induced to enroll in the Nazi party by his children, and so on. Taken together, these two points tend to indicate that Heidegger was unaware of the consequences of, and hence not responsible for, his political actions, while holding open the possibility, which he later never renounced, of the true gathering of the metaphysical *Volk*.

Towarnicki's version of the official view is at least partly false.[41] He suggests that Heidegger was unanimously elected rector, although that is now known to be untrue. Towarnicki quotes Heidegger to the effect that the death of Röhm opened his eyes to the true nature of Nazism, which he later criticized in his courses on Nietzsche; but we know that Heidegger continued to affirm his belief in an authentic form of National Socialism. The article ends with an affirmation, in the form of a direct quotation, of Heidegger's emotional proclamation of the spiritual importance of France to the world. When we recall that Heidegger also justified his turn to Nazism through the concern with the spiritual welfare of the German people, this remark appears less uplifting.

Löwith's discussion, which was written outside Germany in 1939, hence at the beginning of the war that was to devastate Europe, is still surprisingly complete.[42] It mentions topics that continue to occur and recur in the later debate, such as the link between Heidegger's turn toward Nazism and his famous description of resoluteness in paragraph 74 of *Being and Time,* an analysis of the *Rektoratsrede,* Heidegger's praise of Schlageter, Heidegger's relation to the students of Freiburg, the role of E. Jünger, and so on. Löwith's analysis can be summarized as follows: In the final analysis *Being and Time* represents a theory of historical existence. It was only possible for Heidegger to turn toward Nazism on this basis since an interpretation of his thought in this sense was possible. Further, Heidegger's turn to National Socialism follows from his prior philosophy, in fact is squarely based on a main principle of his thought: existence reduced to itself reposes only on itself in the face of nothing. Finally, this principle expresses the identification of Heidegger's thought with the radical political situation in which it arose.

Löwith's analysis is a clear attempt to understand Heidegger's Nazism as following from Heidegger's position, and his position as the expression of the historical situation, in Hegelian terms as the times comprehended in thought. Löwith contradicts two points maintained by all subsequent defenders of Heidegger: Löwith denies that Heidegger's philosophy can be understood otherwise than through its social and political context. Accordingly, he contradicts in advance the well-known "textualist" approach, especially prevalent in French circles, to Heidegger's writings without reference to the wider social, political, and historical context in which they arose. He further denies the "official" view of Heidegger's National Socialism—most prominently represented in the French debate by Fédier and Aubenque, and from a different perspective by Derrida and Lacoue-Labarthe—which tends to minimize, even to excuse, Heidegger's turn toward Nazism as unfortunate, temporary, and above all contingent with respect to Heidegger's thought.

At the outset of the French debate, the opposition between Löwith on the one hand and Gandillac and Towarnicki on the other already symbolizes the two basic alternatives in their respective readings of Heidegger's Nazism as either necessary or contingent. Every other, later debate both within and without the French context only varies, but does not fundamentally modify, these two main options. Obviously, these two extremes are incompatible. Since Löwith traces Heidegger's actions to his thought and Heidegger's thought to the historical context, Löwith disputes Towarnicki, who regards Heidegger's link to National Socialism as temporary, regrettable, and unmotivated by the underlying position; and Löwith disputes as well Gandillac's assertion that Heidegger was unaware of what he did.

The disagreement gave rise to a debate. In the debate Weil, who correctly qualifies Towarnicki's article as a plea for Heidegger, or as he says rather by Heidegger, intervenes against the necessitarian thesis, whereas De Waelhens defends the contingency view. Weil criticizes Heidegger for a supposed failure to assume the responsibility of his acts and as the sole important philosopher who took up Hitler's cause.[43] But he denies the necessitarian thesis on the grounds that even by Heideggerian standards the link between Heidegger's thought and National Socialism is illegitimate. According to Weil, what he incorrectly calls Heideggerian existentialism is intrinsically defective since it leads to a decision in general, but not to any particular decision. From this perspective, Weil claims that Heidegger has falsified his own thought in merely pretending *a contrario* that a political decision could be derived from his apolitical thought. Although it is correct to point to the open-ended quality of Heidegger's view of resoluteness, this does not impede the derivation of a political consequence from another aspect of Heidegger's position, such as his conception of authenticity.

This effort to deconstruct the necessitarian reading is peculiar—not because of the amalgam between Heideggerian phenomenology and existentialism, which Heidegger took pains to deny in the "Letter on Humanism," nor in virtue of the denial that Heidegger is a privileged interpreter of his own thought, since there is no need to accord him this interpretative privilege—but because it fails to address the claim that a clear political decision follows from Heidegger's view of authenticity. Now Alphonse De Waelhens—who also identifies Heidegger's thought as an existential phenomenology—suggests, through an attack on the necessitarian thesis, that the theme of Heidegger's fidelity to his own position is less significant than its possibly intrinsic relation to National Socialism.[44]

De Waelhens's attack on the necessitarian thesis is remarkable for two reasons. On the one hand, he raises the issue of who really understands Heidegger as a precondition for the critique of the latter's thought. Later in the discussion, even when the defenders of Heidegger are led to ac-knowledge that Nazism is central to his position, Derrida and others, including numerous writers outside the French debate, continue to insist that only someone deeply steeped in Heidegger's thought, by inference an unconditional adherent, is possibly competent to measure its defects. On the other hand, De Waelhens formulates a kind of transcendental argument meant to demonstrate that Heidegger's political turning could not have followed from his philosophy. According to De Waelhens, who has obviously been contradicted by history, an analysis of Heidegger's conception of historicality shows that its author could not accept fascism, a doctrine incompatible with the ideas of *Being and Time*. And he dis-poses of Löwith's version of the necessitarian thesis through a rapid but unconvincing effort to demonstrate that Heidegger's former colleague did not always possess a sufficient grasp of the master's texts.

When we compare the views of Weil and De Waelhens, we see at once that since both deny that Heidegger's thought bears an intrinsic relation to Nazism, each is obliged to interpret what Heidegger thought and did as an instance of Heidegger's infidelity to Heidegger's own position. Yet since Heidegger rapidly abandoned an "inauthentic" type of Nazism in favor of an "authentic form" which he never forsook, the effort to defuse the necessitarian thesis undertaken by Weil and De Waelhens is insufficient to demonstrate that the relation in question is contingent. At best, their respective arguments could show only that Heidegger was mistaken on the basis of his thought in turning toward National Social-ism as it in fact existed, which he himself later admitted, but not that he was mistaken on the basis of his thought in turning toward National Socialism as he desired it to exist, that is, from the futural perspective intrinsic to his position.

De Waehlens is more radical than Weil since he does not assert that Hei-degger misunderstood his own thought, but rather claims—a point widely asserted in the later discussion—that the action of the individual Heideg-ger is without philosophical interest. Perhaps for that reason, he drew a response by Löwith, who does not take up the issue of who is capable of judging Heidegger.[45] This omission is important, since it is always possible to claim that a criticism, any criticism at all, is based on an insufficient awareness of the position. Rather, Löwith restates his own conviction that Heidegger's relation to Nazism is a necessary consequence of Heidegger's philosophy of existence. He further affirms that it is curious to defend Heidegger against Heidegger's own voluntary political engagement. In his rejoinder[46] De Waelhens insists that his attempt to show that Heidegger's political action did not, and cannot, follow from the latter's philosophy is only a specific instance of the more general claim that one cannot deduce a particular political stance from a philosophy.

De Waelhens's rejoinder invokes a principle, which, if followed, would effectively suppress the possibility of analyzing the relation between thought and action. His principle, which contradicts the entire ethical tradition, whose unexpressed premise is that reasons can be causes, is false for at least two reasons: First, throughout history, at present in eastern Europe, millions of people have been motivated to political action on behalf of ideas. This is a point De Waehlens can accommodate only on pain of denying that such ideas are philosophical. Second, De Waelhens calls on us to abandon the political act of an analysis of the link between Heidegger's philosophy and politics, which precisely assumes the political efficacy of philosophy he is concerned to deny.

The initial phase of the French discussion of Heidegger's relation to Nazism records a calm, scholarly exchange. In retrospect, this exchange is interesting as a clear statement of the necessitarian and contingent analyses, and for the anticipation of later variants of the effort to "deconstruct" the necessitarian thesis on a priori grounds. These include the effort to construct an a priori impossibility argument and the related claim—from the perspective of conceptual orthodoxy—that whoever criticizes is uninformed. It is notable that the two attempts to deconstruct the necessitarian thesis canvassed here, due to Weil and De Waelhens, avoid a direct analysis of the relevant passages in Heidegger's texts in favor of more general statements. This is specifically the case for the arguments advanced by De Waehlens—including his a priori argument against the very possibility of an intrinsic link between philosophy and politics as well as his assertion that any possible criticism is impossible because based on insufficient knowledge—each of which responds to any and all criticism in general without engaging the criticism on its merits.

The Second Wave

The initial phase of the debate sets the stage for all later discussion of this theme in France and elsewhere. The second phase of the French debate differed in numerous ways from its predecessor. To begin with, it is less compact, and for that reason more difficult to delimit. It occurred over a number of years, roughly from 1948, when the French first edition of Lukács's book appeared, to the publication of Jean-Michel Palmier's study in 1968, the year of the French student uprising. It further includes articles by François Fédier, Jean-Pierre Faye, François Bondy, Alfred Grosser, Robert Minder, Aimé Patri, and others, and journals such as *Médiations* and *Critique*. Another difference is the increasingly international character of the second phase of the debate, which makes greater reference to materials published in languages other than French. Further, the discussion now takes on an increasingly heated, often overheated, on occasion even strident character, which surpasses the generally polite nature of traditional scholarly discussion. One can speculate that the excited character of the debate indicates the political stakes of the critique or defense of Heidegger's form of National Socialism.

The remarkable change in tone is arguably due to a variety of factors. On the one hand, in the inital phase of the discussion a number of those who took part, including Löwith and Weil, were not native French, but those who intervene in the next stage of the debate are mainly of French origin. It is a fact that debate in French intellectual circles tends to be noisier and more strident than elsewhere. On the other hand, in the meantime the full effect of Heidegger's "Letter on Humanism" had begun to be felt. As a result, Heidegger had already begun to acquire a commanding presence in French intellectual life, whose horizon was increasingly constituted by his thought. The greater identification of French thought with Heidegger even as his position displaced Hegel's in the role of the master thinker meant that French scholars on occasion acted as if they were as much engaged in defending French thought as in defending Heidegger's position. Further, the appearance in the meantime of Guido Schneeberger's collection of relevant documents, as well as other studies, such as those due to Adorno and Hühnerfeld, meant that Heidegger's philosophy, and not only his personal reputation, was now at risk. Finally, France was then approaching a political crisis that would nearly paralyze the country for a number of months beginning in March 1968.

Although in his "Letter" Heidegger implicitly admits his culpability in his stated desire to turn over a new leaf, Beaufret took a more extreme line, which developed only slowly. As early as 1945, when he was close to Marxism, he described Heidegger's adherence to National Socialism as the result of a naïveté linked to a bourgeois character.[47] But Beaufret rapidly abandoned his youthful flirt, common in France at least until 1968, with revolutionary thought. In his letter to Heidegger, he mentions his concern with the relation of ontology to the possibility of an ethics. Beaufret later provided a curious answer to his own concern in two ways: through the denial of a more than casual relation between Heidegger and National Socialism, itself a form of the contingency thesis,[48] but above all in his own later turn to a form of revisionist history in which he simply denied that anyone was murdered in Nazi gas chambers, in effect by denying the very existence of Nazi extermination camps![49] Taken to its extremes, the result is to deny that there could be a problem in the link between Heidegger and National Socialism, which, on Beaufret's demonstrably false reading of history, was intrinsically unproblematic. In a word, Nazism was not Nazism! This is surely the most extreme possible form of the deconstruction of the necessitarian thesis, since from this angle of vision it is fully possible to accept that Heidegger was led by his thought to Nazism but to deny that the acceptance of Nazism is problematic.

We can deal separately with the works by Georg Lukács and Jean-Michel Palmier. Lukács, the important Marxist philosopher and literary critic, is the author of *History and Class Consciousness,* a celebrated book that almost alone created the Hegelian approach to Marxism widely influential in later Marxist discussion.[50] His study of Marxism and existentialism, written during his Stalinist phase, was a consciously polemical intervention in the debate, intended to dismiss existentialism, from an orthodox Marxist perspective.[51] Here, he applied Engels's depiction of the relation between thought and being as the watershed question of all philosophy to oppose the possibility of a putative third way supposedly sought by existentialism between idealism and materialism. According to Lukács, existentialism is merely a form of subjective idealism linked to the defense of bourgeois class interests. In passing, he specifically attacks Heidegger's position as pre-fascist. He developed this criticism at length in an appendix, "Anhang: Heidegger Redivivus"—in direct response to the publication of Heidegger's "Letter on Humanism," the same document that cemented Heidegger's relation to French philosophy—added to the German edition of his book.[52]

Lukács's book seems to have affected the French discussion of Heidegger only marginally, mainly through its influence on Merleau-Ponty and Sartre. Lukács was in part later answered by Merleau-Ponty, who, in a famous discussion, identified Lukács as the founder of so-called Western Marxism.[53] And Lukács clearly influenced Sartre's later turn to Marxism. Writing two decades later, Palmier, a careful student of Heidegger, casts himself in the role of a defender of the master against the various attacks which, for perhaps the first time in the French discussion, he attempts to parry through detailed textual analysis. Palmier's study, which appeared at the close of the sharp exchange between Fédier and Faye, is intended by its author as an initial approach to Heidegger's writings from April 1933 to February 1934, that is, during his period as rector.[54] But by casting his net so narrowly, Palmier perhaps unintentionally takes this period, which he recognizes as belonging to Heidegger's oeuvre, out of context, since he renders it exceedingly difficult to grasp the degree of continuity between it and the later evolution of Heidegger's thought. Perhaps for this reason, despite the serious nature of Palmier's study, it seems not to have attracted attention in the later debate.[55]

In order to characterize the second phase of the discussion, whose conceptual and chronological limits fall between the books by Lukács and Palmier, we do well to turn to the polemic between Fédier and Faye. Unlike the initial phase of the discussion, which began with a defense of Heidegger, the opening shot was fired by an attacker who was met after a short interval by a committed defender, determined to repulse any assault on the house of Being. This phase of the attack, in fact the second battle of the conceptual war concerning Heidegger, was launched by Jean-Pierre Faye in 1961[56] through the publication of the French translation of certain Heideggerian texts, notably the *Rektoratsrede* and the homage to Schlageter. In a short presentation preceding the texts, Faye notes the violence of Heidegger's revolutionary language, particularly in the rectoral speech, and its link to Nazi terminology. In a further article[57] in the same journal, Faye reproduces the famous passage on the essence of authentic Nazism from *An Introduction to Metaphysics,* as well as Heidegger's endorsement—in a letter to *Die Zeit* dated 24 September 1953—of the effort by Christian E. Lewalter to explain away Heidegger's apparent concern with Nazism—published in the same journal on 13 August. Here, Faye develops his earlier discussion by insisting on the relation between Heidegger's views and those of Ernst Krieck. Faye also took the occasion, prodded by Aimé Patri, to correct his earlier translation of Heideggerian texts.

In retrospect, Faye's articles did not break new ground. His main contribution was to make available material that tended to cast doubt on the contingency analysis. The initial intervention by François Fédier, Heidegger's most ardent defender in the French philosophical discussion after Beaufret's death, occurred only some five years after Faye's articles. Even then, Fédier's ire was mainly directed toward other targets. Fédier turns to Faye only when the latter dared to respond to his impassioned defense of Heidegger against all comers. Since that time, Fédier has maintained his visible role—which now after the death of Beaufret, his former teacher, is nearly his alone—as the self-appointed official spokesman for the contingency thesis, determined to deconstruct any and all forms of the necessitarian analysis. With the exception of

Aubenque, at present no other prominent French defender of Heidegger argues that the link between Heidegger's philosophy and politics is merely contingent.

Fédier's initial article[58] was prompted by his perception of attacks on Heidegger by Guido Schneeberger, Theodor Adorno, and Paul Hühnerfeld. Instead of a response to a polemic, the author describes his intent as an examination of the presuppositions of so-called hostile arguments. In each case, Fédier shows to his satisfaction that the writer in question is methodologically incapable of comprehending Heidegger's Nazism before describing what he calls reality through a simple statement of the "main facts" of the case. According to Fédier, who does not examine other, later evidence, with the exception of the *Spiegel* interview, an analysis of Heidegger's courses between 1934 and 1944 suffices to perceive the exact meaning of Heidegger's opposition to Nazism and, for the same reason, to understand why he desired in 1933 to contribute to the realization of something other than what Nazism became.

It is noteworthy that none of the works to which Fédier responds here is due to a French author or published in French. Fédier's discussion, which is a form of the contingency thesis, specifically a further version of the claim that the critics of Heidegger are insufficiently familiar with the object of their criticism, is innovative only as an early attempt within the French context to respond to foreign criticism of Heidegger. Although Fédier's *défense tous azimuts* did not even consider the nascent French effort to come to grips with the problem, it is not surprising that he was quickly answered by three French writers, including Patri, Minder, and Faye, which in turn evoked a rapid rejoinder from Fédier.

Fédier is defended by Patri. In his short paper, he argues in support of Fédier and against Faye that—on linguistic grounds alone—one cannot identify a relation between Heidegger and Nazism, since the adjective "*völkisch*" was already used by Fichte, who was not a member of the SS.[59] This version of the attack on the necessitarian thesis because the critic is allegedly misinformed was immediately contradicted in another short paper by Minder, who asserts that even a cursory examination of Heidegger's language supposes an acceptance of some fundamental principles of the Third Reich.[60] He further notes, as Farias and especially Ott later argue in detail, that Heidegger was strongly influenced by a certain rustic but politically reactionary form of Roman Catholicism.

The latter point is a form of the necessitarian thesis interpreted in a historicist manner directly counter to the evolution of Heidegger's thought after the famous turning. For the claim that anyone, including the author of fundamental ontology, is not in part a product of the surrounding environment precisely contradicts Heidegger's own claim that we are all determined by the modern world, by technology, ultimately by metaphysics, even by Being. In his response, Faye returns to the attack with a perceptive comment on nascent right-wing Heideggerianism.[61] He notes in an ironic remark that there is at present a Parisian sect devoted to protecting its masters in the way that the ASPCA is devoted to protecting animals! He provides a discussion of the history of the term *"völkisch"* and its relation to racism, in particular anti-Semitism, later developed by Bourdieu, before turning his critical gaze on the difference, crucial in his eyes, between being in the world and transforming it.

Faye's article could only have been perceived as it was in part intended: as a provocation. In his article, Faye commits a strategic error, since he attempts to show that he has the appropriate knowledge which Fédier accuses him of lacking. The argument cannot be won on such terms, since it is always possible to maintain that the critic knew some things but not others, and the other things are relevant, indeed crucial. In short, it is always possible to claim and in effect to make out the claim that one who opposes a doctrine, any doctrine, is not sufficiently informed. This insight was not lost on Fédier, who quickly responded in this way in order to show that *après tout* Faye was uninformed, in any case not sufficiently informed to criticize such a difficult thinker as Heidegger, since he did not know German sufficiently well. This is a technique which Fédier has continued to employ with frequency in his now numerous attempts to defend the "sacred" cause.[62]

In his response, Fédier concedes that Heidegger did use certain incriminating expressions over a ten-month period, but he denies that as a result Heidegger's thought is compromised in any way. In the course of a veritable demonstration of why no translation is safe from "deconstruction," which anticipates Derrida's use of this method in his best days, Fédier goes so far as to say that a "real" translation of the rectoral address will remove the vestiges of Nazism which Faye has "injected" into it. He further advances a claim—which he later developed at length in a book—that although Heidegger was mistaken in 1933 in his allegiance to Hitler, it was impossible to understand at the time what Hitler would become. He closes with a triple criticism of Heidegger's failure: to foresee the consequences of Nazism, to measure the powerlessness of thought with respect to Nazism, and to grasp that thought could not modify what was under way. The latter two points are different versions of the same idea of the weakness of thought, which represent an application of Heidegger's own later view, in the "Letter on Humanism" and elsewhere, of thought as different from and opposed to philosophy.

For present purposes, Fédier's argument is interesting as the basic statement of the contingentist attack on the necessitarian analysis. More than twenty years later, one can no longer doubt in good faith the existence of a form of right-wing Heideggerianism determined to save Heidegger at all costs, even if to do so on occasion requires one to deny the clearly evident. At this early stage, with the exception of Beaufret, Gandillac, and De Waelhens, and to a lesser extent such secondary figures as Patri, Fédier was virtually isolated as the keeper of the grail of Being. But as early as his first skirmish, he identified the basic form of his response to any form of the necessitarian argument.

Fédier's strategy is obviously dependent on that of such pioneer defenders of Heidegger in the French-language discussion as De Waelhens, who formulated the initial version of the attack on the necessitarian thesis for insufficient evidence. Now De Waelhens's version of this gambit was unconvincing since it was no more than the claim, which can always be made, that the critic is uninformed. But this claim was unconvincing, or at least not sufficiently convincing to be acceptable to such a truly knowledgeable observer as Löwith. Yet if he does not perfect this strategy, Fédier at least takes it much further by developing it into a coherent defense, much as in chess the difference between an isolated move and a viable defense consists in the articulation of the various elements. Fédier's counter consists in the following elements, all calculated to make it difficult, even impossible, to make out a claim for a durable, or even a transitory, link between Heidegger and Nazism: the assertion that Heidegger was naive, but not culpable since he did not, or could not, know the nature of Nazism; the intimation that the critic is inadequately informed, for instance about Heidegger, as concerns the German language, and so on; and the pretension that a simple statement of the "facts," including a look at the statements of others who were there and hence by implication know the "real" story is sufficient to separate the "real" Heidegger from the mythic figure who is the target of his critics. Combined in different ways, all of these elements later return in the third phase of the French debate on Heidegger and National Socialism.

The Onset of the Third Wave

The third, most recent phase of the French debate began when Farias's study burst onto the intellectual scene in the fall of 1987. Any account of this phase needs to distinguish between the immediate reaction to Farias's book in French circles and the more measured but often still heated discussion that followed and at the present time is still under way. The immediate French reaction to Farias's book was part of a rapid response which, it is fair to say, swept over western Europe. The major newspapers and many magazines in all the major European countries carried articles concerning this study, often with a kind of concealed amusement directed at the French reception of the work.

Two examples from the West German press and one from an Italian newspaper are typical. In an article in a well-known liberal German daily, the author, apparently unaware of the preceding discussion, comments that the question of the negative influence on Heidegger's thought will henceforth be raised in France as well as in Germany.[63] In a respected intellectual German weekly, another writer concludes that Heidegger's letter to Jean Beaufret did not remain without a response, since it led to French postmodernism, although none of the postmodernists, who are all staunchly antitotalitarian, can be simply assimilated to Heidegger in a political manner.[64] Both of these articles are cautious and, in the best German sense, *sachlich,* concerned more to report than to pass judgment.

We find a much sharper, less journalistic reaction in an Italian daily newspaper which counterposes articles by two well-known Italian philosophers: Roberto Maggiori, an anti-Heideggerian; and Gianni Vattimo, a well-known Heideggerian. Responding to an earlier review by Vattimo of the Farias book, Maggiori criticizes Vattimo's view that the whole *"affaire Heidegger"* is an operation directed against certain Parisian thinkers. In a sharp response, which recalls Beaufret's estimate of Heidegger as a conceptual giant among pygmies, Vattimo dismisses Farias's work as of little historical consequence.[65]

The sharp exchange between Maggiori and Vattimo is similar in content, but not in tone, to the often much sharper character of the French discussion. The immediate reaction, what in French is aptly called the *réaction à chaud,* was precisely that, namely heated, in fact overheated to a degree unusual even in French intellectual circles. This phase of the controversy, which was more symptomatic of the depth of feeling than of insight into the problem, was uncharacteristically played out in the pages of the daily papers, the weekly magazines, in art and literary journals, on television, and so on—in short, through forms of communication not often associated with the measured tread of philosophical debate. It involved such well-known figures on the French intellectual scene as Derrida, Finkielkraut, E. de Fontenay, Baudrillard, Levinas, Aubenque, Blanchot, Bourdieu, Renaut, Ferry, Daix, and so on, as well as a large number of less well known figures, all of whom felt called upon to comment on the situation; it involved as well foreign scholars imported for the occasion such as Gadamer. What had earlier been a philosophical debate, a disagreement between scholars on a theme concerning a famous but obscure German thinker, quickly became a kind of intellectual free-for-all in which opinions, even frank accusations, were voiced in rapid fashion. The result was to guarantee a *succès de scandale* for a book that rapidly became a *cause célèbre.*

One way to indicate the amplitude of the immediate reaction, which lasted for weeks in certain cases, is by a simple list, in no particular order, of some of the newspapers and journals that ran articles, sometimes numerous articles, on the topic: *Art Press, La Quinzaine Littéraire, Le Monde, Le Matin, Libération, La Croix, Le Quotidien de Paris, Le Figaro, Le Magazine Littéraire, Le Canard Enchaîné,* and so on. The tone of the debate to follow was given by the opening shot, fired by Christian Jambet, a former *nouveau philosophe,* in his preface to the French edition of Farias's work. His sharply worded preface begins with a reference to the traditional belief in the virtue of philosophy for life, before building to remarks on the manner in which Heidegger allegedly identifies authentic existence with a mere semblance, itself representative of the politics of extermination. Jambet ends with a statement intended to sum up Heidegger's thought in a reference to a well-known film, *Night and Fog (Nuit et brouillard)* on the Nazi concentration camps: "Heidegger has the merit of making ontology the question of our time. But how can we accept that philosophy, born of Socrates' trial for leading a just life, ends in the twilight where Heidegger wanted to see the end of the gods, but which was only the time of *Night and Fog?*"[66]

In his preface, Jambet raises the question of the specific difference that opposes, or seems to oppose, Heidegger to the entire philosophical tradition through the relation between his own thought and absolute evil. Yet Jambet does not raise the other theme, highly relevant in the French context, of the specific link between Heidegger's philosophy and French thought. Certainly, the latter topic is partially responsible for the inflamed, passionate character of the immediate French reaction. Perhaps Hugo Ott, the Freiburg historian, caught the mood best in the opening comment of his review of Farias's book: "In France a sky has fallen in—*the sky of the philosophers.*"[67]

Even a small selection will communicate the sheer breadth of opinion in the immediate response to Farias's study in French circles. In a sober article, Roger-Pol Droit states that as a result of his study Farias has dismantled the "official" view of Heidegger's merely contingent relation with National Socialism, long maintained by Beaufret and other friends.[68] According to Droit, who clearly denies De Waelhens's claim, in the future it will be impossible to separate Heidegger the philosopher from Heidegger the man, and it will be necessary to think the link that unites them. Georges-Arthur Goldschmidt, a French refugee from German Nazism, welcomes Farias's study for swelling the meager ranks of those bothered by Heidegger's Nazi past; he regards Farias's book as a means to impede the normal business of the Parisian Heideggerians, henceforth obliged to confront the issues.[69] In a response, Emmanuel Martineau, the author of the pirated translation of *Being and Time,* a friend and student of Beaufret, admits that the latter became part of Heideggerian fascism, which he regards as matched by a hystericial anti-Heideggerian fascism. He accuses Goldschmidt of falling prey, not to the hate of Nazi cruelty, but purely and simply to the hatred of thought.[70]

Alain Finkielkraut complains that in noting the connection between *Being and Time* and *Mein Kampf,* there is a concealed risk of promoting a kind of fascist reaction against philosophy.[71] In a response to Finkielkraut, Goldschmidt suggests that in France there is little real knowledge of Nazism; there is further an incapacity to see that a kind of Nazism rooted in German thought since Fichte is central to Heidegger's thought.[72] Jean Baudrillard observes that the so-called necrological discussion concerning Heidegger has no intrinsic philosophical meaning. He maintains that this discussion only betrays a transition from the stage of history to the stage of myth in which events, which we cannot grasp on the plane of reality, give rise to a convulsion indicative of a loss of reality.[73]

Martineau's version of the lack of critical competence, already in evidence in earlier discussions, is further developed by Jacques Derrida in an interview.[74] According to Derrida, then on the point of publishing a book coincidentally concerned with Heidegger and politics, the so-called facts discovered by Farias are not new for anyone seriously interested in Heidegger; and the interpretation of their relation to the master's thought is so insufficient as to raise the question of whether Farias has devoted more than an hour to reading Heidegger. Yet Derrida also concedes the need to show the deep link between Heidegger's thought and actions to the possibility and reality of what he calls all the Nazisms.

In the face of Derrida's claim that Farias is not a competent reader of Heidegger's texts, Farias's enumeration, in his response, of a list of facts, supposedly brought to the attention of scholars for the first time, seems vaguely unsatisfactory.[75] A still more radical response is furnished by Pierre Aubenque, the well-known Aristotle scholar, who in a bitter article[76] simply denies all the relevant points, including the relevance of Farias's book, the intellectual honesty of his analysis, the need for a study of this kind, and the lack of a significant connection between Heidegger's thought and Nazism. Aubenque's analysis is supported by Pascal David, who ends a review of Farias's study with a quotation from Abraham a Santa Clara—the Augustinian anti-Semite whom Farias regards as influential on Heidegger—to the effect that God loves fools, not foolishness.[77]

In his article, Aubenque refers approvingly to Derrida, but the difference between their respective readings of Heidegger's Nazism places them in different camps. Although infinitely more clever than Fédier, in his avowal of a version of the contingency thesis Aubenque is finally close to Fédier's wholly unyielding defense, which simply denies that there is a problem worthy of consideration. In comparison, Derrida's response is more innovative in "deconstructing" the opposition between representatives of the necessitarian and contingentist analyses. In essence, Derrida proposes that we can acknowledge the intrinsic link between Heidegger and Nazism, although he continues to insist that only the anointed few can comprehend it in the correct manner.

The result is to concede the main point of the necessitarian approach but to restrict its development by continuing to insist, as the contingentists have all along, that only the "orthodox," or more precisely the "orthodox" critic of Heidegger, can measure the problem. An appropriate analogy is the claim made by a former Stalinist that only Stalin's victims can legitimately judge his crimes. This new standard of criticism, which couples an admission of the problem—which can no longer be denied, and is in fact no longer denied in any straightforward fashion by any observer with the clear exception of Fédier and Aubenque, who continue to represent the original form of the contingentist view—with the insistence on expert knowledge of Heidegger's thought as a precondition for valid discussion of Heidegger's Nazism, represents a significant evolution in the scholarly French discussion of this theme. As a result, the gap between the discussants has narrowed considerably since the point at issue is no longer whether there was a real and durable link between Heidegger and Nazism—something perhaps only Aubenque among the more significant French intellectuals still denies—but rather how to understand this link, in particular how to understand its significance for his philosophy.

In philosophy, because of the length of the gestation period the debate normally unfolds rather slowly, over a period measured at best in years and more often in decades or centuries. Now in French circles, where the half-life of a theory is very short, the debate usually unfolds more quickly since to publish slowly would be to run the risk of being able to comment on a topic only as it was in the process of disappearing from the intellectual scene. Until recently, that is, until the publication of Farias's work, with the exception of Palmier's study, no books wholly, or even mainly, centered on the theme of Heidegger and Nazism had appeared. This lacuna, if it is one, was now rapidly corrected, at a speed extraordinary even by the standards of the French intellectual discussion. Farias's book was published in October 1987. From that period until the following May, even as a steady, but steadily diminishing, stream of articles devoted to the topic continued to pour out, in an extraordinary burst of scholarly creativity no fewer than six studies devoted to this theme appeared.[78] Not surprisingly, in most cases they reflected the new consensus that there was a problem, although they differed widely on its description and analysis.

The Third Wave

Let us discuss these books in the order in which they appeared, which corresponds at least roughly to the order of their composition. We can begin with three rather different studies by Pierre Bourdieu, by Jean-François Lyotard, one of the main representatives of the postmodern tendency in French philosophy, and by Fédier. Bourdieu's discussion of what he, following Heidegger's concern with Being, calls Heidegger's political ontology, is the second edition of a text originally published in 1975, rewritten and adapted to recent revelations about Heidegger. Lyotard's study is the apparent result of the desire, or at least the felt need, of every well-known Parisian intellectual who desires to avoid regression to the state of mere anonymity to comment rapidly on any major topic. Fédier's work is a further example of his continued effort, which in the meantime has lost any semblance of scholarly credibility, to maintain the contingentist thesis in its original but now outmoded form. These three disparate works nicely illustrate the range of the next strand in the scholarly discussion by those whose relation to Heidegger is either tangential or, if the relation is on the contrary close, at least tangential to the further evolution of the Heidegger debate.

In a short introduction to his short study, Bourdieu, a well-known Marxist sociologist, indicates that his analysis of methodology has been updated in the footnotes and by placing at the end three chapters concerning the analysis of Heideggerian language.[79] In an evident reference to the first edition of his book, he remarks—with a certain self-approval—that, despite the image of sociology, a close reading of Heidegger's work already revealed such themes as anti-Semitism, his refusal to break with Nazism, his ultrarevolutionary conservative tendencies, as well as his disappointment in the lack of recognition of his revolutionary aspirations as the philosophical *Führer*.[80] In a clear allusion to the prior debate on Heidegger and politics, Bourdieu states that the failure to understand what has occurred was aided by Heidegger's erection of a wall between anthropology and ontology,[81] although we need now to examine the intrinsic blindness of these "professionals of lucidity."[82]

Bourdieu is prescient in his allusion to Heidegger's anti-Semitism, which has only recently been established.[83] His comments are significant in raising the second-order question of how so-called professionals of lucidity are able to respond to a situation of this kind. He provides an answer as to how one ought to proceed in a manner that reveals the politically conservative thrust of purely textual analysis, favored most prominently in the current French discussion by Derrida and other so-called deconstructionists. According to Bourdieu, even the most determined adversaries of Heidegger have missed some of the signs concerning his Nazism since they unfortunately accept the form of immanent textual hermeneutics on which others, that is, Heidegger's epigones, insist. An approach of this kind, even its most radical form, can at best be only partially successful since it concerns certain presuppositions only.[84] In fact, this sort of approach is dangerous since when rigorously applied it has the effect not only of sanitizing what is unsavory but of turning attention away from the political dimension to which the texts in question, even by their failure to state their aim, nonetheless refer. A striking example provided by Bourdieu concerns the manner in which a variety of participants in the French discussion, for example Beaufret, Lefebvre, Châtelet, and Axelos—in fact those who accept Heidegger's own effort in the "Letter on Humanism" to measure his thought in terms of Marx's—see a convergence between Heidegger and Marx.[85]

Bourdieu insists that we must abandon the separation between a political and a philosophical interpretation in order to institute a double reading (*lecture double*) that is both political and philosophical for Heideggerian texts characterized by an intrinsic ambiguity.[86] His aim is to break out of the circle formed by an exclusively immanent reading of the text, doubly confined within the text and to professionals, such as professional philosophers, or even confined to those philosophers who profess allegiance to Heidegger.[87] He regards Heidegger as representative of extremely conservative revolutionary tendencies that arose in Germany between the two world wars. And he agrees in part with the tendency of French defenders of Heidegger to discern two basically different stages in his thought. According to Bourdieu, Heidegger II constitutes a series of commentaries on Heidegger I in which, as the master himself notes, nothing is abandoned but, in Bourdieu's words, the celebrated author now absolutizes his practical choices in philosophical language.[88] He regards Heidegger's denial of a relation between his and any other position as an exercise in negative political ontology.[89] In Bourdieu's view, only those sensitive to the situation beyond the internal approach to the reading of the text can finally decode it.[90]

Bourdieu is in part correct that Heidegger refused to explain his relation to Nazism since to do so would have been to admit that the essential thought never thought the essential, since Heidegger did not and could not grasp Nazism on the basis of his thought of Being. Bourdieu's error, which reveals a problem in his methodology, is to trivialize Heidegger's position by reducing it merely to an unconscious component which it supposedly later erects as a philosophical standard. Yet when we consider Heidegger's texts, not only in the context of his position but against the social and political background, we clearly have access to a dimension not accessible if we limit ourselves to a more immanent textual approach. Bourdieu's point tends to undermine various forms of immanent hermeneutics, including the celebrated view of intertextuality. It further reveals a conscious or unconscious strategy on the part of some right-wing Heideggerians, the reason for its relative success, and the way in which, as Bourdieu's own essay demonstrates, one can surpass its limits.

Bourdieu's book is a significant effort, altogether too rare in the discussion, to come to grips with the political dimension of Heidegger's thought against the historical background. The limitation of his account is that he mainly relies on an essay already in hand with only minor changes to react to more recent discussion. Although both Lyotard and Fédier make greater efforts to confront the latest research, their books are less impressive. Like Bourdieu, Lyotard also refuses to amalgamate Heidegger's thought and his politics.[91] Yet in comparison with Bourdieu's book and his own earlier writing, Lyotard's essay appears hasty and unsatisfactory. Bourdieu's work is saturated with references to English and German discussion and is particularly rich in allusions to the constitution of the Weimar ethos against the nineteenth-century German background. Bourdieu's analysis of the relation between Heidegger's thought and the historical, cultural, and political background is still unsurpassed in the French discussion. With the exception of the obligatory tipping of the hat to Freud and Kant, Lyotard is exclusively concerned with French sources, something unsurprising since he holds that the "problem" is essentially French.

Despite Habermas's effort[92] to portray him and his colleagues as cryptoconservatives, Lyotard's approach reveals a fashionable, postmodernist form of liberalism. The term "Jews" ("les juifs") in the title refers not only to the Jews but to all those who in Europe have always been assimilated to them. This slight volume is divided into two chapters, respectively titled "The 'Jews' " and "Heidegger." According to Lyotard, who seems to like quotation marks, what he refers to as the Heidegger problem is a "French" problem.[93] He holds that "the Jews," those outcasts of society, demonstrate that man's misery is constitutive of his being.[94] Lyotard insists on the need to think the Heidegger problem[95] without accepting the modish view that Nazism can either be deduced from *Being and Time* or that this book arose from an ethos that was already Nazi or pre-Nazi.[96] After stating that both Farias and Derrida are correct, Lyotard asserts that there is, however, something unforgettable but still forgotten that constitutes the real problem—that is, that Heidegger could possibly have thought that in and through his collaboration with the Nazi party a real opportunity existed.[97]

Lyotard is close to Bourdieu with respect to the famous turning, which he describes in difficult language as "the amnesiac meditation of what will occur in Heideggerian 'politics.' "[98] He suggests that *Being and Time* makes possible, but does not require, Heidegger's political engagement,[99] as witness the political reading Heidegger gave of his own thought during the rectoral episode.[100] The remainder of the book consists in a serial critique of the views of other French commentators, including Derrida, Lacoue-Labarthe, and Nancy. For Lyotard, all of them fail to grasp that—as Lyotard notes in a comment on Heidegger's "Essence of Truth"—in Heidegger's turn toward Being and, by inference, away from the Jews, or "Jews," Heidegger's thought commits a cardinal "fault" since it is still the hostage of the Law (*la Loi*).[101]

This discussion is perhaps most enlightening as an undeveloped but correct suggestion: although not an overtly political book, *Being and Time* could be and in fact was read by Heidegger in a political sense as the basis of his turn toward Nazism.[102] The suggestion that the basic flaw in Heidegger's thought resides in its relation to the Law, perhaps by extension in its dependency on the nondifferentiated other, or other than itself, calls attention to a possible relation to the German idealist tradition; but it is unfortunately too vague to state clearly, much less to evaluate. This is not the defect of Fédier's work, which could hardly be clearer in its intent or weaker in its arguments.

Fédier's book[103] is the latest—and final, one hopes—expression of his unremitting faith as an orthodox Heideggerian not swayed, or even chastened, by new information or the intervening debate. He displays this point of view in his study with increased ardor even as he becomes the most prominent and certainly most persistent representative of this angle of vision, a sort of living dinosaur. Like the mythical author in Camus's *La Peste,* the entire bibliography of certain writers is wholly composed of multiple versions of a single text, which they write again and again in different forms. Fédier's scenario follows in detail the meanders of his initial defense of the master in articles published more than two decades ago. The relevant difference is that here the *rappel des faits,* meant to exonerate Heidegger, is not due to Fédier and does not follow but precedes the discussion. In a "biographical essay" (*"essai biographique"*) that begins the work, and which opens and closes with comments on the tranquil little city of Messkirch where Heidegger was born and is buried, François Vezin declares that the period of the rectorate is no more than a parenthesis in Heidegger's life.[104]

Like the earliest forms of the contingentist analysis, Fédier's book is intended to defend Heidegger by attacking his detractors, in particular Farias. In the course of a difficult defense, the author is compelled to take extreme measures. Two examples worth noting are the tortured distinction introduced between anti-Judaism and anti-Semitism,[105] and the defense of the German bishops for their 1933 decision to remove the interdiction that prevented Roman Catholics from adhering to National Socialism. In his introduction, Fédier indicates that his book is meant as an apology in a supposed Socratic sense in order to dispose of the charges.[106] Like a good defense lawyer, he begins by exaggerating the "crime" in order to show that his client could not possibly be guilty of it. According to Fédier, who perhaps had Adorno in mind, Farias holds that Heidegger never said nor thought essentially anything other than Nazism, a charge which Fédier affirms to be a calumny.[107]

This attempted defense is problematic, since neither Farias nor anyone else has ever criticized Heidegger as broadly as Fédier pretends. Although he is concerned to refute all the charges brought against Heidegger, Fédier mainly concentrates on the rectoral period. He claims that whereas it is permissible to accuse Heidegger of adherence to Nazism in 1933–1934, it is slanderous to describe the adherence as total, since he never adhered to biological racism and so on.[108] But, then, by this standard there never were many total adherents of Nazism, especially among German academics, since few wholly accepted all aspects of the doctrine. Fédier's main argument consists in a perverse form of skepticism, according to which in 1933 it was not possible to foresee the future of National Socialism.[109] He even asserts that the definitive form of Nazism was not known prior to 1 September 1939.[110] But although many aspects of what would occur were indeed unclear in 1933, and by definition the future is what has not yet happened, the situation was already sufficiently clear then, well before the outbreak of the war, for many, including numerous Jewish philosophers, such as Cassirer, Marcuse, Weil, Benjamin, Löwith, Arendt, and others, to choose exile. For instance, as early as the Nazi party program, formulated in July 1920, the fledgling political party insisted that a Jew could not be a member of the German community,[111] and Hitler left no doubt of his intentions toward Jews in *Mein Kampf*. In fact, even Fédier is not convinced by his argument, since he also concedes that when Heidegger took up the cause of a National Socialism it already carried with it the signs of an essential perversity.[112]

The first part of Fédier's discussion, entitled "Un pseudo-événement," is a long attack on Farias's book because of what Fédier alleges to be its inquisitorial tone,[113] obfuscation,[114] unconscious appeal to Freudian mechanisms of condensation and displacement,[115] failure to respect the rules of honest scientific procedure,[116] and so on. Alone at this late

date, when so much is known, indeed when even such *croyants* as Derrida claim incorrectly that everything is known, Fédier explains Farias's
study as a sheer invention (*montage*) of which almost no page can with-
stand serious study.[117] In the second part of the discussion, entitled "Heidegger et la politique," having disposed of Farias to his satisfaction,
Fédier provides his own analysis of the problem raised by the rectoral
period, which he attributes to Heidegger's impatience.[118]

In the course of his defense, Fédier makes the following controversial
points: the rectoral address does not show an acceptance of Nazism but
only a concern to defend academic science in the university,[119] Heidegger
later distinguished himself in his opposition to Nazism,[120] the source of
his action lies in a philosophical error leading to a need to modify the
position,[121] and Heidegger's later silence is to be respected after the
martyrdom he endured.[122] Yet unfortunately the rectoral address shows
not only an interest in the defense of science but an explicit concern,
which Heidegger underlines here and specifically admits in the article on
the rectorate, to utilize the university to attain a common goal shared
with the Nazis: the destiny of the German people; and Heidegger's
silence is neither honorable nor acceptable. And examination of Heidegger's texts refutes Heidegger's own claim to have confronted Nazism in
his later writings.

Fédier's most interesting point is his claim in passing that a philosophical error necessitates a modification of the position, which suggests,
reasoning by *modus tollens,* that if a position leads to an incorrect form
of action there is something mistaken in its very heart. In different ways
this theme is developed in three further books on Heidegger and politics, due to Jacques Derrida, Philippe Lacoue-Labarthe, and Luc Ferry
and Alain Renaut. Derrida requires no introduction. Lacoue-Labarthe,
Derrida's former student, is a well-known Heidegger specialist who has
worked closely in the past with Jean-Luc Nancy, another of Derrida's
close associates.[123] Ferry and Renaut are two young antiestablishment
philosophers who have collaborated on several other works. Derrida's
book, which coincidentally appeared almost immediately after Farias's
study, caused a stir in Heideggerian circles. Lacoue-Labarthe's work is
an effort to think through the problem in a manner related to, but also
significantly different from, Derrida's analysis, itself apparently dependent on Lacoue-Labarthe's earlier writing. The study by Ferry and
Renaut is an attack on French right-wing Heideggerianism as a form of
antihumanism due ultimately to Heidegger.

Derrida is an important thinker as well as presently the leading Heideggerian in France. His thought is deeply marked by, in fact inconceiv-
able without, the encounter with Heidegger; he has also commented on
Heidegger's position in numerous writings.[124] His influential but unortho-

dox Heideggerianism is itself an important form of Heideggerian "ortho-doxy," especially in France.[125] Derrida's study, which can be viewed as a long meditation on Heidegger, is thoroughly Heideggerian since it pro-poses to thematize the concept of spirit, something Heidegger never does, in fact avoids. It can be read from at least two perspectives: as a Heideggerian analysis of Heidegger; and as an indirect, but pointed response to the theme of Heidegger and politics.[126]

Derrida's defense of Heidegger, like so much of the French discussion of Heidegger, rests on a creative use of the "Letter on Humanism." Derrida applies Heidegger's remark that humanism is metaphysical to characterize Heidegger's own Nazism as a metaphysical humanism which, in his later writings, he supposedly overcomes in a nonmeta-physical, deeper form of humanism announced in this text. This analysis presupposes on the one hand that the later Heidegger, but not the early Heidegger, is antimetaphysical, or more precisely beyond metaphysics in any ordinary sense—precisely what Heidegger himself claimed in his later writings, such as the *Beiträge*—and on the other hand that there is a break between the early and later phases of Heidegger's thought.

As a defense of the importance of Heidegger's thought while acknowl-edging the clear, undeniable link to Nazism, Derrida's strategy is reminis-cent of a form of "orthodox" Marxism, most clearly represented by Althusser and his associates, which argued for a break situated within Marx's thought. On this reading—already foreshadowed in Marx's view of the break between prehistory and human history in the transition from capitalism to communism—Marx's thought allegedly decomposes into two chronologically separable positions, the first of which can be described as philosophy but not yet as science, and the second of which breaks with philosophy in order to assume the form of science that is supposedly beyond philosophy. Althusser, who was obliged by the tardy publication of Marx's early writings to acknowledge the philosophical tenor of the early position, sought to defend the nonphilosophical, alleg-edly scientific character of the later theory, that is, the supposedly ma-ture form taken by Marx's theory after it broke with philosophy. In a similar manner, apparently relying on the concept of the turning in Hei-degger's thought, which he does not, however, discuss, Derrida corre-lates the initial Heideggerian critique of metaphysics with Heidegger's supposedly still metaphysical philosophy, which then later gives way to what Heidegger later describes as an antimetaphysical view of thinking beyond philosophy. According to Derrida, in his still metaphysical phase Heidegger turned to Nazism, which he renounced in his later move away from metaphysics and beyond philosophy.

Derrida's Heidegger interpretation takes shape as a meditation on the terms *"Geist," "geistig,"* and *"geistlich"* in Heidegger's thought.[127]

His defense of Heidegger includes a reading of Heidegger's supposed deconstruction of spirit (*Geist*) and its significance for an appreciation of Heidegger's relation to National Socialism.[128] Derrida points out that in *Being and Time* Heidegger warns against the use of *Geist,* which he puts in quotation marks; but twenty-five years later in an essay on Trakl[129] he speaks freely of the same term, which he now employs without quotation marks.[130] Derrida's hypothesis is that for Heidegger this term refers to such supposedly metaphysical concepts as unity (*l'Un*) and gathering (*Versammlung*).[131] According to Derrida, for Heidegger spirit is neither *pneuma* nor *spiritus,* but finally a flame more originary than either the Christian or the Platonico-metaphysical concepts.[132] He maintains that even in 1933, for instance in the rectoral address, Heidegger rejected the reduction of spirit to reason[133] in order to spiritualize Nazism,[134] as can be seen in the role of spirit in the rectoral address.[135] It follows, then, that Heidegger's Nazism was metaphysical, and that he overcame it when he overcame the metaphysical element in his own thought.

This attempted defense is problematic for various reasons. To begin with, in his self-described Heideggerian effort to think the unthought, Derrida exaggerates the importance of a concept which Heidegger never thematizes precisely because it is not fundamental but ancillary to or even insignificant in his position. Derrida is unconvincing in his claim that spirit is central to Heidegger's thought, in which this concept seems at best a minor concern. Derrida unfortunately trivializes Heidegger's commitment to Nazism as following from a residually metaphysical turn of mind, in effect by reducing a practical political engagement to a philosophical commitment from which it apparently followed but with which it cannot reasonably be equated. A form of thought that makes it possible to accept a particular political approach, no matter of what kind, must not be confused with its consequence. Obviously, metaphysics as such does not necessarily lead to Nazism, since there are many metaphysicians who did not become Nazis. Yet when Heidegger renounced metaphysics after the turning in his thought, he did not give up Nazism. Further, Derrida is obviously incorrect if he means to suggest that when Heidegger employs the term "*Geist*" without quotation marks in the 1953 article on Trakl, Heidegger has overcome both metaphysics and Nazism. For in the same year he republished *An Introduction to Metaphysics* in which he publicly reaffirmed his commitment to a form of Nazism present, in Heideggerian terminology, under the mode of absence. At most, Heidegger turned away from Nazism as it was, although there is no evidence that he ever accepted it without reservations, but he never turned away from it as he still desired it to be. Finally, the interpretation of the turning in Heidegger's thought, on which Derrida's defense of Heidegger rests, is basically mistaken if judged by Heidegger's texts. As the *Beiträge zur Philosophie* shows in detail, the turning is not intended to indicate a break or discontinuity between phases of Heidegger's thought; rather, it is intended to point to further progress from a first beginning to another, deeper beginning more originary than, and a condition of, his initial but more superficial starting point. Since there is, then, no break in Heidegger's thought, his position cannot fairly be defended in this way.

Lacoue-Labarthe presents a clearer, even more extreme, less acceptable form of a similar argument. Lacoue-Labarthe's consideration of "*la question*" antedated Farias's book. In a recent collection[136] he includes two earlier papers concerning Heidegger and politics which preceded and obviously influenced both his and Derrida's later discussions of Heidegger and politics: "La transcendance finie/ dans la politique" from 1981, and "Poétique et politique" from 1984. In the former, he poses the question of the possibility of a politics that takes into account Heidegger's thought. Here, he examines the rectoral speech in order to show its link to the destruction of the history of ontology and, by extension, to the effort to rethink the problem of the meaning of Being. In this paper, he makes two points: the rectoral speech is not an occasional document but a reflection on science, which is metaphysics as such; and this speech is intended as a philosophical foundation of the political. According to Lacoue-Labarthe, Heidegger's political engagement in 1933 was metaphysical and its basic result is the collapse of Heidegger's fundamental ontology. In the latter paper, in an examination of the question why the poetical dimension arose within political discourse, he argues that Heidegger's effort at the leadership (*Führung*) of National Socialism was essentially spiritual.[137]

There is an obvious, striking continuity between the views of Derrida and Lacoue-Labarthe in their joint insistence on the metaphysical nature of Heidegger's turning toward Nazism and the spiritual component of Heidgger's view of politics. But there is an even more important difference in Lacoue-Labarthe's stress on the link between the political and the philosophical in Heidegger's thought, in virtue of which Heidegger's original philosophical project is compromised by the political action to which it led. The assertion that Heidegger's effort at fundamental ontology was irreparably compromised by his turn to Nazism derives from the recognition—now rarely denied, and explicitly affirmed by Heidegger—that at least his initial enthusiasm for National Socialism followed from his position. This insight is significant for an understanding of the link between Heidegger's thought and Nazism. It leads to a conclusion which Lacoue-Labarthe does not draw, and which Heidegger means to deny in his description of the rectoral episode as meaningless (*beudeutungslos*): the later evolution of the Heideggerian position, perhaps even the famous turning in his thought, must be understood, in fact cannot be understood otherwise than, in relation to Heidegger's Nazism.

I stress this unstated but important consequence of Lacoue-Labarthe's article since he mainly develops other themes from his earlier analysis of the relation of poetry and politics, less menacing for the faith of a Heideggerian, in his later treatment of the political as fiction.[138] Unlike some others in the French discussion, who are concerned mainly, or even solely, to defend Heidegger at all costs, and hence unconcerned to present a full record, Lacoue-Labarthe does not hesitate to mention items rarely evoked in the French debate, such as the problem of anti-Semitism, the comments by Löwith and Jaspers, Heidegger's denunciation of Baumgarten, Heidegger's meditation on the nature of the Holocaust, and so on. It is especially significant, in view of the author's obvious identification with Heidegger as incontestably the best thinker of our time,[139] that he does not hesitate clearly to denounce Heidegger's failure to decry the Holocaust, which, from Heidegger's conception of history as the unfolding of metaphysics, supposedly constitutes a metaphysical event.[140]

In his book, Lacoue-Labarthe modifes his earlier analysis. According to Lacoue-Labarthe, Heidegger's political engagement in 1933 was based on the idea of the hegemony of the spiritual and the philosophical over the political[141]—a stance in obvious continuity with *Being and Time*[142] and coherent with all his earlier thought[143]—which cannot be explained as an error[144] but must be viewed as a consequence.[145] Now abandoning his earlier insistence on the significance of the rectoral speech, Lacoue-Labarthe argues for a caesura (*césure*) in the sense of Hölderlin.[146] Heidegger's understanding of the political does not lie in his texts from 1933, including the rectoral address, but in writings after the break with Nazism, specifically those on technology. In this respect, Lacoue-Labarthe makes two important points: On the one hand, he suggests that there is a beginning of the *Verwindung* of nihilism in the poet's thought,[147] since for Heidegger art opens the possibility of the historicity of Dasein;[148] on the other hand, he maintains that Heidegger's discourse on art throws light on the essence of Nazism as a national-estheticism.[149]

These suggestions are independent of each other and must be discussed separately. Lacoue-Labarthe is certainly correct that Heidegger never abandoned his concern to seize the destiny of the German people, and that he later linked this possibility to an interest in the alethic qualities of poetry. Yet this point is inconsistent in two ways with his own analysis. For whereas he insists on a break in Heidegger's position, this point requires an acknowledgment of the essential continuity of Heidegger's thought over time as concerns the destiny of the Dasein. And as a further, direct consequence, it requires an acknowledgment of a conceptual kinship with Nazism, which Lacoue-Labarthe strongly denies in his critique of Adorno's well-known claim that Heidegger's thought was Nazi to its core.[150] It is further inaccurate to regard Heidegger's discussion of art or technology as illuminating the essence of Nazism. One can concede a certain perverse aestheticism in Nazi ideology, for instance in the writings of Albert Speer, the Nazi architect. But one must resist the idea that the massive political phenomenon of German fascism is solely, or even mainly, or essentially, aesthetic.

The usefulness of Lacoue-Labarthe's book is limited by the depth of his own commitment to Heidegger's thought. As a result of his basic acceptance of Heidegger's position, Lacoue-Labarthe is unable to draw the consequences of his own critique of it. For instance, Lacoue-Labarthe cites a passage from an unpublished conference on technology, already cited above, where Heidegger likens agricultural technology to the Nazi gas chambers.[151] Despite his criticism of the patent inadequacy of Heidegger's dreadful comparison, Lacoue-Labarthe, the Heideggerian, is unable to perceive the full implication of Heidegger's statement in at least two ways: in his quasi-Heideggerian claim that this phenomenon somehow reveals the essence of the West,[152] which Heidegger allegedly failed to perceive, which in turn supposes the Heideggerian view that technology is the extension of metaphysics; and in his inability to draw the obvious consequence of his own indictment of Heidegger's failure, due to the inadequacy of fundamental ontology, to grasp the essence of the Nazi phenomenon.

Lacoue-Labarthe's analysis—patient, sober, careful, informed, considerate of other points of view—exhibits virtues unsurpassed in the present French Heidegger debate. This comprehension and tolerance gives way in Ferry and Renaut's work to an accusatory, pamphletary, confrontational style, more characteristic of recent French philosophy. In their attack on the separations between various forms of French Heideggerianism as in effect distinctions without a difference—which they paradoxically represent as an effort to surpass mere polemics[153]—they deny the shared assumption, common to Derrida and Lacoue-Labarthe, of a break in Heidegger's thought. Their book is the successor of their earlier work on contemporary antihumanism, centered mainly on French varieties of Heideggerianism.[154]

Ferry and Renaut are most original in their effort to develop Lyotard's suggestion of the link between the defense of Heidegger and French philosophy. They draw attention to the parallel between the French controversy about Marxist antihumanism in the 1970s and the current Heidegger controversy.[155] Their aim is to diagnose a link between Heidegger's antihumanism, which they comprehend as the rejection of modernity[156] and the supposed *erreur par excellence* of contemporary French philosophy.[157] They illustrate this error by Lacoue-Labarthe's strange, even wild comment, in the course of his attempt to differentiate the later Heidegger from the earlier Nazi enthusiast, that "Nazism is a humanism."[158]

After some remarks on the significance of Farias's book in the context of the French debate, Ferry and Renaut develop their indictment of contemporary French philosophy through the identification of the common thread of various forms of French Heideggerianism. They isolate three variants: the so-called zero degree, represented by Beaufret, which simply denies any relation between Heidegger and Nazism; Heideggerian orthodoxy, which admits, by playing Heidegger II off against Heidegger I, that in 1933 the master was not yet free of the metaphysics of subjectivity; and Derridian, or unorthodox, Heideggerianism, which relies on Heidegger's purported later deconstruction of the concept of spirit. According to Ferry and Renaut, in the final analysis there is no difference between Derridian and orthodox Heideggerianism since at best the Derridian approach innovates on a strategic plane only.[159]

Apart from their remarks on Farias's work, the main contribution of Ferry and Renault lies in their survey of various factions of the French debate about Heidegger's politics. They are most helpful in their suggestion of a relation between French postmodernism, or antihumanism, and Heidegger's own Nazi proclivities. They usefully relate Heidegger's well-known reading of modernity as the reign of technology to his view that democracy and totalitarianism are similar in their domination by subjectivity, and his further adherence to the possibility of a good form of National Socialism[160] as by inference postmodernist and antimodernist.[161] They criticize Heidegger's general incapacity to think subjectivity[162] because of an inability to think humanism in a nonmetaphysical manner,[163] an inattention to the plural character of modernity,[164] and the inconsistency in his rejection of a humanist vision of man in his view of Dasein in terms of Being. And they invoke a certain humanism in his view of man as transcendental in order to criticize Nazi biologism and racism.[165]

These criticisms are well taken in virtue of Heidegger's identification of humanism with metaphysics. The relation of postmodernism and "antihumanism" in the work of recent French thinkers such as Derrida, Lyotard, Foucault, and Lévi-Strauss among others is too well-known to require detailed commentary. The most original point is insistence on Heidegger's supposed inability to differentiate the various forms of modernity while implying the point, clearly articulated only by Lacoue-Labarthe among Heidegger's French disciples, that Nazism is humanism of a different, supposedly acceptable kind. Beyond its indictment of the

French identification with the Heideggerian rejection of Cartesian subjectivity—manifest in the ongoing effort to decenter the subject—the most important result of this work is to question Heidegger's conception of the subject as transcendence, a theme present throughout his writings from his dissertation on Duns Scotus onwards.[166]

After the Third Wave

The French discussion of Heidegger's relation to politics is still under way. Its most recent phases include a continuing debate that has most recently opposed Fédier to Nicolas Tertulian, the well-known Lukács specialist,[167] Janicaud's sober, insightful discussion of the intrinsic link between Heidegger's conception of Being and Heidegger's Nazism,[168] and aspects of Meschonnic's discussion of Heidegger's language.[169] The primary lesson of this review of the French debate on Heidegger's Nazism concerns the delicate relation between thought and the context in which it arises. We do not know how a philosophical theory takes shape; but we do know that it can be neither reduced to nor separated from the context in which it emerges, including the social and political context on the one hand and the network of competing views against which it strives on the other. Heidegger's position—despite his repeated but apparently strategic claims, clearly meant to create his own legend, by stressing a positive relation of his position to pre-Socratic thought only—needs to be understood against the complex background of theology, Kant's thought, German neo-Kantianism, particularly Lask, and medieval Aristotelianism, as well as the social, political and historical situation in Germany between the two world wars.

The French debate offers a particularly interesting example of the delicate relation between thought and its context. With the exceptions noted, it is distinguished by its concern even now to defuse the problematic relation between Heidegger's thought and politics by arguing for a discontinuity between Heidegger's early and later position in order to "save" his thought and—insofar as the French discussion is dependent on Heidegger's theory—itself. Yet Heidegger only turned against one form of Nazism, not Nazism as such. To fail to see this point, to confuse his withdrawal from the historical form of National Socialism with an unproven rejection of the essence of a movement Heidegger continued to embrace, is to fall victim to the problem of the emperor's new clothes.

Now French philosophers are not less intelligent or well informed than those elsewhere. How can we explain their reluctance to see that the emperor has no clothes on? I believe that the reason lies in a persistent, unhealthy degree of identification of contemporary French philosophy with Heidegger's position, which literally forms its horizon. We can formulate what is clearly an existential predicament in the form of a paradox: to the extent that the horizon of contemporary French philosophy is constituted by Heidegger's thought, it cannot examine Heidegger's link to Nazism without putting itself in question, that is, without simultaneously criticizing the Heideggerian position. In a word, Heidegger's French connection prevents, or impedes, the French thinkers from perceiving that the emperor has no clothes.

The French example is unusual for the extent to which Heidegger's thought dominates French philosophy. The result of this domination is to remain attentive to the unthought in Heidegger's position, at the cost of obstructing any attempt to place the Heideggerian horizon into question. This consequence is useful to the extent that French philosophy remains within the Heideggerian orbit, but it is also philosophically dangerous. For at least since Plato philosophy has consisted in the refusal to accept undemonstrated assumptions, in the constant effort to examine itself in order to clarify, demonstrate, or eliminate what it merely presupposed, in order to move forward by moving backward through an examination of its presuppositions.

The recent effort of some dissident French thinkers, especially Bourdieu, Janicaud, Tertulian, and from another angle of vision Ferry and Renaut, to examine the roots of French Heideggerianism, to reflect on the so-called French problem, is a healthy sign. Despite Heidegger's oft-cited claim that when French philosophers begin to think they think in German—or by implication think about Heidegger, or even within the ambit of Heidegger's thought—it indicates that French thought will be even more robust, and accordingly able to grow in new and different ways, when it has finally examined its own Heideggerianism. For to the extent that Heidegger still forms the horizon of French philosophy, to appreciate the limits of his thought is to go beyond Heidegger and hence beyond French philosophy. But this move beyond Heidegger is, however, necessary if French thought is to advance beyond its present level.

The French discussion is an extreme example of the problem posed by the reception of Heidegger's Nazism. For a variety of reasons, philosophers in general, not just Heideggerians, have been slow in confronting Heidegger's Nazism. Now the process of the understanding of the thought of any important thinker, of someone who breaks new ground in a significant sense, cannot be immediate since new ways must be found to comprehend the genuinely novel aspects of the position. But Heidegger's Nazism is deeply rooted in, indeed basic to, his philosophy, which cannot be comprehended in isolation from his political turning. At least since De Waelhens, a number of Heideggerians, particularly in France, although elsewhere as well, have insisted that the link between Heidegger's philosophy and politics can be understood only by someone so deeply versed in Heidegger's thought as to be a follower of the master. If we accept this claim, then the result is still another paradox, which can be formulated as follows: only a Heideggerian can grasp Heidegger's thought, including the relation between Heidegger's Nazism and his philosophy; but as our discussion of the French debate illustrates, the link between Heidegger's Nazism and his philosophy can only be grasped from a vantage point located outside of Heidegger's position. It follows, then, on this Heideggerian hypothesis for the understanding of Heidegger's thought, that Heidegger's political engagement is literally beyond criticism: for either it can only be understood by Heideggerians, who cannot confront the problem within the framework of Heidegger's own theory, to which they are committed; or it must be understood by non-Heideggerians who, according to the Heideggerian claim about understanding Heidegger, also cannot understand it. The result, then, of the Heideggerian view of Heidegger is to render this aspect of Heidegger's thought strictly unknowable, a kind of thing in itself, a theory about which anything can be believed but nothing can be known.

This result, which follows from the Heideggerian approach to Heidegger, is obviously unsatisfactory, since it suggests that in the final analysis a careful, responsible, but critical reception of the complex issues raised by Heidegger's turning on the basis of his thought to National Socialism is impossible. On the contrary, I believe that we can best, and perhaps only, understand Heidegger's position, including his Nazism, if we are informed about it but also not committed to it as in principle correct. The preceding discussion has shown that Heidegger's thought cannot be understood apart from his Nazism, but that his Nazism cannot be comprehended by those unconditionally committed to the truth of his thought. If Heidegger's Nazism cannot be grasped by someone already committed to his thought and if his Nazism is integral to his philosophy, then his philosophy, including his Nazism, can finally best be understood, and perhaps only grasped at all, by someone prepared, without presuppositions or prior commitments, to let the conceptual chips fall where they may, but not by someone whose main investment is in the defense of Heidegger's thought.

8

Being, the *Volk*, and Nazism

Interpretations of Heidegger's Nazism

In this book we have examined the nature and significance of the relation between Heidegger's Nazism and philosophy. There is a maximally wide range of opinion encompassing virtually all possible views of this relation. While aware of the various views, I have attempted to steer an independent course through examination of the full range of Heidegger materials now available for scholarly study.

At present—leaving aside the widespread idea that the best way to deal with the problem is to ignore it—we can isolate six main lines of analysis[1] of Heidegger's philosophy and Nazism in the Heidegger literature: First, there is Adorno's extreme view that everything that Heidegger ever said and did was Nazi to the core.[2] Second, there is the conviction that Nazism is not Nazism, most prominently associated with Beaufret, through his acceptance of the French historian Faurisson's radical form of historical revisionism, in fact a denial of the historical reality of National Socialism.[3]

Third, there is the idea, now most prominently represented by Fédier, that Heidegger is not responsible for the political consequences of Nazism since they could not have been foreseen.[4] Fourth, there is the belief, following Heidegger's own view of the matter, that Heidegger's Nazism was merely an insignificant moment in his biography unrelated to his thought, developed by Aubenque[5] and Vietta,[6] and hinted at by Habermas[7] and Rorty,[8] based on a distinction in kind between Heidegger the thinker and Heidegger the man. Fifth, there is the claim—rooted in Heidegger's conception of the turning in his thought—due mainly to Derrida[9] and Lacoue-Labarthe,[10] that Heidegger's early thought led to Nazism, but his later thought led away from it, a reading presupposing a break between the earlier and the later Heidegger. Sixth, there is the organic analysis, presented by Löwith,[11] and more recently by Bourdieu,[12] Janicaud,[13] Zimmerman,[14] Wolin,[15] Thomä,[16] and myself, according to which Heidegger's philosophical thought and his Nazism are inseparable.

With the exception of Beaufret's effort, quite mad at this late date, to deny the historical reality of Nazism, the various lines of analysis tending to exculpate Heidegger's Nazism were suggested by Heidegger as part of his effort after the Second World War to limit the damage to himself and to his thought, and then only later adopted by his followers. The views that Heidegger is not responsible for his adherence to Nazism, that his Nazism was meaningless, or that he later moved away from Nazism are all claims that he himself raises. The central point at issue, of course, on which all of these explanatory models divide, is how to understand the relation between Heidegger's Nazism and his philosophical thought. My basic response is to argue that any interpretation of Heidegger's Nazism which denies the intrinsic link between his theory of Being and his Nazi politics is unable to comprehend the origin of his Nazism, which becomes a merely inexplicable, contingent fact; and it is unable as well to comprehend the later development of Heidegger's thought, specifically including its turning beyond philosophy. In short, whatever their respective virtues, the other lines of analysis all fall short of accounting for central items required in any comprehensive interpretation of Heidegger's Nazism and philosophy.

It is important to be clear about what is being said, since one of the favorite strategies to defend Heidegger's thought consists in equating any criticism of it with a simple dismissal of its value in general in order then to dismiss the criticism of the position. This protective mechanism should be seen for what it is: an effort to remove Heidegger's position from critical evaluation, to prevent it from being addressed in the normal course of discussion as part of the process of reception of an important body of thought. There is no suggestion here that Heidegger's thought can merely be reduced to his Nazism or even to politics. What I am suggesting is that for Heidegger, ontology and politics are basically conjoined. For a denial of the historical reality of Nazism, which underlies the second approach, is simply not credible, no more so than assertions that the earth is flat. If the exculpation of Heidegger's Nazism depends on the demonstration of the unreality of Nazism, then it would seem that no such argument can reasonably be made.

The third and fourth approaches, which are variations on the theme of the supposed difference in kind beween Heidegger the man and Heidegger the thinker, are refuted by examination of Heidegger's texts. Study of his thought, and what he says about it, shows that Heidegger was also led to Nazism on the basis of his philosophical position, as he himself admitted. His Nazi turning is, then, not merely due to external factors, such as the decline of the Weimar Republic, and the concern with reactionary German *Volksideologie,* nor to his inability to comprehend politics, nor even to his psychological need to achieve a powerful position in the German university. None of these factors should be omitted from a comprehensive analysis. Yet from the narrow philosophical perspective, the decisive point is the political nature of Heidegger's ontology which led him into the realm of practice, and toward Nazism as an authoritarian political conception compatible with, and made necessary by, his own view of Being. The effort to pry apart Heidegger the thinker and Heidegger the man should further be rejected on Heideggerian grounds as inconsistent with the theory it intends to defend. It is because there is an intrinsic link between Heidegger's philosophical position and his Nazism that from a philosophical perspective nothing, nothing at all would have been altered had Heidegger simply said it was all a mistake, that he was sorry about his acceptance of Nazism, that it was all a dreadful mistake in judgment, and so on. Heidegger's acceptance of Nazism is surely a contingent fact, since it might have been the case that Nazism had not existed. Yet his thought literally demands some type of antidemocratic, totalitarian politics in virtue of his own conception of Being. For Heidegger's ontology and politics are intrinsically and inseparably linked through his conception of authenticity, his lifelong quasi-Platonic understanding of the political vocation of the thinker of Being, and his commitment to the destiny of the German *Volk,* all aspects of his understanding of Being.

The fifth line of analysis, which is particularly prominent in the French discussion, depends on a supposed discontinuity in the evolution of Heidegger's position, based on the interpretation of the turning in his thought as a break. This approach, which is presently the most philosophically sophisticated alternative to the organic approach favored here, presents a subtle restatement of Heidegger's own effort to protect his thought by invoking the conception of the turning, understood as turning over a new conceptual leaf, so to speak. But the suggestion that the turning represents a break between Heidegger's early and later thought, between Heidegger I and II as it were, is clearly refuted through the obvious continuity of his intellectual development and through his own understanding of the turning as a deepening of his theory of Being beyond the original beginning through the introduction of a new beginning.

In arguing for a break in Heidegger's thought—similar to the supposed, but finally fictitious, break in Marx's development recently popular in French Marxism—Heidegger's French adherents take seriously Heidegger's suggestion in the "Letter on Humanism" that there has been a turning in his thought, in fact a reversal. There is an obvious analogy between the view that Heidegger's turning constitutes a fundamental break and Marxism's traditional view of Marx's supposed materialism as the reversal of Hegelian idealism, as a break between Marxism and philosophy. Yet Marx's thought does not reverse Hegel's, and Marx's later position develops further but does not break with his own earlier theory. Similarly, Heidegger's later theory of Being carries further, develops, modifies, transforms, but does not break with, his earlier thought. As study of Heidegger's texts show, above all the recently published *Beiträge zur Philosophie,* Heidegger understood the concept of the turning as a further development but not as a break in his thought.

Heidegger's thought exhibits a continuous development, but certain aspects of his position remain virtually unchanged. The idea of the *Volk* as an authentic community, which Heidegger takes over from German *Volksideologie* and grounds philosophically in *Being and Time* in his conception of plural authenticity, remains a permanent part of his position throughout its later development. Beginning with the rectoral address, Heidegger continues to hold one or more versions of the venerable Platonic view that philosophy can found politics as the necessary condition of the good life, as the real presupposition of the radiant future. Heidegger never abandoned the familiar philosophical conviction in the cognitive privilege of philosophy, what after the turning in his position became new thought, with its familiar link to antidemocratic, totalitarian politics.

I favor the sixth, organic line of analysis of Heidegger's philosophy and politics as integrally, in fact inseparably, connected. In my view, none of the other approaches to this theme can provide a satisfactory account of what is now known, above all the durable nature of Heidegger's concern with the destiny of the Germans, his tardy insistence when it was no longer even advantageous on the misunderstood essence of Nazism. In their own ways, each of the other approaches to this problem also overestimates the importance of Heidegger's connection to National Socialism, that is real Nazism. There is a widespread tendency in the debate about Heidegger's politics to analyze its relation to Nazism mainly or solely in terms of his link to real National Socialism. Yet this tendency is wrong on two counts. For it fails to consider the possibility that Heidegger's allegiance to Nazism was always to his own, idiosyncratic idea of Nazism. And it further ignores Heidegger's later, more consistent, and certainly deeper fidelity to an ideal form of Nazism.

It is important to understand the limits of Heidegger's initial, enthusiastic commitment to National Socialism. Although Heidegger became a member of the NSDAP and a Nazi in that sense, starting in 1933 he continued to insist on the cognitive privilege of his "philosophy," to found authentic politics. Even after his resignation as rector, he never abandoned, or even dampened, the enthusiasm about destiny of the Germans, which he initially shared with real National Socialism, and which he continued to seek in his ideal concept of National Socialism. Derrida is correct that Heidegger's thought is open to a whole variety of Nazisms,[17] both real and imaginary. Yet Derrida does not appear sufficiently aware of Heidegger's later writings, especially the important *Beiträge zur Philosophie*. This explains his failure to realize that Heidegger's Nazism did not disappear in Heidegger's later thought, in which it remained a central component in imaginary, ideal form.

Even real Nazism is more present in Heidegger's later thought than is often understood. Stress on the later development of Heidegger's theory is often employed to suggest a clean break with real Nazism. Yet Heidegger's later view of Being after the turning conserves important elements of continuity with some National Socialist views. Consider, for example, the following passage from an article by Ernst Krieck, a leading philosophical theoretician of the Nazi *Weltanschauung:*

> The revolutionary upheaval made itself known in a dispacement of emphasis. Instead of the individual person, the *völkische* whole is central, as a result of which the basic reality of life comes into view. . . . The individual does not arrive at his worldview through reason according to his individual situation and inclination to arbitrariness and choice. Rather, we are subject to the movement of forces over us and directed in common. We do not seize, but we are seized and driven.[18]

If we overlook the idea of a *Weltanschauung*, which Heidegger consistently rejected, common elements between this Nazi view and Heidegger's later thought, after the supposed turn away from his earlier thought and Nazism, include a displacement of emphasis from the individual to the group taken as a whole, the reliance on extrarational forces which we do not choose, but which choose us and operate through us, and so on.

Heidegger invokes and never abandons the destiny of the Germans in virtue of his theory of Being. His position, even in its later formulation, turns on the authentic thought of Being. According to Heidegger, metaphysics, his later name for an inauthentic form of ontology, tends to cover up, or to hide, an authentic understanding of Being. If the authentic thought of Being requires authenticity, if authenticity is defined as the acceptance of one's being as defined by the concern with Being, and if the only metaphysical people is the German people which alone can know Being as the true heirs of the Greeks, then there is an easy, obvious transition from Heidegger's ontology to the concern with the German *Volk*. Heidegger's position, Nazism, German *Volk* ideology, and the interest throughout the Weimar Republic in the resurrection of a Germany still suffering from the effects of the First World War come together in the desire for a vibrant development of the German people. The problem is not due to Heidegger's political naïveté; nor can it merely be ascribed to a casual interest in a political phenomenon; nor is it due to a change from his initial view of Being to a view of Being as historical and destinal, to a change in the initial view; rather it is due to the initial view itself as Heidegger understood it. Perhaps Heidegger's theory of Being can be interpreted in different ways; perhaps one can argue, as he himself argued about others' theories, that Heidegger did not understand his own theory or that others failed to understand it; but this is the way in which Heidegger comprehended it, in my view correctly understood it.

The conception of the German *Volk*, which Heidegger stressed, means different things from different perspectives. What for the Nazis was a step to world domination was for the average German a way to restore self-esteem, a means to correct the perceived injustices of the First World War, even a way to win back what was lost in the war and perhaps finally to win the war. For Heidegger, it is mainly a means for the authentic thought of Being. Hence, the problem does not lie in Heidegger's Nazism but in his ontology, on whose soil his Nazism flourished. Specifically, the problem follows from his assumption that genuine ontology required a certain purity of mind, what he called authenticity, an effort to be oneself, not in order to overcome alienation, for that was never Heidegger's goal, but rather in order authentically to think Being. Heidegger's Nazism should not be excused as merely momentary or meaningless. For it was not momentary, a mere incident; and it is philosophically meaningful within the context of his ontology. Yet the basic problem does not lie in Heidegger's Nazism, which is an effect of a deeper cause, but in his theory of Being, which requires for its realization an authentic subject.

Heidegger is an important, perhaps even a great thinker. Yet if Nazism is significant, his thought is fundamentally flawed. The problem of Being has no necessary connection with Nazism, but Heidegger's view of the problem points directly to this or similar kinds of political practice. It is not a simple accident, a merely contingent fact that Heidegger's effort to reawaken the long-forgotten question of Being leads seamlessly to Nazism and his consistent but finally grotesque comprehension of Nazism as a necessary step to the authentic comprehension of Being. If human being is important, if at this late date human being is more important than Being, then the project of the authentic thought of Being is intrinsically compromised. It is time, then, to reaffirm human being, which Heidegger sacrificed in the name of the thought of Being. For we need to hold fast to humanism, if necessary even by renouncing an antihumanism intended to lead to Being through the way station of Nazi barbarism, hence to renounce a thought of Being which denies and necessarily denies human Being.

This problem is not ameliorated but only complicated by the character of the Heidegger reception, which has not always been worthy of the reputation of philosophy as the main form of the search for truth. While some have sought for truth in disinterested fashion, others have sought to protect themselves, their reputations, their investment in what must be true to uphold their views of Heidegger and of themselves. Still others have routinely reaffirmed the traditional philosophical claim that philosophical theories occur in time but are not of time, that if they are determined by anything at all, it is only by other theories in a form of epistemological behaviorism. It is held that philosophy, say Heidegger's philosophy, has nothing to do with the type of person one is. Heidegger, we are told, was a bad person, a terrible man, *ein richtiges Schwein,* but his thought is completely independent of who he was.[19]

This fashionable "liberal" approach is based more on a reaffirmation of the traditional dogma of philosophy as independent of the context in which it arises than on careful study of the Heideggerian texts. It avoids coming to grips with the harder issues that arise as soon as one realizes that thought in general belongs to time. For Heidegger contributes powerfully to the demise of the traditional philosophical dogma of the independence of thought and time, and the depths of Heidegger's own thought literally can only be plumbed against the background of the period in which it arose.

At this late date, at least two things should be clear to anyone who examines the relevant writings: Heidegger's theory, like that of most important thinkers, was never static, never fixed in final form, always under way. Yet as examination of Heidegger's writings has shown, Heidegger's Nazism is deeply seated in his thought, so profoundly rooted as to remain unchanged throughout evolution of his position over forty-two years from the end of his rectorate to the end of his life; and the philosophical discussion of his political engagement both during and after the rectorate has often contrived to conceal rather than to reveal his Nazism. The remaining task is to build on this knowledge, to examine the philosophical significance of Heidegger's Nazism and the complex discussion to which it has given rise both for Heidegger's thought and for philosophy.

Heidegger's Nazism and the
Limits of His Philosophy

Heidegger's Nazism and the failure to confront it are philosophically significant for Heidegger's philosophy, for its reception, and for philosophy itself. At a time when some are still concerned to deny the existence of the Holocaust, in effect to deny that Nazism was Nazism, and many still deny that Nazism had a more than tangential appeal to one of the most significant theories of this century, merely to assert the philosophical significance of an abject philosophical failure to seize the historical moment for the German *Volk* and Being is not likely to win the day. Yet there is something absurd, even grotesque about the conjunction of the statement that Heidegger is an important, even a great philosopher, perhaps one of the few seminal thinkers in the history of the tradition, with the realization that he, like many of his followers, entirely failed, in fact failed in the most dismal manner, to grasp or even to confront Nazism. If philosophy is its time captured in thought, and if Heidegger and his epigones have basically failed to grasp their epoch, can we avoid the conclusion that they have also failed this test, failed as philosophers?

Since even those thinkers who hold that we need to begin again, to begin from the beginning, rely on a reading of the history of the philosophical tradition, philosophy is inseparable from its past. If philosophy is a historical discipline, then it is unavoidably under obligation to come to grips with what has come before in order to progress. Yet it is significant that after some twenty-five hundred years of practice, there are no widely accepted standards as to how to judge prior philosophical views. In the absence of clear guidelines, we can measure the failure of Heidegger and some of his students to come to grips with Nazism in his thought or even with Nazism as it existed, parenthetically like so many other philosophers and academics in general, against the idea of the philosophical pursuit offered by the philosophers themselves.

At the dawn of the Western tradition, a flattering view of philosophy was formulated as the ultimate source of truth and social goodness, as the only way to know in an ultimate sense and as indispensable for the good life. The question of what philosophy can know finds a partial response in an assessment of what Heidegger in fact knew and what he claimed to know. He claimed to know how to go about arriving at an authentic thought of Being, and perhaps how to think Being, as well as to be able to interpret the present and even the future through Jünger's reading of Nietzsche's philosophy. At the end of the Second World War, he foresaw difficult times ahead; but by then he was scarcely alone in that perception. He was also hardly isolated in his initial enthusiasm for Nazism as the express route to German greatness, a misapprehension widely shared by the literati—among them candidates for the title of master thinker, heirs to the great German philosophical tradition in our time—and the illiterati, the uneducated, many of whom were equally mistaken about the prospects of the Nazi movement. It is sobering to realize, despite Heidegger's claims as a philosophical seer, a prophet of Being, that his theory was of no comparative advantage when it came time to confront the present and to foresee its consequences. Although Heidegger reacted against nihilism as early as the rectoral address, in the same talk he publicly threw in his lot with a leading example of nihilism in our troubled century.

There is an old view that the thinker needs to preserve a distance, to be alienated from reality in order to know it. Supposedly, it is because one is distant from what one wants to know, not caught up within it, that objectivity becomes possible; out of the distance one is paradoxically nearer to what one seeks to know. Similarly, Heidegger insists in his own way that the thinker needs to withdraw, to be oneself alone, in order to be able to know Being. Yet if we discount bad faith as an explanation, in which case anything is possible, Heidegger genuinely did not seem to know, never seemed to recognize, that there was something absolutely new about Nazism, which made it different in kind from, and for that reason literally incomparable with, anything else. Here and there one can point to a word, even a sentence in his wider corpus, that perhaps indicates an obscure awareness of the problem. But even to allow this kind of interpretative license, in order retrospectively to isolate in Heidegger's voluminous writings a passage or two in his works that might charitably be read as showing a minimal sensitivity to the issues, is in effect to confirm the essential poverty of his understanding of the entire Nazi phenomenon.

The problem posed by Nazism is a human problem in the most basic meaning of the term "human." It is widely known that Nazism posed a decisive threat to values, to human beings, to the democratic form of life, to the idea of human and racial equality, to concepts of mutual tolerance—in short, was a menace to the small advances of human beings concerned to realize, as Hegel put it, the idea of freedom. Heidegger either could not understand or was unconcerned with the problem posed by Nazism to human beings since he consistently offered the main role to Being. Heidegger's philosophy is rooted in his antihumanistic subordination of human being to Being, to which he subordinated his own entire life, and to which his students on occasion seem willing to subordinate themselves and others in the increasingly unavailing effort to excuse Heidegger the philosopher and sometimes even Heidegger the man. Heidegger's understanding of the problem of Being required him to reject values and anything linked to value as incompatible with thought in the deepest sense, which is limited to contemplation of the idea of Being. According to Heidegger, any concept of value is inextricably linked to the philosophies of the worldview which are philosophy in name only, since they fall below the genuine thought necessary to think Being.

It is often said by Heidegger's supporters that his later thought is a confrontation with Nazism. Heidegger himself makes this claim more than once. It is also possible that Heidegger's claim expressed his deep conviction and not merely what it was convenient to state, that it was not finally a statement of what the many in their unwisdom desired to hear from him. Heidegger may sincerely have believed that he was confronting Nazism. But he did not and could not since his thought of Being, as he understood it, required him to turn away from human values and human being. Yet Nazism's threat to human values and human beings cannot be usefully understood through the lens provided by technology or even inauthentic metaphysics. The reason why Heidegger's critique of Nazism is limited precisely and solely to its philosophical status, its character as a *Weltanschauung* that falls short of philosophy as he conceives it, is that this is the only aspect of the problem which falls within the domain of "philosophy" or authentic thought as Heidegger understood it. In a position that puts Being before human being, and argues that Being is literally the only question, there is literally no way to differentiate the extermination of people in gas chambers from agricultural technology. As his statement of this point makes clear, Heidegger's position simply does not possess the conceptual resources necessary for this end. If to name reality is the paramount philosophical task, Heidegger's thought suffers from its paradoxical incapacity, despite its emphasis on concreteness, to do so.

Heidegger's philosophical insight is accompanied by a pervasive blindness to what perhaps is visible to almost everyone, with the possible exception of those rare individuals who at this late date continue to deny the existence or the importance of the Holocaust. A novel philosophical position offers a perspective that uncovers whole new regions of thought, vast domains that become salient through the formulation of new ideas that circumscribe and give meaning to regions they literally render visible. Heidegger's thought, as he repeatedly emphasized, was limited to the single task of thinking Being. In Heidegger's wake, a whole cottage industry of philosophers has arisen who share his view that Being is the central question of the discipline. But the same perspective that has uncovered the problem of Being for our time also conceals while it reveals, covering up from view what for most of us is so starkly visible. It is difficult to know what is more important: Heidegger's insight in uncovering Being or his blindness to Nazism which lay concealed to his ontological gaze.

Heidegger's embarrassment reflects the limits of his thought. A painter might reasonably be expected to focus on painting and all that pertains to it, as would a literary critic with literary topics. An issue such as Nazism falls outside the immediate ken of painting or literary criticism. Yet it would be surprising if either a painter or a literary critic not only did not but in fact could not find a way to evoke the most significant example of moral and political evil in this century. If philosophy were peculiarly handicapped in this regard, we would need to think seriously about what we could expect from the love of wisdom. Fortunately, this strange forgetfulness has not afflicted the entire community or even very many among us. Heidegger objected to the forgetfulness of Being (*Seinsvergessenheit*). Yet if attention to Nazism is the criterion, he is the only major thinker who seems to suffer in a serious, incurable way from an even more important lapse of memory: the forgetfulness of human being (*Menschensvergessenheit*). One need not hold that philosophy is as rigid and unconnected with reality as schizophrenia[20] to conclude that something is basically amiss in philosophy if a major representative neither notices nor can notice the series of issues raised by Nazism.

Heidegger's claim for the significance of his thought is based on the idea that in Being he has uncovered the forgotten, central question of philosophy. Yet Heidegger's approach to metaphysics is preferable to others, such as those defended in our time by Kant and Hegel, only if we accept it as normative. His view of Being is an illustration of the contemporary thought of Being, more precisely the contemporary reading of what he regarded as the recapturing of the original insight into Being. But there is a difficulty in Heidegger's inability to engage the contemporary epoch in a more direct way. The Socratic view of philosophy is intended to respond to the felt need to examine life. But Heidegger's position fails the Socratic test since, despite its frequently repeated claims about insight into concrete human being, life is merely a secondary theme that must inevitably be sacrificed for a deeper concern.

Heidegger later realized that his thought required him to reject not only Cartesianism but Platonism in all its forms. But we need to reaffirm the value of the Socratic stress on critical thought about human existence. A lesson of the behavior of intellectuals in this century is that it is too easy to invoke mitigating circumstances in which intellectuals account for the abandonment of the critical intellectual role, such as the supposed political incompetence of philosophers.[21] What an intellectual of any kind needs to do, including a philosopher, even in difficult circumstances, is to contribute to separating the intellectual wheat from the rhetorical chaff, to continue, as philosophers have always done, to separate good arguments from bad ones. In his thought, Heidegger claimed to be critical with respect to a tradition that covered up and hence served to obscure genuine insights about Being. We in turn need to be critical about this claim in order to judge it on its merits since not to do so is to contribute to the consequences of this thought, albeit unwillingly, and to abnegate our intellectual responsibility.

What we can hope for from philosophy depends as much on the way we exercise our intellectual responsibility as on philosophy itself. It is becoming ever clearer, if it was not clear already, that philosophy is not what it seems and seems to be what it is not and cannot be. Despite the flattering image of their discipline which philosophers have long presented, it is not in itself a source of perfect knowledge, nor intrinsically linked with virtue. It is merely one way among others, with no particular cognitive privilege of any obvious kind, to contribute to the truth and perhaps to serve the good.[22]

Despite the urging of others in the discussion, we cannot simply turn away from Heidegger's turn to Nazism—that is, not if we still desire to understand his thought. Heidegger obscurely held that his thought went back behind the distinction of theory and practice,[23] although he continued to insist even in his later position on the political relevance of his thought. Yet Heidegger's view of thought as retaining the relevance of pure theory, which satisfies our desire to know, nonetheless falls below the standard supposedly ingredient in all the other sciences: the human good. For even if we accept the idea of a good for the German people, a good that is one only for them is obviously not the general human good. And how are we to make out the claim that the question of Being is the central question of human history?

Heidegger's Thought, Its Reception, and the Role of the Intellectual

A different point, concerning the responsibility of intellectuals, needs to be made about the frequent failure in the Heidegger literature to come to grips with Heidegger's Nazism.[24] The French discussion is an extreme example of the problem posed by the reception of Heidegger's Nazism. Philosophers in general, not just Heideggerians, have been slow in confronting this theme for all the reasons already cited. Although certainly less gifted than the master, Heidegger's interpreters have a comparative advantage which they need to exploit. Philosophy as such is essentially critical since its role is not to celebrate but to know. Yet philosophy only remains critical in the continual effort to uncover and to evaluate previously undisclosed presuppositions. Heidegger manifests his commitment to this view in two ways: in his effort, in confronting another thinker's thought, to think what is unthought, to bring to light what is still obscure within it; and in the long conceptual journey, leading from what he later came to call the first beginning to the other beginning, which is in fact a journey back behind the original formulation of his thought of Being through its presuppositions to a deeper approach to Being.

When philosophers fail even to make this attempt, they cross the fragile line separating their discipline from theology, the study of revealed truth. Like all positions, Heidegger's reflects and embodies themes current in the context in which it took shape. Obviously, the capacity of any thinker to engage the surrounding conceptual framework is limited by one's very nearness to the themes that prevail at any given moment. It is difficult even for a gifted thinker to come to grips with ideas and concepts that shape one's consciousness at any given moment but of which one may be at most only dimly aware. But philosophy demands that one who would interpret Heidegger do battle with what is unthought in his position—with an idea or ideas, as Kant would say, which he knows how to employ but which he may not have been able to make clear to himself or analyze correctly.[25]

Heidegger's responsibility in his unquestioning acceptance of many of the themes of the Weimar Republic is tempered by the way in which his personal fate was inextricably linked to the events of the time. But the immediate proximity that hinders Heidegger's appreciation of his surroundings cannot be invoked by later interpreters of his thought, who enjoy the advantage of a temporal and cultural remove. The recent discussion of Heidegger's Nazism provoked by Farias and Ott is not a mere episode in the reception of his thought, a trend we are at liberty to accept or reject as we like. Obviously, all is not yet known and may never be known about Heidegger's Nazism. Nonetheless, enough is now known to make it less than fully philosophical, even intellectually irresponsible, to continue as before, to go on reading Heidegger's texts without so much as acknowledging the significance of his Nazism.

Ironically, the desire to understand Heidegger in an apolitical way by putting his Nazism in parentheses threatens the possibility of the comprehension it wishes to preserve, the comprehension of his thought of Being. If it is ever the case that philosophy and politics are separable, it is not true with respect to Heidegger, since his political commitment and his thought are inseparable. Obviously, someone who has important new ideas cannot be understood immediately since a way must be found to comprehend a position that differs significantly from previous views. If this is true, then no original thinker is ever grasped without an intervening process of reception since a claim to instant comprehension can only be based on a misunderstanding. Perhaps, then, we have not yet fully grasped Heidegger's thought. Perhaps his view is so original that we still lack adequate ways to understand it. Whether or not this is true, it is obvious that no one's thought can be comprehended if an essential element is omitted. In Heidegger's case, his Nazism is indeed an essential element, without which his position is literally incomprehensible. It follows that those who are concerned to protect Heidegger's position by any conceptual means at all often do not, in fact cannot, fully understand what they intend to shield. Their actions indicate more a commitment on faith than a grasp of the ideas.

The failure to come to grips with Heidegger's Nazism is further important for philosophy. The only difference between the reception of Heidegger's position and others lies in the public controversy to which his Nazism has given rise. If our reading of the prior tradition, our reception of earlier views, merely provides what we wanted to believe, then it is mainly useful as a form of reassurance. Certainly, in that sense the failure to engage Heidegger's Nazism stands for the incapacity of philosophy as some have understood it to make good on its promise to supply truth and, accordingly, to be useful in a general sense.

Can we speak of guilt with respect to or following from Heidegger's Nazism? If we employ Jaspers's useful fourfold distinction,[26] we must immediately exclude criminal guilt since, to the best of my knowledge, there is no evidence that Heidegger ever violated a criminal statute. If one is responsible for the form of government under which one lives, certainly Heidegger, although not necessarily his defenders, must bear the responsibility of voluntarily submitting to Nazism. Heidegger must also accept the moral guilt deriving from certain questionable acts committed because of his Nazi affiliation, such as the denunciations of Baumgarten and Staudinger, perhaps also his questionable behavior in respect to Husserl. Since definitive proof of Heidegger's anti-Semitism, which his followers have denied for decades, has only recently come to light,[27] we cannot exclude the possibility that other revelations may yet be forthcoming.

There is further a deeper, more pervasive so-called metaphysical guilt shared by Heidegger and those followers who excuse his Nazism for whatever reason. If one can speak of solidarity among human beings, then whoever identifies in any fashion with a movement that exalts one group above another, unquestionably the aim of Nazi ideology, shares a metaphysical guilt. If it is wrong to comprehend Heidegger's thought in a reductive fashion, to reduce it to Nazism, then it is equally wrong to exempt him from responsibility and blame for what he did in his turning toward National Socialism. And if it is important to comprehend the

Nazi constituent of his thought in order to maintain solidarity with every-one excluded by the Nazi option, then all of us concerned with Heidegger bear a responsibility to examine this aspect and a blame for failing to do so.

Heidegger interpreted Nietzsche's racism as not biological but metaphysical.[28] Whatever his own racial views may have been, one must wonder if Heidegger's concern with the German as a distinct historical entity is a form of philosophical, even metaphysical "racism" based on the exaltation of this people alone among all others. In his "Letter on Humanism," Heidegger maintained that "every humanism is either grounded in a metaphysics or made to be one,"[29] and he further offered his own "humanism that thinks the humanity of man from nearness to Being."[30] If all humanisms are metaphysical, then so also is Heidegger's. His specific attachment to the *Volk* as a potentially authentic community presupposes an intrinsic superiority of the Germans as German above all other contemporary peoples. What I am calling Heidegger's metaphysical "racism"—which is neither biological[31] nor anti-Semitic as such—surpasses a merely nationalistic attachment to the German people in his conviction that the Germans are the true heirs to undistorted Greek metaphysics, the idea that philosophy in the deepest sense can only be thought in German, the claim that only the Germans can save us from the decline of the West, and so on, in short in the conception of the specifically German as a different and better human species, alone adequate to Being, and in his implicit denigration, for the same reasons, of others.

What are we to say about Heidegger's view of Nazism? There is a tendency, since Heidegger is also a powerful philosopher, to accord disproportionate respect to his ideas in areas where he has no comparative advantage. Certainly, one of these areas is his conception of Nazism, and his related claims to understand the present and to foresee the future. In this crucial respect, Heidegger's correspondence with Jaspers is illuminating. In a letter to Jaspers, he finally admits that in 1933 and earlier the Jews and the left-wing politicians, who were directly menaced by events, saw further than he did; and he privately accepts the existentialist conception of blame for the acts of the individual. In respect to Stalin, Heidegger writes:

Stalin does not need to declare war any more. He wins a battle every day. But "one" does not see it. For us there is no possible evasion. And every word and every text is in itself a counterattack, if all this does not play itself out in the sphere of the "political," which is itself long since outwitted through other relations of Being and leads [only] a false existence.[32]

And he continues:

> Despite all, dear Jaspers, despite death and tears, despite suffering and horror, despite need and torment, despite landlessness and exile, *in this lack of a homeland* it is not that nothing occurs; here is hidden an Advent, whose most distant hint we can perhaps experience and must take up in [the form of] a mild [wind] blowing, in order to preserve it for a future, which no historical construction, above all not the contemporary one, most certainly not one that thinks in technical ways, will decipher.[33]

Jaspers's response, written by a fellow philosopher and friend, who unfortunately greeted the rectoral address as a conceptual breakthrough surpassing Nietzsche, is important. After quoting the passage about Stalin, Jaspers writes in part:

> To read something like this frightens me. If you were in front of me, as decades ago so today you would experience my flood of words in anger and plea for reason. I find the questions urgent: Is [not] such a view of things through their imprecision the promotion of ruin? Isn't the possibility of doing whatever is possible spoiled by the appearance of the greatness of such visions? . . . Isn't the power of evil in Germany also what has steadily grown and in fact prepared the victory of Stalin: the covering up and the forgetting of what has occurred, the new so-called nationalism, the return to the old ways of thought and all the ghosts, which, although null and void, ruin us? Is not this power the imprecision in all thought (imprecise because it accompanies the life and activity of the thinker)? Is not a philosophy, which one perceives and composes in such propositions in your letter, that which brings about the vision of the monstrous, again the preparation of the victory of the totalitarian in that it separates itself from reality?[34]

And Jaspers continues, after citing Heidegger's passage on the Advent, as follows:

> My fright grew as I read this. It is, so far as I can think, pure fantasy, in line with so many other fantasies, which, each "in its own time"—has made fools of us during this half century. Do you mean to come forward as a prophet, who shows the transcendent from hidden knowledge, as a philosopher, who was misled through reality? Who neglects the possible for fictions? The same questions can be put to your views of full power and preservation.[35]

I submit that Jaspers's alarmed reaction to Heidegger's troubling view of social reality is essentially correct. There is something irrational, fantastic, and frightening in Heidegger's conviction that the future of the

German people could be attained through real National Socialism, even more in his later insistence on an ideal form of Nazism. Beyond Heidegger's psychological inability to confront his mistake, present even in his continued insistence on what Jaspers correctly diagnoses as Heidegger's self-characterization of himself as a prophet of Being, whose errors are due to reality itself, there is Heidegger's obvious inability to provide the concrete analysis of experience, especially social experience, for which he increasingly substituted a complex mythology.

Despite his undeniable philosophical capacities, Heidegger's thought is weakened by his evident failure to understand the world in which he lived, for which he increasingly substituted a rich fantasy that he presented as ultimate reality itself. Whatever the merits of Heidegger's original position, its later evolution is also an increasing turning away from the concrete analysis of the world he sought in his fundamental ontology, whose grasp was increasingly impeded and imperiled by the conceptual framework meant to interpret it. There is no reason to believe that anyone, including a philosopher, even a gifted philosopher has direct access to "reality," however that term is understood. Yet if philosophy still has meaning for the good life, it must continue to strive to name reality, mindful of the danger that what appears most evident and even true might still be illusion. The role of the philosopher and all intellectuals can only be to speak the truth as best we can, to defend the distinction between blindness and insight, to refuse the dangerous confusion between fact and fiction which has lately become fashionable.[36] For in the final analysis, we can only do this, we can only play a responsible role as intellectuals, we can indeed only construct a philosophical theory of social value on the basis of a true grasp of the world in which we live.

Heidegger's thought finally remains paradoxical. Ever since its origins in ancient Greece, there has been a flattering view about philosophy making the rounds, which numerous philosophers have been content to repeat. According to this view, philosophy is the source of reason in the highest sense, productive of truth and intrinsically linked to goodness. Yet Heidegger failed to come to grips with Nazism, the main instance of evil in our time, toward which his own thought led. If the true is good and Nazism is evil, then by implication it is also false, certainly false as a political option. Heidegger's thought is not useful, and certainly not true when evaluated by its capacity effectively to confront Nazism. The consequence is a paradox, since it is paradoxical to acknowledge that Heidegger is a powerful, perhaps even a great philosopher on the one hand and a proponent of Nazism on the other. But unless we merely overlook Nazism and turn away from a central moral problem of our epoch, it is not possible to maintain that great philosophy preserves the link between truth and goodness and to describe Heidegger as a great philosopher.

Conclusion: On Heidegger's Nazism and Philosophy

For obvious reasons, the present discussion is, in fact must be, provisional. As part of our inability to understand the relation between thought and action, we do not comprehend the link between Heidegger the man and Heidegger the thinker. Any effort to elucidate this connection is forced to develop its own way of going about things, since there is no well-established procedure or even a firm idea of what that would look like. This discussion is further limited by the unfortunate fact that, even now, portions of Heidegger's corpus are still unavailable for scholarly study. We cannot exclude the possibility that writings or documents may later emerge which will alter our present picture of what we now know about Heidegger's Nazism. Since the documents are held by Heidegger's closest admirers, presumably everything is already released which tends to exculpate the master. It is more likely that future publication will chip away little by little at the surrounding wall his unconditional defenders have erected to shield him from critical discussion. A likely source of incriminating evidence is Heidegger's correspondence from his period as rector. It is no accident that perhaps alone of all the major thinkers, the publication of Heidegger's complete works will not include his correspondence.

The basic claims of this essay are that Heidegger's Nazism is influenced by a series of contemporary factors, particularly German *Volk* ideology, but is finally based on his philosophy; and that the later evolution of his philosophy in the period after his service as rector of the University of Freiburg cannot be understood without, in fact must be understood through, his continued interest in an ideal form of Nazism. Heidegger stressed the concept of the turning to describe the evolution of his thought. The relation between his philosophical thought and his Nazism can be understood as a series of three turnings: an initial turning on the basis of his philosophy to National Socialism as it existed, a turning in which social, political, and historical factors, including German *Volk* ideology, and Heidegger's own philosophy of Being come together; a second turning away from really existent National Socialism when Heidegger became aware that the rectorate had failed; and a third turning—still based on his personal and philosophical acceptance of the manifest destiny of the German *Volk*—toward an ideal form of Nazism, from which he never later averted his gaze, and whose acceptance influenced the later evolution of his theory of Being.

The framework proposed here provides a coherent, plausible reading of the relation between Heidegger's philosophical thought and his own philosophy. Yet in the present, overheated atmosphere, in which the political stakes are high, in which scholarly careers are tied to the defense of Heidegger the man and above all Heidegger the thinker, no reading can be judged squarely on its merits. It would be illusory to anticipate that even best possible study could produce widespread assent, least of all among those Heidegger scholars who, following the master's lead, have already worked out various strategies for damage control. Just as Heidegger repeatedly hinted at a confrontation with Nazism but in fact finally never addressed it otherwise than as a rival theory of Being, there is no reason to forecast that Heidegger's closest supporters will confront the issues raised by the link between Heidegger's thought and his Nazism. In short, like the master himself, whenever possible they will continue business as usual.[37] Yet to do so, to fail to confront this problem, clearly reflects badly not only on Heidegger's philosophy but on philosophy in general.

As the materials about Heidegger's Nazism continue to accumulate, as the discussion expands, as more and more philosophers become aware of the complex issues, as we become ever more cognizant that the Holocaust is a central event of our time from which we cannot simply turn away, it becomes increasingly difficult, even for Heidegger's closest admirers, simply to pretend that his fateful decision for National Socialism was, is, or even could be essentially meaningless, or that it might be sufficient merely to deplore it. The point is emphatically not to discard Heidegger's philosophy, to consign it to the dustheap of history, as he so candidly consigned the history of ontology he intended to "destroy." It is rather to understand what remains of value in his thought through a thorough evaluation comprising all the relevant factors, including his attachment to Nazism.

As the master conception of his later thought is the event, it is appropriate to utilize the event of his lengthy adherence to Nazism as the turning point for a detailed examination of his entire corpus, to sift his ideas, to measure their worth, cognizant of the intrinsic link in his philosophical thought between ontology and politics. The effort to analyze and evaluate the basic concepts is a necessary part of the arduous process of coming to grips with the theory of an important thinker, someone who introduces new ideas. In that sense, what is necessary for Heidegger is what is required for any novel thinker. The difference, however, is that unlike any other philosopher in this century, Heidegger clearly and unambiguously, on the basis of his philosophical thought, identified with Nazism.

It is too late to expunge Heidegger's Nazism from the historical record or from the interpretation of his thought. Examination of Heidegger's corpus shows that Heidegger's Nazism, real and ideal, is a permanent feature of his thought beginning in 1933. To fail to take his Nazism into account in the interpretation of his philosophical and "postphilosophical" thought, to endeavor to be more friendly to Heidegger than to the truth, is finally to distance oneself from the concern with truth.

Notes

Introduction: On Heidegger's Nazism
and Philosophy

1. To avoid any ambiguity, "philosophical position" will be understood throughout this book to be roughly synonymous with a given "philosopher's thought" or "philosophy."

2. See Karl Löwith, "Les implications politiques de la philosophie de l'existence chez Heidegger," *Les Temps Modernes* 2, no. 14 (novembre 1946): 343–360.

3. See Hugo Ott, *Martin Heidegger: Unterwegs zu seiner Biographie* (Frankfurt a.M. and New York: Campus, 1988).

4. See Victor Farias, *Heidegger and Nazism,* ed. Joseph Margolis and Tom Rockmore, French materials trans. Paul Burrell with the advice of Dominic Di Bernardi, German materials trans. Gabriel R. Ricci (Philadelphia: Temple University Press, 1989). The original French edition of this work appeared in 1987.

5. For Levinas's view of Heidegger, see Emmanuel Levinas, *Éthique et infini: Dialogues avec Philippe Nemo* (Paris: Fayard, 1982), pp. 27–34.

6. See Dieter Thomä, *Die Zeit des Selbst und die Zeit danach: Zur Kritik der Textgeschichte Martin Heideggers 1910–1976* (Frankfurt a.M.: Suhrkamp, 1990), pp. 31–35.

7. The disagreement is instructive. Janicaud, for example, proposes a so-called iron triangle consisting of the *Führerprinzip,* anti-Semitism, and imperialistic nationalism, none of which he finds in Heidegger's position. See Janicaud, *L'ombre de cette pensée. Heidegger et la question politique* (Grenoble: Jérôme Millon, 1990), chap. 2, esp. pp. 35–50. Others have denied that anti-Semitism is central to Nazism as Hitler originally conceived it. For Baum, the main themes were "sovereignty of the German people . . . ; a national community without

class conflict; militant anti-Marxism; the leadership principle; a frank espousal of meritocratic principles whereby, as in contemporary Western societies, rank was to be attained by achievement and talent rather than birth; chauvinism and glorification of war; and, of course, the antidemocratic stance." Rainer C. Baum, "HOLOCAUST: Moral Indifference as *the* Form of Modern Evil," in *Echoes from the Holocaust: Philosophical Reflections from a Dark Time*, ed. Alan Rosenberg and Gerald E. Myers (Philadelphia: Temple University Press, 1988), p. 67. For a wide-ranging survey of fascism in general, see Eugen Weber, *Varieties of Fascism: Doctrines of Revolution in the Twentieth Century* (Malabar, Fla.: Robert E. Krieger Publishing Company, 1982).

8. Paul de Man, *Allegories of Reading: Figural Language in Rousseau, Nietzsche, Rilke, and Proust* (New Haven and London: Yale University Press, 1979), p. 293.

9. See, e.g., Karsten Harries's introduction to *Martin Heidegger and National Socialism: Questions and Answers,* ed. Günther Neske and Emil Kettering, trans. Lisa Harries and Joachim Neugroschel (New York: Paragon House, 1990), p. xii.

10. See, e.g., John Sallis, *Echoes: After Heidegger* (Bloomington and Indianapolis: Indiana University Press, 1990). Sallis employs the now familiar view that we have to let Heidegger's texts speak to us in order to suggest that when we take into account Heidegger's politics we cannot do so and, literally, cannot think. See ibid., p. 11.

11. See Charles E. Scott, *The Question of Ethics: Nietzsche, Foucault, Heidegger* (Bloomington and Indianapolis: Indiana University Press, 1990). Scott considers ethics while suspending the very idea of its practical application, surely a questionable approach since ethics has always been understood as concerning proper action. See ibid., p. 4. Since he refers to none of the prior discussion concerning Heidegger's application of his philosophical thought to political practice, Scott at this late date is able to read the rectoral address without noticing Heidegger's concern in it to put his thought at the service of Nazism. See ibid., pp. 178–192.

12. Löwith already noted this tendency in the foreword to the second edition of his study of Heidegger, which elicited almost no real discussion in the literature. "Desgleichen hat des Verfassers Schrift zwar Ärgernis und Zustimmung erregt, aber keine kritische Entgegnung bekommen." Karl Löwith, "Vorwort zur zweiten Auflage," *Denker in dürftiger Zeit,* in Karl Löwith, *Sämtliche Schriften,* ed. Klaus Stichweh and Marc de Launay (Stuttgart: Metzler, 1984), 1:124.

13. For Rawls's view of the veil of ignorance, see John Rawls, *A Theory of Justice* (Cambridge, Mass.: Harvard University Press, 1971).

14. Blitz is correct to write: "The peculiar need to analyze *Being and Time* is even more obvious when we remember that Heidegger collaborated with the Nazi regime in the first year of its power. Many argue that Heidegger's 'politics' is completely irrelevant for understanding his thought. This argument is useful because indignation seriously interferes with understanding. Ultimately, however, this dismissal of Heidegger's politics is both philosophically ridiculous and

politically dangerous. The precise nature of the connection between a thinker's thought and his practical speeches and deeds is a difficult and revealing subject, hardly to be dismissed with the prejudice that no connection is relevant. It would be both philosophically strange and politically frightening to discover that the thought of the deepest thinkers does not, cannot, inform their practical concerns." Mark Blitz, *Heidegger's Being and Time and the Possibility of Political Philosophy* (Cornell: Cornell University Press, 1981), p. 18. See also Karsten Harries's introduction to *Martin Heidegger and National Socialism: Questions and Answers,* pp. xviii-xix.

Chapter 1: Revealing Concealed Nazism

1. On this point, see Richard Wolin, *The Politics of Being: The Political Thought of Martin Heidegger* (New York: Columbia University Press, 1990), p. xi.

2. For the *locus classicus* of Marx's view of ideology, see Karl Marx and Friedrich Engels, *The German Ideology, Part One,* ed. C. J. Arthur (New York: International Publishers, 1970). For a form of Marxism that maintains Marx's claim that ideology tends to conceal the state of society which would otherwise be transformed as a result of becoming aware of it, see Georg Lukács, *History and Class Consciousness: Studies in Marxist Dialectics,* trans. Rodney Livingstone (Cambridge, Mass.: MIT Press, 1971).

3. See Martin Heidegger, *Being and Time,* trans. John Macquarrie and Edward Robinson (New York and Evanston: Harper and Row, 1962), pp. 60ff.

4. See ibid., p. 60.

5. Ibid., p. 51.

6. For Heidegger's theory, which is crucial to his entire view of Being, see *Being and Time,* § 44, "Dasein, Disclosedness, and Truth," pp. 256–273. For criticism of Heidegger's supposed confusion of disclosure with truth, see Ernst Tugendhat, "Heideggers Idee von Wahrheit," in *Heidegger: Perspektiven zur Deutung seines Werkes,* ed. Otto Pöggeler (Köln and Berlin: Kiepenhauer and Witsch, 1969), pp. 286–297. See also Ernst Tugendhat, *Der Wahrheitsbegriff bei Husserl und Heidegger* (Berlin: Walter de Gruyter, 1967).

7. See Heidegger, *Being and Time,* p. 260.

8. See ibid., p. 264.

9. For discussion of the conception of concealment in Heidegger's theory, see Hans-Georg Gadamer, *Philosophical Hermeneutics,* trans. and ed. David E. Linge (Berkeley, Los Angeles, London: University of California Press, 1977), p. 234.

10. See Martin Heidegger, *Basic Writings,* ed. David Farrell Krell (New York: Harper and Row, 1977), p. 132.

11. Martin Heidegger, *On Time and Being,* trans. Joan Stambaugh (New York: Harper and Row, 1972), p. 69; Heidegger's emphases.

12. Kant held that an original thinker is likely not to be aware of the nature of his or her own thought, which is only later established by epigones who bring out ideas applied but not completely understood by the original thinker. See

Immanuel Kant, *Immanuel Kant's Critique of Pure Reason,* trans. Norman Kemp Smith (London: Macmillan and New York: St. Martin's Press, 1961), B 862, pp. 654–655.

13. Heidegger's main work concerns, as its title suggests, the relation of Being and time. Although there is an immense literature concerning his thought, Dastur says that with the exception of a single dissertation, apparently none of it, besides her own recent work, directly addresses the topics of the temporality and of time. See Françoise Dastur, *Heidegger et la question du temps* (Paris: Presses universitaires de France, 1990), p. 126.

14. See Heidegger, *Being and Time,* pp. 138–139.

15. See ibid., p. 62.

16. See ibid., § 32, pp. 188–194.

17. This problem is ingredient in much of the later hermeneutic discussion, for instance in the work of Gadamer. See Hans-Georg Gadamer, *Truth and Method,* trans. Garrett Barden and John Cumming (New York: Crossroad, 1988).

18. See Kant, *Critique of Pure Reason,* B 864, p. 655.

19. See Heinrich W. Petzet, *Auf einen Stern zugehen: Begegnungen mit Martin Heidegger 1929–1976* (Frankfurt a.M., 1983).

20. For Heidegger's view of "destruction," see Martin Heidegger, *Being and Time,* § 6, "The Task of Destroying the History of Ontology."

21. See John D. Caputo, *Radical Hermeneutics: Repetition, Deconstruction, and the Hermeneutic Project* (Bloomington and Indianapolis: Indiana University Press, 1987), pp. 82–83. According to Dreyfus, Heidegger incompletely acknowledges his debt to Kierkegaard. See Hubert L. Dreyfus, *Being-in-the-World: A Commentary on Heidegger's Being and Time, Division I* (Cambridge, Mass., and London: MIT Press, 1991), p. 298. Dreyfus provides an extensive discussion of the relation of Heidegger to Kierkegaard. See Dreyfus, *Being-in-the-World,* pp. 283–340.

22. See Jacques Taminiaux, "La présence de Nietzsche dans 'Etre et Temps,' " in *"Etre et Temps" de Martin Heidegger. Questions de méthode et voies de recherche,* ed. Jean-Pierre Cometti and Dominique Janicaud (Marseilles: Sud, 1989), pp. 59–76.

23. See Michael Zimmerman, *Heidegger's Confrontation with Modernity. Technology, Politics, Art* (Bloomington and Indianapolis: Indiana University Press, 1990).

24. See Kant, *Critique of Pure Reason,* trans. Smith, B xiii, p. 20.

25. For Ryle's view of a category mistake, which may well be derived from Heidegger, whose thought he admired, see Gilbert Ryle, *The Concept of Mind* (New York: Barnes and Noble, 1949).

26. For instance, in a recent letter to me Prof. Friedrich-Wilhelm von Herrmann specifically denied permission to see the manuscript of a lecture on technology, "Die Gefahr," delivered by Heidegger in Bremen in 1949, and already cited in the literature, on the grounds that none of Heidegger's *Nachlass* could be seen prior to publication. Heidegger's *Beiträge zur Philosophie,* his longest work, has recently been published. See Heidegger, *Gesamtausgabe,* vol.

65, *Beiträge zur Philosophie* (*Vom Ereignis*), ed. Friedrich-Wilhelm von Herrmann (Frankfurt a.M.: Vittorio Klostermann, 1989). According to Thomä, there are at least two other unpublished manuscripts of comparable size in the Heidegger Archives. See Thomä, *Die Zeit des Selbst* (see introd., n. 6), pp. 761–762.

27. Nazism is a form of totalitarianism. Heidegger is certainly not the only major thinker to adhere to totalitarianism. An example that comes readily to mind is the adherence of the Hungarian philosopher, Georg Lukács, to Stalinism. His justification of his adherence to Stalinism on the grounds that it was necessary to defeat Nazism is the obverse of hints in Heidegger's writings that Heidegger's Nazism was partially motivated by anticommunism. Heidegger's anticommunism was typical among conservative intellectuals and also part of National Socialist ideology.

28. For instance, Derrida's limitation of his recent study of Heidegger's Nazism to Heidegger's relation to official, Hitlerian Nazism, simply excludes from consideration Heidegger's later interest in an ideal form of Nazism. See Jacques Derrida, *De l'esprit: Heidegger et la question* (Paris: Éditions Galilée, 1988). If for no other reason, Derrida's explanation that in 1933 Heidegger was himself prey to the metaphysics which he had not yet overcome in his *Fundamentalontologie* is unconvincing in its failure to explain Heidegger's continued concern with Nazism in later years.

29. For the concept of the turning, which Heidegger applies to his own thought, see "The Letter on Humanism," in Heidegger, *Basic Writings,* p. 208. Derrida's interpretation of Heidegger's *Fundamentalontologie* as still not having overcome metaphysics represents the application to Heidegger's position of the critique that in this text Heidegger applies to humanism, particularly to Sartre.

30. See "Only a God Can Save Us: Der Spiegel's Interview with Martin Heidegger," *Philosophy Today* 20 (Winter 1976): 275: "I gave a lecture course with the title, *Poetizing and Thinking.* This was in a certain sense a continuation of my Nietzsche lectures, that is to say, a confrontation with National Socialism."

31. For the most recent, full-scale defense, see Silvio Vietta, *Heideggers Kritik am Nationalsozialismus und an der Technik* (Tübingen: Niemeyer Verlag, 1989). Wolin identifies an example of the politically evasive ways in which some Heideggerians describe their own actions in a review of Hans-Georg Gadamer's *Philosophical Apprenticeships.* See Sheldon Wolin, "Under Siege in the 'German Ivory Tower,' " *New York Times Book Review,* 28 July 1985, p. 12.

32. For the passage in question, see Martin Heidegger, *An Introduction to Metaphysics,* trans. Ralph Mannheim (New Haven and London: Yale University Press, 1977), p. 199.

33. See Wolfgang Schirmacher, *Technik und Gelassenheit* (Freiburg: Alber, 1983), p. 25: "Ackerbau ist jetzt motorisierte Ernährungsindustrie, im Wesen das Selbe wie die Fabrikation von Leichen in Gaskammern und Vernichtungslagern, das Selbe wie die Blockade und Aushungerung von Ländern, das Selbe wie die Fabrikation von Wasserstoffbomben."

34. For instance, Schneeberger's book, which is the first documentary study, was published by the author himself in order to protect against legal action from

the Heidegger family. See Guido Schneeberger, *Nachlese zu Heidegger: Dokumente zu seinem Leben und Denken* (Bern, 1962).

Chapter 2: The Nazi Turning and the Rectoral Address

1. Steiner sees this as the question which Heidegger's critics, including Adorno and Habermas, have failed to answer. See George Steiner, "Heidegger, abermals," *Merkur* 43, no. 2 (February 1989): 95.

2. Sartre seems to have thought that in principle a total explanation of human behavior was indeed possible. See Jean-Paul Sartre, *L'idiot de la famille: Gustave Flaubert de 1821 à 1857,* 3 vols. (Paris: Gallimard, 1971).

3. The distinction between philosophical and nonphilosophical analyses of Heidegger's turn to Nazism neatly divides the French discussion of his politics into two camps. On the one hand, there are those who regard his Nazism as an isolated episode, unrelated to his position, such as Fédier and Aubenque. On the other, there are those, such as Derrida and Lacoue-Labarthe, more sophisticated, who accept a link between his thought and Nazism, which, they argue, is overcome in the later evolution of his thought.

4. For this list and discussion, see Gerald E. Myers, "The Psychology of Man after Auschwitz," in *Echoes from the Holocaust* (see Introd., n. 7), p. 313. Myers insists on the role of Hitler as a central cause of the Holocaust.

5. This information is derived from Fritz Stern, *Dreams and Delusions. National Socialism in the Drama of the German Past* (New York: Vintage, 1989), pp. 130–131.

6. For a classic formulation of this argument, see Franz Neumann, *Behemoth: The Structure and Practice of National Socialism 1933–1944* (Toronto: Oxford University Press, 1944), p. 3.

7. For a recent effort to present a synthetic view of the Weimar Republic in its entirety, see Reinhard Kühnl, *Die Weimarer Republik: Errichtung, Machtstruktur und Zerstörung einer Demokratie* (Hamburg: Rowohlt, 1985).

8. Löwith reports a series of articles that appeared in the *Frankfurter Zeitung* in December 1931 by Paul Tillich, Eduard Spranger, Karl Jaspers, and others under the title "Gibt es noch eine Universität?" See Karl Löwith, *Mein Leben in Deutschland vor und nach 1933: Ein Bericht* (Frankfurt a.M.: Fischer, 1989), p. 24.

9. Peter Gay, *Weimar Culture: The Outsider as Insider* (New York: Harper and Row, 1970), p. 144.

10. See Neumann, *Behemoth,* p. 14.

11. See Leonard Krieger, *The German Idea of Freedom: History of a Political Tradition* (Boston: Beacon, 1957), p. 467.

12. For a discussion of the rise of Nazism as a conservative revolution, see Jeffrey Herf, *Reactionary Modernism: Technology, Culture, and Politics in Weimar and the Third Reich* (Cambridge: Cambridge University Press, 1984), chap. 2, "The Conservative Revolution in Weimar," pp. 18–48.

13. For a presentation of these possibilities, see Kühnl, *Die Weimarer*

Republik, pp. 8–9. He argues that like the First World War, the demise of the Weimar Republic is due not to economic determinism but to conscious action on the part of those who controlled the economic levers of power. See ibid., "Nachwort," pp. 241–248.

14. For a short summary, see Peter Gay, "A Short Political History of the Weimar Republic," in Gay, *Weimar Culture,* pp. 147–164.

˙15. For a discussion of the Nazi assumption of power, see Karl Dietrich Bracher, Wolfgang Sauer, and Gerhard Schulz, *Die nationalsozialistische Machtergreifung: Studien zur Errichtung des totalitären Herrschaftssystems in Deutschland, 1933–1934* (Cologne: Westdeutscher Verlag, 1960).

16. Löwith has expressed a similar view. "Die deutsche Revolution von 1933 begann mit dem Ausbruch des Weltkriegs. Was seit 1933 in Deutschland geschieht, ist der Versuch, den verlorenen Krieg zu gewinnen. Das Dritte Reich ist das Bismarcksche Reich in zweiter Potenz und der 'Hitlerismus' ein gesteigerter 'Wilhelmismus,' zwischen denen die Weimarer Republik nur ein Zwischenakt war." Löwith, *Mein Leben in Deutschland,* p. 1.

17. For an account of German intellectuals up to the Nazi seizure of power, see Fritz Ringer, *The Decline of the German Mandarins: The Academic Community 1890–1933* (Cambridge, Mass.: Harvard University Press, 1969).

18. For a discussion of romantic anti-capitalism, see Michael Löwy, *Georg Lukács–From Romanticism to Bolshevism,* trans. by Patrick Camiller (London: New Left Books, 1979), pp. 22–66.

19. See Rainer Lepsius, cited by Baum "HOLOCAUST" (see Introd., n. 7), p. 63.

20. See Dagmar Barnouw, *Weimar Intellectuals and the Threat of Modernity* (Bloomington and Indianapolis:Indiana University Press, 1988), p. 18. For a good survey of the attitude of German intellectuals toward the Weimar Republic, see ibid., pt. 1: "Tempted by Distance: Intellectuals and the Grey Republic," pp. 11–42.

21. See Max Scheler, *Man's Place in Nature,* trans. Hans Meyerhoff (Boston: Beacon, 1961), p. 4.

22. Cited in Barnouw, *Weimar Intellectuals,* p. 2.

23. See Hans Blumenberg, *The Legitimacy of the Modern Age,* trans. Robert M. Wallace (Cambridge, Mass.: MIT Press, 1985).

24. See Martin Heidegger, *Heraklit: Freiburger Vorlesungen Sommersemester 1943 und Sommersemester 1944,* ed. Manfred S. Frings (Frankfurt a.M.: Vittorio Klostermann, 1987), p. 181.

25. For exceptions, see W. F. Haug, ed., *Deutsche Philosophen 1933* (Hamburg: Argument, 1989), and Thomas Laugstien, *Philosophieverhältnisse im deutschen Faschismus* (Hamburg: Argument, 1990).

26. See Helmut Kuhn, "German Philosophy and National Socialism," in *Encyclopedia of Philosophy,* ed. Paul Edwards (New York and London: Macmillan, 1967), 3–4:310.

27. See Martin Heidegger to Karl Jaspers, Marburg, 2 Dec. 1926, in *Martin Heidegger-Karl Jaspers, Briefwechsel 1920–1963,* ed. Walter Biemel and Hans Saner (Frankfurt a.M., München and Zürich: Vittorio Klostermann and Piper,

1990), p. 69. Jaspers seems to have become aware of the problem of anti-Semitism very late. For instance, in a letter of 20 April 1933 to Heidegger, when Hitler had already come to power and Heidegger was about to become the philosophical *Führer* of the University of Freiburg, after a visit to Berlin Jaspers routinely distinguished between Jewish and German nationalist intellectual circles. See ibid., p. 153.

28. See George M. Kren, "The Holocaust as History," in *Echoes from the Holocaust* (see Introd., n. 7), pp. 37–38.

29. For discussion of Ian Kershaw's view, which omits anti-Semitism from Hitler's main themes in his rise to power, see Baum, "HOLOCAUST," pp. 66–67.

30. See Edmund Husserl, *The Crisis of European Sciences and Transcendental Phenomenology: An Introduction to Phenomenological Philosophy,* trans. David Carr (Evanston, Ill.: Northwestern University Press, 1970), p. 12.

31. See Laugstien, *Philosophieverhältnisse,* p. 52.

32. See ibid., p. 79.

33. See ibid., p. 25.

34. See ibid., p. 202.

35. See ibid.

36. See ibid., p. 27.

37. See ibid.

38. See ibid., p. 90.

39. See ibid., pp. 85–86.

40. See ibid., p. 90.

41. Löwith insists on the relation between Schmitt's view of resoluteness and Hitler's rise to power. "Das Pathos der Entscheidung für die nackte Entschiedenheit hatte zwischen den beiden Weltkriegen einen allgemeinen Anklang gefunden. Es hat die Entscheidung für Hitlers Entschiedenheit vorbereitet und den politischen Umsturz als 'Revolution des Nihilismus' möglich gemacht." Karl Löwith, "Der okkasionnelle Dezisionismus von C. Schmitt," in Löwith, *Sämtliche Schriften* (see Introd., n. 12), 1:61

42. Hitler wrote: "So ist die Voraussetzung zum Bestehen eines höheren Menschentums nicht der Staat, sondern das Volkstum, das hierzu befähigt ist." Cited in Thomä, *Die Zeit des Selbt* (see Introd., n. 6), p. 559. Thomä points to the way in which Heidegger's view that the state can only be understood on the basis of the *Volk* coincides with Hitler's view. See ibid., p. 559.

43. G. W. F. Hegel, *Jenaer Realphilosophie I: Die Vorlesungen von 1803/4,* ed. J. Hoffmeister (Leipzig, 1932), p. 239, cited in Shlomo Avineri, *Hegel's Theory of the Modern State* (London: Cambridge University Press, 1972), p. 93.

44. Lukács has shown that alienation is a central theme in Hegel's thought. See Georg Lukács, *The Young Hegel: Studies in the Relations between Dialectics and Economics,* trans. Rodney Livingstone (Cambridge, Mass.: MIT Press, 1976).

45. For a discussion of this point, see Karl Löwith, *From Hegel to Nietzsche:*

The Revolution in Nineteenth Century Thought, trans. David E. Green (Garden City, N.Y.: Doubleday, 1967).

46. Bürger has argued that the difference between aestheticism and the avant-garde lies in the latter's concern to erect a theory of art into a theory of life. See Peter Bürger, *Theory of the Avant-Garde,* trans. Michael Shaw (Minneapolis: University of Minnesota Press, 1984).

47. See Craine Brinton, "Romanticism," in *Encyclopedia of Philosophy,* ed. Edwards, 7–8:209.

48. See Jacques Droz, "Romanticism in Political Thought," in *Dictionary of the History of Ideas,* ed. Philip P. Wiener (New York: Charles Scribner's Sons, 1973), 4:205–208.

49. See Herf, *Reactionary Modernism* (see n. 12), p. 15.

50. See Nathan Rotenstreich, "Volksgeist," in *Dictionary of the History of Ideas,* ed. Weiner, 4:490–496.

51. See G. W. F. Hegel, "Fragmente über Volksreligion und Christentum (1793–1794)," in G. W. F. Hegel, *Werke in zwanzig Bänden,* ed. Eva Moldenhauer and Karl Markus Michel (Frankfurt a.M.: Suhrkamp, 1971), vol. 1, *Frühe Schriften,* pp. 9–103, e.g., pp. 34, 42, etc.

52. See Rotenstreich, "Volksgeist," p. 493.

53. See Pierre Bourdieu, *L'ontologie politique de Martin Heidegger* (Paris: Éditions de minuit, 1988), pp. 16–18.

54. See George Mosse, *The Crisis of German Ideology: Intellectual Origins of the Third Reich* (New York: Grosset and Dunlap, 1964), pp. 14–15. For a description of the conception of the *Volk* in the context of modern German anti-Semitism, see Lucy S. Dawidowicz, *The War against the Jews 1933–1945* (New York: Bantam, 1986), pp. 23–48.

55. See Alfred Rosenberg, *Der Mythus des zwanzigsten Jahrhunderts: Eine Wertung der seelisch-geistigen Gestaltenkämpfe unserer Zeit* (Munich: Hoheneichen, 1930).

56. For the category of romantic disillusionment, see Georg Lukács, *La théorie du roman,* trans. Jean Clarevoye (Paris: Éditions Gonthier, 1963), pp. 115ff.

57. Isaiah Berlin, "Joseph de Maistre and the Origins of Fascism," *The New York Review of Books* 37, no. 14 (27 September 1990): 64. For a fuller account of Berlin's effort to revise the usual antiromantic reading of Maistre, see Isaiah Berlin, *The Crooked Timber of Humanity* (London: John Murray; New York: Knopf, 1991).

58. On this point, see Michael Dummett, *Frege: Philosophy of Language* (London: Duckworth, 1973), p. xii. Although he died in 1925, Frege was also an early enthusiast of National Socialism. Entries in his *Tagebuch* (that has not yet been published) from 10 March to 9 May 1924 record: his desire for someone, although not a centrist, to free Germany from French pressure; his conviction that there were too many Jews in Germany and that he finally understood anti-Semitism; his preoccupation with, in his words, the "enormous difficulty" of distinguishing Jews from others; his suggestion that when new racial laws are

established Jews should wear something that enables one to recognize them as Jews; and so on. (I owe this reference to Hans Sluga.)

59. See Pierre Aubenque, "Encore Heidegger et le nazisme," *Le Débat* no. 48 (janvier-février 1988): 119.

60. See Janicaud, *L'ombre de cette pensée* (see Introd., n. 7), p. 58. But note that Janicaud holds that Heidegger's rejection of politics is in effect an "apolitic" (*apolitique*), that is, a particular form of political theory. See ibid., pp. 51–76.

61. See Wolin, *The Politics of Being* (see chap. 1, n. 1).

62. See *Plato's Republic,* trans. G. M. A. Grube (Indianapolis: Hackett, 1974) 1.352, p. 25.

63. See Aristotle, *Nicomachean Ethics,* trans. Martin Ostwald (New York: Library of Liberal Arts, 1962), 1.2.1094b, p. 4.

64. For a discussion of Heidegger's critique of the Aristotelian conception of human being, see Janicaud, *L'ombre de cette pensée,* pp. 58–64.

65. See Aristotle, *Nicomachean Ethics,* 10.9.1181b, p. 302.

66. See Heidegger, *Being and Time,* § 74, "The Basic Constitution of Historicality."

67. Martin Heidegger, *Der Satz vom Grund* (Pfullingen: Neske, 1957), pp. 210–211.

68. For an example of the argument that Stalinism is contained in Marx's theory, see Leszek Kolakowski, "Marxist Roots of Stalinism," in *Stalinism: Essays in Historical Interpretation,* ed. Robert C. Tucker (New York: Norton, 1979); and Leszek Kolakowski, "Die sogenannte Entfremdung," *Zukunft,* February 1978. For an analysis, see Tom Rockmore, "Kolakowski and Markovic on Stalinism, Marxist and Marx," *Philosophy and Social Criticism* 6, no. 3 (1979).

69. There is an enormous and rapidly growing secondary literature on Heidegger's position. The best general account of Heidegger's thought of which I am aware is Pöggeler's classic study. See Otto Pöggeler, *Der Denkweg Martin Heideggers* (Pfullingen: Neske, 1963, 3d ed., 1990).

70. Heidegger, *Being and Time,* p. 19.

71. See ibid., §4, p. 32: "As ways in which man behaves, sciences have the manner of Being which this entity—man himself—possesses. This entity we denote by the term '*Dasein.*' "

72. See Heidegger, *Being and Time,* § 4, p. 32.

73. Ibid.

74. Ibid., § 4, p. 33.

75. Ibid.

76. See ibid.

77. Ibid., § 4, p. 34; see also p. 35.

78. Ibid., § 5, p. 38.

79. See ibid.

80. Goldmann has argued that *Being and Time* is intended as a response to Lukács's *History and Class Consciousness.* See Lucien Goldmann, *Lukács and Heidegger: Towards a New Philosophy,* trans. William Q. Boelhower (London: Routledge and Kegan Paul, 1977).

81. Heidegger's analysis includes numerous aspects that appear to be based on an appropriation or rethinking of Kierkegaardian concepts, including fear, death, anxiety, authenticity, repetition, etc.

82. See Heidegger, *Being and Time,* § 2, p. 24.

83. See ibid., § 9, p. 68.

84. See ibid., § 9, p. 67.

85. Ibid., p. 68.

86. See ibid., p. 69.

87. See ibid., § 10, "How the Analytic of Dasein Is to Be Distinguished from Anthropology, Psychology, and Biology," pp. 71–77.

88. Heidegger's view of authentic thought bears a close relation to Kant's idea of maturity, of thinking for oneself as the criterion of appropriate thought. For Kant's view, see "An Answer to the Question: What Is Enlightenment?" in Immanuel Kant, *Perpetual Peace and Other Essays,* trans. Ted Humphrey (Indianapolis: Hackett, 1985).

89. Heidegger does not claim that authenticity must be realized in practice, although it would make sense to do so. Wolin argues that authenticity is meaningful only if it is in fact realized. But the passage he cites, from *Being and Time,* p. 312, merely indicates that Heidegger is concerned at that point with a form of authenticity which is in fact realized, not that authenticity is meaningful only when this is the case. See Wolin, *The Politics of Being,* p. 34.

90. See Heidegger, *Being and Time,* § 44, p. 264.

91. Ibid.

92. See ibid., § 60, p. 344. For a general discussion of resoluteness that does not emphasize the lack of criteria nor discuss the political consequences, see Charles M. Sherover, "The Hermeneutic Structure of Resoluteness: A Preliminary Exploration," in *Hermeneutic Phenomenology: Lectures and Essays,* ed. Joseph J. Kockelmans (Washington, D.C.: Center for Advanced Research in Phenomenology and University Press of America, 1988), pp. 41–66.

93. Heidegger, *Being and Time,* § 61, p. 349.

94. See ibid., § 74, "The Basic Constitution of History."

95. For an expression of this view, see Caputo, *Radical Hermeneutics* (see chap. 1, n. 21), pp. 88–89.

96. See Heidegger, *Being and Time,* § 74, p. 435.

97. See ibid., § 74, pp. 435–436.

98. See ibid., § 74, p. 436; see also § 26, p. 159.

99. See ibid., § 74, p. 436.

100. See ibid., §74, p. 437.

101. In partial defense, it should be noted that not only the National Socialists but other segments of society also, apparently including Communists as well as Catholics, likewise honored Schlageter's memory. For an analysis of Heidegger's homage to Schlageter, see Farias, *Heidegger and Nazism* (see Introd., n. 4), pp. 87–95. According to Löwith, Heidegger's praise of Schlageter was based on Tolstoy's "Death of Ivan Ilitch." See Löwith, *Mein Leben in Deutschland* (see n. 8), p. 36.

102. See Heidegger, *Being and Time,* § 74, p. 438. This concept has attracted extensive attention in the literature. For a survey of the main approaches, see Thomä, *Die Zeit des Selbst und die Zeit danach* (see Introd., n. 6), pp. 153–162.

103. For instance, in the *Gutachten* that formed the basis for Heidegger's suspension from his teaching functions after the Second World War, Jaspers stated that Heidegger's personal excuse should be partly acknowledged since Heidegger was by his very nature not political. See Ott, *Martin Heidegger* (see Introd., n. 3), p. 316.

104. See Martin Heidegger, *Die Grundbegriffe der Metaphysik. Welt— Endlichkeit—Einsamkeit: Freiburger Vorlesung Wintersemester 1929/30,* ed. Friedrich-Wilhelm von Herrmann (Frankfurt a.M.: Vittorio Klostermann, 1983). For an analysis of the significance of this text for Heidegger's Nazism, see Winfried Franzen, "Die Sehnsucht nach Härte und Schwere: Über ein zum NS-Engagement disponierendes Motiv in Heideggers Vorlesung 'Die Grundbegriffe der Metaphysik' von 1929/30," in *Heidegger und die praktische Philosophie,* ed. Annemarie Gethmann-Siefert and Otto Pöggeler (Frankfurt a.M.: Suhrkamp, 1989).

105. See Heidegger, *Being and Time,* § 29: "Being There as State-of-Mind," pp. 172–179.

106. See ibid., p. 178.

107. Heidegger's formulation reads in part (*Die Grundbegriffe der Metaphysik,* p. 244): "aber keiner ist der Verwalter der inneren Grösse des Daseins und seiner Notwendigkeiten." This passage calls for two comments. First, it is possible, as Zimmerman thinks, that Heidegger is here thinking of a *Führer.* See Zimmerman, *Heidegger's Confrontation with Modernity* (see chap. 1, n. 23), p. 33. But it is also equally likely that he is saying that no one is really master of himself or herself. Second, it is startling to see that Heidegger here employs a locution, viz. "the inner greatness," very similar to the locution employed after his period as rector, in the *Introduction to Metaphysics,* where he speaks of the "inner truth and greatness of National Socialism." The significant point, beyond the linguistic similarity, is that in both cases he is referring to the problems of the authenticity of Dasein and ultimately to knowledge of Being.

108. Heidegger, *Die Grundbegriffe der Metaphysik,* p. 243.

109. See ibid., § 18c, "Die tiefe Langeweile als die verborgene Grundstimmung der kulturphilosophischen Deutungen unserer Lage," pp. 111–116.

110. See ibid., p. 243.

111. Ibid., p. 248; Heidegger's emphases.

112. Ibid.

113. See ibid., p. 249.

114. Mosse describes this concept as follows: " 'Volk' is one of those perplexing German terms which connotes far more than its specific meaning. 'Volk' is a much more comprehensive term than 'people,' for to German thinkers ever since the birth of German romanticism in the late eighteenth century 'Volk' signified the union of a group of people with a transcendental 'essence.' The 'essence' might be called 'nature' or 'cosmos' or 'mythos,' but in each instance it

was fused to man's innermost nature, and represented the essence of his creativity, his depth of feeling, his individuality, and his unity with other members of the Volk." Mosse, *The Crisis of German Ideology* (see n. 54), p. 4.

115. There are at present two available translations into English due respectively to Karsten Harries and to Lisa Harries in collaboration with Karsten Harries. See "The Self-Assertion of the German University: Address, Delivered on the Solemn Assumption of the Rectorate of the University Freiburg [and] The Rectorate 1933/34: Facts and Thoughts," trans. Karsten Harries, *Review of Metaphysics* 38 (March 1985): 467–502, and "The Self-Assertion of the German University," in *Martin Heidegger and National Socialism: Questions and Answers* (see Introd., n. 9), pp. 5–14. The same volume also has a translation of Heidegger's article, "The Rectorate: Facts and Thoughts," pp. 15–32. To avoid confusion, and because of the relatively greater availability of the earlier translations of the speech and the article, I shall refer to Karsten Harries's translations of both the rectoral address and the article "Facts and Thoughts" as "Rectoral Address–Facts and Thoughts," followed by the page number.

116. On this point, see Karl Jaspers, *Die Schuldfrage: Zur politischen Haftung Deutschlands* (Munich and Zurich: Piper, 1987), p. 64.

117. For discussion, see Farias, *Heidegger and Nazism* (see Introd., n. 4), pp. 96–112; Ott, *Martin Heidegger,* pp. 146–166; and Reiner Alisch, "Heideggers Rektoratsrede im Kontext," in *Deutsche Philosophen 1933,* ed. Haug (see n. 25).

118. For detailed discussion of this speech, see Farias, *Heidegger and Nazism,* chap. 9, "The Rector's Address: Its Assumptions and Its Effects," pp. 99–112; Ott, *Martin Heidegger,* "Das soldatische Umfeld der Rektoratsrede," pp. 146–166; and Alisch, "Heideggers Rektoratsrede im Kontext," pp. 69–98. For Ott's analysis of Heidegger's use of Göring as a model, see Ott, *Martin Heidegger,* pp. 145–148. For a recent analysis which largely follows Heidegger's self-justification of his actions, see Scott, *The Question of Ethics* (see Introd., n. 11), chap. 5, pp. 148–172.

119. See Ott, *Martin Heidegger,* pp. 147f.

120. See Löwith, *Mein Leben in Deutschland,* pp. 57–58.

121. Cited in Emil L. Fackenheim, *To Mend the World: Foundations of Future Jewish Thought* (New York: Schocken Books, 1982), p. 267.

122. See Fackenheim, *To Mend the World,* pp. 266–267. According to Fackenheim, this was Fichte's sole moment of truth. On Huber, see also Laugstien, *Philosophieverhältnisse* (see n. 25), pp. 58ff.

123. The Platonism of Heidegger's turn to politics has been seen, particularly in the French discussion, where stress has been placed on the metaphysical aspect of Heidegger's political turn in order to argue that his later thought overcomes the metaphysical dimension by bringing his position in line with its own attempt to "destroy" the history of ontology. See Philippe Lacoue-Labarthe, *L'imitation des modernes. Typographies II* (Paris: Éditions Galilée, 1986), pp. 135–200, and Jacques Derrida, *De l'esprit* (see chap. 1, n. 28). I am less interested here in the internal consistency of Heidegger's position than in his apparent reliance on a quasi-Platonic model for the political role of philosophy.

124. The parallels in this respect between Lukács and Heidegger are rarely explored. For an interesting discussion, see István M. Fehér, "Heidegger und Lukács. Eine Hunderjahrebilanz," in *Wege und Irrwege des neueren Umgangs mit Heideggers Werk: Ein deutsch-ungarisches Symposium* (Berlin: Duncker und Humblot, forthcoming).

125. See Leszek Kolakowski, *Main Currents of Marxism*, trans. P. S. Falla (Oxford: Clarendon Press, 1978), vol. 3, chap. 7, "György Lukács: Reason in the Service of Dogma," pp. 253–307.

126. Harries helpfully notes the first two senses of "*Selbstbehauptung*" but apparently misses the third, relevantly philosophical sense that was presupposed in Heidegger's claim for the role of philosophy in the realization of Nazism. See "Rectoral Address–Facts and Thoughts," p. 468.

127. Ibid., p. 470.

128. Thomä, who fails to notice the discussion of the conception of the *Volk* in *Being and Time,* sees a shift in position between the conception of Dasein in Heidegger's fundamental ontology and the conception of the *Volk* developed here. See Thomä, *Die Zeit des Selbst und die Zeit danach,* p. 553.

129. For the term "spiritual leader," see "Ernennung eines Kanzlers an der Universität Freiburg," *Der Alemanne: Kampfblatt der Nationalsozialisten Oberbadens . . .* , Folge 178, 30 June 1933, p. 2, cited in Schneeberger, *Nachlese zu Heidegger* (see chap. 1, n. 34), p. 73. For an analysis of Heidegger's Nazism through the concept of leadership (*Führung*) and the leader (*Führer*), see Hans Ebeling, *Geschichte einer Täuschung* (Würzburg: Königshausen und Neumann, 1990), "Das Ereignis des Führers: Heidegger's Antwort," pp. 9–34.

130. On the leading role of the party, see V. I. Lenin, *What Is to Be Done?,* trans. Joe Fineberg and George Hanna, ed. Victor J. Jerome (New York: International Publishers, 1969). For Marx's view of the philosophers as the head of the revolution and the proletariat as its heart, see "Contribution to the Critique of Hegel's Philosophy of Right," in Karl Marx, *Early Writings,* trans. and ed. T. B. Bottomore (New York: McGraw-Hill, 1963).

131. See Ernst Cassirer, *The Myth of the State* (New Haven and London: Yale University Press, 1971), p. 290ff.

132. See Plato's account of the Myth of Er, in *Plato's Republic,* trans. G. M. A. Grube (Indianapolis: Hackett Publishing Company, 1974), 10.616f., pp. 258f.

133. Heidegger, *Being and Time,* p. 436.

134. For a good discussion of this point, see Otto Pöggeler, "Den Führer führen? Heidegger und kein Ende," *Philosophischer Rundschau* 32, no. 1/2 (1985): 26–67.

135. The same reaction was produced by Spengler, who enthusiastically welcomed the Nazi accession to power without ever mentioning Hitler. See Oswald Spengler, *Jahre der Entscheidung, Erster Teil, Deutschland und die weltgeschichtliche Entwicklung* (Munich: C. H. Beck, 1933).

136. "Rectoral address—Facts and Thoughts," p. 471.

137. See *Hegel's Phenomenology of Spirit,* trans. A. V. Miller (Oxford: Oxford University Press, 1977), p. 6.

138. "Rectoral Address—Facts and Thoughts," p. 471.

139. Ibid., p. 472.

140. See, e.g., Martin Heidegger, *Nietzsche* (Pfullingen: Neske, 1961) 2:398, 413.

141. "Rectoral Address—Facts and Thoughts," p. 473.

142. Heidegger renders the Greek word "*techne*" as "*Wissen*," or "knowledge." In a recent translation of Plato's *Symposium* the term is rendered as "profession," "science," and "expertise." See *Plato: Symposium*, trans. Alexander Nehemas and Paul Woodruff (Indianapolis and Cambridge: Hackett, 1989), p. xxvii. According to Liddell and Scott, the Greek term means "art," "skill," "craft," "cunning of hand," etc. These are all forms of knowing how, but not knowledge in the ordinary sense of the word. See Henry George Liddell and Robert Scott, *A Greek-English Lexicon*, 9th ed. (Oxford: Clarendon Press, 1978), p. 1785.

143. For this argument, related to his turn to the concept of thought (*Denken*) as distinguished from philosophy, see "The Letter on Humanism."

144. For a classic statement of this reading of Plato's theory, see Werner Jaeger, *Aristotle: Fundamentals of the History of His Development*, trans. Richard Robinson (Oxford: Clarendon Press, 1962).

145. "Rectoral Address—Facts and Thoughts," p. 474.

146. See Martin Heidegger, *Hölderlins Hymne "Der Ister": Freibürger Vorlesung, Sommersemester 1942*, ed. Walter Biemel (Frankfurt a.M.: Vittorio Klostermann, 1984), pp. 98, 106.

147. On the relation between Heidegger's language, the language of Messkirch, and the terminology of National Socialism, see Robert Minder, "Heidegger und Hebel oder die Sprache von Messkirch," in Robert Minder, "*Hölderlin unter den deutschen*" *und andere Aufsätze zur deutschen Literatur* (Frankfurt a.M.: Suhrkamp, 1968). For a specific study of Nazi language, see Berel Lang, "Language and Genocide," in Berel Lang, *Act and Idea in the Nazi Genocide* (Chicago and London: University of Chicago Press, 1990), pp. 81–102.

148. "Rectoral Address—Facts and Thoughts," p. 475; translation modified.

149. See for this view Hegel's letter of 28 October 1808 to Niethammer, in *Briefe von und an Hegel*, ed. J. Hoffmeister, Hamburg: Meiner, 1952), 1:253: "Die theoretische Arbeit, überzeuge ich mich täglich mehr, bringt mehr zustande in der Welt als die praktische; ist erst das Reich der Vorstellung revolutioniert, so hält die Wirklichkeit nicht aus."

150. See, e.g., Herbert Marcuse, *Five Lectures* (Boston: Beacon, 1970).

151. "Rectoral Address—Facts and Thoughts," p. 475.

152. For Marx's view, see "Contribution to the Critique of Hegel's Philosophy of Right," in Marx, *Early Writings*, pp. 41–60.

153. See Immanuel Kant, *Fundamental Principles of the Metaphysic of Morals*, trans. Thomas K. Abbott (New York: Library of Liberal Arts, 1949), p. 12.

154. *Freiburger Studentenzeitung* . . . 8. Semester (15), Nr. 1, 3. November 1933, p. 1, cited in Schneeberger, *Nachlese zu Heidegger*, p. 136.

155. See "Only a God Can Save Us" (see chap. 1, n. 30), p. 271.

156. "Rectoral Address—Facts and Thoughts," p. 498.

157. See Kolakowski, *Main Currents of Marxism* 3:307.

158. "Rectoral Address—Facts and Thoughts," p. 476.

159. Heidegger's enumeration of three bonds of the German student recalls the appeal in May 1933 by von Papen for the cooperation of the Nazi movement, "Stalhelm" and "Konservative," which he regarded as "die drei grossen Säulen der nationalen Bewegung." See Haug, *Deutsche Philosophen 1933* (see n. 25), p. 159.

160. See *Being and Time,* § 26, p. 159. This idea of authentic being with others is never developed by Heidegger either in this work or in his later writings, although it is presupposed in his conception of the *Volk.* It apparently serves as the basis of Sartre's later view of the distinction between seriality and the group in fusion. See Jean-Paul Sartre, *Critique de la raison dialectique* (Paris: Gallimard, 1960), trans. Alan Sheridan Smith as *Critique of Dialectical Reason* (London: New Left Books, 1976).

161. See *Being and Time,* §§ 46–53.

162. This episode is still not fully clarified. For a discussion, see Ott, *Martin Heidegger,* pp. 214–223.

163. "Rectoral Address—Facts and Thoughts," p. 477.

164. Ibid.; see also p. 478 for a restatement of the same theme.

165. Ibid., p. 477.

166. Heidegger's stress on *Kampf,* in connection with the realization of the *Volk,* which is one of the most noticeable aspects of this speech, directly recalls Hitler's view in *Mein Kampf.* See Adolf Hitler, *Mein Kampf* (Munich, 1934), p. 418, cited in George Mosse, *Nazi Culture: A Documentary History* (New York: Schocken Books, 1981), p. xxiii: "Every world-view, be it correct and useful a thousand times over, will be without importance for the life of a *Volk* unless its basic tenets are written upon the banners of a fighting movement." In this text, neither Hitler nor the National Socialist movement is directly mentioned. But there is an obvious link between Heidegger's repeated stress on the concept of *Kampf* and Hitler's book. Heidegger's awareness of this obvious link is a plausible reason for his determined effort in his article on the rectorate, at a time when he wishes to project the view that he has officially broken with Nazism of every form, to reinterpret the concept of *Kampf* in terms of Heraclitus's thought.

167. "Rectoral Address—Facts and Thoughts," p. 479.

168. Ibid.

169. Heidegger, *Being and Time,* p. 436.

170. The extent of Spengler's influence on Heidegger is not often acknowledged. But it is important, particularly for the analysis of technology, as will emerge below. See chap. 6.

171. "Rectoral Address—Facts and Thoughts," pp. 479–480.

172. Ibid., p. 480.

173. Ibid.

174. See "Le dossier d'un nazi 'ordinaire,' " *Le Monde,* 14 October 1988, p. 12.

175. "Rectoral Address—Facts and Thoughts," p. 480. Once again, Hei-

degger appears deliberately to have taken liberties with the Greek, which does not mention a storm and literally reads "the great [things] are precarious."

176. For a detailed discussion of Heidegger's mistranslation of this passage, see Bernd Martin, " 'Alles Grosse ist gefährdet'—Der Fall Heidegger(s)," in *Martin Heidegger und das "Dritte Reich": Ein Kompendium,* ed. Bernd Martin (Darmstadt: Wissenschaftliche Buchgesellschaft, 1989), pp. 3–13.

177. Thomä, who throughout his study relatively deemphasizes the central role of Being in Heidegger's thought, curiously insists on the importance of Heidegger's effort to find a solution for the problem of the self, arising out of *Being and Time,* in the Nazi turn in 1933: "Die 'Lösung' des Jahres 1933 besteht dann darin, Handeln und Sprache gewaltsam zusammenzuzwingen." Thomä, *Die Zeit des Selbt und die Zeit danach,* p. 643. Thomä maintains that Heidegger finally finds the solution he was seeking in National Socialism in his theory of art. See ibid., p. 704.

178. For a well-known attack on the antidemocratic consequences of Platonism, see Karl Popper, *The Open Society and Its Enemies,* 2 vols. (London: Routledge and Kegan Paul, 1945).

Chapter 3: The "Official" View and "Facts and Thoughts"

1. For some representative reactions, see Schneeberger, *Nachlese zu Heidegger* (see chap. 1, n. 34), pp. 50–51, 76–80, 82–84, 84–87.

2. See Löwith, *Mein Leben in Deutschland* (see chap 2, n. 8), p. 57.

3. For Heidegger's admission that he briefly saw the Nazi rise to power as a propitious moment, see "Only a God Can Save Us" (see chap. 1, n. 30).

4. See Georg Lukács, *Existentialismus oder Marxismus?* (Berlin: Aufbau-Verlag, 1951).

5. See Jean-Paul Sartre, *Search for a Method,* trans. Hazel E. Barnes (New York: Vintage, 1968), p. 38; Sartre's emphasis.

6. See "Rectoral Address—Facts and Thoughts" (see chap. 2, n. 115), pp. 468–469. For another short statement of the "official" view, see Michael Haller, "Der Philosophen-Streit zwischen Nazi-Rechtfertigung und postmodernner Öko-Philosophie," in *Die Heidegger Kontroverse,* ed. Jürg Altwegg (Frankfurt a.M.: Athenäum, 1988), p. 202.

7. See Rectoral Address—Facts and Thoughts, p. 468.

8. In the United States, a major step in the transition from the arcane level of professional philosophical debate, which obviously repels rather than attracts wider attention, to the general public was taken by Michiko Kakutani's recent, withering review of the English-language translation of *Antwort: Martin Heidegger im Gespräch* (see n. 111 below), which appeared in German closely after Farias's book was published in French in order to limit the damage, so to speak. See "Friends of Heidegger and the Nazi Question," *The New York Times,* 14 December 1990.

9. The 1945 article appeared under the title "Das Rektorat 1933/34: Tatsachen und Gedanken" in the little volume edited by Hermann Heidegger.

Curiously, the translator omits the section headings in the translation, although he inserts roman numerals to divide the text. The result, in the absence of the section headings which the original text contained, is to render the interpretation more, not less, difficult.

10. For a brief discussion, see "The End of the War and the Beginning of *Polemos,*" in Farias, *Heidegger and Nazism* (see Introd., n. 4), pp. 278–280. For a more detailed discussion, see "Die Auseinandersetzung um die politische Vergangenheit," in Ott, *Martin Heidegger* (see Introd., n. 3), pp. 291–327. My brief statement of the historical background is based on these two sources.

11. The relations between Heidegger and Jaspers are highly complex. The best record of their friendship, and of Jaspers's later disillusionment with Heidegger as a friend and a philosopher, is provided by their letters, which have recently been published. See *Briefwechsel 1920–1963* (see chap. 2, n. 27). For Jaspers's never-completed effort to write a critical study of Heidegger's thought, see Karl Jaspers, *Notizen zu Martin Heidegger,* ed. Hans Saner (Muchin and Zurich: Piper, 1989).

12. For Jaspers's *Gutachten* on Heidegger, which was the basis of the decision, see Ott, *Martin Heidegger,* pp. 315–317.

13. For the report by the committee, see Ott, *Martin Heidegger,* pp. 305–307. For a good analysis of this entire episode, see ibid., pp. 291–327.

14. See ibid., p. 296.

15. For Heidegger's own explanation of why he chose to remain in Freiburg, see Martin Heidegger, "Schöpferische Landschaft: Warum bleiben wir in der Provinz?" in Martin Heidegger, *Gesamtausgabe,* vol. 13, *Aus der Erfahrung des Denkens 1910–1976,* ed. Hermann Heidegger (Frankfurt a.M.: Vittorio Klostermann, 1983).

16. Ott, *Martin Heidegger,* p. 305.

17. See Jaspers's letter to Heidegger of 23 August 1933, cited in Ott, *Martin Heidegger,* pp. 192–193.

18. For Croce's correspondence with Vossler, see Schneeberger, *Nachlese zu Heidegger,* pp. 110–112.

19. See Martin Heidegger, "Rectoral Address—Facts and Thoughts."

20. That the text is repetitive is easily shown through the almost obsessive recurrence of certain themes, in similar language, e.g., the problem of science, "Rectoral Address—Facts and Thoughts," pp. 481, 497; technology, pp. 482, 497; historical vocation of the Western world, pp. 483, 497; political science, pp. 483, 496; Nietzsche and the will to power, pp. 485, 498; etc.

21. Ibid., pp. 492–493.

22. See Hugo Ott, "Martin Heidegger und der Nationalsozialismus," in *Heidegger und die praktische Philosophie* (see chap. 2, n. 104), p. 67.

23. For a detailed study of how Heidegger was elected, see H. Ott, "Wie Heidegger Rektor wurde," in *Heidegger und die praktische Philosophie,* pp. 138–147.

24. I follow Thomä on this point. See Thomä, *Die Zeit des Selbst* (see Introd., n. 6), p. 628.

25. "Rectoral Address—Facts and Thoughts," p. 481.

26. This is the same difference that Aristotle formalizes in his distinction between activity (*energeia*) and movement (*kinesis*). An activity is complete in itself and has no end external to it to which it serves as a means; a movement is a means to an end which is external to it and which is only reached when the means ceases to be. See Aristotle, *Metaphysics*, 9.6.1048b18–35.

27. Jaspers, *Notizen zu Martin Heidegger*, p. 18.

28. See Heidegger, *Basic Writings*, ed. Krell (see Introd., n. 11), pp. 91–112.

29. There is a close link between Heidegger's inaugural lecture, delivered in 1929, and his study of metaphysics in a wide variety of other writings, including his work on Kant's view of metaphysics and his own introduction to metaphysics. See Martin Heidegger, *Kant and the Problem of Metaphysics*, trans. James S. Churchill (Bloomington and London: Indiana University Press, 1962), and Heidegger, *An Introduction to Metaphysics*, trans. Mannheim (see chap. 1, n. 32).

30. See "What Is Metaphysics?" in Heidegger, *Basic Writings*, p. 95.

31. Carnap held that Heidegger's analysis of nothing was an example of a meaningless statement and argued for the elimination of metaphysics. See Rudolf Carnap, "The Elimination of Metaphysics through Logical Analysis of Language," in *Logical Positivism*, ed. A. J. Ayer (New York: Free Press, 1959). It is not impossible that Carnap, the apostle of rigorous thought from a scientific perspective, was put off by Heidegger's view, expressed in his lecture, that such forms of "exact" knowledge as mathematics are no more rigorous than others. See Heidegger, *Basic Writings*, p. 96.

32. See Heidegger, *Basic Writings*, p. 112.

33. Martin Heidegger, "Nachwort zu: 'Was Ist Metaphysik?' " in *Wegmarken* (Frankfurt a.M.: Vittorio Klostermann, 1967), p. 100.

34. Heidegger, *Wegmarken*, p. 107.

35. "Einleitung zu: 'Was Ist Metaphysik?' " in Heidegger, *Wegmarken*.

36. "Rectoral Address—Facts and Thoughts," pp. 481–482.

37. Ibid., p. 482.

38. Ibid., pp. 482–483.

39. For Husserl's view of objectivism, see Husserl, *The Crisis of European Sciences and Transcendental Phenomenology* (see chap. 2, n. 30), para. 14: "Precursory characterization of objectivism and transcendentalism. The struggle between these two ideas as the sense of the struggle of modern spiritual history," pp. 68–70. For Heidegger's view that as reflective phenomenology is deeper than the positive sciences, see *Being and Time*, § 10, "How the Analytic of Dasein Is to Be Distinguished from Anthropology, Psychology, and Biology," pp. 71–77.

40. For his view of the relation of the special sciences to philosophical science, see the discussion of the divided line in Plato, *The Republic*, bk. 6, 509–511E.

41. "Rectoral Address—Facts and Thoughts," p. 486.

42. Ibid., p. 488.

43. Ibid., p. 496.

44. I agree with Lacoue-Labarthe on this point, who writes: "Et tel est très

précisément ce que le 'Discours de rectorat' *rappelle:* en tous sens, le philosophique est la raison ou le fondement du politique." Lacoue-Labarthe, *L'imitation des modernes: Typographies II* (see chap. 2, n. 123), pp. 156–157.

45. This point is significant, and will be developed in the discussion of Heidegger's own Nietzsche interpretation. It is sufficient to note at this point that Heidegger's concern to provide an authentic reading of Nietzsche is doubly determined on the one hand by his view that National Socialism has provided an insufficient interpretation of Nietzsche's thought and on the other by his dissatisfaction with Baeumler. Jaspers points out that like C. Schmitt and Heidegger, Baeumler also sought to lead National Socialism. See his letter to Oehlkers of 22 December 1945, reprinted in Ott, *Martin Heidegger,* p. 317. For Baeumler's Nietzsche interpretation, see Alfred Baeumler, *Nietzsche, der Philosoph und Politiker* (Leipzig: Reclam, 1931). For a discussion of Baeumler's view, which is largely parallel to Heidegger's Nietzsche reading, in particular in the emphasis on the will to power and the negation and overcoming of the preceding tradition, see Endre Kiss, "Nietzsche, Baeumler oder über die Möglichkeit einer positiven faschistischen Metaphysik," in *Annales* 16 (1982): 157–174. For discussion of Nietzsche and Nazism in general, see Konrad Algermissen, *Nietzsche und das Dritte Reich* (Celle: Verlag Joseph Giesel, 1947). Heidegger further had a personal reason to dislike Baeumler because of the latter's vulgarization of the concept of resoluteness (*Entschlossenheit*), developed in *Being and Time,* in his own work, *Männerbund und Wissenschaft* (Berlin: Junker und Dünnhaupt, 1934), p. 108. On this aspect of the relation between Heidegger and Bäumler, see Karl Löwith, "Der okkasionelle Dezisionismus von C. Schmitt," in Löwith, *Sämtliche Schriften* (see Introd., n. 12), 1:64, n. 88.

46. This idea was a commonplace in the Third Reich. In an essay written in 1934, Bauemler portrays Nietzsche as a prophet who was able to foresee the future. See Alfred Bauemler, "Nietzsche und der Nationalsozialismus," in Alfred Bauemler, *Studien zur deutschen Geistesgeschichte* (Berlin: Junker und Dünnhaupt, 1943), p. 282. For a statement of the same idea in the context of Nietzsche's thought, see also his *Nachwort* to Friedrich Nietzsche, *Der Wille zur Macht: Versuch einer Umwertung aller Werte* (Leipzig: Alfred Kröner Verlag, 1930), p. 705.

47. "Rectoral Address—Facts and Thoughts," p. 483.

48. Ibid., pp. 483–484. The translation of the first passage seems to me not to communicate adequately the strength of Heidegger's statement, although I am unable to improve on the rendering.

49. One can argue that in the attribution of a vocation to the German people, Heidegger is merely developing the concept of the vocation of man earlier sketched by Fichte and applied to the German nation. See Johann Gottlieb Fichte, *Die Bestimmung des Menschen,* in *Fichtes Werke,* ed. I. H. Fichte (Berlin: Walter de Gruyter, 1971), 2:165–320, and *Reden an die deutsche Nation,* ibid., 7:257–502. For this argument, see André Glucksmann, *Les maîtres penseurs* (Paris: Grasset, 1977).

50. This idea was in the air at the time. For instance, Theodor Lessing, a philosopher who was assassinated by the Gestapo on 30 August 1933, shortly

after Heidegger became rector, with an eye on the evolution of German politics wrote as early as 1925 in opposition to Hindenburg: "Nach Plato sollen die Philosophen Führer der Völker sein. Ein Philosoph würde mit Hindenburg nun eben nicht den Thronstuhl besteigen. Nun ein repräsentives Symbol, ein Fragezeichen, ein Zero. Man kann sagen: 'Besser ein Zero als ein Nero.' Leider zeigt die Geschichte, dass hinter einem Zero immer ein künftiger Nero verborgen steht." Cited in Laugstien, *Philosophieverhältnisse* (see chap. 2, n. 25), p. 80.

51. Letter from Martin Heidegger to Prof. Schuchardt, dean of the philosophy faculty, 19 July 1943, in Heidegger records, cited in Farias, *Heidegger and Nazism*, p. 269.

52. "And so far there seems to be no end in sight to this abuse of Nietzsche's work. In speaking here of Nietzsche, we mean to have nothing to do with all that—or with blind hero worship for that matter. The task in hand is too crucial and at the same time too sobering. It consists first of all, if we are to gain a true grasp of Nietzsche, in bringing his accomplishment to a full unfolding." Heidegger, *An Introduction to Metaphysics*, p. 36.

53. Heidegger, *An Introduction to Metaphysics*, pp. 36–37; translation modified.

54. See *Being and Time*, pt. 2, chap. 5: "Temporality and Historicality," particularly § 74, "The Basic Constitution of Historicality."

55. See "Rectoral Address—Facts and Thoughts," p. 485. Heidegger never seems to realize that this doctrine is not original with Nietzsche. Others had, of course, considered this view before Heidegger. For Hegel's opinion that modern atheism and modern nihilism were like a generalization of the historical Good Friday, see G. W. F. Hegel, *Faith and Knowledge*, trans. Walter Cerf and H. S. Harris (Albany: SUNY Press, 1977), pp. 190–191. For Feuerbach's understanding of the death of God, see Ludwig Feuerbach, *Principles of the Philosophy of the Future*, trans. Manfred H. Vogel (Indianapolis and New York: Bobbs-Merrill, 1966), § 21, pp. 31–34.

56. See "The World of Nietzsche: 'God is Dead,' " in Martin Heidegger, *The Question concerning Technology and Other Essays*, trans. by William Lovitt (New York: Harper and Row, 1977), pp. 53–112. The remark on the death of God is taken almost verbatim from the lecture. See ibid., p. 57. For an interpretation of this claim as a factual ascertainment of the turn away from religion by a leading Nietzsche specialist of the time, see Bauemler, "Nietzsche und der Nationalsozialismus," p. 286.

57. See Heidegger, *The Question concerning Technology and Other Essays*, p. 53.

58. See ibid., pp. 75–76.

59. See ibid., p. 76.

60. Ibid., p. 75.

61. These remarks recur in somewhat different form in a later essay. See "Zur Seinsfrage," in Heidegger, *Wegmarken*, pp. 218–219.

62. "Rectoral Address—Facts and Thoughts," pp. 484–485.

63. Ibid., p. 485.

64. Ibid. It is noteworthy that in a variant of this theme, Ott suggests that had Heidegger not withdrawn from the Catholic Church his turn toward Nazism could have been avoided. See Ott, *Martin Heidegger,* pp. 344–346.

65. See, e.g., "The Question concerning Technology," in Heidegger, *The Question concerning Technology and Other Essays,* pp. 3–35.

66. "Rectoral Address—Facts and Thoughts," p. 485.

67. The German "ins Feld zu führen," which does not mention a battle, literally means "to lead into the field," although "to lead into battle" is perhaps an acceptable rendering of Heidegger's military metaphor.

68. "Rectoral Address—Facts and Thoughts," pp. 485–486; translation modified.

69. See François Fédier, *Heidegger: Anatomie d'un scandale* (Paris: Éditions Robert Laffont, 1988). We will return to this interpretation in chap. 7 below.

70. See "Rectoral Address—Facts and Thoughts," pp. 491–492.

71. Ibid., p. 486.

72. See, e.g., Heidegger, *Being and Time,* pp. 57, 59–60.

73. See "Rectoral Address—Facts and Thoughts," p. 487; translation modified. The translator's omission here of the term "translation" turns attention away from Heidegger's suggestion that his text requires interpretation according to his own theory of the relation between understanding and interpretation. See Heidegger, *Being and Time,* § 32, "Understanding and Interpretation," pp. 188–194.

74. For this analysis, see Gadamer, *Truth and Method* (see chap. 1, n. 17), "Heidegger's Disclosure of the Fore-structure of the Understanding," pp. 235–240.

75. "Rectoral Address—Facts and Thoughts," p. 487.

76. Ibid..

77. Ibid., p. 492.

78. The distinction between the letter and the spirit is already present in the Bible. Kant, who was concerned that his work was misunderstood by his critics, complained that it was easy to find contradictions by comparing passages out of context, in order to arrive at an unfavorable impression of a work. For Kant's restatement of this distinction, see the "Preface to the Second Edition," in Immanuel Kant's *Critique of Pure Reason,* trans. Smith (see chap. 1, n. 12), B xliv, p. 37. Kant's distinction was widely influential in German idealism. See my article, "Idealist Hermeneutics and the Hermeneutics of Idealism," *Idealistic Studies* 12, no. 2 (1982): 91–102.

79. I am by no means alone in this way of reading the *Rektoratsrede.* Even Vietta, the author of the most complete effort to date to defend Heidegger, acknowledges that in the rectoral Address Heidegger was concerned with the future role of science in National Socialism. See Vietta, *Heideggers Kritik am Nationalsozialismus und an der Technik* (see chap. 1, n. 31), p. 21.

80. See "Rectoral Address—Facts and Thoughts," p. 476.

81. See ibid., p. 477.

82. See ibid., p. 487.

83. Ibid.; translation modified. The translator's rendition of *"Notwehr"* as

"self-defense" fails to capture the sense of need, from "*Not*," prominent in Heidegger's repeated allusions to the historical occasion represented by the Nazi rise to power in a time of historical need.

84. For Heidegger's well-known criticism of Descartes, see, e.g., *Being and Time*, §§ 14–24.

85. "Rectoral Address—Facts and Thoughts," p. 476.

86. Ibid.

87. Ibid., p. 487.

88. See ibid., p. 472.

89. For a statement of this view in Heidegger's early and middle periods, see *Being and Time*, § 44, and "On the Essence of Truth," in Heidegger, *Basic Writings*.

90. See Heidegger, *An Introduction to Metaphysics*, p. 62.

91. For a close reading of Heidegger's conception of *polemos*, see Gregory Fried, "Heidegger's *Polemos*," *Journal of Philosophical Research*, forthcoming.

92. "Rectoral Address—Facts and Thoughts," p. 486.

93. For Hegel's famous master-slave discussion, see *Hegel's Phenomenology of Spirit*, trans. Miller (see chap. 2, n. 137), "Independence and Dependence of Self-Consciousness: Lordship and Bondage," pp. 111–118. For the analysis of mutual recognition, see *Hegel's Philosophy of Mind*, trans. A. V. Miller (Oxford: Clarendon Press, 1971), sec. 1, "Mind Subjective," subsection B, "Phenomenology of Mind: Consciousness," a. "Self-Consciousness," pt. γ, "Universal Self-Consciousness," pp. 176–177.

94. "Rectoral Address—Facts and Thoughts," pp. 488–489.

95. See ibid., p. 479.

96. See ibid., p. 489.

97. G. S. Kirk, J. E. Raven, and M. Schofield, *The Presocratic Philosophers*, 2d ed. (Cambridge: Cambridge University Press, 1983), p. 194.

98. "Rectoral Address—Facts and Thoughts," p. 489.

99. Ibid., p. 470.

100. Ibid., p. 489.

101. Ibid.

102. See Heidegger, *Being and Time*, § 35, "Idle Talk."

103. "Rectoral Address—Facts and Thoughts," pp. 489–490. It is important to point to two slips in the translation of this important passage, in which Heidegger seeks to exonerate himself of blame by confronting the obvious reading of his rectoral address. The translator's substitution of "National Socialism" for " 'the' National Socialism" makes it appear that Heidegger is questioning National Socialism in general when he is rather making the point, by putting the accusative form of the definite article in scare quotes, that there is more than one form of Nazism. This is a crucial point for a comprehension of Heidegger's later Nazism. In his own careful way, through these linguistic devices Heidegger is holding open the possibility for a better, more authentic form of National Socialism than the vulgar variety in practice associated with the NSDAP. The rendering of "*politischen Wissenschaft*" or "political science" as "the political character of science" is an example of the substitution of an interpretation for a transla-

tion. The most recent translation of Heidegger's article by Lisa Harries in collaboration with Karsten Harries silently corrects the latter misreading. But it preserves the crucial misrendering of " 'den' Nationalsozialismus" as "National Socialism" that continues to obscure Heidegger's steadfast adherence, at a time when he claims to have broken his ties to the so-called movement, to the possibility of an authentic form of Nazism. See *Martin Heidegger and National Socialism: Questions and Answers* (see Introd., n. 9), p. 22.

104. See Heidegger, *Being and Time,* § 9 and passim.

105. For a discussion along these lines, see Mark Okrent, *Heidegger's Transcendental Pragmatism* (Ithaca, N.Y., and London: Cornell University Press, 1989). On the contrary, Dreyfus considers Okrent's analysis as a trivializing reduction of Husserl's. See Dreyfus, *Being-in-the-World* (see chap. 1, n. 21), p. 345n.

106. There is no evidence that Heidegger ever adopted the Nazi view of race, although it is plausible to interpret his stress on the German people as a kind of metaphysical "racism." With the exception of an overt form of racism, in his failure to cite either the Nazi party or Hitler, Heidegger resembled Spengler. See Spengler, *Jahre der Entscheidung* (see chap. 2, n. 135).

107. In a letter to Prof. Dietz, Heidegger explicitly disclaims his intention to realize Nazi party doctrine in any other sense than through the respect for the university, whose spirit he intended to transform. "[E]s war nicht und nie meine Absicht, die Universität an die Parteidoktrin auszuliefern, sondern umgekehrt zu versuchen, *innerhalb* des Nationalsozialismus und in bezug auf diesen eine geistige Wandlung in Gang zu bringen." Letter of Heidegger to the president of the *politischer Bereinigungsausschuss,* Prof. v. Dietze (15 Dec. 1945), cited in *Martin Heidegger und das "Dritte Reich,"* ed. Martin (see chap. 2, n. 176), p. 208. In the same letter, Heidegger further presents himself as opposed to National Socialism but devoted to Hitler, who he believed would transcend Nazism after 1933: "Ich stand schon 1933/34 in derselben Opposition gegen die n.s. Weltanschauungslehre, war damals aber des Glaubens, dass die Bewegung geistig in andere Bahnen gelenkt werden könne und hielt diesen Versuch vereinbar mit den sozialen und allgemein politischen Tendenzen der Bewegung. Ich glaubte, Hitler werde, nachdem er 1933 in der Verantwortung für das ganze Volk stand, über die Partei und ihre Doktrin hinauswachsen und alles würde sich auf den Boden einer Erneuerung und Sammlung zu einer abendländischen Verantwortung zusammenfinden." Ibid., p. 210.

108. "Rectoral Address—Facts and Thoughts," p. 491.

109. In the discussion concerning Heidegger's anti-Semitism, his defenders attach great weight to the fact that he interceded to help his student, Werner Brock, migrate to England. Müller, who notes this fact, also notes that from the moment that he became rector, Heidegger did not permit any of his Jewish students to finish their degrees. See Martin, *Martin Heidegger und das "Dritte Reich,"* p. 106. This view has recently been corroborated by Helene Weiss's niece. See letter by Miriam Lewin to *The New York Times Book Review,* 11 February 1990.

110. In a letter to Dietrich Mahnke dated 4 May 1933, that is, immediately

after Heidegger and other German academics publicly joined the NSDAP, Husserl openly speaks of Heidegger's well known anti-Semitism. See Martin, *Martin Heidegger und das "Dritte Reich,"* p. 149. Husserl's claim of Heidegger's anti-Semitism is routinely denied in the secondary literature. But it is supported by Jaspers, who, in his *Gutachten,* states that in a certain sense in 1933, although not earlier, Heidegger was an anti-Semite. See Jaspers's letter to Friedrich Oehlkers of 22 December 1945, cited in Ott, *Martin Heidegger,* p. 316.

111. See, e.g., Hans L. Gottschalk, "Heideggers Rektorenzeit," in *Antwort: Martin Heidegger in Gespräch,* ed. Günther Neske and Emil Kettering (Pfullingen: Neske, 1988), p. 187.

112. See "Rectoral Address—Facts and Thoughts," pp. 491–492.

113. See Fédier, *Heidegger* (see n. 69), p. 67.

114. For this letter and a discussion of it, see Ulrich Sieg, "Die Verjudung des deutschen Geistes," *Die Zeit,* no. 52 (22 December 1989): 50. The vulgar term *"Verjudung,"* which is not contained in standard dictionaries, was common in contemporary forms of anti-Semitism, and was used by Hitler in *Mein Kampf,* especially in his discussion of "Volk und Rasse" in vol. 1, chap. 11. See, e.g., Adolf Hitler, *Mein Kampf* (Munich: Zentralverlag der NSDAP, 1935), pp. 348–349: "Wie weit dabei die innere Verjudung unseres Volkes schon fortgeschritten ist. . . ." I owe this reference to Gregory Fried.

115. Heidegger expresses his opposition to biological reductionism in various places, including the "Letter on Humanism" (see chap. 1, n. 29), p. 231. For an example of the view that Heidegger's antibiologism is incompatible with Nazism, see Alexander Schwan, *Politische Philosophie im Denken Heideggers* (Opladen: Westdeutscher Verlag, 1989), p. 103. See also Luc Ferry and Alain Reinaut, *Heidegger et les modernes* (Paris: Bernard Grasset, 1988), pp. 224–225. Schwan erroneously sees Heidegger's refusal of biologism as leading to a break with Nazism. Ferry and Renaut erroneously infer that because Heidegger rejects biologism, he was also not anti-Semitic.

116. For passages from Luther's book *From the Jews and Their Lies,* see Raul Hilberg, *The Destruction of the European Jews* (New York: Harper and Row, 1961), p. 9.

117. For passages from a speech given before the Reichstag in 1895, see Hilberg, *The Destruction of the European Jews,* pp. 10–11.

118. For discussion of how and why the definition of an "Aryan" was formulated and applied, see Hilberg, *The Destruction of the European Jews,* 4: "Definition," pp. 43–53, esp. p. 45.

119. See "Rectoral Address—Facts and Thoughts," pp. 491–492.

120. The rectoral address took place on 27 May 1933. Heidegger became a member of the NSDAP on 1 May 1933. For a discussion, see Max Müller, "Bekenntnisse: Ein Gespräch mit Max Müller," in *Martin Heidegger und das "Dritte Reich,"* ed. Martin, p. 95. Other well-known philosophers who joined the NSDAP on 1 May 1933 include E. Rothacker, A. Gehlen, and J. Ritter. See Haug, *Deutsche Philosophen 1933* (see chap. 2, n. 25), pp. 17, 190, 235. For newspaper reports on Heidegger's adherence to the Nazi party, see Schneeberger, *Nachlese zu Heidegger* (see chap. 1, n. 34), pp. 23–35.

121. Pöggeler reports that Mörchen was surprised to discover in 1931 that the entire Heidegger family had been converted to National Socialism. See Martin, *Martin Heidegger und das "Dritte Reich,"* p. 84. Pöggeler bases his comment on a radio talk by Mörchen. See ibid., p. 91, n. 21.

122. See Otto Pöggeler, " 'Praktische Philosophie' als Antwort an Heidegger," in *Martin Heidegger und das "Dritte Reich,"* ed. Martin, p. 66: "Wenn es um Philosophie geht, dann muss mann damit fertig werden, dass 1933 Heidegger als der 'führende' Philosoph alle Hoffnungen auf den neuen 'Führer' Hitler setzte." This claim is supported by Weil. According to Weil, in 1932 at the latest Heidegger was a known Nazi. See Eric Weil, "Le cas Heidgger," reported in *Lignes.* 2 February 1988, p. 140.

123. Martin makes this point persuasively. See Martin, *Martin Heidegger und das "Dritte Reich,"* p. 36: "Doch auch nach seinem offiziellen Rückzug von der Hochschulpolitik blieb er der Partei als Mitglied bis zum Zusammenbruch des Reiches verbunden und die NSDAP wiederum in einer Art von Dankesschuld dem Philosophen bis in die letzten Kriegsmonate gewogen."

124. This claim is rejected by most of Heidegger's defenders. Vietta, for instance, argues that the incorrect objection that Heidegger remained close to fascism is contradicted by the texts. See Vietta, *Heideggers Kritik am Nationalsozialismus und an der Technik,* p. 46.

125. See "Rectoral Address—Facts and Thoughts," p. 494.

126. See ibid.

127. See Farias, *Heidegger and Nazism,* chap. 14: "The End of the Rectorate," pp. 177–187.

128. See "Rectoral Address—Facts and Thoughts," p. 494.

129. See Farias, *Heidegger and Nazism,* "Attacks from Ernst Krieck and His Faction," pp. 168–169.

130. On this point, see Laugstien, *Philosophieverhältnisse* (see chap. 2, n. 25), p. 109.

131. In different ways, this point is made by Jaspers, Gadamer, and Schorcht. See Laugstien, *Philosophieverhältnisse,* pp. 107, 108, and 193 n. 28.

132. "Rectoral Address—Facts and Thoughts," p. 497; translation modified. It is better to translate "*Zwiespalt*" here by "discrepancy" since "rift," which the translator uses, suggests a prior relation that has later been torn asunder, which in fact is what happened, although Heidegger suggests that there never was any significant area of agreement. The translation of "*wohl*" as "presumably" creates a doubt, whereas Heidegger insists that his view and National Socialism are incompatible.

133. For the effort by some National Socialists to depict Nazism as a *Weltanschauung,* see Alfred Baeumler, "Nietzsche and National Socialism," in Mosse, *Nazi Culture* (see chap. 2, n. 166), p. 97.

134. See the discussion of historicism and *Weltanschauungphilosophie* in Edmund Husserl, "Philosophy as Rigorous Science," in *Phenomenology and the Crisis of Philosophy,* trans. Quentin Lauer (New York: Harper, 1965), sec. 2: "The Concept of Philosophy and the World-View," pp. 4–11, and Heidegger, *Beiträge zur Philosophie* (see chap. 1, n. 26), § 14, pp. 36–41. Another factor in

Heidegger's opposition to the conception of a *Weltanschaaung* was his early review of Jaspers's *Philosophie der Weltanschauungen.*

135. Rosenberg rejected philosophy in favor of a *Weltanschauung.* Rosenberg, Krieck, Alfred Klemmt, Heinrich Härtle, and others worked to develop a Nazi *Weltanschauung.* See Laugstein, *Philosophieverhältnisse,* pp. 72–77.

136. Like Heidegger, Krieck was also concerned to ground National Socialism, but as a *Weltanschauung,* in his *Völkisch-politischen Anthropologie,* published in Leipzig from 1936 to 1938. See Laugstien, *Philosophieverhältnisse,* p. 73.

137. "Rectoral Address—Facts and Thoughts," p. 497; translation modified.

138. See Martin Heidegger, "The Age of the World Picture," in Heidegger, *The Question concerning Technology* (see n. 56), pp. 115–154. Vietta follows this indication in his effort to show that, after 1938, Heidegger adopted a critical attitude toward National Socialism. See Vietta, *Heideggers Kritik am Nationalsozialismus und an der Technik,* chap. 3: "Heideggers metaphysikkritischer Ansatz und die Grundzüge seiner Kritik am Nationalsozialismus," pp. 19–47.

139. "Rectoral Address—Facts and Thoughts," p. 498.

140. For a representative view of the matter, see Frederick Ferré, *Philosophy of Technology* (Englewood Cliffs, N.J.: Prentice-Hall, 1988), p. 44: "Modern science, as it has developed since the seventeenth century, is the joint product of theoretical and practical intelligence, and so is modern technology. Neither gave birth to the other. They are non-identical twins of the same parents."

141. See "Rectoral Address—Facts and Thoughts," p. 483.

142. See ibid., p. 487 and passim.

143. Ibid., p. 498.

144. Heidegger came to this conclusion at least as early as 1934, that is, immediately after his resignation from the rectorate. The idea that national salvation lies in poetry underlies his turn to Hölderlin as the poet of poets, as the one who sees into the German future. For an early form of this view, see Martin Heidegger, *Hölderlins Hymnen "Germanien" und "Der Rhein": Freiburger Vorlesung, Wintersemester 1934/35,* ed. Susanne Ziegler (Frankfurt a.M.: Vittorio Klostermann, 1980).

145. "Rectoral Address—Facts and Thoughts," p. 502.

146. Ibid., p. 499.

147. See Fédier, *Heidegger* (see n. 69), p. 162.

148. See Jaspers's letter of 22 December 1945 to Oehlkers, cited in Ott, *Martin Heidegger,* p. 317.

149. See Jaspers, *Die Schuldfrage* (see chap. 2, n. 116), p. 85.

150. See Heidegger's letter of 8 April 1950 to Jaspers, in *Briefwechsel 1920–1963* (see chap. 2, n. 27), p. 202.

151. For Heidegger's view of the hero, see *Being and Time,* § 74. For an analysis of his talk on Schlageter, see Farias, *Heidegger and Nazism,* pp. 87–95.

152. "Rectoral Address—Facts and Thoughts," pp. 498–499.

153. Ibid., p. 502.

154. See ibid., p. 461.

155. "Wege zur Aussprache," in *Alemannenland: Ein Buch von Volkstum*

und Sendung, ed. Dr. Franz Kerber (Stuttgart: J. Engelhorns Nachf. 1937), pp. 135–139, reprinted in Schneeberger, *Nachlese zu Heidegger,* pp. 258–262.

156. Schneeberg, *Nachlese zu Heidegger,* p. 262.

157. Ibid., p. 258.

158. "Rectoral Address—Facts and Thoughts," p. 497.

159. Schneeberger, *Nachlese zu Heidegger,* p. 260.

160. For this view in the early Marx, see his essay, "Contributions to the Critique of Hegel's *Philosophy of Right:* Introduction," in Marx, *Early Writings* (see chap. 2, n. 130), pp. 41–60. Lukács bases his own influential reading of Marx on the supposed efficacy of class consciousness. See Lukács, *History and Class Consciousness* (see chap. 1, n. 2).

161. Schneeberger, *Nachlese zu Heidegger,* p. 260.

162. Lukács's own effort to enlist Marxism as a revolutionary form of thought in the service of oppressed humanity, relevantly similar to Heidegger's view here, is a constant in his long Marxist period.

163. Heidegger, "Letter on Humanism" (see chap. 1, n. 29), p. 239.

Chapter 4: The History of Philosophy: Nietzsche and the History of Ontology

1. For instance, Grondin writes, in the context of a brief remark on the evolution of Heidegger's position: "Dans cet itinéraire, le rectorat n'aura sans doute été qu'un épisode (il fut en effet étonnament court, dont on aurait tort d'exagérer la portée philosophique, même si Heidegger lui-même a peut-être été le premier à se fourvoyer sur ce point." Jean Grondin, review of Martin Heidegger, *Beiträge zur Philosophie* and of *Vom Wesen der Wahrheit,* in *Archives de philosophie* 53, no. 3 (July-September 1990): 523.

2. See Aubenque, "Encore Heidegger et le nazisme" (see chap. 2, n. 59), pp. 113–128, and Vietta, *Heideggers Kritik am Nationalsozialismus und an der Technik* (see chap. 1, n. 31).

3. It is significant that Heidegger associates the purported failure to perceive the essence of National Socialism with a commitment to axiology, or values. See Heidegger, *An Introduction to Metaphysics,* trans. Mannheim (see chap. 1, n. 32), p. 199. This recalls Nietzsche's view of a transvaluation of values, which in turn suggests that Nietzsche may well have been ingredient in Heidegger's turning to real Nazism.

4. Heidegger initially took a softer line on the conception of a *Weltanschauung.* In his initial lecture series, he depicted the *Weltanschauung* as the immanent task of philosophy and finally identical with philosophy on the one hand, and as the limit of philosophy on the other. See Martin Heidegger, *Zur Bestimmung der Philosophie: Frühe Freiburger Vorlesungen, Kriegsnotsemester 1919 und Sommersemester 1919,* ed. Bernd Heimbüchel (Frankfurt a.M.: Vittorio Klostermann, 1987), p. 10. The volume includes lectures titled "Die Idee der Philosophie und das Weltanschauungsproblem" and "Phänomenologie und Wertphilosophie" and an abridged version of a course titled "Über das Wesen der Universität und des akademischen Studiums."

5. "Only a God Can Save Us" (see chap. 1, n. 30), p. 274.

6. Aubenque, "Encore Heidegger et le nazisme," p. 121.

7. See Vietta, *Heideggers Kritik am Nationalsozialismus und an der Technik,* p. 50.

8 This lecture series was given during the summer semester 1935. See Martin Heidegger, *Einführung in die Metaphysik: Freiburger Vorlesung Sommersemester 1935* (Tübingen: Max Niemeyer, 1953).

9. See Martin Heidegger, *Hölderlins Hymne "Andenken":* *Freibürger Vorlesung Wintersemester 1941/42,* ed. Curd Ochwadt (Frankfurt a.M.: Vittorio Klostermann, 1982), and *Hölderlins Hymne "Der Ister"* (see chap. 2, n. 146).

10. Heidegger, *Hölderlins Hymnen "Germanien" und "Der Rhein"* (see chap. 3, n. 144).

11. See Beda Allemann, *Hölderlin und Heidegger* (Zurich: Atlantis Verlag, 1956), and Else Buddeberg, "Heidegger und die Dichtung: Hölderlin," *Deutsche Vierteljahrschrift für Literaturwissenschaft und Geistesgeschichte* 26, no. 3 (1952): 293–330. See also Michel Deguy, "Sur le commentaire heideggérien de Hölderlin," *Tel Quel,* no. 8 (1962): 57–65; Otto Pöggeler, "Heidegger's Begegnung mit Hölderlin," *Man and World* 10 (1977): 13–61, and Paul de Man, "Heidegger's Exegeses of Hölderlin," in Paul de Man, *Blindness and Insight. Essays in the Rhetoric of Contemporary Fiction* (Minneapolis: University of Minnesota Press, 1983), pp. 246–266.

12. See Jaspers, *Notizen zu Martin Heidegger* (see chap. 3, n. 11), esp. § 47, pp. 75–76. Jaspers thought that Heidegger, as a result of the abandonment of science, and hence of metaphysics, was led finally to a form of irrationalism and gnosticism. See ibid., §§ 38 and 187, pp. 68, 208–209.

13. See Heidegger, *Being and Time,* § 44, "Dasein, Disclosedness, and Truth."

14. This essay first appeared in 1964. See Heidegger, *On Time and Being,* trans. Stambaugh (see chap. 1, n. 11), pp. 55–73.

15. Heidegger, *Hölderlins Hymnen "Germanien" und "Der Rhein,"* p. 1.

16. Ibid.

17. See "Only a God Can Save Us," p. 277.

18. This theme recurs in almost exactly the same terminology three times. See Heidegger, *Hölderlins Hymnen "Germanien" und "Der Rhein,"* pp. 50, 58, 226.

19. See ibid., p. 213.

20. See ibid., p. 252.

21. See ibid., p. 294.

22. See ibid., p. 226: ". . . denn die Götter sind geflohen, wer der Mensch ist, wissen wir nicht."

23. See ibid., p. 30.

24. See ibid., p. 40.

25. See ibid., p. 51

26. See ibid., p. 74.

27. See ibid., p. 76.

28. See ibid., p. 116.

29. See ibid., pp. 121–122.

30. See ibid., p. 220.

31. Ibid., p. 221.

32. Ibid., p. 237.

33. Ibid., p. 255.

34. See ibid., p. 284.

35. Ibid., p. 294.

36. For a statement of the idea of the poet as divinely inspired, see *Ion,* 534e: "By this example, above all, it seems to me, the god would show us, lest we doubt, that these lovely poems are not of man or human workmanship, but are divine and from the gods, and that the poets are nothing but interpreters of the gods, each one possessed by the divinity to whom he is in bondage." *Ion,* trans. Lane Cooper, in *The Collected Dialogues of Plato including the Letters,* ed. Edith Hamilton and Huntington Cairns (New York: Pantheon, 1961), p. 220. For the more developed critique of this view, see *Republic,* book 10.

37. According to Szilasi, with the exception of Hegel and Schelling no other important philosopher spent so much time interpreting other thinkers. See W. Szilasi, *M. Heideggers Einfluss auf die Wissenschaften* (Bern, 1949), pp. 73ff., cited in Löwith, *Sämtliche Schriften* (see Introd., n. 12), 1:196.

38. According to Heidegger, Hegel's history of philosophy is and will remain the only philosophical history until philosophy is forced to think historically. See Martin Heidegger, *Nietzsche* (see n. 143 below), vol. 2, *The Eternal Recurrence of the Same* (San Francisco: Harper and Row, 1984), p. 186.

39. The widely accepted Young Hegelian view of the end of philosophy in Hegel's thought, a claim which Hegel never makes, is formulated by Heine in a famous passage. "Our philosophical revolution is concluded; Hegel has closed its great circle." Heinrich Heine, *Religion and Philosophy in Germany: A Fragment,* trans. John Snodgrass (1882; reprint, Albany: State University of New York Press, 1986), p. 156.

40. For instance, in a typical passage, Bochenski writes: "Heidegger is an extremely original thinker. The problem of his historical affiliations is not of primary concern here and we need only mention that he borrows his method from Husserl, that he is in many ways influenced by Dilthey, and that his general thesis is largely inspired by Kierkegaard." I. M. Bochenski, *Contemporary European Philosophy* (Berkeley and Los Angeles: University of California Press, 1961), p. 161. For a more detailed study, see Walter Schulz, "Über den philosophiegeschichtlichen Ort Martin Heideggers," *Philosophische Rundschau* 1 (1953–54): 65–93, 211–232.

41. See Martin Heidegger, *Die Lehre vom Urteil im Psychologismus. Ein kritisch-positiver Beitrag zur Logik* (Leipzig: Johann Ambrosius Barth, 1913).

42. See Martin Heidegger, *Die Kategorien- und Bedeutungslehre des Duns Scotus* (Tübingen: Paul Siebeck, 1916).

43. For recent discussion of Heidegger's treatment of Hegel, see Denise Souche-Dagues, *Hégélianisme et dualisme: Réflexions sur le phénomène* (Paris: Vrin, 1990), pp. 20–31.

44. Löwith, who as Heidegger's student and later colleague knew him well,

describes his relation to Kierkegaard as follows: "In dieser Suche nach dem Einen, was not tut und darum notwendig ist, orientierte sich Heidegger vor allem an Kierkegaard, mit dem er jedoch nicht verwechselt sein wollte, denn das Motiv und Ziel seiner Existentzialphilosophie war ja kein 'Aufmerksammachen aufs Christliche', sondern eine 'formale Anzeige' der weltlichen Existenz." Löwith, *Mein Leben in Deutschland* (see chap. 2, n. 8), p. 28.

45. Löwith links Heidegger's interest in both Kierkegaard and Luther as follows (Löwith, *Mein Leben in Deutschland,* p. 30): "Aus Luther stammte auch das unausgesprochene Motto seiner Existenzialontologie: 'Unus quisque robustus sit in existentia sua' was sich Heidegger ohne den Glauben an Christus damit verdeutlichte, dass er immer wieder betonte, es komme nur darauf an, 'dass jeder das macht, was er kann', auf 'das je eigene Sein-können' oder die 'existentielle Beschränkung auf die eigene, historische Faktizität.' Dieses Können nahm er zugleich als ein Müssen in Anspruch oder als 'Schicksal.' Er schrieb mir 1921: 'Ich mache lediglich, was ich muss und was ich für nötig halte, und mache es so, wie ich es kann—ich frisiere meine philosophische Arbeit nicht auf Kulturaufgaben für ein allgemeines Heute. Ich habe auch nicht die Tendenz Kierkegaards. Ich arbeite aus meinem "ich bin" und meiner geistigen, überhaupt faktischen Herkunft. Mit dieser Faktizität wütet (sic!) das Existieren.' "

46. See Heidegger, *Being and Time,* §§ 19–21.

47. See ibid., § 43a.

48. See ibid., § 77.

49. See ibid., § 82.

50. See ibid., § 1, p. 2.

51. See ibid., § 6.

52. See ibid., p. 42.

53. Ibid., p. 43.

54. Ibid., p. 44.

55. See Martin Heidegger, *Gesamtausgabe,* vol. 24, *Die Grundprobleme der Phänomenologie* (Frankfurt a.M.: Vittorio Klostermann, 1989), "Nachwort des Herausgebers," p. 471.

56. See Martin Heidegger, *The Basic Problems of Phenomenology,* trans. Albert Hofstadter (Bloomington: Indiana University Press, 1982), § 6, p. 23.

57. See Heidegger, *The Basic Problems of Phenomenology,* p. 35. These include Kant's thesis that being is not a real predicate, the medieval form of the Aristotelian view that the being of a being includes essence and existence, the modern ontological thesis that the basic ways of being include the being of nature or *res extensa* and the being of mind or *res cogitans*, and the logical thesis that all kinds of being can be discussed in terms of the "is" or copula.

58. See Heidegger, *The Basic Problems of Phenomenology,* p. 37.

59. See "Author's Preface to the Second Edition," in Heidegger, *Kant and the Problem of Metaphysics,* trans. Churchill (see chap. 3, n. 29), p. xxiii.

60. See Heidegger, *Kant and the Problem of Metaphysics,* p. xxiii.

61. See Heidegger, *Being and Time,* p. 45

62. See ibid., p. 49.

63. See "Vorbemerkung zur dritten Auflage," in Martin Heidegger, *Kant und das Problem der Metaphysik* (Frankfurt a.M.: Vittorio Klostermann, 1965), p. 8. This passage does not appear in the English translation, which was made from the second German edition.

64. By the term "repetition" Heidegger roughly means "to rethink what was possible beyond what in fact took place," in his words "the disclosure of the primordial possibilities concealed in it." Heidegger, *Kant and the Problem of Metaphysics,* p. 211. The concept of repetition is already present, in undeveloped form, in *Being and Time.* For instance, in a passage on the limitations of the positive sciences, particularly ethnology, Heidegger states that they cannot wait for philosophy, which needs to repeat ontologically what has already been accomplished ontically. See Heidegger, *Being and Time,* p. 76. For an application of the concept of repetition to the problem of being in general, see Heidegger, *An Introduction to Metaphysics,* p. 36.

65. For Cassirer's view of Heidegger's Kant interpretation, see Ernst Cassirer, "Kant und das Problem der Metaphysik: Bemerkungen zu Martin Heideggers Kant-Interpretation," *Kant-Studien* 36 (1931): pp. 1–26.

66. See foreword to Heidegger, *Kant and the Problem of Metaphysics,* pp. xii-xiii.

67. See Heidegger, *Kant and the Problem of Metaphysics,* § 35, "The Basic Originality of the Established Ground," pp. 201–208, and "Author's Preface to the Second Edition," p. xxv.

68. See ibid., p. 206.

69. See ibid., p. 207.

70. Ibid.

71. See Alexandre Kojève, *Introduction to the Reading of Hegel: Lectures on the Phenomenology of Spirit,* trans. James H. Nichols, Jr. (New York: Basic Books, 1969). For Kojève's enormous influence on later French thought, or what Heidegger would call the "confirmation" of his textually arbitrary interpretation, see Vincent Descombes, *Le même et l'autre. Quarante-cinq ans de philosophie française (1933–1978)* (Paris: Éditions de Minuit, 1979).

72. Heidegger, *Kant and the Problem of Metaphysics,* p. xxv.

73. For Kant's distinction between the letter and the spirit, see Kant, *Immanuel Kant's Critique of Pure Reason,* trans. Smith (see chap. 1, n. 12), B xliv, p. 37. For a recent, quasi-Heideggerian approach to the history of philosophy, see Jürgen Habermas, *Zur Rekonstruktion des historischen Materialismus* (Frankfurt a.M.: Suhrkamp, 1976), p. 9. What Habermas here refers to as "reconstruction" is a version of Heidegger's view of the historical and philosophical approach, which excludes a philological approach.

74. This is the reworked version of a lecture course delivered in the spring semester 1935.

75. See Heidegger, *An Introduction to Metaphysics,* p. 13. For another example, see Heidegger's remarks on the translation of *energeia* as *actus* in Heidegger, *Nietzsche* (see n. 85 below), 2:399, 413.

76. Heidegger, *An Introduction to Metaphysics,* p. 13.

77. For Quine's argument for the indeterminacy of translation, see his article "Ontological Relativity," in W. V. Quine, *Ontological Relativity and Other Essays* (New York: Columbia University Press, 1969), pp. 26–68.

78. See Heidegger, *An Introduction to Metaphysics*, p. 176.

79. Ibid.

80. See Martin Heidegger, *Holzwege* (Frankfurt a.M.: Vittorio Klostermann, 1950); *Vorträge und Aufsätze* (Pfullingen: Neske, 1954); *Wegmarken* (see chap. 3, n. 33).

81. Volume 50 of the *Gesamtausgabe* includes the course on Nietzsche's metaphysics announced for 1941/42, which was never given, as well as "Einleitung in die Philosophie—Denken und Dichten," 1944/45.

82. See Martin Heidegger, *Gesamtausgabe*, vol. 43, *Nietzsche: Der Wille zur Macht als Kunst: Wintersemester 1936/37;* vol. 44, *Nietzsches metaphysische Grundstellung im abendländischen Denken: Die Lehre von der ewigen Wiederkehr des Gleichen: Sommersemester 1937;* vol. 46, *Nietzsche II: Unzeitgemässe Betrachtung: Wintersemester 1938–39;* vol. 47, *Nietzsches Lehre vom Willen zur Macht als Erkenntnis: Sommersemester 1939;* vol. 48, *Nietzsche, der europäische Nihilismus. II. Trimester 1940;* vol. 50, *Nietzsches Metaphysik,* announced for winter semester 1941/42, but not given; *Einleitung in die Philosophie—Denken und Dichten: Wintersemester 1944/45.*

83. According to Vietta, between 1936 and the end of the war, Nietzsche was perhaps Heidegger's most important companion. See Vietta, *Heideggers Kritik am Nationalsozialismus und an der Technik,* p. 51.

84. See Martin Heidegger, "Nietzsches Wort 'Gott ist tot,' " in *Holzwege;* and "Wer ist Nietzsches Zarathustra," in *Vorträge und Aufsätze.*

85. See Martin Heidegger, *Nietzsche,* 2 vols. (Pfullingen: Neske, 1961).

86. See David Farrell Krell, "Analysis," in Martin Heidegger, *Nietzsche,* vol. 1, *The Will to Power as Art,* trans. David Farrell Krell (San Francisco: Harper and Row, 1979), p. 241.

87. See Gay, *Weimar Culture* (chap. 2, n. 9), pp. 31, 49, 125. See also Ernst Bertram, *Nietzsche: Versuch einer Mythologie* (Berlin: Georg Biondi, 1918). For more discussion on the interest of the George-Kreis in Nietzsche, see Walter Kaufmann, *Nietzsche: Philosopher, Psychologist, Antichrist* (Princeton: Princeton University Press, 1968), pp. 9–16 and 415–418.

88. See Ernst Gundolf and Kurt Hildebrandt, *Nietzsche als Richter unsrer Zeit* (Breslau: F. Hirt, 1922); see also Kurt Hildebrandt, *Nietzsches Wettkampf mit Sokrates und Plato* (Dresden: Sibyllenverlag, 1922), and Kurt Hildebrandt, *Wagner und Nietzsche: Ihr Kampf gegen das neunzehnte Jarhhundert* (Breslau, 1924).

89. See Wilhelm Windelband, *A History of Philosophy,* trans. James H. Tufts (New York: Harper and Brothers, 1958), p. 676.

90. For an appreciation of the relation between Nietzsche and Spengler, see Paul Hühnerfeld, *In Sachen Heideggers: Versuch über ein deutsches Genie* (Hamburg: Hoffmann und Campe), 1959, pp. 47–48: "Er [Spengler] gab Goethe und Nietzsche als die beiden Vorbilder an, denen er all verdanke. Aber es ist schwer, den weitsichtigen und weltmännischen Einfluss des Weimaraners in Spenglers

überpointiertem Buch [*Untergang des Abendlandes*] wiederzufinden (wenn man einmal von einigen Termini, wie zum Beispiel dem der 'Morphologie,' absieht). Und es ist ebenso schwer, in Spenglers Bemühung etwas anderes zu spüren als das typische Missverständnis, in dem sich das *fin de siècle* und das beginnende zwanzigste Jahrhundert Nietzsche gegenüber so kontinuierlich befand." Kaufmann suggests that Spengler accepts Nietzsche's denial of the unity of history but gives up Nietzsche's central point that the individual is not the pawn of the historical process. See Kaufmann, *Nietzsche: Philosopher, Psychologist, Antichrist*, p. 415.

91. See Hans Vaihinger, *Nietzsche als Philosoph* (Berlin, 1902); and the chapter entitled "Nietzsche und seine Lehre vom bewusst gewollten Schein," in *Die Philosophie des Als-Ob* (Berlin, 1911).

92. Georg Simmel, *Schopenhauer and Nietzsche,* trans. Helmut Loiskandl, Deena Weinstein, and Michael Weinstein (Amherst: University of Massachusetts Press, 1986).

93. Krell ties these three approaches respectively to Bauemler, Klages, and Jaspers. See Heidegger, *Nietzsche,* vol. 1, *The Will to Power as Art,* pp. 241–243.

94. Jaspers, who is the main representative of the existentialist reading of Nietzsche, also represents the Christian reading of his thought. See Karl Jaspers, *Nietzsche und das Christentum* (Hameln: Verlag der Bücherstube Fritz Seifert, n.d.).

95. For a fuller discussion, see Eckhard Heftrich, "Nietzsche im Denken Heideggers," in *Durchblicke* (Frankfurt a.M.: Vittorio Klostermann, 1970).

96. See Gadamer, *Truth and Method* (see chap. 1, n. 17), p. 228.

97. See Pöggeler, *Der Denkweg Martin Heideggers* (see chap. 2, n. 69), p. 105 (1963ed.). See also Otto Pöggeler, *Philosophie und Politik bei Heidegger* (Freiburg and Munich: Karl Alber, 1972), p. 25.

98. See Heidegger, *Nietzsche,* vol. 1, *The Will to Power as Art,* pp. 245–246.

99. See Heidegger, *Being and Time,* pp. 308, 317 n. 6, and 448.

100. See Taminiaux, "La présence de Nietzsche dans 'Etre et temps' " (see chap. 1, n. 22), p. 73: "Seul le traitement réservé à Nietzsche a l'allure d'un geste univoque de réappropriation sans distance."

101. See "Rectoral Address—Facts and Thoughts" (see chap. 2, n. 115), p. 474.

102. See ibid., pp. 484–485.

103. See Heidegger, *An Introduction to Metaphysics,* p. 36: "The task in hand is too crucial and at the same time too sobering. It consists first of all, if we are to gain a true grasp of Nietzsche, in bringing his accomplishment to a full unfolding."

104. See her *Nachwort* to Heidegger, *Gesamtausgabe,* vol. 44, *Nietzsches metaphysische Grundstellung im abendländischen Denken,* pp. 252–254. This paragraph is based on her discussion.

105. Cited in Heidegger, *Nietzsches metaphysische Grundstellung,* p. 254.

106. See *Was heisst Denken?* (Tübingen, 1954). This volume is available in translation as Martin Heidegger, *What Is Called Thinking?* trans. J. Glenn Gray (New York: Harper and Row, 1968).

107. Heidegger, *Being and Time,* p. 44.

108. See ibid., pp. 43–44. For an explicit description of Suarez's role in systematizing and transmitting Aristotle's metaphysical views, which were originally stated in unsystematic fashion, see Heidegger, *The Basic Problems of Phenomenology,* pp. 79–80.

109. Heidegger, *Being and Time,* p. 95.

110. On this point, see the *Beiträge zur Philosophie* (see chap. 1, n. 26), "The Age of the World Picture" (see chap. 3, n. 138), and the "Letter on Humanism" (see chap. 1, n. 29).

111. See Heidegger, *Being and Time,* pp. 94–95.

112. See ibid., p. 45.

113. See Heidegger, *Kant and the Problem of Metaphysics,* p. 208.

114. See Heidegger, *Being and Time,* p. 127.

115. See Heidegger, *The Basic Problems of Phenomenology,* p. 49.

116. See ibid., p. 55.

117. Ibid., p. 76.

118. See Heidegger, *Being and Time,* p. 250.

119. See ibid.

120. See ibid., p. 367.

121. See ibid., p. 369.

122. For Sartre's view of Marx, see Sartre, *Search for a Method* (see chap. 3, n. 5), and Sartre, *Critique de la raison dialectique* (see chap. 2, n. 160).

123. See G. W. F. Hegel, *The Difference between Fichte's and Schelling's System of Philosophy,* trans. H. S. Harris and Walter Cerf (Albany, N.Y.: State University of New York Press, 1977).

124. For a discussion of Hegel centered on the *Differenzschrift,* see Tom Rockmore, *Hegel's Circular Epistemology* (Bloomington and London: Indiana University Press, 1986).

125. See Alfred Baeumler, "Nietzsche und der Nationalsozialismus," in Baeumler, *Studien zur deutschen Geistesgeschichte* (see chap. 3, n. 46), pp. 281–294.

126. Carl August Emge, VB 6.4.1932, cited in Laugstien, *Philosophieverhältnisse* (see chap. 2, n. 25), p. 25.

127. See Algermissen, *Nietzsche und das Dritte Reich* (see chap. 3, n. 45), pp. 3–4. This paragraph is based on this passage from his book. See also D. Gawronsky, *Friedrich Nietzsche und das Dritte Reich* (Bern, 1935).

128. Cited in Algermissen, Nietzsche und das Dritte Reich, p. 3.

129. Cited ibid., p. 3.

130. Cited ibid.

131. See Ludwig Klages, *Die psychologischen Errungenschaften Nietzsches* (Leipzig: J. A. Barth, 1926).

132. See Baeumler, *Nietzsche, der Philosoph und Politiker (see chap. 3, n. 45).*

133. For a first acquaintance with the Nietzsche discussion in the Third Reich, see Alfredo Guzzoni, ed., *Neunzig Jahre philosophische Nietzsche-Rezeption* (Königstein, 1979); Wolfgang Müller-Lauter, *Aufnahme und*

Auseinandersetzung: Nietzsche im 20. Jahrhundert (Berlin, 1982); Algermissen, *Nietzsche und das Dritte Reich;* Karl Löwith, *Nietzsches Philosophie der ewigen Wiederkehr des Gleichen* (Stuttgart: Kohlhammer, 1956), "Anhang: Zur Geschichte der Nietzsche-Deutung (1894–1954)," pp. 199–225.

134. See Georg Lukács, *The Destruction of Reason,* trans. Peter Palmer (Atlantic Highlands, N.J.: Humanities Press, 1980), chap. 3, "Nietzsche as Founder of Irrationalism in the Modern Period," pp. 309–402.

135. See Lukács, *The Destruction of Reason,* pp. 536–537.

136. See Roderick Stackelberg, *Idealism Debased. From Völkisch Ideology to National Socialism* (Kent, Ohio: The Kent State University Press, 1981).

137. See Cassirer, *The Myth of the State* (see chap. 2, n. 131).

138. See Löwith, *Nietzsches Philosophie der ewigen Wiederkehr des Gleichen,* "Anhang: Zur Geschichte der Nietzsche-Deutung (1994–1954)," pp. 199–225.

139. See Jaspers's letter to Oehlkers, 22 December 1945, in Ott, *Martin Heidegger,* p. 317.

140. See Ott, *Martin Heidegger,* p. 186.

141. Derrida, for instance, has made this point. Before listing Heidegger's *mises en garde* concerning Nietzsche, Derrida correctly states that Heidegger's study of Nietzsche is less simple than it is commonly thought to be. See Jacques Derrida, *Éperons. Les styles de Nietzsche* (Paris: Flammarion, 1973), p.60.

142. See Heidegger, *Nietzsche* (German ed.; see n. 85).

143. See Martin Heidegger, *Nietzsche,* trans. David Farrell Krell [et al.], 4 vols. (San Francisco: Harper and Row, 1979–1987).

144. See Martin Heidegger, *Nietzsche: Der Wille zur Macht als Kunst, Wintersemester 1936/37,* ed. Bernd Heimbuchel (Frankfurt a.M.: Vittorio Klostermann, 1985), and Martin Heidegger, *Nietzsches metaphysisiche Grundstellung im abendländischen Denken: Die ewige Wiederkehr des Gleichen: Sommersemester 1937,* ed. Marion Heinz (Frankfurt a.M.: Vittorio Klostermann, 1986).

145. Heidegger, *The Will to Power as Art,* p. 5.

146. The approach to Plato in terms of his unwritten dialogues has become popular in recent years. Two of the foremost examples of this approach in English are Whitehead and Findlay. See Alfred North Whitehead, "Mathematics and the Good," in A. N. Whitehead, *The Interpretation of Science* (Indianapolis and New York: Bobbs-Merrill, 1961), pp. 187–203, and John Findlay, *Plato: The Written and Unwritten Dialogues* (New York: Humanities Press, 1974). For the influential Tübingen School discussion, see K. Geiser, *Platons ungeschriebene Lehre* (Stuttgart: Ernst Klett Verlag, 1963), and H. J. Krämer, *Arete bei Platon und Aristoteles: Zum Wesen und zur Geschichte der platonischen Ontologie* (Heidelberg: Carl Winter Universitätsbuchhandlung, 1959).

147. Heidegger, *The Will to Power as Art,* p. 3.

148. See ibid., p. 10.

149. Ibid., p. 17.

150. See ibid., p. 21.

151. See ibid., p. 10.

152. See ibid., p. 11.

153. See ibid., chap. 4, "The Unity of Will to Power, Eternal Recurrence, and Revaluation," p. 18–24.

154. Heidegger's discussion is highly selective. It picks out Baeumler and Jaspers among all the many interpreters, and it is further limited to two works only: Baeumler, *Nietzsche, der Philosoph und Politiker,* and Karl Jaspers, *Nietzsche: Einführung in das Verständnis seines Philosophierens* (Berlin and Leipzig: Walter de Gruyter, 1936). Significantly, he fails to take into account Jaspers's book on Nietzsche and Christianity as well as the many other writings by Bauemler in this domain.

155. The relation to the Nazi party is a significant factor. Ott reports that in 1936, Baeumler served as a Heidegger expert for the evaluation of Heidegger's personality by the Rosenberg Amt. See Ott, *Martin Heidegger,* p. 253.

156. See Heidegger, *The Will to Power as Art,* pp. 21–22. Heidegger's objections to Bauemler's reading concern his interpretation of the idea of the eternal recurrence. Löwith further reports that Bauemler misinterpreted the will to power as the will as power. See Löwith, *Mein Leben in Deutschland* (see chap. 2, n. 8), p. 140.

157. See Heidegger, *The Will to Power as Art,* pp. 22–23.

158. In a later passage in the lectures, which was omitted in the version published by Heidegger, he sharply attacks what he regards as Bauemler's clear misinterpretation of Nietzsche's doctrine of the will to power, which Bauemler allegedly tries merely to interpret away. See Heidegger, *Gesamtausgabe,* vol. 44, *Nietzsches metaphysische Grundstellung im abendländlischen Denken,* p. 229.

159. As concerns Jaspers, see, e.g., Richard Lowell Howey, *Heidegger and Jaspers on Nietzsche: A Critical Examination of Heidegger's and Jaspers's Interpretations of Nietzsche* (The Hague: Martinus Nijhoff, 1973). See also Kaufmann, *Nietzsche: Philosopher, Psychologist, Antichrist,* p. 34.

160. See Heidegger, *The Will to Power as Art,* p. 23

161. See ibid.

162. See Jaspers, *Notizen zu Martin Heidegger* (chap. 3, n. 11), §187, §38.

163. "Die bisherige Verfälschung der Philosophie Nietzsches," in Heidegger, *Gesamtausgabe,* vol. 43, *Nietzsche: Der Wille zur Macht als Kunst,* p. 278. This passage contrasts oddly with Heidegger's friendly remarks in two letters to Jaspers greeting the news that Jaspers is working on a book on Nietzsche. See Letter 120, Martin Heidegger to Karl Jaspers, 1 July 1935, Freiburg i.B., in *Briefwechsel 1920–1963* (see chap. 2, n. 27), pp. 157f. Heidegger writes in part (p. 157): "Irgendwer berichtet mir gelegentlich, dass Sie an einem Nietzschebuch arbeiteten, so darf ich mich darüber freuen, wie sehr das Strömen bei Ihnen auch nach dem großen Werk anhält." See also Letter 122, Martin Heidegger to Karl Jaspers, Freiburg, 16 May 1936, p. 160: "In Rom, wo ich den beiliegenden Vortrag über Hölderlin hielt, erfuhr ich, dass Sie an einem Werk über Nietzsche arbeiten. Im Februar dieses Jahres hatte ich für den kommenden Winter eine Vorlesung über Nietzsches 'Willen zur Macht' angekündigt; meine erste sollte es werden. Nur Ihr Werk vorliegt, brauche ich diesen Versuch nicht zu machen; denn eben dies war meine Absicht, was Sie im Vorwort klar und

einfach sagen: zu zeigen, dass es an der Zeit sei, vom Nietzsche-Lesen zur Arbeit überzugehen. Nun kann ich in der nächsten Stunde einfach auf Ihr Werk, das zudem für die Studenten erschwinglich ist, hinweisen. Und für den Winter werde ich eine andere Vorlesung wählen."

164. For instance, at the beginning of the long discussion of the doctrine of the eternal return of the same, he comments negatively on Ernst Bertram's view in his book, *Nietzsche: Versuch einer Mythologie* (see n. 87). See Heidegger, *The Eternal Recurrence of the Same*, pp. 5–6.

165. See Heidegger, *The Will to Power as Art*, p. 18.

166. To take a single example, according to Moehling, Heidegger's Nietzsche lectures were "outspoken assaults upon the Nazis' attempts to assimilate Nietzsche into the pantheon of National Socialist forerunners." See Karl A. Moehling, "Heidegger and the Nazis," in *Heidegger: The Man and the Thinker*, ed. Thomas Sheehan (Chicago: Precedent, 1981), p. 38.

167. See Walter Kaufmann, "Editor's Introduction," in Friedrich Nietzsche, *The Will to Power*, trans. Walter Kaufmann and R. J. Hollingdale, ed. Walter Kaufmann (New York: Vintage, 1968), pp. xii–xiv.

168. "Nachwort" to Friedrich Nietzsche, *Der Wille zur Macht*, ed. Alfred Baeumler (Leipzig: Alfred Kröner Verlag, 1930), p. 699.

169. On this point, see Kaufmann, "Editor's Introduction," p. xvi.

170. See Heidegger, *An Introduction to Metaphysics*, pp. 36f.

171. See ibid., p. 57.

172. See ibid., pp. 39, 91.

173. See ibid., p. 175.

174. See ibid., p. 45.

175. See ibid., p. 36.

176. See ibid., pp. 16, 159–160.

177. Heidegger, *The Will to Power as Art*, p. 18.

178. See ibid., p. 19.

179 See ibid., p. 18.

180. Ibid.

181. Ibid., p. 20.

182. Heidegger, *Being and Time*, § 45, p. 278. See further "Time and Being," in Heidegger, *On Time and Being*, trans. Stambaugh (see chap. 1, n. 11), pp. 1–24.

183. Heidegger, *Gesamtausgabe*, vol. 43, *Nietzsche: Der Wille zur Macht als Kunst*, p. 278.

184. See ibid., pp. 275–290 passim. For further mention of the crucial distinction between the *Leitfrage*, which designates all earlier metaphysical thought, including Heidegger's own initial position, and the *Grundfrage*, toward which Heidegger now turns, see, e.g., Heidegger, *The Eternal Recurrence of the Same* (see n. 38), par. 25, "The Essence of a Fundamental Metaphysical Position: The Possibility of Such Positions in the History of Western Philosophy," pp. 184–197 passim.

185. Heidegger, *The Will to Power as Art*, p. 20; translation modified.

186. See ibid.

187. Ibid., p. 24. The translator's use of the word "genuine" rather than "authentic" to translate "*eigentlich*" in this and other passages conceals rather than reveals the link between Heidegger's claim here and elsewhere to provide an authentic reading, which by implication differs in kind from others, and the concept of authenticity (*Eigentlichkeit*) in *Being and Time*.

188. Ibid.

189. Derrida, who seems to suggest an opposition between metaphysics and nonmetaphysics, is wrong to attribute it to Heidegger. See Derrida, *Éperons. Les styles de Nietzsche*, p. 96.

190. See Immanuel Kant, *Prolegomena to Any Future Metaphysics,* introd. Lewis White Beck (Indianapolis and New York: Library of Liberal Arts, 1950).

191. This is the theme of Heidegger's brief meditation on the relation of the eternal return of the same and the will to power, which opens the second volume of the Nietzsche lectures. See "Die ewige Wiederkehr des Gleichen und der Wille zur Macht," in Heidegger, *Nietzsche* (German ed.; see n. 85), 2:7–29. The second volume opens with the following sentence, which provides a categorical statement of Heidegger's view (ibid., p. 7): "Kaum eine Spur von Recht besteht zunächst, Nietzsches Philosophie als die *Vollendung* der abendländischen Metaphysik in Anspruch zu nehmen; denn sie ist durch die Abschaffung der 'übersinnlichen Welt' als der 'wahren' eher schon die Absage an alle Metaphysik und der Schritt zu ihrer endgültigen Verleugnung."

192. Any version of the claim to provide the authentic interpretation of a position is controversial. It is unclear whether Heidegger in fact "hears" or even "listens to" Nietzsche, into whose thought he may well "read" his own, in order to "find" what he was seeking. Derrida, for instance, who is deeply sympathetic to Heidegger, is sufficiently suspicious of his reading of Nietzsche to evoke the problem of how to save Nietzsche from the possibility of a Heideggerian type of reading. See Derrida, *Éperons,* p. 32. Heidegger supports the perception of this danger in his scornful rejection of the idea of capturing Nietzsche's view in itself. See Heidegger, *Gesamtausgabe,* vol. 43, *Nietzsche: Der Wille zur Macht als Kunst,* p. 277: "Der 'wirkliche' Nietzsche 'an sich'—nein!"

193. On this point, the unrevised lecture notes give an even clearer indication. See Heidegger, *Gesamtausgabe,* vol. 43, *Nietzsche: Der Wille zur Macht als Kunst,* p. 278, where he writes: "*Nietzsche* ist ein Übergang—das Höchste, was von einem Denker gesagt werden kann."

194. It will be useful to follow the German original for this purpose. The English translation, which includes a variety of other Heidegger materials on Nietzsche but omits portions of the two-volume format of the version prepared by him for publication, differs significantly. Such differences include material not available in the original as well as material that it omits but which is available elsewhere.

195. For a more detailed, but still not exhaustive, list of references to Nietzsche in Heidegger's writings, see Hildegard Feick, *Index zu Heideggers "Sein und Zeit"* (Tübingen: Niemeyer Verlag, 1968), p. 120.

196. On the relation of art and truth, see his 1935 essay, "The Origin of the Work of Art," in Heidegger, *Basic Writings,* trans. Krell, pp. 143–188, esp. pp. 178–188.

197. Heidegger, *The Will to Power as Art,* p. 218; translation modified.

198. See Heidegger, *The Eternal Recurrence of the Same,* p. 205.

199. See ibid.

200. See ibid., p. 206.

201. See Heidegger, *Nietzsche* (German ed.), 1:639.

202. See ibid., vol. 1, part 3, *Der Wille zur Macht als Erkenntnis,* "Nietzsches angeblicher Biologismus," pp. 517–526.

203. See Heidegger, *Nietzsche* (German ed.), 1:642.

204. See ibid., p. 656.

205. See ibid., vol. 2, *Der europäische Nihilismus,* pp. 31–256. The volume contains 481 pages, including the *Inhalt* and *Übersicht.* This discussion of European nihilism is available in translation under the title *Nihilism.* See Heidegger, *Nietzsche* (see n. 143), vol. 4, *Nihilism,* trans. Frank A. Capuzzi.

206. See, e.g., Hermann Rauschning, *The Revolution of Nihilism: Warning to the West,* trans. E. W. Dickes (New York: Alliance Book Corporation, Longmans, Green and Co., 1939). Rauschning argues that National Socialism, which has no doctrine, leads to nihilism. See ibid., chap. 1: "The Road to Nihilism," pp. 3–58. See further Carl Schmitt, *Political Romanticism,* trans. Guy Oakes (Cambridge, Mass.: MIT Press, 1986). Schmitt argues, in a book published in 1919, in a striking anticipation of Heidegger's reading of Nietzsche, that a nihilism has been created by the death of the traditional concept of God. See ibid., pp. 58–59, 82, 91.

207. See Heidegger, *Being and Time,* p. 69.

208. See ibid., p. 223.

209. "What Is Metaphysics?" in Heidegger, *Basic Writings,* p. 105.

210. See Heidegger, *Basic Writings,* pp. 105–106. Heidegger's opposition between being and nothingness is transformed by Sartre as the basis of his existential position. See Jean-Paul Sartre, *Being and Nothingness,* trans. Hazel Barnes (New York: Washington Square Press, 1973).

211. See Heidegger, *Basic Writings,* p. 110.

212. See "Rectoral Address—Facts and Thoughts" (see chap. 2, n. 115), p. 474.

213. Heidegger refers to *Being and Time,* § 38, pp. 223–224.

214. Heidegger, *An Introduction to Metaphysics,* p. 37; translation modified.

215. See ibid., pp. 38–39.

216. Ibid., p. 39; translation modified.

217. Heidegger, *Nihilism,* p. 4.

218. See ibid., pp. 59–60.

219. Ibid., p. 4.

220. Ibid., p. 5.

221. See ibid., p. 132.

222. See ibid., p. 123.

223. See ibid., p. 103.

224. See ibid., p. 136.

225. See ibid., p. 195.

226. Ibid., p. 196; translation modified.

227. Krell argues for the replacement of "*Geschehnis*" by "*Ereignis*" beginning with chapter 20 of *The Will to Power as Art* but fails to perceive how that replacement is related either to the *Beiträge*, whose unpublished text he may not have known, or to the problem of the turning in Heidegger's thought. "Note that the 'event' of nihilism, cited four times in this and the following paragraphs, occasions perhaps the earliest 'terminological' use of the word *Ereignis* in Heidegger's published writings." Heidegger, *The Will to Power as Art*, p. 156n. This observation is only correct if Heidegger's lecture courses are omitted. In fact, words such as "*Ereignis*" and "*ereignen*" occur much earlier in Heidegger's writings, beginning with his initial lecture series during the *Kriegsnotsemester* in 1919. See Heidegger, *Gesamtausgabe*, vol. 56/57, *Zur Bestimmung der Philosophie*, ed. Bernd Heimbüchel (Frankfurt a.M.: Vittorio Klostermann, 1987), passim.

228. See Heidegger, *An Introduction to Metaphysics*, p. 37; Heidegger, *Einführung in die Metaphysik* (see n. 8), p. 28; Heidegger, *Gesamtausgabe*, vol. 40, *Einführung in die Metaphysik*, par. 10, p. 40.

229. See the parallel passages in Heidegger, *The Will to Power as Art*, par. 20, and *Nihilism*, par. 29; Heidegger, *Nietzsche* (German ed.), vol. 1, *Wahrheit im Platonismus und im Positivismus: Nietzsches Versuch einer Umdrehung des Platonismus aus der Grunderfahrung des Nihilismus*, and vol. 2, *Der europäische Nihilismus*, chap. 5, "Das Sein als die Leere und der Reichtum"; Heidegger, *Gesamtausgabe*, vol. 48, *Nietzsche: Der europäische Nihilismus* (Frankfurt a.M.: Vittorio Klostermann, 1986), "Schluss: Der vergessene Unterschied des Seins und des Seienden und das Ende der abendländischen Philosophie als Metaphysik," pars. 32–35.

230. See Heidegger, *Basic Writings*, p. 208. For Heidegger's interpretation of the turning in his thought, see his preface to William Richardson, *Heidegger: Through Phenomenology to Thought* (The Hague: Martinus Nijhoff, 1974), pp. viii–xxii. For a recent summary of discussion concerning the turning, see Thomä, *Die Zeit des Selbst und die Zeit danach* (see Introd., n. 6), pp. 459–465. Thomä denies the existence of a *Kehre* in Heidegger's thought. For a version of this view, see Lacoue-Labarthe, *L'imitation des modernes* (see chap. 2, n. 123), p. 236. For a detailed study of the turning in Heidegger's thought, see Jean Grondin, *Le tournant dans la pensée de Martin Heidegger* (Paris: Presses universitaires de France, 1987). See also Alberto Rosales, "Zum Problem der Kehre im Denken Heideggers," *Zeitschrift für philosophische Forschung*, 1984: 241–262. According to Thomä, the term occurs for the first time in Heidegger's 1928 summer lecture series: "Diese temporale Analytik ist (. . .) zugleich die *Kehre*." Heidegger, *Gesamtausgabe*, vol. 26, *Metaphysische Anfangsgründe der Logik im Ausgang von Leibniz*, ed. Klaus Held (Frankfurt a.M.: Vittorio Klostermann, 1978), p. 201 (Heidegger's emphasis), cited in Thomä, *Die Zeit des Selbst und die Zeit danach*, p. 458.

231. See Karl Marx, *Capital*, ed. Friedrich Engels, trans. Samuel Moore and

Edward Aveling (New York: International Publishers, 1967), 1:20. For a discussion of various forms of philosophical reversal, see Jean-François Mattéi, "Le chiasme heideggérien," in Dominique Janicaud and Jean-François Mattéi, *La métaphysique à la limite* (Paris: Presses universitaires de France, 1983), pp. 49–162.

232. See Heidegger, *Basic Writings*, p. 208.

233. See ibid.

234. See chap. 5, "The Structure of the 'Major Work': Nietzsche's Manner of Thinking as Reversal [Umkehrung]," in Heidegger, *The Will to Power as Art*, pp. 25–33, and chap. 20, "Truth in Platonism and Positivism: Nietzsche's Overturning [Umdrehung] of Platonism," ibid., pp. 151–161.

235. See Heidegger, *The Will to Power as Art*, pp. 29, 30.

236. See ibid., p. 210.

237. See Heidegger, *Nietzsche* (German ed.), 1:654.

238. For an effort to correlate the turning in Heidegger's thought to his Nietzsche lectures, see Hannah Arendt, *The Life of the Mind: Willing* (New York and London: Harcourt Brace Jovanovich, 1978), "Heidegger's Will-not-to-will," pp. 172–194. Her interpretation of the turning as primarily a turn against the will to will is hardly plausible. It is plausible only if his turning is mainly directed against Nietzsche, whereas there is abundant evidence that (1) in *Being and Time* the connection of Heidegger's view with Nietzsche is not central; (2) in the course of these lectures, Heidegger took Nietzsche increasingly seriously; (3) in the attempt to think with Nietzsche against Nietzsche, Heidegger does not turn against Nietzsche, or even against the idea of the will to power, which he seeks to realize even against Nietzsche.

239. I disagree with Grondin's thesis that the turning is a turning of Being, since there is an obvious turning in Heidegger's thought as a result of his reading of the turning of Being through Nietzsche's insight. See Grondin, *Le tournant dans la pensée de Martin Heidegger*, p. 101.

240. Heidegger, *Introduction to Metaphysics*, p. 39.

241. Ibid., pp. 38–39; translation modified. According to Heidegger, Nietzsche's failure to attain the true center is due to his stubborn adherence to a theory of values. See ibid., p. 199.

242. "Only a God Can Save Us" (see chap. 1, n. 30), p. 275.

243. See Arendt, *The Life of the Mind: Willing*, p. 173. Pöggeler specifically disputes her claim that Nietzsche helped Heidegger to turn against Nazism. He argues it was precisely the study of Nietzsche and the pre-Socratics which led to the turn to National Socialism. See Otto Pöggeler, "Heidegger, Nietzsche, and Politics," in *Heidegger and Politics*, ed. Tom Rockmore and Joseph Margolis (Philadelphia: Temple University Press, forthcoming).

244. See Aubenque, "Encore Heidegger et le nazisme" (chap. 2, n. 59) p. 121.

245. See Heidegger, *Basic Writings*, pp. 27–28.

246. See Vietta, *Heideggers Kritik am Nationalsozialismus und an der Technik*, chap. 4, "Heideggers Nietzsche-Lektüre: Kritik der Weltanschauungen und Nihilismusbegriff," pp. 48–68, esp. pp. 66–68.

247. Heidegger, *Gesamtausgabe,* vol. 42, *Schelling: Vom Wesen der menschlichen Freiheit* (Frankfurt a.M.: Vittorio Klostermann, 1988), pp. 40–41. Carl Ulmer called attention to this passage in *Der Spiegel,* 2 May 1977, p. 152.

248. Heidegger, *Gesamtausgabe,* vol. 43, *Nietzsche: Der Wille zur Macht als Kunst,* p. 193. Heidegger was apparently concerned with the relation between Nietzsche's aphorism about the death of God and atheism. He evokes this theme in the first series of Hölderlin lectures as well. See Heidegger, *Hölderlins Hymnen "Germanien" und "Der Rhein"* (see chap. 3, n. 144), p. 95.

249. Krell accepts, with reservations, the claim that there is a shift in tone but denies that there is a polemic with Nietzsche. See Heidegger, *Nihilism,* pp. 272–273.

250. The controversy with Nietzsche is not confined to Nietzsche lectures. It is a main theme in the first part of the 1951/52 lecture series. See Heidegger, *What Is Called Thinking?* trans. Gray (see n. 106), passim, esp. p. 70. The controversy continues in later writings. It is present as an underlying theme in the subsequent analysis of technology which in part supposes a Nietzschean orientation.

251. Heidegger, *Nihilism,* p. 196.

Chapter 5: Nazism and the *Beiträge zur Philosophie*

1. More than a quarter of a century ago, Pöggeler provided a helpful but overly brief introduction to this text. See Pöggeler, *Der Denkweg Martin Heideggers* (see chap. 2, n. 69), pp. 143–145.

2. Unless otherwise indicated, all translations from the *Beiträge* are my own.

3. In a work that has just appeared, Vietta devotes a large part of a chapter to this text. See Vietta, *Heideggers Kritik am Nationalsozialismus und an der Technik* (see chap. 1, n. 31), chap. 5, "Kritik am Nationalsozialismus und an der Technik in den 'Beiträgen zur Philosophie' in der Spätphilosophie," pp. 69–94. See also Reiner Schürmann, "Riveted to a Monstrous Site: On Heidegger's *Beiträge zur Philosophie,*" in *Heidegger and Politics,* ed. Rockmore and Margolis (see chap. 4, n. 243).

4. According to Vietta, it is possible that Heidegger's work on the book lasted until the beginning of 1939. See Vietta, *Heideggers Kritik am Nationalsozialismus und an der Technik,* p. 70.

5. See Heidegger, *Beiträge* (see chap. 1, n. 26), p. 514. This description is controversial. Vietta, who had possession of the handwritten original that was used for the edition printed in the *Gesamtausgabe,* reports that the manuscript consists of loose sheets of format DIN A4 and some of format DIN A5, bundled together in the form of *Konvoluten* with other sheets of format DIN A4 attached in the middle. See Vietta, *Heideggers Kritik am Nationalsozialismus und an der Technik,* p. 71.

6. The editor notes that the publication of this work in Heidegger's *Gesamtausgabe* was retarded to a point fourteen years after the beginning of the

publication of his complete writings by Heidegger's conviction that it needed to be preceded by publication of his lecture courses. Heidegger held that study of his lecture courses constituted an indispensable condition for the understanding of his writings from the 1930s and first half of the 1940s. See Heidegger, *Beiträge,* p. 513.

7. According to Thomä, it is merely the outline of a work which was never written. See Thomä, *Die Zeit des Selbst und die Zeit danach* (see Introd., n. 6), p. 763.

8. For a section in which the main discussion is interrupted in the middle for another discussion, see Heidegger, *Beiträge,* § 110, pp. 208–222, discussed below. For a section that lacks verbs, see Heidegger, *Beiträge,* § 247, p. 392, which ends with the following passage: "Maschinenerziehung; die Machenschaft und das Geschäft. Welche Umwandlung des Menschen setzt hier ein? (Welt—Erde?) Machenschaft und das Geschäft. Die grosse Zahl, das Riesige, reine Ausdehnung und wachsende Verflachung und Entleerung. Das notwendige Verfallen dem Kitsch und dem Unechten."

9. An example, picked at random, is the verb "*vergötzen*," obviously related to the noun "*Götze*," meaning an "essence or image worshiped as a deity; a false god," or further "*Götzenbild*," namely "the representation of such a false god." See Heidegger, *Beiträge,* § 251, p. 398.

10. Heidegger writes: " 'Das Seyn' als Abschnitt II ist nicht richtig eingereiht; als Versuch, das Ganze noch einmal zu fassen, gehört er nicht an diese Stelle." Cited in Heidegger, *Beiträge,* p. 514. For von Herrmann's defense of his editorial decision concerning the proper place of this part of the manuscript, see ibid., pp. 514–515.

11. See Heidegger, *Beiträge,* p. 514.

12. In the "Afterword to the Second Edition" of his well-known study of Heidegger, Pöggeler wrote: "The *Beiträge* were for me Heidegger's major work." Otto Pöggeler, *Martin Heidegger's Path of Thinking,* trans. David Magurshak and Sigmund Barber (Atlantic Highlands, N.J.: Humanities Press, 1987), pp. 286–287. In a more recent passage, written after this text appeared, in a description of the loneliness which Heidegger endured after his withdrawal from the rectorate, Pöggeler writes: "In dieser Einsamkeit schrieb Heidegger 1936–38 sein eigentliches Hauptwerk, die 'Beiträge zur Philosophie'." Otto Pöggeler, " 'Praktische Philosophie' als Antwort an Heidegger," in *Martin Heidegger und das "Dritte Reich,"* ed. Martin (see chap. 2, n. 176), p. 85.

13. See Alexander Schwan, "Verliebt in Untergang und Abgrund," *Rheinischer Merkur, Christ und Welt,* no. 17 (28 April 1989), p. 15.

14. See Schwan, "Verliebt in Untergang und Abgrund," p. 15: "Die 'Beiträge' sind ein einziges grosses Dementi für Victor Farias' Behauptung, Heidegger sei anhaltend, auch im ideologischen Sinne, ein überzeugter Nationalsozialist gewesen!"

15. See Schwan, "Verliebt in Untergang und Abgrund," p. 15: "Die 'Beiträge' sind jedoch eine eindeutige Absage an die Verstrickungen von 1933, die sich als Folge verhängnisvoller Verquickungen von Seinsdenken und politischem Aktionismus erweisen."

16. See Schwan, "Verliebt in Untergang und Abgrund," p. 15: "So werden die 'Beiträge' zum grossen Widerruf alles dessen, was für Heidegger mit 1933 verbunden war. Sie führen jedoch nicht zur aktiven Wende gegen die zur blanken Tyrranei ausgearteten 'Machenschaften' des Nationalsozialismus, sondern lediglich zur 'Einkehr' in den Verzicht auf jegliches Tun, allerdings unter fortwährenden Unmutsbekundungen, also doch nicht aus gänzlich freien Stücken." Already in his book on Heidegger's political philosophy, Schwan claimed that the relation between Heidegger's thought and Nazism could not be maintained after 1933 to the same degree as in 1933 unless Heidegger simply abandoned philosophy. See Schwan, *Politische Philosophie im Denken Heideggers* (see chap. 3, n. 115), p. 101. Schwan seems not fully to have realized the extent of the compatibility between Heidegger's thought and Nazism and the durable nature of his commitment.

17. "Mehr als fünzig Jahre nach ihrer Entstehung erscheinen im Jubiläumsjahr des 100. Geburtstages des Denkers als ein weiteres Hauptwerk erstmals Martin Heideggers 'Beiträge zur Philosophie (Vom Ereignis)'." Heidegger, *Beiträge*, p. 511.

18. See Vietta, *Heideggers Kritik am Nationalsozialismus und an der Technik*, p. 69: "Die anlässlich des 100. Geburtstages Martin Heideggers veröffentlichten 'Beiträgen zur Philosophie' sind das wohl wichtigste Hauptwerk Heideggers nach 'Sein und Zeit'."

19. Vietta builds his case for Heidegger as someone who later became a staunch opponent of Nazism on his analysis of this text. See Vietta, *Heideggers Kritik am Nationalsozialismus und an der Technik*.

20. See Otto Pöggeler, "Heidegger, Nietzsche, and Politics," in *Heidegger and Politics*, ed. Rockmore and Margolis (see chap. 4, n. 243).

21. See Thomä, *Die Zeit des Selbst und die Zeit danach*, p. 767.

22. See Nicolas Tertulian, "Histoire de l'être et révolution politique: Réflexions sur un ouvrage posthume de Heidegger," in *Heidegger and Politics*, ed. Rockmore and Margolis.

23. Vietta, who was in possession of the original manuscript, states that when Heidegger numbered the pages so that his brother Fritz Heidegger could retype the handwritten manuscript, he left out a number of *Zetteln* that were also not published in the *Gesamtausgabe*. See Vietta, *Heideggers Kritik am Nationalsozialismus und an der Technik*, p. 71. He has further published an important fragment which, if it indeed comes from the manuscript, amply demonstrates his point. See ibid., pp. 93–94.

24. See Heidegger, "Letter on Humanism" (see chap. 1, n. 29), pp. 207–208. Grondin's discussion of the *Kehre* appeared prior to the first publication of the *Beiträge*. See Grondin, *Le tournant dans la pensée de Martin Heidegger* (see chap. 4, n. 230).

25. Heidegger, *Basic Writings* (see chap. 1, n. 10), p. 242.

26. For Heidegger's own self-interpretation, see his "Letter to Richardson," in William J. Richardson, *Heidegger: Through Phenomenology to Thought* (The Hague: Nijhoff, 1963), pp. ix-xxiii.

27. See Heidegger, *Beiträge*, p. 4: "Die 'Beiträge' fragen in einer Bahn, die

durch den *Übergang* zum anderen Anfang, in den jetzt das abendländische Denken einrückt, erst gebahnt wird."

28. See Heidegger, *Gesamtausgabe*, vol. 45, *Grundfragen der Philosophie: Ausgewählte "Probleme" der "Logik," Freiburger Vorlesung Wintersemester 1937/38,* ed. Wilhelm-Friedrich von Herrmann (Frankfurt a.M.: Vittorio Klostermann, 1984).

29. Heidegger, *Being and Time,* p. 261

30. Ibid., p. 265.

31. Ibid., p. 269.

32. Ibid.

33. "On the Essence of Truth," in Heidegger, *Basic Writings,* p. 138.

34. See Heidegger, *Beiträge,* p. 3: "Der öffentliche Titel: Beiträge zur Philosophie und die wesentliche Überschrift: Vom Ereignis." For further discussion of the title, see ibid., § 39, "Das Ereignis," pp. 80–82.

35. Apparently emphasizing the preliminary form of the manuscript that is the basis of the published version of the work, Heidegger states that its correct title would be "Das Ereignis." See Heidegger, *Beiträge,* p. 77.

36. In this work, Heidegger consistently writes "Sein" as "Seyn" in order to emphasize that he is attempting to make a new beginning.

37. Heidegger, *Beiträge,* p. 3. See also ibid., p. 31.

38. Ibid., p. 3.

39. Heidegger does not strictly observe this convention prior to this text. So in the first series of Hölderlin lectures, where he is already beginning to make this distinction, he does not consistently maintain this linguistic distinction. See "Nachwort des Herausgebers" in Heidegger, *Hölderlins Hymnen "Germanien" und "Der Rhein"* (see chap. 3, n. 144), p. 295.

40. See Heidegger, *Beiträge,* §§ 3, 4, 7, 8, 10.

41. See ibid., §§ 35 and 39.

42. See ibid., §§ 20, 21, 22, 23, 24, 27, 28, 29, 30, 31.

43. See ibid., §§ 43, 44, 45, 46, 47, 48, 49.

44. Michael Zimmerman emphasizes its fugue-like character in his review of it in the *Times Literary Supplement,* 16–22 March 1990, p. 295.

45. See *Beiträge,* p. 132. The concept of enframing is prominent in the later discussion on technology. See in particular "The Question concerning Technology," in Heidegger, *The Question concerning Technology and Other Essays* (see chap. 3, n. 56).

46. Heidegger, *Beiträge,* p. 407. It is difficult to translate this passage since Heidegger here avails himself of two terms, namely *"Zirkel"* and *"Kreis,"* where English has only the single word "circle."

47. See Heidegger, *Beiträge,* pp. 408–409.

48. This section is 103 pages long, in a book 510 pages in length.

49. See Heidegger, *Beiträge,* p. 5.

50. See ibid., p. 6.

51. See ibid., p. 7.

52. Ibid., p. 8.

53. Ibid., p. 10.

54. See ibid., p. 11.

55. Ibid., p. 31.

56. See ibid., p. 32.

57. Heidegger, *Being and Time*, § 45, p. 274.

58. See Heidegger, *Beiträge*, p. 35. One of Heidegger's problems in the transition to a new beginning is to find a way to reconceptualize his basic distinctions from *Being and Time*. Slightly earlier, in the initial Hölderlin lecture series, he describes care as the metaphysical basic essence of Dasein. See Heidegger, *Hölderlins Hymnen "Germanien" und "Der Rhein,"* p. 281.

59. Heidegger, *Beiträge*, p. 52.

60. See Frederick Engels, *Ludwig Feuerbach and the Outcome of Classical German Philosophy*, ed. C. P. Dutt (New York: International Publishers, 1941).

61. Heidegger, *Beiträge*, p. 59.

62. Ibid., p. 65.

63. Ibid., p. 76.

64. See ibid., p. 75.

65. Ibid., p. 85.

66. Ibid., p. 93.

67. Ibid., p. 94.

68. Ibid., p. 95.

69. Vietta's overly selective effort to discuss this theme merely in terms of the second part of the *Beiträge* means that in effect he takes the part for the whole. The inevitable result is a distortion of Heidegger's understanding of National Socialism in this work. See Vietta, *Heideggers Kritik am Nationalsozialismus und an der Technik*, chap. 5, pp. 69–94, esp. p. 72.

70. See "Rectoral Address—Facts and Thoughts" (chap. 2, n. 115), p. 490.

71. See Heidegger, *Beiträge*, § 273, "Geschichte," p. 493: "Blut und Rasse werden zu Trägern der Geschichte." For Heidegger's distinction between history and historicality, see Heidegger, *Being and Time*, part 2, chap. 5, "Temporality and Historicality."

72. According to Vietta, who has had access to the manuscript material conserved in the Heidegger Archives at Marbach, when the material becomes accessible it will be seen that Heidegger was deeply ashamed of what he had done. See Vietta, *Heideggers Kritik am Nationalsozialismus und an der Technik*, p. 101. This point is confirmed indirectly by a letter from Heidegger to Jaspers in which the following passage occurs: "Ich bin seit 1935 nicht deshalb nicht mehr in Ihr Haus gekommen, weil dort eine jüdische Frau wohnte, sondern *weil ich mich einfach schämte.*" See Letter 141, Heidegger to Jaspers, Freiburg i.B., 7 March 1950, in *Briefwechsel 1920–1963* (see chap. 2, n. 27), p. 196; Heidegger's emphases.

73. In the appendix to this lecture, in the published version, after a reference to Descartes's supposedly anthropological approach, Heidegger writes: "Through this, the intellectual situation finds some clarification, while the laborious fabrications of such absurd off-shoots as the national-socialist philosophies produce nothing but confusion." Heidegger, *The Question concerning Technology and Other Essays*, p. 140. Vietta refers to a passage present in the handwrit-

ten manuscript in which Heidegger objects to the approach taken in the *Rekoratsrede*. See Vietta, *Heideggers Kritik am Nationalsozialismus und an der Technik*, p. 32. But it is important to see that Heidegger does not criticize his earlier adherence to Nazism; rather, from the vantage point of the other beginning he is now critical of his earlier philosophical commitment to a "philosophically" unacceptable form of theory.

74. See Martin Heidegger, "Anmerkungen zu Karl Jaspers 'Psychologie der Weltanschauungen' (1919/21)," in *Gesamtausgabe*, vol. 9, *Wegmarken*, ed. F. W. von Herrmann (Frankfurt a.M.: Vittorio Klostermann, 1976), pp. 1–44. For Jaspers's response to Heidegger's criticism, see "Vorwort zur dritten Auflage (1925)," cited ibid., pp. 481–482.

75. See Heidegger, *The Basic Problems of Phenomenology*, trans. Hofstadter (see chap. 4, n. 56), § 2, p. 7.

76. Heidegger is, of course, not the only philosophical critic of the Nazi worldview. For another criticism, from the perspective of orthodox Marxism, see Lukács, *The Destruction of Reason* (see chap. 4, n. 134), esp. chap. 7, part 5: "The 'National-Socialist Philosophy' ["national-sozialistische Weltanschauung"] as the demagogic synthesis of German imperialist philosophy," pp. 714–764. There is a striking difference in the ways that the Marxist Lukács and the Nazi Heidegger analyze the same phenomenon. The former sees the philosophy of the worldview as the result of the rise of irrationalism due ultimately to the capitalist form of political economy, whereas the latter attributes it to the age of metaphysics and hence ultimately to Being.

77. Heidegger, *Beiträge*, p. 25.

78. Ibid.

79. Ibid., p. 26.

80. See Heidegger, *Hölderlins Hymnen "Germanien" und "Der Rhein,"* p. 1.

81. See Heidegger, *Beiträge*, § 45, "Die Entscheidung," pp. 96–99.

82. Heidegger, *Beiträge*, p. 96.

83. There is a clear analogy between Heidegger's view of the historical conditions under which individuals become a people and the later Sartre's view of the revolutionary situation, or *groupe-en-fusion*. See Sartre, *Critique de la raison dialectique* (see chap. 2, n. 160).

84. Heidegger, *Beiträge*, p. 97.

85. See ibid., § 56: "The lasting nature [das Währen] of the abandonment of Being [Seinsverlassenheit] in the hidden way of the forgetfulness of Being [Seinsvergessenheit]," pp. 116–119.

86. Ibid., pp. 116–117. The observation that *Seiende* is subordinate to *Seyn* shows that in the remark on the prevailing understanding of Being (*das herrschende Seinsverständnis*) Heidegger does not have in mind something as concrete as National Socialism. Rather, he is referring to the continued rule of the first beginning, itself a consequence of the age of metaphysics, whereas his aim is to progress beyond this initial stage to the other beginning beyond metaphysics.

87. See Ibid., pp. 117–119.

88. Ibid., p. 117.

89. It is possible that Heidegger's objection to a supposed insensitivity to the ambiguous character of experience is a distant echo of his initial phenomenological fascination with Franz Brentano's dissertation on the manifold forms of being in Aristotle, "Von der mannigfachen Bedeutung des Seienden nach Aristoteles." For Heidegger's later description of the importance of his reading of Brentano's dissertation for *Being and Time*, see Martin Heidegger, in *Sitzungsberichte der Heidelberger Akademie der Wissenschaften*, 1957/58:20f., quoted in Ott, *Martin Heidegger* (see Introd., n. 4), p. 54.

90. According to Pechman, Rosenberg was highly dismayed to learn at the Nuremberg trials that the "Nazi-Bonzen" had not in fact read his work. See Laugstien, *Philosophieverhältnisse* (see chap. 2, n. 25), p. 51.

91. See Heidegger, *Beiträge,* § 69, "Das Erlebnis und die Anthropologie," pp. 134–135.

92. Ibid., p. 134.

93. It is also possible that Heidegger's objection is directed against contemporary thinkers who attempted to combine the National Socialist worldview with an anthropological perspective, such as Rothacker and especially Gehlen. See Haug, *Deutsche Philosophen 1933* (see chap. 2, n. 25), pp. 137 and 188–218.

94. See Heidegger, *Beiträge,* § 72, "Der Nihilismus," pp. 138–141.

95. Ibid., p. 139.

96. See ibid., pp. 141–143.

97. Ibid., p. 142.

98. See ibid., p. 208.

99. See ibid., § 110, pp. 208–222.

100. See ibid., pp. 218–219. The significance of the rejection of biologism here is unclear. It might refer to the Nazi insistence on race, or it might refer to Nietzsche's biological interpretation of knowledge.

101. Heidegger, *Beiträge,* p. 219. There is an obvious similarity between this passage and Heidegger's claim in the article on the rectorate that through Nietzsche's metaphysics, as interpreted by Jünger, one is able to see and foresee the history and present day of the Western world. See "Rectoral Address—Facts and Thoughts," p. 484.

102. Heidegger, *Beiträge,* p. 219.

103. See ibid., part 5, a) "Da-sein und Seinsentwurf," §§ 168–186, and b) "Das Da-sein," §§ 187–203, pp. 293–326.

104. See ibid., § 194, "Der Mensch und das Da-sein," pp. 317–318.

105. See ibid., § 195, "Da-sein und Mensch," p. 318.

106. Ibid., § 196, "Da-sein und Volk," p. 319.

107. See Heidegger, *Being and Time,* § 29: "Being-there as State-of-mind [Stimmung]," pp. 172–179, etc.

108. Heidegger, *Beiträge,* p. 319. It does not seem possible to reproduce gracefully in English Heidegger's play in German on the distinctions between *bilden* and *verbilden* in this passage.

109. See ibid., part 7, "Der letzte Gott," §§ 253–256, pp. 405–416.

110. See ibid., part 6: "Die Zu-künftigen," §§ 248–252, pp. 396–401: § 251, "Das Wesen des Volkes und Da-sein," and § 252, "Das Da-sein und die Zukünftigen des letzten Gottes."

111. See ibid., § 256, p. 411. The reference to the "last god" in Heidegger's antifoundationalist approach is consistent with the earlier adumbration of nihilism in the *Rektoratsrede* and elsewhere on the basis of Nietzsche's assertion that God is dead.

112. See ibid., § 248, p. 395.

113. See ibid., § 250, p. 396.

114. See ibid., § 251, "Das Wesen des Volkes und Da-sein," pp. 398–399. This view appears earlier in ibid., § 196, p. 319.

115. See Heidegger, *Being and Time,* § 26, p. 159.

116. Heidegger, *Beiträge,* pp. 398–399.

117. Ibid., p. 399.

118. See Kant, *Immanuel Kant's Critique of Pure Reason,* trans. Smith (see chap. 1, n. 12), B 867, p. 658.

119. See Heidegger, *Beiträge,* § 252, pp. 399–401.

120. Ibid., p. 399.

121. Marx's view of the difference between human prehistory and human history, which will begin when the transition from capitalism to communism has been undertaken, is developed in a number of places, for instance in the third of the "Paris Manuscripts of 1844." See Marx, *Early Writings* (see chap. 2, n. 130), pp. 135–144. For Heidegger's clear statement of a similar view, see Heidegger, *Beiträge,* § 273, p. 492: "Bisher *war* der Mensch noch niemals geschichtlich."

122. See Heidegger, *Beiträge,* part 8, "Das Seyn," § 275, "Das Seiende," pp. 495–497.

123. See ibid., § 274, "Das Seiende und die Berechnung," pp. 494–495.

124. Ibid., p. 496. "*Verklärung*" normally means "Erhöhung ins Über-erdische" as Christ is said to have been raised up.

125. Vietta, who has to date provided the most extensive philosophical defense of Heidegger's supposed turn away from Nazism, writes in a summary passage of his view: "Als Gesamtergebnis kann festgehalten werden: der von Habermas und anderen vorgebrachte Vorwurf einer gleichbleibenden Nähe Heideggers zum Faschismus ist nicht haltbar. Der Vorwurf ist durch die Texte widerlegt." Vietta, *Heideggers Kritik am Nationalsozialismus und an der Technik,* p. 46. Since Vietta states his case in terms of an unchanged relation to Nazism, he would be correct if in this and later texts Heidegger's link to National Socialism were in fact strengthened.

126. For a different analysis, which attributes a deep personal shame to Heidegger because of his silence but fails otherwise to explain the existence of that silence, see Vietta, *Heideggers Kritik am Nationalsozialismus und an der Technik,* pp. 101–103. For still another reading, which connects silence to "the antique tradition of secret and mystery," for instance in Plato's Seventh Letter, see Gerald L. Bruns, *Heidegger's Language, Truth, and Poetry: Estrangements in the Later Writings* (New Haven and London: Yale University Press, 1989), pp. 52–53.

127. On the problem of silence as in itself problematic, see Nadezhda Mandelstam, *Hope against Hope: A Memoir* (New York, 1976), p. 43, cited in Fritz Stern, *Dreams and Delusions: National Socialism in the Drama of the German Past* (New York: Vintage, 1989), p. 146: "Silence is the real crime against humanity." An analogous point is developed by Levinas. See Emmanuel Levinas, "As If Consenting to Horror," *Critical Inquiry* 15, no. 2 (Winter 1989): 485–489.

128. See Heidegger, *Being and Time*, § 34: "Being-there and Discourse. Language," p. 204.

129. Heidegger, *Being and Time*, § 34, p. 208. "He who never says anything cannot keep silent at any given moment. Keeping silent authentically is possible only in genuine discourse."

130. Ibid., § 60, "The Existential Structure of the Authentic Potentiality-for-Being Which Is Attested in the Conscience," p. 342. "In the appeal Dasein gives itself to understand its ownmost potentiality-for-Being. This calling is a therefore a keeping-silent."

131. See Heidegger, *Hölderlins Hymnen "Germanien" und "Der Rhein,"* p. 70.

132. See ibid., p. 218.

133. See Heidegger, *The Eternal Recurrence of the Same* (see chap. 4, n. 38), p. 208: "Supremely thoughtful utterance does not consist simply in growing taciturn when it is a matter of saying what is properly to be said; it consists in saying the matter in such a way that it is named in nonsaying. The utterance of thinking is a telling silence."

134. A similar view was apparently held by others as well at the time. For instance, the Russian philosopher Keyserling, of Baltic extraction, who, like Heidegger, rejected Nazi biologism, and took a more cosmopolitan point of view, shared Heidegger's fascination with Hitler. In an article published in 1933, in which he stressed the importance of *Gleichschaltung*, which Heidegger carried out in the university, Keyserling emphasized the importance of silence: "Auch das Schweigen ist ein positives; in Zeiten allgemeiner Lautheit verkörpert es sogar sehr grosse Macht. Und wem das Schweigen schwer fällt,—nun, der wächst desto mehr innerlich, je schwerer er es hat. In jedem Fall aber zwingt das Dasein echter anderer Überzeugung diejenigen, die als Nationalsozialisten überzeugt sind, *allen* lebendigen Kräften Deutschlands Rechnung zu tragen. Denn Deutschlands endgültiger neuer Zustand wird . . . dem Gleichgewicht *aller* Kräfte entsprechen und nicht irgendeine vorausgesetzte Theorie verwirklichen." Graf Hermann Keyserling, "Gleichschaltung und Zusammenhang," *Der Weg zur Vollendung: Mitteilungen der Schule der Weisheit* 22:7, cited in Laugstien, *Philosophieverhältnisse*, p. 154.

135. See Heidegger, *Beiträge*, part 1, "Vorblick," § 37, "Das Seyn und seine Erschweigung (die Sigetik)," pp. 78–79, and § 38, "Die Erschweigung," pp. 79–80.

136. See Liddell and Scott, *A Greek-English Lexicon* (see chap. 2, n. 142), p. 1596.

137. See Heidegger, *Beiträge*, part 8, "Das Seyn," § 281, "Die Sprache (ihr Ursprung)," p. 510.

138. Ibid.
139. See Ludwig Wittgenstein, *Tractatus Logico-Philosophicus,* trans. D. F. Pears and B. F. McGuinness, introd. Bertrand Russell (London: Routledge and Kegan Paul; New York: Humanities Press, 1961), proposition 7, p. 151.

Chapter 6: Nazism and Technology

1. For an account, see Pöggeler, *Der Denkweg Martin Heideggers* (see chap. 2, n. 69), chap. 9, "Die Befreiung zum Eigenen," pp. 236–267. For a more recent series of papers, see Walter Biemel and Friedrich-Wilhelm von Herrmann, *Kunst und Technik: Gedächtnisschrift zum 100. Geburtstag von Martin Heidegger* (Frankfurt a.m.: Vittorio Klostermann, 1989). For studies of technology influenced by Heidegger's view, see Albert Borgmann, *Technology and the Character of Contemporary Life: A Philosophical Inquiry* (Chicago and London: University of Chicago Press, 1984), and Wolfgang Schirmacher, *Technik und Gelassenheit, Zeitkritik nach Heidegger* (Freiburg and Munich, 1983). For an analysis of Heidegger's view of technology in the context of a discussion of twentieth-century views of progress, see G. M. Tavrizian, *Tekhnika, kul'tura, chelovek: Kriticheskij analiz kontseptsij tekhnicheskovo progressa v burzhyanznoj filosofij xx veka* (Moscow: Nauka, 1986), esp. "Ontologicheskoe obosnovanie syshchnosti tekhniki M. Xajdeggerom," pp. 115–131. For an account of the relation of Heidegger's view of technology to modernity, see Zimmerman, *Heidegger's Confrontation with Modernity* (see chap. 1, n. 23). For a study of Heidegger's view of technology and nihilism, see Phillip R. Fandozzi, *Nihilism and Technology: A Heideggerian Investigation* (Washington, D.C.: University Press of America, 1982). For a recent survey of literature on Heidegger's view of technology, see Albert Borgmann and Carl Mitcham, "The Question of Heidegger and Technology: A Review of the Literature," *Philosophy Today* 31, no. 2 (Summer 1987).

2. See Otto Pöggeler, "Heideggers politisches Selbstverständnis," in *Heidegger und die praktische Philosophie* (see chap. 2, n. 104), and Silvio Vietta, *Heideggers Kritik am Nationalsozialismus und an der Technik* (see chap. 1, n. 31). The claim for an intrinsic link between Heidegger's critique of Nazism and technology is the main thesis of Vietta's book.

3. See "Only a God Can Save Us" (see chap. 1, n. 30), p. 276.
4. See ibid.
5. See ibid. For an analysis of the relation between Heidegger's views of technology and democracy, see my paper, "Heidegger on Technology and Democracy," forthcoming.
6. See "Only a God Can Save Us," p. 276.
7. See ibid., p. 277.
8. For a statement of this side of his thought, see "Building Dwelling Thinking," in Martin Heidegger, *Poetry, Language, Thought,* trans. Albert Hofstadter (New York: Harper and Row, 1975).
9. See "Only a God Can Save Us," p. 279.
10. See ibid., p. 278.

11. See ibid.

12. See ibid., p. 280.

13. See ibid., p. 281. Heidegger's view that Nazism can be understood as a failed attempt to confront technology is easily challenged on the basis of the texts. Consider the following passage by Joseph Goebbels, written in 1939: "While bourgeois reaction was alien to and filled with incomprehension, if not outright hostility to technology, and while modern skeptics believed the deepest roots of the collapse of European culture lay in it, National Socialism undertood how to take the soulless framework of technology and fill it with the rhythm and hot impulses of our time." Joseph Goebbels, *Deutsche Technik*, March 1939, pp. 105–106 (speech at the opening of the Berlin Auto Show, 17 February 1939), cited in Herf, *Reactionary Modernism* (see chap. 2, n. 12), p. 196.

14. Some commentators have seen Heidegger's Nazism as following out of his concern to respond, in Moehling's words, to "the spiritual crisis engendered by modern, post-industrial man's encounter with the meaning of his own tehnological devices." See Moehling, "Heidegger and the Nazis" (see chap. 4, n. 166), p. 40.

15. For an example, see Steven T. Katz, "Technology and Genocide: Techology as a 'Form of Life,'" in *Echoes from the Holocaust* (see Introd., n. 7), pp. 262–291. Katz suggests that many writers fail to given sufficient weight to the role of techology in Nazism since they overemphasize the reactionary, romantic aspects of National Socialism. For a list of such writers, see ibid., p. 285 n. 6. For an extensive analysis of the way that Nazism combined technology and bureaucracy in the service of genocide, see Hilberg, *The Destruction of the European Jews* (see chap. 3, n. 116).

16. If Katz is correct that technology functioned as a main cog in Nazi genocide, then Heidegger's reading of Nazism as directly opposed to technology is related to his inability to comprehend the event of the Holocaust. For Katz's claim, see *Echoes from the Holocaust*, p. 262.

17. "Only a God Can Save Us," p. 280.

18. Ibid., p. 281.

19. Heidegger, *Being and Time*, p. 409.

20. Ibid., § 15, p. 100.

21. Ibid., p. 101.

22. Heidegger, *An Introduction to Metaphysics,* trans. Mannheim (see chap. 1, n. 32), p. 16.

23. Ibid., p. 158. *Machenshaft* is a persistent theme in the *Beiträge zur Philosophie,* where Heidegger insists on the relation between *Weltanschauung* and *Machenschaft.* See *Beiträge zur Philosophie (Vom Ereignis)* (see chap. 1, n. 26), p. 38 and passim.

24. Heidegger, *Introduction to Metaphysics,* p. 159; translation modified.

25. Heidegger further calls attention to the relation of understanding of art and technology in his essay on art. See "The Origin of the Work of Art," in Heidegger, *Poetry, Language, Thought,* pp. 15–87, esp. "Addendum," pp. 82–87.

26. See Heidegger, *Beiträge,* pp. 120, 274. Heidegger's view closely resem-

bles Husserl's explanation of the rise of modern science through Galileo's mathematization of nature. See Husserl, *The Crisis of European Sciences and Transcendental Phenomenology* (see chap. 2, n. 30), part 2, §§ 8 and 9, pp. 21–60. Heidegger stresses the turn away from being whereas Husserl emphasizes the failure to appreciate the life-world as the precondition of modern science.

27. See *Beiträge*, p. 392.

28. See ibid., p. 336. Heidegger makes this point elsewhere as well, for instance in his analysis of the concept of representation.

29. Heidegger, "The Age of the World Picture" (see chap. 3, n. 138), p. 116.

30. See Heidegger, *Basic Writings*, p. 219.

31. See ibid., p. 220.

32. The official aim of Sartre's later, Marxist phase is to dialogue with Marxism understood as a theory of history. See Sartre, *Critique de la raison dialectique* (see chap. 2, n. 160).

33. For this argument, see George L. Kline, "The Myth of Marx's Materialism," in *Philosophical Sovietology: The Pursuit of a Science*, ed. Helmut Dahm, Thomas J. Blakeley, and George L. Kline (Dordrecht: D. Reidel Publishing Co., 1988), pp. 158–203.

34. Heidegger, *Basic Writings*, pp. 220–221.

35. Aubenque, for instance, situates the turning in Heidegger's thought in 1935–1936 in order to make it coincide with the *Introduction to Metaphysics* and the beginning of the Nietzsche lectures. See Aubenque, "Encore Heidegger et le nazisme" (see chap. 2, n. 59), p. 123.

36. For an account of the discussion of technology during this period, see Friedrich Dessauer, *Streit um die Technik* (Frankfurt a.M.: J. Knecht, 1956).

37. See Rudolph Haym, *Hegel und seine Zeit: Vorlesungen über Entstehung und Entwickelung, Wesen und Werth der Hegel'schen Philosophie* (Berlin, 1857; reprint, Hildesheim: Georg Olms, 1962), p. 5.

38. Karl Jaspers, "Spannung von technischer Massenordnung und menschlicher Daseinswelt," in *Die geistige Situation der Zeit* (Berlin: de Gruyter, 1965), pp. 32ff., cited in Barnouw, *Weimar Intellectuals and the Threat of Modernity* (see chap. 2, n. 20), p. 13.

39. See "Rectoral Address—Facts and Thoughts" (see chap. 2, n. 115), p. 474.

40. See ibid., p. 473.

41. Heidegger, *Nietzsche*, vol. 4, *Nihilism*, trans. Capuzzi (see chap. 4, n. 205), p. 196; translation modified.

42. The topic of the Jünger-Heidegger link has received extensive attention, particularly among politically conservative Heideggerians. Among the writings concerning the Heidegger-Jünger relation, see Christian Graf von Krockow, *Die Entscheidung: Eine Unterscheidung über Ernst Jünger, Carl Schmitt, Martin Heidegger* (Stuttgart: Felke, 1958); Jean-Michel Palmier, *Les écrits politiques de Heidegger* (Paris: L'Herne, 1968); Fréderic de Towarnicki, "Le travailleur planétaire: Entretien avec Ernst Jünger," in *Martin Heidegger*, ed. Michel Haar, *L'Herne*, no. 45 (Paris: L'Herne, 1983), pp. 145–150. See also Krell's remarks in Heidegger, *Nietzsche* (see chap. 4, n. 143), vol. 3, *The Will to Power as Knowl-*

edge and Metaphysics, pp. 263–268, and *Nietzsche,* vol. 4, *Nihilism,* pp. 286–291. For an extensive recent reading of Jünger's relation to Heidegger, see Zimmerman, *Heidegger's Confrontation with Modernity* (see chap. 1, n. 23). Following Herf, Zimmerman sees the convergence between Heidegger and Jünger in the effort, characteristic of other reactionary conservatives, to understand technology in particular and modernity in general in categories that transcended the so-called causal-material realm. See Zimmerman, *Heidegger's Confrontation with Modernity,* p. 46. Zimmerham holds, however, that Heidegger finally rejects Jünger's vision of technological nihilism. See ibid., p. 67.

43. See "Rectoral Address—Facts and Thoughts," pp. 484–485.

44. See Martin Heidegger, "Zur Seinsfrage," in Heidegger, *Wegmarken* (see chap. 3, n. 33), pp. 217–219.

45. See ibid., p. 219.

46. See Ernst Jünger, *Der Arbeiter. Herrschaft und Gestalt* (Stuttgart: Ernst Klett, 1981). The attraction of the thought of this rather weak thinker for Heidegger is unclear. Thomä, relying on Schneeberger, cites a list of passages on *Arbeit* in Heidegger's writings on *Arbeit* and *Arbeiter* from 1933. See Thomä, *Die Zeit des Selbst und die Zeit danach,* pp. 595–596. He also cites a passsage from a radio talk by Hitler given on 10 May 1933, ending with the words: "In diesem Sinne ist das Deutsche Reich das Reich des deutschen Sozialismus, ein Staat der Arbeit und der Arbeiter." Cited in Thomä, *Die Zeit des Selbst und die Zeit danach,* p. 595. In view of the fact that Heidegger's interest in Jünger began as early as 1932, when he formed the first group to study Jünger's thought, it is difficult to accept Thomä's suggestion that Heidegger's concern with Jünger's *Arbeiter* represents a turn away from Nazism. See Thomä, *Die Zeit des Selbst und die Zeit danach,* p. 600.

47. See Jünger, *Der Arbeiter,* p. 9.

48. See ibid., p. 7.

49. See ibid.

50. In several letters written many years later, he denied any anti-Marxist motivation, claiming to go further than Marx down the same road. See Jünger, *Der Arbeiter,* pp. 316, 317.

51. See ibid., p. 15.

52. See ibid., p. 16.

53. See ibid., p. 27.

54. See ibid., p. 31.

55. See ibid., p. 45.

56. See ibid., p. 68.

57. Heidegger, *Wegmarken,* p. 215.

58. See ibid., p. 224.

59. See ibid., p. 228.

60. See ibid., p. 242. For further discussion of *Verwindung,* see his essay "Überwindung der Metaphysik," in Heidegger, *Vorträge und Aufsätze* (see chap. 4, n. 80), pp. 67–95.

61. See Heidegger, *Wegmarken,* p. 244.

62. For a recent account of Spengler's influence on Heidegger's view of

technology, see Zimmerman, "Heidegger's Critical Appropriation of Spengler in the Fight against Modern Technology," in *Heidegger's Confrontation with Modernity,* pp. 26–33. Zimmerman points to Heidegger's lectures in order to maintain that Heidegger's account of the history of being is an attempt to provide the authentic philosophy of history allegedly missing in Spengler. See ibid., p. 27.

63. For Heidegger's reference to his Spengler lectures, see his letter to Karl Jaspers, 21 April 1920, in *Briefwechsel 1920–1963* (see chap. 2, n. 27), p. 15.

64. See Otto Pöggeler, "Heideggers politisches Selbstverständnis," in *Heidegger und die praktische Philosophie* (see chap. 2, n. 104), p. 26.

65. See Oswald Spengler, *Der Mensch und die Technik: Beitrag zu einer Philosophie des Lebens* (Münich: C. H. Beck'sche Verlagsbuchhandlung, 1931). This book was rapidly made available in translation. See Oswald Spengler, *Man and Technics: A Contribution to a Philosophy of Life,* trans. Charles Francis Atkinson (New York: Alfred A. Knopf, 1932).

66. For such themes, see Spengler, *Jahre der Entscheidung* (see chap. 2, n. 135).

67. See Spengler, *Man and Technics,* preface.

68. For details, see Martin Heidegger, *Die Technik und die Kehre* (Neske: Pfullingen, 1962), *Vorbemerkung,* p. 3. According to Zimmerman, nearly all the basic aspects of Heidegger's view of technology are found in his lecture notes and writings between 1934 and 1944. See Zimmerman, *Heidegger's Confrontation with Modernity,* p. 35. But this lecture series in which Heidegger expounded the main features of his view occurs later, and the essay entitled "Die Frage nach der Technik," which is Heidegger's major text on technology, occurs still later.

69. Access to Heidegger's writings continues to pose a major interpretative problem. A recent request for a copy of the manuscript of Heidegger's unpublished lecture entitled "Die Gefahr" was denied in a letter from Prof. Friedrich-Wilhelm von Herrmann, general editor of the edition of the collected works now under way, who said in part that no access could be permitted until the lecture is published in a future volume. See unpublished letter dated 28 March 1990. This denial is unfortunate since it is important to study the complete record. The refusal to grant access to this particular document is further curious, in fact inconsistent, since it has been already cited in the literature by others. See, e.g., Thomas Sheehan, "Heidegger and the Nazis," *The New York Review of Books* 35, no. 10 (16 June 1988): 42.

70. See "The Thing," in Heidegger, *Poetry, Language, Thought,* pp. 163–186.

71. "The Question concerning Technology" and "The Turning" in Heidegger, *The Question concerning Technology,* pp. 3–35 and 36–49.

72. An example, among many, is the term "*Bestand,*" an ordinary German word, modeled on the verb "*bestehen,*" which has the meanings of "existence, stock, inventory, cash on hand, inventory," etc., but which is rendered as "standing-reserve." See Heidegger, *The Question concerning Technology and Other Essays,* p. 17. Although Heidegger uses the term, as he states, in his own way, it is not a neologism in German. But to introduce a neologism for it in

English, when other words are apparently available, is to introduce a supplementary difficulty in the comprehension of the text.

73. See Heidegger, *The Essence of Technology,* p. 4.

74. See ibid., p. 31.

75. For further discussion of this point, see his chapter entitled "Der Wandel der energeia zur actualitas," in Heidegger, *Nietzsche* (German ed.; see chap. 4, n. 85), 2:410–421.

76. See Heidegger, *The Question concerning Technology,* p. 5.

77. For an example, see Spengler's analysis of technology as a vital tactic in *Der Mensch und die Technik,* chap. 1.

78. See Heidegger, *The Question concerning Technology,* p. 6.

79. See ibid., p. 9.

80. Ibid., p. 12.

81. For Aristotle's influential attempt to sort out the differences between such terms as *"episteme," "sophia," "poiesis," "techne,"* etc., see his *Nicomachean Ethics,* book 6.

82. See Heidegger, *The Question concerning Technology,* p. 13.

83. Ibid., p. 14.

84. Ibid., p. 15; translation modified.

85. Zimmerman regards Heidegger's thought as important for so-called deep, or nonanthropological, ecology. See Zimmerman, *Heidegger's Confrontation with Technology,* pp. 241–244.

86. See Heidegger, *The Question concerning Technology,* p. 17.

87. Ibid., p. 18.

88. Ibid., p. 19.

89. See ibid., p. 20.

90. Ibid.

91. Ibid., p. 23; translation modified.

92. Ibid., p. 24.

93. This claim is already formulated much earlier in his thought, for instance during the Hölderlin lectures: "Denn das Schickliche bestimmt das Geschick und dieses die Geschichte." Heidegger, *Hölderlins Hymne "Der Ister"* (see chap. 2, n. 146), p. 101.

94. Heidegger, *The Question concerning Technology,* p. 25.

95. Ibid., p. 26.

96. Ibid.

97. Ibid., p. 28; translation modified.

98. Ibid., translation modified.

99. Ibid., p. 31, Heidegger's emphases; translation modified.

100. Ibid., p. 32.

101. Ibid., p. 34; translation modified.

102. See Immanuel Kant, *Critique of Practical Reason,* trans. Lewis White Beck (Indianapolis and New York: Library of Liberal Arts, 1956), book 2, chaps. 5 and 6, pp. 126–136.

103. See Heidegger, *The Question concerning Technology,* p. 35.

104. For an expression of this view, see John D. Caputo, "Demythologizing

Heidegger: *Aletheia* and the History of Being," *Review of Metaphysics* 41 (March 1988): 542.

105. Theodore Kisiel called this to my attention.

106. We have noted Heidegger's discussion of Marx in "The Letter on Humanism" (see chap. 1, n. 29), pp. 219–220.

107. See the article on "technology," in *A Dictionary of Marxist Thought,* ed. Tom Bottomore et al. (Cambridge, Mass.: Harvard University Press, 1983), p. 478.

108. Marx's view of agency, which is influenced by Fichte's similar view, contains an unresolved tension. On this point, see my *Fichte, Marx and the German Philosophical Tradition* (Carbondale, Ill.: Southern Illinois University Press, 1980), pp. 91–94.

109. For a general statement of his awareness of this hermeneutical problem, see Heidegger, *An Introduction to Metaphysics,* p. 176.

110. For a well-known critique of Plato as an enemy of democracy, see Popper, *The Open Society and Its Enemies* (see chap. 2, n. 178), vol. 1, *The Spell of Plato.*

111. Kant argues that the concept of freedom grounds the autonomy of the will and must be presupposed. See Kant's discussion of freedom in Kant, *Fundamental Principles of the Metaphysics of Morals* (see chap. 2, n. 153), pp. 63–65

112. See H. Kimmerle, "Motiven in het denken van Heidegger als verklarende elementen voor zijn politieke houding," in *Heidegger en het nazisme: Een symposium,* ed. H. A. F. Oosterling and A. W. Prins (Rotterddam: Faculteit der Wijsbegeerte van de Erasmus Universiteit Rotterdam, n.d.), pp. 37–45. Kimmerle attributes Heidegger's difficulty to a mistakenly Hegelian reading of Hölderlin. See ibid., p. 45.

113. These views are expressed by Pöggeler. See Pöggeler, "Heideggers politisches Selbstverständnis" (see n. 64), pp. 33 and 47.

114. Vietta argues strongly, but inconsistently, that Heidegger's critique of technology follows from his critique of National Socialism and that his critique of technology is also a critique of National Socialism. See Vietta, *Heideggers Kritik am Nationalsozialismus und an der Technik.*

115. For a summary, see Sheehan, "Heidegger and the Nazis," pp. 42–43.

116. Marten has described this incident. See Rainer Marten, "Ein rassistisches Konzept von Humanität," *Badische Zeitung,* 19–20 December 1987, p. 14. The relevant passage is cited in Farias, *Heidegger and Nazism* (see Introd., n. 4), pp. 227–228.

117. See "Mit Heidegger gegen Heideggers Denken: Zur Veröffentlichung von Vorlesungen aus dem Jahre 1935," *Frankfürter Allgemeine Zeitung,* 25 July 1953, reprinted as "Zur Veröffentlichung von Vorlesungen aus dem Jahre 1935 (1953)," in Jürgen Habermas, *Philosophisch-politische Profile* (Frankfurt a.M.: Suhrkamp Verlag, 1973), pp. 67–75.

118. See Christian E. Lewalter, "Wie liest man 1953 Sätze von 1935?" *Die Zeit,* 13 August 1953, p. 6.

119. See "Heidegger über Heidegger," *Die Zeit,* 24 September 1953, p. 18, reprinted in Martin Heidegger, *Gesamtausgabe,* vol. 40, *Einführung in die*

Metaphysik, ed. Petra Jaeger (Frankfurt a.M.: Vittorio Klostermann, 1976), pp. 232–233.

120. Letter of 18 March 1968 to S. Zemach, cited in Heidegger, *Einführung in die Metaphysik,* p. 233.

121. See "Only a God Can Save Us," p. 276.

122. See the *Nachwort* by Petra Jaeger, in Heidegger, *Einführung in die Metaphysik,* p. 234.

123. See Pöggeler, "Heideggers politisches Selbstverständnis," p. 38.

124. Heidegger, *An Introduction to Metaphysics,* p. 199. This passage is susceptible of different interpretations. According to Zimmerman, it indicates Heidegger's belief that the Nazis would bring forth a new kind of human being endowed with the qualities favored by Jünger but devoid of the interest in production related to technology. See Zimmerman, *Heidegger's Confrontation with Modernity,* p. 190. The most detailed interpretation of which I am aware is due to Janicaud. See Janicaud, *L'ombre de cette pensée* (see Introd., n. 7), chap. 7, "La lettre volée," pp. 77–96.

125. Vietta here refers to a personal communication from Heribert Heinrichs. See Vietta, *Heideggers Kritik am Nationalsozialismus und an der Technik,* pp. 46–47.

126. See Heidegger, *Vorträge und Aufsätze* (see chap. 4, n. 80), p. 18.

127. Heidegger, *The Question concerning Technology,* p 15.

128. This passage was first published by Schirmacher. See Wolfgang Schirmacher, *Technik und Gelassenheit: Zeitkritik nach Heidegger* (Freiburg and Munich, 1983), p. 25. The passage cited is given in Farias, *Heidegger and Nazism,* p. 287; translation modified.

129. For a closely Heideggerian claim that Heidegger's insensitivity is terrible but that the Holocaust reveals the essential nature of the West, see Philippe Lacoue-Labarthe, *La fiction du politique* (Paris: Christian Bourgois, 1987), pp. 57–63.

130. This passage is from the manuscript of a lecture entitled "Die Gefahr," p. 47, cited in Sheehan, "Heidegger and the Nazis" (see n. 69), p. 42; translation modified.

131. Cited in Farias, *Heidegger and Nazism,* p. 285. For Marcuse's astonished response, which rejects the implied comparison between forcible displacement and the annihilation of peoples, see ibid., pp. 285–287.

Chapter 7: The French Reception of Heidegger's Nazism

1. For a brief introduction, see Richard Wolin, "Introduction to 'Martin Heidegger and Politics: A Dossier,' " *The New German Critique,* no. 45 (Fall 1988): 91–95. Wolin regards the problem as concerning Heidegger and politics, whereas in fact it more narrowly concerns Heidegger and Nazism.

2. For a selection of the newspaper reports, see Schneeberger, *Nachlese zu Heidegger* (see chap. 1, n. 34), passim, esp. secs. 79 and 82. See also Farias, *Heidegger and Nazism* (see Introd., n. 4), pp. 109–112.

3. For Croce's letters to Vossler, particularly the letter of 10 August 1933, see Schneeberger, *Nachlese zu Heidegger,* sec. 93, pp. 110–112.

4. See Jaspers's letter to Heidegger dated 23 August 1933, cited in Ott, *Martin Heidegger* (see Introd., n. 3), pp. 192–193.

5. With the exception of a version of Löwith's contribution, this debate is still not available in English. See Karl Löwith, "Political Implications of Heidegger's Existentialism," *New German Critique,* no. 45 (Fall 1988): 117–134.

6. See Guido Schneeberger, *Ergänzungen zu einer Heidegger-Bibliographie* (Bern, 1960). The reaction of Heideggerians has been predictable. For Harries, Schneeberger's collection of materials is valuable but one-sided. See Karsten Harries's introduction to *Martin Heidegger and National Socialism: Questions and Answers* (see Introd., n. 9), p. xvii. Yet it is unclear how a collection of materials meant to document the extent of Heidegger's involvement with Nazism, which some of Heidegger's closest students, following Heidegger's lead, have long striven to conceal, could be anything other than "one-sided."

7. See Schneeberger, *Nachlese zu Heidegger.* Schneeberger's compilation is the indispensable basis for Runes's collection of materials in English. See Dagobert D. Runes, *Martin Heidegger: German Existentialism* (New York: Philosophical Library, 1965).

8. See Karsten Harries, "Heidegger as a Political Thinker," *The Review of Metaphysics* 29, no. 4 (June 1976): 642–669, reprinted in *Heidegger and Modern Philosophy,* ed. Michael Murray (New Haven and London: Yale University Press, 1978), pp. 306–307 n. 10.

9. See Victor Farias, *Heidegger et le nazisme* (Paris: Éditions Verdier, 1987).

10. See Ott, *Martin Heidegger.*

11. See particularly Zimmerman, *Heidegger's Confrontation with Modernity* (see chap. 1, n. 23), and Wolin, *The Politics of Being* (see chap. 1, n. 1).

12. For a recent, short discussion of the French reception of Heidegger, see Jürg Altwegg, "Heidegger in Frankreich—und zurück?" in *Die Heidegger Kontroverse,* ed. Altwegg (see chap. 3, n. 6), pp. 14–25. See also Haar, *Martin Heidegger* (see chap. 6, n. 42), and *Magazine Littéraire,* no. 235 (novembre 1986). It is significant that as late as this period, in a special issue containing a "dossier" specifically devoted to "Martin Heidegger: *l'Etre et le Temps,*" there was only a brief discussion of the problem of politics. See François Fédier, "La question politique," *Magazine Littéraire,* no. 235 (November 1986): 51–52.

13. For a discussion of the reception of Heidegger's Nazism in French philosophy, see Jean Quillien, "Philosophie et politique: Heidegger, le nazisme et la pensée française," in *Germanica* no. 8 (1990): 103–142. For an account from a different perspective, see Richard Wolin, "The French Heidegger Debate," *New German Critique,* no. 45 (Fall 1988): 135–160.

14. The texts omitted include Georges Friedmann, in *Cahiers de Sociologie* 16 (1954), and *Mélanges Lucien Febvre* (1954); Robert Minder, "Hebel and Heidegger: Lumières et obscurantisme," in *Utopies et institutions au XVIIIe siècle,* ed. P. Francastel (Paris and The Hague: Mouton, 1963), and "Heidegger und Hebel oder die Sprache von Meßkirch," in Robert Minder, *Dichter in der*

Gesellschaft (Frankfurt a.M.: Insel Verlag, 1966), pp. 210–264; and Alexandre Koyré, "L'évolution philosophique de Heidegger," in *Critique*, 1946, no. 1:73–82, and ibid., 1946, no. 2:161–183.

15. Despite the "violence" of the recent French reception of Heidegger's Nazism, interest in the discussion seems now to have noticeably waned. Significantly, the recent publication of a French translation of Ott's book has attracted little attention. For a review in the best academic style, written by Thomas Ferenczi, see "Douze ans dans la vie de Heidegger: L'historien allemand Hugo Ott confirme que, de 1933 à 1945, le philosophe est resté fidèle au régime hitlérien," *Le Monde*, 16 novembre 1990, p. 26.

16. For a classic French study of postmodernism, see François Lyotard, *La condition postmoderne* (Paris: Éditions de minuit, 1979).

17. It has been suggested that the rapid pace of change in French thought indicates that it is in crisis. See de Man, *Blindness and Insight* (see chap. 4, n. 11), pp. 3–5.

18. This is perhaps the significance of the enthusiastic reception of Rorty's recent work, which is less an attack on philosophy in general than on analytic philosophy in all its various forms.

19. For an objective review of Farias's book, unthinkable in recent decades in Soviet philosophy, see A. M. Rytkevich, "Gaidegger i Natsizm," *Voprosy filosofij*, 1988, no. 11:157–165. This is not the first time that Heidegger's politics has attracted attention in eastern Europe. For an earlier discussion touching on Heidegger's Nazism, see the special issue of the Polish journal *Znak*, no. 240 (June 1974), published in Krakow. See especially Krzysztof Pomian, "Z okazji marcina Heideggera," ibid., pp. 702–713.

20. The tenth article of the "Déclaration des droits de l'homme et du citoyen," promulgated by the Assemblée nationale in August 1789, reads: "Nul ne doit être inquiété pour ses opinions, même religieuses, pourvu que leur manifestation ne trouble pas l'ordre public établi par la loi."

21. For a recent example, see André Glucksmann, *Descartes, c'est la France* (Paris: Flammarion, 1987).

22. See Kojève, *Introduction to the Reading of Hegel* (see chap. 4, n. 71).

23. For an analysis of Hegel's residual Cartesianism, see Tom Rockmore, *Hegel's Circular Epistemology* (Bloomington and London: Indiana University Press, 1986), chap. 6, esp. pp. 142–154.

24. In his otherwise excellent study of Hegel as the central thinker in recent French philosophy, Descombes fails to appreciate the sense in which his role in French thought was in part dependent on his relation to Descartes. See Descombes, *Le même et l'autre* (see chap. 4, n. 71).

25. For a recent analysis of the role of Heidegger in French philosophy, see Alain Badiou, *Manifeste pour la philosophie* (Paris: Éditions du Seuil, 1989), chap. 4, "Heidegger envisagé comme lieu commun," pp. 27–32.

26. For Heidegger's later criticism of philosophical anthropology as deriving from Descartes, see "The Age of the World Picture" (see chap. 3, n. 138), pp. 115–154.

27. Sartre's basic statement of the humanist thrust of his existentialism is

contained in his popular lecture, "Existentialism Is a Humanism." Heidegger's rejection of humanism as a metaphysical concept is developed in his "Letter on Humanism."

28. See "Only a God Can Save Us" (see chap. 1, n. 30), p. 282.

29. The main exception to this tendency in the French discussion is the work of Bourdieu. See Bourdieu, *L'ontologie politique de Martin Heidegger* (see chap. 2, n. 53).

30. For a representative sample of how *Being and Time* is received in the French discussion, see "Dossier: Martin Heidegger," *Magazine Littéraire*, no. 235 (novembre 1986): 16–58.

31. See Martin Heidegger, *Lettre sur l'humanisme,* trans. Roger Munier (Paris: Aubier, 1964), p. 7.

32. See Heidegger, "Letter on Humanism" (see chap. 1, n. 29), p. 221.

33. See ibid., p. 231.

34. See ibid., p. 202.

35. See ibid., pp. 221, 224, 227.

36. Ibid., Heidegger's emphases.

37. See "Deux documents sur Heidegger," *Les Temps Modernes* 1, no. 4 (janvier 1946): 713.

38. See Karl Löwith, *Heidegger. Denker in dürftiger Zeit: Zur Stellung der Philosophie im 20. Jahrhundert* (Stuttgart: J. B. Metzler, 1984).

39. See Eric Weil, *Logique de la philosophie* (Paris: Vrin, 1950).

40. See Maurice de Gandillac, "Entretien avec Martin Heidegger," *Les Temps Modernes* 1, no. 4 (janvier 1946): 713–716.

41. See Alfred de Towarnicki, "Visite à Martin Heidegger," *Les Temps Modernes* 1, no. 4 (janvier 1946): 717–724.

42. See Löwith, "Les implications politiques de la philosophie de l'existence chez Heidegger" (see Introd., n. 2).

43. See Eric Weil, "Le cas Heidegger," *Les Temps Modernes*, juillet 1947, pp. 128–138.

44. See Alphonse De Waelhens, "La philosophie de Heidegger et le nazisme," *Les Temps Modernes* 3 (1947): 115–127.

45. See Karl Löwith, "Réponse à M. de Waelhens," *Les Temps Modernes*, no. 35 (août 1948): 370–373.

46. See Alphonse De Waelhens, "Réponse à cette réponse," *Les Temps Modernes*, no. 35 (août 1948): 374–377.

47. See Jean Beaufret, *Introduction aux philosophies de l'existence, Bibliothèque Médiations, 85* (Paris: Denoël/Gonthier, 1971), p. 30, reprinted as *De l'existentialisme à Heidegger* (Paris: Vrin, 1986), p. 25.

48. See, e.g., his article, "En chemin avec Heidegger," in *Martin Heidegger,* ed. Haar (see chap. 6, n. 42), pp. 205–233; see also his statement, in J. Beaufret, *Entretien avec F. de Towarnicki* (Paris: Presses universitaires de France, 1984), p. 87: "Heidegger n'a jamais rien fait qui ait pu motiver les allégations formulés contre lui" and the examination of his philosophy from a political perspective represents "la conspiration des médiocres au nom de la médiocrité." Essentially

the same defense is offered later by Vattimo in his claim that Heidegger's thought is more important than that of his accusers.

49. See *Annales d'histoire révisionniste*, no. 3 (automne-hiver 1987): 204–205; for a discussion of the link between Beaufret and Robert Faurisson, see Michel Kajman, *Le Monde*, 22 janvier 1988, pp. 1, 18. The following passage (cited in Jean-François Lyotard, *The Differend: Phrases in Dispute*, trans. Georges Van Den Abbeele [Minneapolis: University of Minnesota Press, 1988], p. 3) provides an idea of Faurisson's view: "I have analyzed thousands of documents. I have tirelessly pursued specialists and historians with my questions. I have tried in vain to find a single former deportee capable of proving to me that he had really seen, with his own eyes, a gas chamber." This form of historical revisionism is fundamentally different from the more benign discussion in German intellectual circles where the controversy does not concern the existence but rather the interpretation of the so-called Final Solution. See *"Historikerstreit": Die Dokumentation der Kontroverse um die Einzigartigkeit der national-sozialistischen Judenvernichtung* (Zurich and Munich: Piper Verlag, 1987). For a philosophical reaction to Faurisson, see Lyotard, *The Differend*, pp. 3–4. For a summary of recent revisionist readings of the Holocaust in English, see Dawidowicz, *The War against the Jews* (see chap. 2, n. 54), pp. xxi–xxxii.

50. For a good recent survey of his thought, see Werner Jung, *Georg Lukács* (Stuttgart: J. B. Metzler, 1989).

51. See Georg Lukács, *Existentialisme ou Marxisme?* (Paris: Nagel, 1948).

52. See Georg Lukács, *Existentialismus oder Marxismus?* (Berlin: Aufbau Verlag, 1951).

53. See Maurice Merleau-Ponty, *Les aventures de la dialectique* (Paris: Gallimard, 1955), chap. 2: "Le marxisme 'occidental,' " pp. 43–80.

54. See Jean-Michel Palmier, *Les écrits politiques de Heidegger* (Paris: L'Herne, 1968).

55. Palmier argues that Heidegger made two basic mistakes: he thought that through the Nazi party he could realize an intuition he perceived in Ernst Jünger's book, *Der Arbeiter;* and he thought that within Nazism he could develop a philosophical dimension since he deluded himself into perceiving within it a spiritual potentiality. For a statement of his view, see Jean-Michel Palmier, "Heidegger et le national-socialisme," in *Martin Heidegger,* ed. Haar, pp. 409–446. For a summary of Palmier's criticism, see ibid., pp. 443–444.

56. See Jean-Pierre Faye, "Heidegger et la révolution," *Médiations,* no. 3 (automne 1961): 151–159. Faye has continued to develop his critique of Heidegger. For its most recent form, see Jean-Pierre Faye, *La raison narrative* (Paris: Balland, 1990).

57. See Jean-Pierre Faye, "Attaques Nazies contre Heidegger," *Médiations,* no. 5 (été 1962): 137–151.

58. See François Fédier, "Trois attaques contre Heidegger," *Critique,* no. 234 (novembre 1966): 883–904. The discussion begun by Fédier, including a series of responses and rejoinders, ended with contributions by Bondy and

Fédier. See François Bondy, "Une lettre de Heidegger à François Bondy," *Critique*, 1968:433–435, and François Fédier, "Le point," ibid., pp. 435–437.

59. See Aimé Patri, "Serait-ce une querelle d'allemands?" *Critique*, no. 237 (février 1967): 296–297.

60. See Robert Minder, "Langage et nazisme," *Critique*, no. 237 (février 1967): 284–287.

61. See Jean-Pierre Faye, "La lecture et l'énoncé," *Critique*, no. 237 (février 1967): 288–295.

62. See François Fédier, "A propos de Heidegger: Une lecture dénoncée," *Critique*, no. 242, pp. 672–686.

63. See the *Frankfurter Rundschau*, 22 October 1987, no. 245, "Bis zuletzt ein Nazi Heidegger im grellen Licht / Eine Pariser Sensation," p. 11

64. See *Die Zeit*, no. 46 (6 November 1987), "Wie braun war Heidegger? Die postmodernen Grossfurthsen und ihr deutscher Ahnherr."

65. See Gianni Vattimo, "Il pensiero di Heidegger più forte di chi lo accusa," *La Stampa*, 14 November 1987.

66. Christian Jambet, preface to Farias, *Heidegger et le nazisme* (see n. 9), p. 14.

67. Hugo Ott, "Wege und Abwege: Zu Victor Farias' kritischer Heidegger-Studie," *Neue Zürcher Zeitung*, no. 275 (27 November 1987): 67: "In Frankreich ist ein Himmel eingestürzt—*le ciel des philosophes.*"

68. See Roger-Pol Droit, "Heidegger était-il Nazi? Une minitieuse enquête de Victor Farias révèle les liens entre le philosophe, mort en 1976, et le national-socialisme," *Le Monde*, 14 octobre 1987, p. 2.

69. See Georges-Arthur Goldschmidt, "Heidegger, militant et penseur nazi," *Le Matin*, 15 octobre 1987, p. 16.

70. See Emmanuel Martineau, "De la haine de la pensée aux 'faurisonneries,' " *Le Matin*, 26 octobre 1987.

71. See Alain Finkielkraut, "Heidegger: La question et le procès," *Le Monde*, 5 janvier 1988, p. 2.

72. See Georges-Arthur Goldschmidt, "Heidegger: L'allemand et le ressentiment," *Le Monde*, 13 janvier 1988, p. 2.

73. See Jean Baudrillard, "Nécrospective autour de Martin Heidegger," *Libération*, 27 janvier 1988, pp. 1–2.

74. See "Un entretien avec Jacques Derrida. Heidegger, l'enfer des philosophes," *Le Nouvel Observateur*, 6–12 novembre 1988.

75. See Victor Farias, "Victor Farias: Pas d'accord avec Jacques Derrida," *Le Nouvel Observateur,* no. 47 (27 novembre–3 décembre 1987).

76. See Aubenque, "Encore Heidegger et le nazisme" (see chap. 2, n. 59), pp. 113–123. This issue, which provides a good point of entry into the recent French discussion of Heidegger and Nazism, contains a diverse collection of articles by P. Aubenque, H. Crétella, M. Deguy, F. Fédier, G. Granel, S. Moses, and A. Renaut under the heading of "Heidegger, la philosophie et le nazisme" as well as a collection of twelve texts under the heading of "Martin Heidegger: Textes politiques 1933–1934."

77. See Pascal David, "*Heidegger et le nazisme:* A propos du livre de V.

Farias de même intitulé," *Les Études Philosophiques*, avril-juin 1988, pp. 257–263.

78. See also *Heidegger: Questions ouvertes,* Collège international de philosophie (Paris: Éditions Osiris, 1988). This volume contains a diverse collection of articles on different themes presented at a seminar organized by the Collège international de philosophie. Under the heading of "Histoire, Politique," there is a series of articles by J. Rolland, Eliane Escoubas, P. Lacoue-Labarthe, J. Derrida, M. Abensour, and E. Levinas on various aspects of the theme of Heidegger and Nazism. For a review covering the works by Fédier, Bourdieu, Lacoue-Labarthe, Renaut and Ferry, and Lyotard, see Jean-Michel Palmier, "Heidegger et le national-socialisme," *Magazine Littéraire*, no. 255 (juin 1988): 89–93.

79. See Bourdieu, *L'ontologie politique de Martin Heidegger* (see chap. 2, n. 53). For a more recent French study of Heidegger's language, see Henri Meschonnic, *Le langage Heidegger* (Paris: Presses universitaires de France, 1990).

80. Bourdieu, *L'ontologie politique de Martin Heidegger,* p. 7.

81. On the importance of Heidegger's refusal of an anthropological reading of his thought, see Martin Heidegger, *La lettre à Jean Wahl,* cited in Bourdieu, *L'ontologie politique de Martin Heidegger,* p. 114.

82. See Bourdieu, *L'ontologie politique de Martin Heidegger,* p. 8.

83. On this point, see ibid., p. 59, where Bourdieu refers to Toni Cassirer's well-known comment, and 61n, where he discusses the influence of H. von Treitschke on later German thought, including the German academy. See also a letter of Husserl to Dietrich Mahnke, dated 4 May 1933, in which Husserl writes: "Vorangegangen ist der von ihm [Heidegger] vollzogene Abbruch des Verkehrs mit mir (und schon bald nach seiner Berufung) und in den letzen Jahren sein immer stärker zum Ausdruck kommenden Antisemitismus—auch gegenüber seiner Gruppe begeisterter jüdischer Schüler und in der Fakultät." Cited by Hugo Ott in *Heidegger und die praktische Philosophie* (see chap. 2, n. 104), p. 69. This contradicts the widespread view, represented by Pöggeler, ibid., p. 17, that the story of Heidegger's anti-Semitism is at best apocryphal.

84. See Bourdieu, *L'ontologie politique de Martin Heidegger,* p. 67.

85. See ibid., pp. 107–108.

86. Ibid., p. 10.

87. See ibid., p. 102.

88. See ibid., p. 115.

89. See ibid., p. 117.

90. See ibid., p. 118.

91. See Jean-François Lyotard, *Heidegger et "les juifs"* (Paris: Éditions Galilée, 1988), pp. 97–101.

92. See Jürgen Habermas, "Die Moderne: Ein unvollendetes Projekt," in Jürgen Habermas, *Kleine politische Schriften I-IV* (Frankfurt a.M.: Suhrkamp Verlag, 1981), pp. 444–464.

93. "L'affaire Heidegger est une affaire 'française,' " in Lyotard, *Heidegger et "les juifs,"* p. 16.

94. See Lyotard, *Heidegger et "les juifs,"* p. 52; see also ibid., p. 71, "judéo-christianisme;" p. 73, "société"; p. 103, "politique"; p. 146, "faute"; p. 153, "Celan"; etc.

95. "Penser l'affaire Heidegger," in Lyotard, *Heidegger et "les juifs,"* p. 87.

96. See Lyotard, *Heidegger et "les juifs,"* p. 90; see also ibid., p. 109.

97. See ibid., p. 95.

98. "La méditation anamnésique de ce qui aura eu lieu dans la 'politique' heideggerienne," in Lyotard, *Heidegger et "les juifs,"* p. 103.

99. See Lyotard, *Heidegger et "les juifs,"* p. 110.

100. See ibid., p. 111; for an initial discussion of this hypothesis, see ibid., pp. 115–120.

101. See ibid., p. 148.

102. Lyotard here contradicts such French commentators as Aubenque, who directly deny the political nature of Heidegger's work. For Aubenque's denial, see Aubenque, "Encore Heidegger et le nazisme."

103. See Fédier, *Heidegger: Anatomie d'un scandale* (see chap. 3, n. 69).

104. "Le rectorat n'a cependant rien d'une parenthèse dans la vie de Heidegger et il vaut la peine de lire les 'textes politiques' de la période de 1933–1934." Ibid., p. 22.

105. See ibid., p. 67.

106. Or as he says, "lever l'accusation portée contre Heidegger." Ibid., p. 30.

107. See ibid., p. 31.

108. See ibid., pp. 31–33.

109. See ibid., p. 37.

110. See ibid., p. 162.

111. Article 4 of the NSDAP program is clear: "Only a member of the community [Volksgenosse] can be a citizen. Only a person with German blood, regardless of his religious adherence, can be a member of the community. No Jew may therefore be a member of the community." Cited in Hilberg, *The Destruction of the European Jews* (see chap. 3, n. 116), p. 18.

112. See Fédier, *Heidegger: anatomie d'un scandale,* p. 185.

113. See ibid., p. 114.

114. See ibid., p. 115.

115. See ibid., pp. 115, 147.

116. See ibid., p. 116.

117. See ibid., p. 136.

118. See ibid., p. 152.

119. See ibid., pp. 198–199.

120. See ibid., p. 234.

121. See ibid., p. 237.

122. See ibid., p. 240.

123. Among the French Heideggerians, Lacoue-Labarthe has been most persistent in pursuing the problem raised by Heidegger's Nazism in all its many variations. Heidegger's later view of the role of poetry in the disclosure of truth led to his encounter with Paul Celan. For a recent effort to study the role of

poetry based on that encounter, see Philippe Lacoue-Labarthe, *La poésie comme expérience* (Paris: Christian Bourgois, 1986).

124. A short list of his writings on or about Heidegger includes *La vérité en peinture, Ousia, Grammé,* "Geschlecht: Différence sexuelle, différence ontologique," "La main de Heidegger (Geschlecht II)," etc. His writings on Heidegger have recently been brought together in a single volume. See Jacques Derrida, *Heidegger et la question* (Paris: Flammarion, 1990).

125. For denial of the importance of the distinction or distinctions between the Derridian approach and so-called orthodox Heideggerianism in France, see Ferry and Renaut, *Heidegger et les modernes* (see chap. 3, n. 115), 99ff.

126. The latter aspect has not been lost on orthodox, or Derridian, Heideggerians. It is significant that his study has in fact been praised by Heideggerians for its Heideggerian quality. For instance, David Krell, in a long review in part intended to defend Heidegger against Farias's criticism, makes this point. See David Farrell Krell, "Spiriting Heidegger: A discussion of *De l'esprit: Heidegger et la question* by Jacques Derrida," in *Research in Phenomenology* 18 (1988): 205–230.

127. See Derrida, *De l'esprit* (see chap. 1, n. 28), p. 11.

128. For a discussion of Derrida's reading of Heidegger's supposed deconstruction of spirit, which does not discuss Derrida's application of his reading to Heidegger's Nazism, see Önay Sözer, "Kommt der Geist fragend zurück? Die Dekonstruktion des Begriffs 'Geist' bei Heidegger nach Derrida," in *Zur philosophischen Aktualität Heideggers: Symposium der Alexander von Humboldt-Stiftung vom 24.-28. April 1989 in Bonn–Bad Godesberg,* vol. 2, *Im Gespräch der Zeit,* ed. Dietrich Papenfuss and Otto Pöggeler (Frankfurt a.M.: Vittorio Klostermann, 1990), pp. 273–283.

129. See Martin Heidegger, "Die Sprache im Gedicht: Eine Erörterung von Georg Trakls Gedicht," 1953, in *Unterwegs zur Sprache* (Pfullingen: Neske, 1959).

130. See Derrida, *De l'esprit,* p. 12.

131. See ibid., p. 24.

132. See ibid., p. 156.

133. See ibid., p. 155.

134. See ibid., p. 64.

135. See ibid., p. 66.

136. See Lacoue-Labarthe, *L'imitation des modernes* (see chap. 2, n. 123).

137. See ibid., p. 184.

138. See Lacoue-Labarthe, *La fiction du politique* (see chap. 6, n. 129).

139. See ibid., p. 14.

140. See ibid., p. 75.

141. See ibid., p. 28.

142. See ibid., p. 35.

143. See ibid., p. 38.

144. See ibid., p. 39.

145. See ibid., p. 43.

146. See ibid., p. 64.

147. See ibid., p. 86.
148. See ibid., p. 87; see also ibid., p. 91.
149. See ibid., p. 91; see also ibid., p. 115.
150. See ibid., p. 150.
151. See ibid., p. 58.
152. See ibid., p. 59.
153. Ferry and Renaut, *Heidegger et les modernes,* p. 12.
154. See Luc Ferry and Alain Renaut, *La pensée 68: Essai sur l'anti-humanisme contemporain* (Paris: Gallimard, 1985).
155. Ferry and Renaut, *Heidegger et les modernes,* p. 40.
156. See ibid., p. 10.
157. See ibid., p. 12.
158. Lacoue-Labarthe, *La fiction du politique,* p. 58.
159. See Ferry and Renaut, *Heidegger et les modernes,* p. 117.
160. See ibid., p. 149.
161. See ibid., p. 155.
162. See ibid., p. 227.
163. See ibid., p. 170.
164. See ibid., p. 172.
165. See ibid., pp. 224–225.
166. See Heidegger, "Die Kategorien- und Bedeutungslehre des Duns Scotus," in Martin Heidegger, *Frühe Schriften* (Frankfurt a.M.: Klostermann, 1972), p. 141: "Es felht dem Mittelalter, was gerade einen Wesenszug des modernen Geistes ausmacht; die Befreiung des Subjekts von der Gebundenheit an die Umgebung, die Befestigung im eigenen Leben."
167. See Nicolas Tertulian, "Trois témoignages: Löwith, Jaspers, Marcuse," *La Quinzaine Littéraire*, no. 496 (1–15 novembre 1987): 10–11; "A propos de Heidegger, la manipulation des textes à tout de même des limites," ibid., no. 515 (1–15 septembre 1988): 18–21; "Quand le discours heideggerien se mue en prise de position politique," ibid., no. 523 (1–5 novembre 1988): 26; "Esquives, abandons et nouvelles inexactitudes: Un tournant dans les recherches sur Heidegger," ibid., no. 526 (16–28 janvier 1989): 19–21; "Heidegger et le national-socialisme: Aspects et points de vue," in *Tramonto dell'occidente?* ed. Gian Mario Cazzaniga, Domenico Losurdo, and Livio Sichirollo (Naples: Istituto per gli Studi Filosofici, 1989), pp. 165–206.
168. See Janicaud, *L'ombre de cette pensée* (see Introd., n. 7).
169. See Meschonnic, *Le langage Heidegger* (see n. 79).

Chapter 8: Being, the *Volk,* and Nazism

1. For a summary of lines of analysis from another angle of vision, see Thomä, *Die Zeit des Selbst und die Zeit danach* (see Introd., n. 6). pp. 474–487. According to Thomä, there is no strict unity between Heidegger's thought and his Nazi engagement. See ibid., p. 468. He maintains that no one has so far understood Heidegger's Nazi turning on the basis of the texts. See ibid., p. 468.

But he emphasizes that Heidegger's later writings are deeply rooted in his commitment to National Socialism. See ibid., p. 796.

2. For Adorno's claim that Heidegger's thought was fascist through and through, see Theodor Adorno, *Musikalische Schriften* (Frankfurt a.M.: Suhrkamp, 1976), 5/6:637–638. The criticism occurs in a letter in which Adorno defended himself against the charge of having collaborated with the Hitler regime. He writes in part (p. 638): "Wer die Kontinuität meiner Arbeit überblickt, dürfte mich nicht mit Heidegger vergleichen, dessen Philosophie bis in ihre innersten Zellen faschistisch ist." For a discussion of Adorno's criticism, see Lacoue-Labarthe, *La fiction du politique* (see chap. 6, n. 129), pp. 150–151n. See also Theodor Adorno, *Jargon der Eigentlichkeit: Zur deutschen Ideologie* (Frankfurt a.M.: Suhrkamp, 1964). See, for a Heideggerian analysis of the Heidegger-Adorno relation, Hermann Mörchen, *Macht und Herrschaft im Denken von Heidegger und Adorno* (Stuttgart: Klett-Cotta, 1980), and *Adorno und Heidegger: Untersuchung einer philosophischen Kommunikationsverweigerung* (Stuttgart: Klett-Cotta, 1981).

3. Beaufret wrote extensively on Heidegger. For his list of publications, many of which concern various aspects of Heidegger's thought, see "Essai de bibliographie de Jean Beaufret," in Jean Beaufret, *De l'existentialisme à Heidegger: Introduction aux philosophies de l'existence* (Paris: Vrin, 1986), pp. 171–182. For a representative sample of his view of Heidegger's politics, see Jean Beaufret, "En chemin avec Heidegger," in *Martin Heidegger,* ed. Haar (see chap. 6, n. 42), pp. 205–232.

4. See Fédier, *Heidegger: Anatomie d'un scandale* (see chap. 3, n. 69).

5. See Aubenque, "Encore Heidegger et le nazisme" (see chap. 2, n. 59), pp. 113–123.

6. See Vietta, *Heideggers Kritik am Nationalsozialismus und an der Technik* (see chap. 1, n. 31).

7. See "Work and Weltanschauung: The Heidegger Controversy from a German Perspective," in Jürgen Habermas, *The New Conservatism: Cultural Criticism and the Historians' Debate,* ed. and trans. Shierry Nicholsen, introd. by Richard Wolin (Cambridge, Mass.: MIT Press, 1989), pp. 140–172.

8. See Richard Rorty, *Contingency, Irony, and Solidarity* (Cambridge: Cambridge University Press, 1989), p. 111: "On the general question of the relation between Heidegger's thought and his Nazism, I am not persuaded that there is much to be said expect perhaps that one of the century's most original thinkers happened to be a pretty nasty character. He was the sort of man who could betray his Jewish colleagues for the sake of his own ambition, and then manage to forget what he had done. But if one holds the view of the self as centerless which I put forth in Chapter 2, one will be prepared to find the relation between the intellectual and moral virtue, and the relation between a writer's books and the other parts of his life, contingent." See also Richard Rorty, "Taking Philosophy Seriously," *The New Republic*, 11 April 1988, pp. 31–34, and Richard Rorty, "Diary," *London Review of Books*, 8 February 1990, p. 21.

9. See Derrida, *De l'esprit: Heidegger et la question* (see chap. 1, n. 28).

10. See Lacoue-Labarthe, *La fiction du politique* (see chap. 6, n. 129). See also Lacoue-Labarthe, *L'imitation des modernes* (see chap. 2, n. 123).

11. See Löwith, "Les implications politiques de la philosophie de l'existence chez Heidegger" (see Introd., n. 2), and Löwith, *Mein Leben in Deutschland* (see chap. 2, n. 8).

12. See Bourdieu, *L'ontologie politique de Martin Heidegger* (see chap. 2, n. 53).

13. See Janicaud, *L'ombre de cette pensée* (see Introd., n. 7).

14. See Zimmerman, *Heidegger's Confrontation with Modernity.* (see chap. 1, n. 23).

15. See Wolin, *The Politics of Being* (see chap. 1, n. 1).

16. See Thomä, *Die Zeit des Selbst und die Zeit danach* (see Introd., n. 6). Thomä, who has provided the most extensive study of Heidegger's texts to date, specifically proposes to demonstrate "die konsequente Ableitung von Heideggers NS-Engagement aus seiner Philosophie." Ibid., p. 30.

17. See "Un entretien avec Jacques Derrida" (see chap. 7, n. 74), p. 172.

18. Ernst Krieck, "Der Wandel der Weltanschauung," *Süddeutsche Monatshefte* 33/34:638–639, cited in Laugstien, *Philosophieverhältnisse* (see chap. 2, n. 25), p. 48.

19. For an expression of this view, see writings by Rorty, cited in n. 8.

20. According to Feyerabend, "Schizophrenics very often hold beliefs which are as rigid, all-pervasive, and unconnected with reality as are the best dogmatic philosophies. However, such beliefs come to them naturally whereas a 'critical' philosopher may sometimes spend his whole life in attempting to find arguments which create a similar state of mind." Paul Feyerabend, *Against Method* (London: Verso, 1978), p. 45.

21. For these views see respectively Hans-Georg Gadamer, "On the Political Incompetence of Philosophers," in *Heidegger and Politics,* ed. Rockmore and Margolis (see chap. 4, n. 243), and Jacques Derrida, "Like the Sound of the Sea Deep within a Shell: Paul de Man's War," *Critical Inquiry* 14 (Spring 1988): pp. 590–652.

22. Among recent thinkers, this point has been perhaps most strongly made by Margolis and Goodman. See Joseph Margolis, *The Persistence of Reality,* 3 vols. (Oxford: Blackwell, 1986–1989), and *The Truth about Relativism* (Oxford: Blackwell, forthcoming). See also Nelson Goodman, *Ways of Worldmaking* (Indianapolis: Hackett, 1978).

23. On the question of theory and practice in Heidegger's thought, see Otto Pöggeler, *Philosophie und Politik bei Heidegger* (Freiburg and Munich: Karl Albers, 1972). See also Schwan, *Politische Philosophie im Denken Heideggers* (see chap. 3, n. 115), and Gerold Prauss, *Erkennen und Handeln in Heideggers "Sein und Zeit"* (Freiburg i. B. and Munich: Albers, 1977).

24. For a recent discussion of the political dimension of this problem, see Ian Maclean, Alan Montefiore, and Peter Winch, eds., *The Political Responsibility of Intellectuals* (Cambridge: Cambridge University Press, 1990).

25. See *Immanuel Kant's Critique of Pure Reason,* trans. Smith (see chap. 1, n. 12), B 862, pp. 654–655.

26. For Jaspers's important distinction between criminal, moral, political, and metaphysical forms of guilt, see Jaspers, *Die Schuldfrage* (see chap. 2, n. 116), pp. 17ff.

27. For a discussion of the letter and its significance, see Sieg, "Die Verjudung des deutschen Geistes" (see chap. 3, n. 114).

28. See Heidegger, *Nietzsche* (German ed.; see chap. 4, n. 85), 2:309.

29. Heidegger, *Basic Writings,* ed. Krell (see chap. 1, n. 10), p. 202.

30. Ibid., p. 222.

31. Heidegger clearly rejected the biological reductionism of National Socialism. See, e.g., his criticism of the Nazi control of culture under Goebbels as tantamount to *Schwängerungsführung* and his objection to the very idea of the production of *Führernaturen,* "Wer ist Nietzsches Zarathustra?" in *Vorträge und Aufsätze* (see chap. 4, n. 80), pp. 91–92.

32. Heidegger's letter of 8 April 1950, in *Briefwechsel 1920–1963* (see chap. 2, n. 27), p. 202.

33. Heidegger's letter to Jaspers of 8 April 1950, in *Briefwechsel 1920–1963,* p. 203.

34. *Briefwechsel 1920–1963,* p. 210.

35. Ibid., pp. 210–211.

36. For the assertion that fiction and reality cannot be distinguished, see de Man, *Blindness and Insight* (see chap. 4, n. 11), pp. 75, 136, and de Man, *Allegories of Reading* (see Introd., n. 8), p. 293. For a recent, semipopular study of the hidden political background of de Man, see David Lehman, *Signs of the Times: Deconstruction and the Fall of Paul de Man* (New York: Poseidon Press, 1991).

37. This seems to have happened in France. For a clear indication, in the response to the French translation of Ott's book, that for Heidegger's closest supporters nothing has changed, see "Réponses à Hugo Ott," *Le Monde,* 14 décembre 1990, p. 24.

Index

Designer: U.C. Press Staff
Compositor: Huron Valley Graphics
Text: 10/12 Times Roman
Display: Times Roman
Printer: Braun-Brumfield, Inc.
Binder: Braun-Brumfield, Inc.